Cristina Dozio

Laugh like an Egyptian

Language Play and Creativity

Editor
Nancy Bell

Volume 5

Cristina Dozio

Laugh like an Egyptian

Humour in the Contemporary Egyptian Novel

DE GRUYTER
MOUTON

ISBN 978-3-11-126726-5
e-ISBN (PDF) 978-3-11-072541-4
e-ISBN (EPUB) 978-3-11-072551-3
ISSN 2363-7749

Library of Congress Control Number: 2021938800

Bibliographic information published by the Deutsche Nationalbibliothek
The Deutsche Nationalbibliothek lists this publication in the Deutsche Nationalbibliografie; detailed bibliographic data are available on the Internet at http://dnb.dnb.de.

This volume is text- and page-identical with the hardback published in 2021.
Cover image: Samuel Zeller Photography
Typesetting: Integra Software Services Pvt. Ltd.
Printing and binding: CPI books GmbH, Leck

www.degruyter.com

To Maya, our hope

Acknowledgments

No pain, no غ

This twist on the saying “no pain, no gain” by inserting an Arabic letter exemplifies how humour can be a powerful tool since the early stages of learning this language. Then, other forms of humour are discovered according to one’s taste and personal experience. In my case, it was Omar Taher’s *Shaklaha bazit*. Reading it brought back to me the sense of humour I had experienced (and sometimes barely understood) as a student in Cairo. Working on this satirical book for my MA dissertation revealed so much about the nuances of the Arabic language and Egyptian culture that I decided to continue this journey by exploring literary humour in my PhD dissertation. So far, this has been a very challenging but also rewarding experience.

I would like to thank my PhD supervisor, Letizia Osti, for guiding me since the beginning of this project and giving me good advice every step of the way. My PhD dissertation was made possible by the financial support I received from Università degli Studi di Milano and the hospitality of the Netherlands-Flemish Institute in Cairo and the Department of the Languages and Cultures of Near and Middle East, SOAS – University of London, where I conducted part of my research. I am grateful to Salvatore Attardo for reading my dissertation, which made me believe in its potential across the fields of Arabic and humour studies. I should also thank Nancy Bell, her editorial team, and the anonymous reviewers for their helpful comments and suggestions.

I feel lucky to work in a stimulating environment surrounded by helpful colleagues: our Arabic Studies team in the Department of Linguistic Mediation and Intercultural Studies at Università degli Studi di Milano, especially Letizia Osti, Marco Golfetto, Francesco De Angelis, Federico Pozzoli, and Asmaa Abdelbary; the staff of our department’s library; my former colleagues at IULM and Università di Pavia; Maria Elena Paniconi, Lorenzo Casini, Richard Jacquemond, and Christian Junge who have often given feedback on this project and my research at large; Lisa Marchi, Alba Rosa Suriano, Fernanda Fischione, Hoda Elhadary, Arturo Monaco, Feras Alkabani, and Peter Konerding who have enriched my attendance to academic conferences with insightful debates and hilarious moments; SSML Vicenza where I have found a second family by meeting Elisabetta Bartuli, Giuliana Schiavi, Giacomo Longhi, Annamaria Bianco, Elena Chiti, Ramona Ciucani, and Ilaria Laghetto. This book would not have been the same without the love of my family and the good company of my friends.

https://doi.org/10.1515/9783110725414-202

Contents

Acknowledgments — VII

Note on transliteration — XIII

Bibliographic reference for the novels— XV

Introduction — 1

1 A laughable tradition — 8
1.1 Literary humour — **8**
1.1.1 Definitions — **8**
1.1.2 Terminology — **12**
1.2 Humour theories — **14**
1.2.1 Phylosophical aesthetic theories: an integrated model — **14**
1.2.2 Linguistic theories and narrative humour — **17**
1.3 Arab humorous tradition — **24**
1.3.1 Jocular anecdotes — **25**
1.3.2 *Maqāmāt* — **27**
1.3.3 Stock characters — **29**
1.3.4 *Arabian Nights* — **33**
1.3.5 Shadow theatre and Ottoman *karagöz* — **35**
1.3.6 Satirical press — **36**
1.3.7 Contemporary literature — **38**
1.4 Egyptian political jokes — **39**
1.5 Literary and popular references — **43**

2 Masters of humour — 45
2.1 Re-designing the canon — **45**
2.2 A canon of humour — **48**
2.3 Analytical framework — **52**
2.4 Authors in their context — **55**
2.4.1 Origins — **55**
2.4.2 Career and recognition — **57**
2.4.3 Literary influences — **60**
2.4.4 From the margins — **62**

3 Reversed epics. Nu‘mān, the village antihero — 68
3.1 Suspended form and unreliable narrator — **70**
3.1.1 Village novel — **70**
3.1.2 Scholarly writing — **76**
3.1.3 Discoursive strategies — **80**
3.2 The puppet — **82**
3.2.1 A folk antihero — **82**
3.2.2 Interrupted rituals — **86**
3.3 Social satire: the village — **92**
3.3.1 Ignorance and superstition — **92**
3.3.2 Entertainment for the elite — **93**
3.4 Conclusion: a tale of incongruities — **96**

4 Ibn Shalabī, a (pre-)modern trickster — 98
4.1 Reviving the past — **100**
4.1.1 Travelogue — **100**
4.1.2 *Maqāmāt* across time — **104**
4.1.3 Historiography — **106**
4.2 The trickster — **109**
4.2.1 Ibn Shalabī and his doubles — **109**
4.2.2 Out of time — **113**
4.2.3 Out of place — **118**
4.3 Humour in the urban world — **119**
4.3.1 Verbal and situational humour — **120**
4.3.2 Egyptian idiosyncrasies — **121**
4.3.3 Comic subversion — **123**
4.4 Conclusion: a very Egyptian story — **127**

5 Laughing together at the hash den — 129
5.1 Social biography of the coterie — **131**
5.1.1 The hash den — **131**
5.1.2 The narrator as a guide — **134**
5.1.3 Aspiring intellectuals — **136**
5.2 Ṣāliḥ, the wise fool — **138**
5.2.1 Appearance — **138**
5.2.2 Philosophy — **140**
5.2.3 Intoxication and collective creativity — **142**
5.2.4 Language and identity — **147**
5.3 What is *hēṣa*? — **150**

5.3.1 From pure fun to political satire — 150
5.3.2 From comedy theatre to farce — 153
5.4 Conclusion: hashish as a metaphor — 155

6 Laughing together at migration — 157
6.1 The labourers — 160
6.1.1 Constructing identity — 160
6.1.2 The city: working sites and accommodation — 162
6.1.3 Tales of labour migration — 164
6.2 Negotiating Bedouin identity — 170
6.2.1 The village: a historical reconstruction — 170
6.2.2 Tales of Bedouin migration — 172
6.3 Which community? — 176
6.4 Conclusion: new forms of nomadism — 179

7 A comparative look — 181
7.1 Narratological aspects — 181
7.1.1 Narrators — 181
7.1.2 Space and time — 184
7.1.3 Characters — 187
7.2 Intertextuality — 190
7.2.1 Literary heritage — 190
7.2.2 Historiography — 192
7.2.3 Across genres — 194
7.3 Themes and style — 195

Conclusions — 198

Bibliography — 205

Websites and videos — 227

Index — 229

Note on transliteration

The transliteration from Modern Standard Arabic (MSA) follows the guidelines of the *International Journal of Middle East Studies* (IJMES). Initial *hamza* is not transliterated and no distinction is made between ā for *alif* or *alif maqṣūra*.

The transliteration from Egyptian Colloquial Arabic (ECA) follows the standards adopted by Booth (1990). The main variations from transliteration of MSA are:

- The definite article *al-* in MSA becomes *il-* in ECA; it is assimilated where appropriate to what precedes (*l-*) and/or follows ([*i*]*s-s*).
- *Tāʾ marbūṭa* in construct *-at* in MSA becomes *-it* in ECA.
- *Jīm* in MSA becomes *gīm* in ECA or, in the cases where reproduction of Delta or Ṣaʿīdī pronunciation is intended, *jīm* (to distinguish it from reproduction of *qāf* as *gīm* in the same context).
- Diphthongs *ay* and *aw* in MSA become *ē* and *ō* respectively in ECA. Where *ū* is pronounced as *ō* (as in *rōḥ*), the latter is also used.

The names of renowned public figures and places are spelt in accordance with their most common English rendition.

https://doi.org/10.1515/9783110725414-204

Bibliographic reference for the novels

When first referred to, the Arabic title of a novel is followed by the year of its first publication, the title and date of its published English translation, or my translation of the title when no English translation is available.

The novels of the corpus are referred to with their English title or its shortened version. For instance, *The Time-Travels of the Man Who Sold Pickles and Sweets* (2010; *Riḥlāt al-ṭurshajī al-ḥalwajī*, 1991a [1981/1983]), shortened as *Time-Travels* in subsequent citations.

When quoting from the novels of the corpus, the first page number refers to the published English translation and is followed by the page number of the original Arabic edition.

https://doi.org/10.1515/9783110725414-205

Introduction

Egyptians are known among the Arabs as *awlād al-nukta*, sons of the joke, for their passion for crafting jokes and their ability to laugh even in hard times. Their proverbial sense of humour tackling socio-political issues emerges in many forms of cultural production, such as comedy films, plays, and cartoons. Humour has been employed as a critical lens to explore certain social phenomena and literary trends in contemporary Egypt: political humour has emerged as a form of creative resistance in the 2011 revolution and its aftermath, whereas wordplay and a biting tone have characterized the satirical writings published since the mid-2000s.

As regards the first aspect, political humour played a significant role in the mass protests of Tahrir Square. It was expressed in slogans, chants, stand-up comedy, placards, and jokes circulating in the square and on social media; in the following months, it also influenced the production of graffiti, videos, TV shows, and cartoons. The Egyptian poet Iman Mersal (Īmān Mirsāl, b. 1966) described the demonstrators' attitude as revolutionary humour, which created a sense of solidarity in the square and challenged the official discourse through its collective creativity (Mersal 2011). Humour circultating in this revolutionary and post-revolutionary context has been framed within Bakhtin's notion of the carnivalesque because of its appropriation of the public space and collective agentivity. The term carnivalesque originally refers to the folk culture of laughter which allows a temporary suspension of official hierarchies during the carnivalesque festivities; as such, it was developed in oral and written forms during the Middle Ages and Renaissance (Bakhtin 1984). Scholars of various fields (sociology, psychology, media studies, linguistics, translation, and popular culture) have monitored the evolution of Egyptian humour after 2011 which commented on, and at the same time was exposed to, changes in the political scenario. These studies illustrate the variety of humorous cultural productions, the involvement of the audience, and the impact of new media (Aboubakr 2013, 2015; Heerbaart 2020).

The central role of humour in the Egyptian uprising challenges two widespread misconceptions according to which the Arabs do not express any political dissent and are devoid of sense of humour. The latter issue became the object of public debate after the publication of cartoons depicting the prophet Muḥammad in a Danish newspaper in 2005 and the killing of the editors of the French satirical magazine *Charlie Hebdo* on January 7, 2015. Western media somehow did not expect that Arab cartoonists, like their international colleagues, drew vignettes in memory of the victims and in defence of freedom of speech (Black

https://doi.org/10.1515/9783110725414-001

2015). Moreover, the work of Arab cartoonists proves that the boundaries of legitimate satire are constantly shifting and not confined to religious extremism.

Moving to the realm of literature, humour in Egypt functions as a political commentary both in times of revolt and oppression. Some years before the 2011 revolution, when the population's discontent was rising, satirical writings criticizing socio-political issues and portraying the incongruities of everyday life became popular among the readers. According to Jacquemond (2013, 2016), these writings revived the genre of *adab sākhir* (satirical literature), which was introduced by the pioneers of modern Egyptian prose at the turn of the 20th century in satirical magazines, fictionalized essays, and early realist fiction, and later developed by some renowned journalists in the Seventies. The new generation of satirical writers connected with the 2011 uprising came mainly from the fields of journalism, scriptwriting, and blogging. They either published satirical books or collected their columns and fictionalized essays in book form, usually under the label of *adab sākhir* to make them recognizable in the book market. These publications enjoyed high sales rates, for instance at the Cairo Book Fair in 2009 and 2010, and still circulate online. Like jokelore and other forms of political humour, these writings offer a satirical commentary of the Egyptian society in years of significant change and are affected by the shifting red lines of freedom of expression: while this cultural outlet represented a limited threat for the authorities before 2011, the situation has changed with the counter-revolution.

In terms of critical recognition, the aesthetic value of these writings has been questioned, as with their antecedents, because of their popular publication venues, the interplay of fact and fiction, and the mixture of Modern Standard Arabic (MSA), Egyptian Colloquial Arabic (ECA), and slang.[1] Despite this skeptical attitude, scholarly interest in these writings is increasing due to their affinity with other emerging genres in the most recent literary production and a broad interest in popular culture. Along with Jacquemond's examination of the bestseller phenomenon, the complex linguistic amalgam of these texts has been tackled to exemplify the evolution of the colloquial as a written language (Håland 2017). Furthermore, the importance of *adab sākhir* was discussed at the 12th Conference of the European Association for Modern Arabic Literature (EURAMAL, University of Oslo, 2016) alongside other literary trends that uphold humanity in a world characterized by socio-political collapse and community disintegration. Translated as carnivalesque or subversive literature, this genre deliberately breaks

1 The literary status of these writings is an object of debate in mainstream media as well as specialized blogs. See, e.g., Fayed 2010; Lynx Qualey 2010b.

with literary conventions while offering a non-serious, often satirical or bitterly sarcastic, form of resistance to reality (Guth & Pepe 2019: ix–xviii, 287–393).

Since the role of humour in contemporary Arabic culture has been approached to understand the recent socio-political scenario and literary production, this book contributes to the current debate by looking at the interplay of humour, satirical criticism, and literature in Egypt. The main goal is to identify how the Egyptian proverbial sense of humour is generated in contemporary fiction and which analytical framework is most suitable for its study. Another concern is the critical reception of writings combining humour and literature, satirical criticism and aesthetic value.

In this respect, the reception of a recent Egyptian novel, *Nisāʾ al-Karantīnā* (2013; *Women of Karantina*, 2014) by Nāʾil al-Ṭūkhī (b. 1978), raises some points that are worthy of consideration. Set in the near future (from 2064 back to 2006), *Women of Karantina* reconstructs the criminal history of Alexandria over three generations of gangsters combining an epic tone, absurdities, and humour. The novel was translated into English and longlisted for the *FT/Oppenheimer Funds Emerging Voices Award*. It was a commercial success and attracted great attention among Arab and Western reviewers, who applauded its stylistic innovations and sarcastic sense of humour. For instance, the Egyptian novelist and critic Mahmoud El-Wardani (Maḥmūd al-Wardānī, b. 1950) praises *Women of Karantina* as "a new twist in the evolution of the form of the Egyptian novel itself" and suggests that "humour marks an essential anchor for the novel, giving it additional glamour" (El-Wardani 2013). The British scholar and translator Paul Starkey (2016a) argues that a sarcastic brand of humour suffuses the whole account in this "exciting and original work, which represents an important contribution to contemporary Egyptian and Arab literature".[2]

During a book launch, al-Ṭūkhī (Eltoukhy 2014 video) was asked why his novel is described as a literary innovation. He answered that the novelty lies in his choice to infuse sense of humour in an artistic work, while humorous books – especially those described as sarcastic or satirical – are usually seen as a second-rate distinct genre in Egyptian literature. Al-Ṭūkhī mentioned the novels of the Palestinian Imīl Ḥabībī (1922–1996) and the Egyptian Ṣunʿallāh Ibrāhīm (b. 1937) as literary works that previously used humour.[3]

While al-Ṭūkhī's assessment is still valid, the past few years have seen an increasing interest toward humour in the writings of contemporary authors and the pioneers of the turn of the 20th century, such as Bayram al-Tūnisī (1893–1961)

2 For other reviews, see: Faraj 2013; Khayr 2013; Lynx Qualey 2014; Nadā 2013.
3 See also: Eltoukhy 2016 video.

and Yaʿqūb Ṣanūʿ (also James Sanua, 1839–1912). Recent studies have shed light on the literary qualities of the works of such pioneers: satire is not only functional for political criticism, but also integrated with the works' thematic focus, narrative, and linguistic strategies. This re-evaluation is the background for the study of other possible combinations of literature and humour. In contrast with the negative attitude toward *adab sākhir*, al-Ṭūkhī explains that the positive recognition of his novel is due to its innovative compositional method combining sense of humour and literary quality. His claim for innovation is justified by the little critical attention to this compositional method in previous novels.

This book investigates the literary context in which *Women of Karantina* emerges by inquiring into whether this novel appears in a vacuum or belongs to a fictional sub-genre. By exploring contemporary Egyptian fiction and the status of comedy within the canon, this study aims at identifying a novelistic sub-genre combining sense of humour and aesthetic qualities. The purpose is to go beyond the labels of satire, sarcasm, irony, cynicism that are often found in book reviews in order to study some common strategies producing the overall humorous effect in these writings. A close textual analysis explores how humour-generating strategies are intertwined with the narrative structure, intertextuality, the construction of the characters, and linguistic variation. The contextual analysis of this literary trend has two main objectives: on the one hand, that of understanding the contribution of humour to literary innovations, in other words how humorous novels revive the comic tradition to innovate the language of fiction; on the other hand, that of adding other masters of humour to the afore-mentioned pioneers of the turn of the 20th century, Ḥabībī, and Ibrāhīm.

To this aim, this study examines literary humour in four novels published from the 1980s till the 2000s by Muḥammad Mustajāb (1938–2005), Khayrī Shalabī (1938–2011), and Ḥamdī Abū Julayyil (b. 1967). The starting assumption is that humour is a key feature in these writings on a thematic, stylistic, and metanarrative level. It is not limited to ironic asides and laughable episodes, but rather constructs the fictional world upon a playful logic and tackles serious issues in an amusing way. In this sense, the examined works can be defined as humorous novels that maintain a recurring comic effect, as opposed to a serious purport, generated by the characters' adventures and misadventures.

As regards the time span, this study covers three decades in which Egyptian fiction moves away from the realist paradigm of representation by introducing multiple formal experimentations. Mustajāb and Shalabī belong to the so-called Generation of the Sixties, whereas Abū Julayyil belongs to the Generation of the Nineties. Both generations developed formal innovations, some of which rely on humour-related phenomena, such as ironic distance, ambiguity, parody, and the absurd. This evolution of the Egyptian novel, which started in the 1970s–1980s, has been extensively studied. In particular, ironic distance has been identified as the main compositional principle of some of the most acclaimed novels published in these decades, such as *al-Lajna* (1981; *The Committee*, 2002) by Ṣunʿallāh Ibrāhīm and *al-Zaynī Barakāt* (1971; *Zayni Barakat*, 1988) by Jamāl al-Ghīṭānī (1945–2015). While scholars have focused mainly on ironic distance and parody so far, this book looks at those novels that employ humour as their main compositional method by combining experimentation and the amusing effects of comedy. Focusing on this period and the following decades contributes to filling the gaps in the canon of Egyptian literary humour, which starts with the re-discovered pioneers of satirical writing and continues till recent publications that are acclaimed or criticized for the way they employ humour. In doing so, the canonical approach to humorous fiction will be questioned. While humour has been hitherto examined as merely one of the stylistic features of some writers, presented almost as exceptions, this volume adopts a comparative approach to identify a literary trend and compare humour-generating strategies in multiple works.

Moreover, the three selected writers are not located outside the canon but on its periphery: Mustajāb, Shalabī, and Abū Julayyil are established novelists who have recently increased their critical recognition but are still understudied in comparison to their contemporaries. While looking at the periphery of the canon, the analysis of the novels reveals a connection between the depiction of marginal communities in liminal spaces and an intense production of humour. This book investigates which characters, themes, and linguistic choices render this local sense of humour in an artistic way.

The study of literary humour combines a local and a cross-cultural dimension, since wordplay and cultural references are highly local, while some humour-generating strategies and characters are recurrent across literatures. In this respect, literary criticism often looks at external influences (Western literary genres and concepts) on the development of trends and sub-genres in Arabic fiction. This study, instead, focuses on internal influences: it illustrates how these humorous novels interact with the writing conventions of the Egyptian canon and revive the rich tradition of Arab literary and popular humour. Nevertheless, Mustajāb, Shalabī, and Abū Julayyil, like other Arab novelists, are influenced by multiple readings and consciously belong to the Egyptian and international literary scenes.

Beside the study of the Egyptian literary field, the close reading of the four selected novels is conducted with analytical tools of humour studies and literary criticism: after looking at the main humour theories to understand the mechanisms of verbal humour, these mechanisms will be applied to the narratological categories, themes, and style. This will enable the investigation of narrative strategies generating humour on the macro-level of structure and rhetorical strategies generating humour on the micro-level of comical episodes. The analysis focuses on the construction of the characters, eccentric types in marginal communities who revive some stock figures of Arabic literature and folklore in an intertextual game that exploits both high and popular cultural references for humorous effects. Placed in the contemporary context, these characters negotiate the relation between the self and the community in a playful way, inviting to investigate the targets of satire and the fictional representation of the culture of laughter in marginal groups. This comparative approach highlights similarities and differences in the selected authors, thus tracing a thematic and stylistic evolution of this subgenre over the decades and investigating the critical recognition, or lack thereof, of their contribution to literary humour.

To address these issues, this study is structured as follows. CHAPTER 1 defines literary humour and its terminology. It illustrates the main philosophical aesthetic theories (incongruity, superiority, and relief) and linguistic theories (General Theory of Verbal Humour, GTVH) as applied to literary texts. Despite their differences, all theories identify two axes for the creation of humour: a cognitive mechanism and an attitudinal positioning. From the adaptation of the General Theory of Verbal Humour for the study of literary texts derives the key concept of humour enhancers, *i.e.* those strategies that are not humorous in themselves but increase the pleasure of reading and the experience of humour. Then, this chapter overviews the main sources of humour in the Arab popular and literary tradition as addressed by recent scholarship. The focus is mainly on pre-modern literature, popular drama, and satirical journalism in the late Ottoman Empire. The last part of this chapter examines political jokes to exemplify what Egyptians laugh at and how multiple approaches (sociological, content-based, linguistic, translation studies) can be combined in the study of verbal humour.

CHAPTER 2 illustrates the status of humorous writings in the canon of Egyptian fiction and outlines the selection criteria of the corpus. Beside the chronological criterion, all four novels have an overall humorous effect achieved through funny characters and comic performances. These peculiarities are recognized in reviews and partially in previous studies. The corpus was also designed according to a thematic criterion, *i.e.* the experience of humour of eccentric characters in marginal environments. This corpus is homogeneous not only for the thematic overlap but also for some biographical affinities among the three authors and their critical reception. In fact, Mustajāb and Shalabī increased their critical recognition at the turn of the millennium, when Abū Julayyil reached his early maturity. Their novels were awarded and translated into English after 2005.

CHAPTERS 3–6 present the four novels of the corpus as case studies: *The Secret History of Nu'man Abd al-Hafiz* (2008; *Min al-tārīkh al-sirrī li-Nuʿmān ʿAbd al-Ḥāfiẓ*, 1986 [1982]) by Mustajāb, *The Time-Travels of the Man Who Sold Pickles and Sweets* (2010; *Riḥlāt al-ṭurshajī al-ḥalwajī*, 1991a [1981/1983]) and *The Hashish Waiter* (2011; *Ṣāliḥ Hēṣa*, 2000) by Shalabī, and *A Dog with No Tail* (2015; *al-Fāʿil*, 2008) by Abū Julayyil. Shalabī features with two novels because he was a very prolific author, whose writings published in the 1990s–2000s represent the linking chain between the old and new generations of writers and readers. Moreover, there is an affinity between the first two novels by Mustajāb and Shalabī, which have an anecdotic structure reminiscent of the *maqāma* and storytelling; conversely, the other two novels by Shalabī and Abū Julayyil share the depiction of the self and its quest for identity in a changing society by mixing social realism with non-mimetic modes of representation. After a summary of the plot, each chapter illustrates how the novel interacts with the literary models and their narrative conventions. Then it examines the construction of the main character through the comical episodes and the juxtaposition of multiple registers. Finally, it identifies the targets of satirical criticism by looking at the thematic threads to which humour is attached.

The titles of these chapters do not classify the type of humour (for instance, comedy, satire of mores, sarcasm, dark humour), but rather refer to the centrality of the character and the writing conventions that are challenged: Nuʿmān is a victim of humour turned into an antihero in the reversed epics of *The Secret History*; Ibn Shalabī is a trickster who combines pre-modern literary references with contemporary popular culture thanks to time-travelling in *Time-Travels*; Ṣāliḥ is a wise fool in the collective biography of a group of friends meeting at the hash den in *The Hashish Waiter*; and finally, Ḥamdī is a Bedouin in the urban underworld of construction workers who tells a collective migration tale in *A Dog with No Tail*.

Chapter 7 compares the main humour-generating strategies found in the analysis of the novels by focusing on four narratological categories (narrating voice, space, time, and characters) and intertextuality. This comparative approach traces an evolution of the themes over the three decades and remarks the peculiarities of each author.

The published translations of all four novels have been an invaluable resource for rendering the quotations into idiomatic English and preserving the comic effect. While the analysis is based on the original Arabic, the quotations are taken from the published English translations. Cross-referring the quotations reveals multiple strategies for transferring humour across texts and cultures. Furthermore, the translators' notes and interviews have also contributed to the appreciation of humour.

1 A laughable tradition

> A man in a coffin was crying and protesting as a multitude of people were taking him to be buried alive. Seeing Qaraqush passing by, he appealed to him. 'What?' said the governor, 'You want me to believe you and disbelieve the hundred mourners walking behind you?'
>
> K. Kishtainy, *Arab Political Humour*, 1985: 54

Placed at the intersection of humour studies and literary criticism, literary humour is related to other phenomena like irony, satire, and parody. This complexity is reflected by the terminology and the criteria for identifying humorous literary texts. After addressing these issues in relation also to Arabic culture, this chapter overviews the main philosophical-aesthetic and linguistic theories applied to the study of verbal humour in literary narratives. An integrated model allows to identify the cognitive mechanism and attitudinal positioning that, combined with the formal aspects of the texts, generate the humorous effect. The Semantic Script Theory of Humour (Raskin 1985) and General Theory of Verbal Humour (Attardo & Raskin 1991) have been enriched by linguistic and narratological studies to account for the mechanisms of humour in narratives that are longer and more complex than jokes. Among these contributions, Triezenberg (2004, 2008) identifies humour enhancers as those textual elements that increase the pleasure of reading and the experience of humour.

One of the humour enhancers is the familiarity with the comic tradition of a certain culture. Therefore, the second part of this chapter overviews the notion of the comic, its forms, and stock characters in the Arab cultural heritage (*turāth*). The focus on prose, rather than poetry and drama, provides a background for the analysis of the contemporary novels conducted in this book. Moreover, the study of humour in contemporary literature is often intertwined with socio-political satire and popular humour. Satire and popular humour are exemplified by political jokes examined in the last part of this chapter to understand the circulation of humour in Egyptian society.

1.1 Literary humour

1.1.1 Definitions

Humour is a human activity functioning as a powerful social tool that is able to ease tension and create affinity. In everyday life, we encounter different forms of humour expressed through verbal, non-verbal, written, and graphic channels. Besides everyday social intercourse, humour circulates on the media in sitcoms,

https://doi.org/10.1515/9783110725414-002

stand-up comedy, drama, cinema, advertisement, cartoons, comics, and political satire. It may be deliberately employed as a rhetorical tool in communication, for example in political speeches and religious sermons.

According to Martin (2007: 10–15), interpersonal humour can be divided into three types: intentional verbal humour when telling jokes and amusing anecdotes; spontaneous conversational humour, which can be verbal (for example, ironic comments and witty repartees) and non-verbal; accidental or unintentional humour, which can be linguistic (the so-called Freudian slips) or physical (for example, slipping on a banana peel). In all these cases, humour entails a relevant communicative dimension: utterances or actions are not humorous in themselves, but somebody should perceive them as funny and have a positive reaction. This communicative dimension implies the relevance of the context. For example, slipping on a banana peel can generate different reactions according to the status of the victim, his/her ability to take things not too seriously, and the context in which the incident happens.

Although humour has been addressed by different disciplines, it is difficult to give a comprehensive definition because of its various functions and forms, as well as its proximity to other phenomena, such as irony, satire, and parody. Scholars have tried to narrow down the common definition of humour as something funny that makes people laugh or smile. To illustrate this, two definitions taken from the fields of psychology and literary criticism respectively are compared:

> humor is essentially an emotional response of mirth invoked in a social context that is elicited by the perception of playful incongruity and is expressed through smiling and laughter. (Martin 2007: 10)

> In a broad sense, humor is connected to the deviation from the ordinary and conventional, which causes relief from the psychological and social restrictions imposed on men, whereas the relief is expressed through smile or laughter. (Tamer 2009: xi)

Both definitions identify a physical reaction to humour, ranging from smile to laughter, a positive emotional response, either in terms of mirth or relief, and a stimulus producing humour, such as incongruity and deviation from the ordinary. Humour theories tackle these key-concepts (cognitive-perceptual process and emotional response) to understand how humour occurs.

Literary criticism acknowledges the difference between experiencing humour and reading about it on paper: the latter may seem a dry record of what it is in social interactions but becomes less ephemeral by circulating among different audiences. Another difference is length since interpersonal humour and some forms of media humour are based on short texts, while humour in literature is developed in longer texts whose complexity is increased by their aesthetic qualities, as Nilsen and Nilsen suggest:

> Among the reasons that comic novels and essays can more easily qualify as "literature" than can stand-up comedy is that the authors have space to include smart allusions and to tie them together. Because of lack of space, jokes and cartoons are necessarily filled with stereotypes, while more sophisticated literary pieces are lexically packed, meaning that several strands of humor are being developed simultaneously. In addition to using such surface structure techniques as puns and word play, authors of fuller pieces make use of such deep structure tropes as metaphors, similes, irony, and synecdoche. They have space to develop truly humorous characters and to establish and break patterns.
>
> (Nilsen & Nilsen 2008: 245)

Studies in this field have looked at single authors, national literary traditions, ethnic and gender-based humour, specific genres such as young-adult fiction, scatological humour, and hate jokes. A preliminary issue is the definition of literary humour and the choice of suitable texts for the analysis. Triezenberg (2008: 524) provides an inclusive definition of literary humour: "anything funny inside any piece of fiction, drama or narrative. What is and is not 'funny' depends on what theory of humor is being subscribed to." Larkin-Galiñanes (2000, 2002), instead, defines humorous novels as those fictional works that have an overall humorous effect, excluding serious novels with elements of humour in them. These definitions raise a relevant question: are short anecdotes told in commercials and satirical newspaper columns with a narrative structure suitable for literary analysis? In other words, what is a humorous literary text?

Transposing these questions to Arabic literature, the categories of *adab hazlī* (jocular literature) and *adab sākhir* (satirical literature) gather various texts with a clearly entertaining aim. This aim, together with the thematic focus and the language variety used in these texts, has often determined the attribution of a lower aesthetic value to these writings compared to literature with a serious purport. The existence of specific categories (*hazlī* and *sākhir*) makes one wonder whether the analysis of literary humour should be confined to texts with a pervasive presence of humour or may include narratives tackling serious issues. At the same time, the term *adab* (literature) drives the attention to the aesthetic qualities that humorous texts should possess to be qualified as literary, which vary according to the cultural context and canon formation. These issues will be addressed in ch.2 in relation to modern and contemporary Egyptian literature, when outlining the selection guidelines for the corpus.

Beside the differences illustrated above, there are also affinities between literary and non-literary humour. In fact, literary humour is placed at the intersection of humour studies and literary criticism, two fields that look at the textual structure and the creative use of the language:

> This means that literary humor scholars have much in common with critics of literature in general because of the extensive overlap between what humor scholars describe as the most common features of humor and the characteristics that literary critics look for in narratives including ambiguity, exaggeration, hostility, irony, superiority, surprise, shock, word play, incongruity and incongruity resolution. (Nilsen & Nilsen 2008: 246)

Thus, humour is the lens to explore the stylistic and thematic features of narratives; conversely, the construction of characters and punch lines in literary texts may confirm something about the general mechanisms of humour. Another common feature is transferability, *i.e.* the possibility of experiencing humour across different contexts. Even though humour is considered a universal phenomenon, it depends on the context which changes synchronically and diachronically. The diachronic perspective reveals the ephemeral nature of humour. For instance, when the contemporary audience reads classical literature, the experience of humour is different because some cultural references are missed or the whole conception of what is funny has changed:

> Shakespeare's comedies are also usually funny, but unlike the Greek bawdy plays and satires, their humour lies in word play – puns, allusions, and double-entendres that are very often lost on today's audience. Careful perusal of an annotated version of *Love's Labours Lost* or *All's Well That Ends Well* will reveal the surprising density of jokes in these plays, which are supposed to have had Elizabethan audiences roaring with laughter. (Triezenberg 2008: 527)

> When I read jokes and amusing anecdotes of court jesters from the Abbasid period, I cannot always laugh at every joke. I regard some of them as even contemptuous and tasteless. My impression of the joke will not change even when I read how the caliph laughed until he nearly died.[4] (Tamer 2009: xii)

To be sure, exploring humour diachronically provides valuable insights about how it is produced and disseminated in a certain culture. Moreover, as a culturally bound phenomenon based on communication, humour goes beyond borders through translation. Translation struggles to make humour accessible in the target language and culture by employing creative strategies and accepting inevitable losses. Chelala (2010) applies translation studies to compare two American and two Arab modern authors (Mark Twain, Edgar Allan Poe, Mīkhā'īl Nu'ayma, and Imīl Ḥabībī). She argues that the humorous effect of the examined short stories is preserved in translation because these narratives share similar cross-cultural humour-generating techniques. Another form of translation, or better said transfer, consists in adapting similar jocular scripts and comic types to different cultures. From an intercultural perspective, humour plays an essential

4 See also: Tamer 2014: 55.

pedagogical role since it unsettles the stereotypes through its unconventional language, creating a space for confrontation within one culture and across cultures. In his essay about teaching humour in Arabic literature and cinema in the United States, El-Ariss illustrates the ability of comedy to humanize the other and aestheticize the text placing it across multiple cultural traditions: "Specifically, strategic use of humor and jest in texts from the Arab and Islamic world was a key to unsettle stereotypes, engage a difficult political context, and communicate aesthetic values without reducing texts to mere representations of a culture or a political situation" (El-Ariss 2017: 130).

The complextity of humour, addressed by multiple often overlapping disciplines, is confirmed by the related terminology that will be illustrated with reference to Arabic language and culture.

1.1.2 Terminology

The Arabic term commonly used as equivalent to humour is *fukāha*. From the same root, the noun *fakīh* (humourist) is derived to describe someone known for his/her sense of humour and inclined to make witty remarks or tell funny stories. Something laughable is *muḍḥik*, from the same root of the verb *aḍḥaka* (to make someone laugh).

Distinguishing humour from other related phenomena is further complicated by the imperfect correspondence of such concepts in the Anglophone and Arabophone traditions and by multiple Arabic equivalents for the English terms (ʿAbd al-Ḥamīd 2003: 13–59, in particular 24; Fatḥī 1986). Following ʿAbd al-Ḥamīd's guideline for Arabic-English equivalents, we have: *fukāha* for humour, *ḥass al-fukāha* for sense of humour, *tahakkum* for irony, *muḥakāh tahakkumiyya* for parody, *sukhriyya* for satire, *tawriyya* for pun, *daʿāba* for wit, and *nukta* for joke.

The privileged form of humorous prose is the anecdote, usually short and self-contained. The most common Arabic terms for anecdote are *nādira* and *laṭīfa*, but other words point out one aspect or another of these narratives, as Marzolph explains:

> *nādira* denotes a short, witty, subtle and amusing anecdote; *laṭīfa* for an elegant, pointed anecdote; *mulḥa* a 'salty', e.g. pleasant, witty anecdote (in contrast to *bārid*, 'cold', dull); *fukāha* (funny, humorous anecdote) and *muḍḥika* (anecdote making somebody laugh) are relatively modern terms. The term *al-adab al-hazlī* might serve best as general denomination.
> (Marzolph 2010c: 294)

Since *al-adab al-hazlī* is a broad category for amusing stories, it is necessary to examine the key-concept of *hazl*, synonymous with *muzāḥ*. It refers to something said in jest, as the antithesis of seriousness (*jidd*). *Al-jidd wa-l-hazl* was a common expression and a literary *topos* in pre-modern Arabic literature; nevertheless, there was no perfect symmetry between the two elements, with *al-hazl* being the less prominent (§1.3.1). Van Gelder's definition of *hazl* illustrates the proximity and considerable overlap with other humour related phenomena, such as joking, the comical, nonsense, folly, or playfulness (van Gelder 1992b: 86).

As Kishtainy (1985: 19–20) notes, the etymology of these terms is linked to food: "*fukāha* (humour) is a derivative of *fākiha* (fruit), *mulḥa* (anecdote) is a derivative of *milḥ* (salt), *nukta* (joke) is associated with *nukat* (ripened dates), *hazl* (jest) also means leanness and *ẓarf* (refined wit) is the vessel used to bring food presents." This etymology suggests, according to De Angelis (2015: 34), that Arabic culture needs humour in everyday life and attributes a life-giving power to it. Another etymological interpretation suggests that effective jokes are something unique, different from the ordinary, providing pleasure. In this sense, Kishtainy (1985: 19) points out that *nādira* derives from *nādir* (rare), whereas Kazarian (2011: 332) argues that *fākiha* (fruit), a rarity in the desert, originally meant sweets.

A discourse mode and genre that makes use of humour is satire (*sukhriyya*). Nilsen and Nilsen summarize the satirical mechanism in literature and its relation to humour:

> [the satirists'] goal is to portray life in such a way that readers will be shocked into a new way of thinking and will then take steps to correct the current wrongs of the world. Writers of satires can be deadly serious, but they often entice readers or listeners to stay with them through using sarcasm, and wit, along with humor that makes people feel wiser than the characters they are reading about. (Nilsen & Nilsen 2008: 248–249)

In other words, satire implies a moral standard, thus things are presented as right or wrong. It is grounded in reality, but this reality is distorted by means of exaggeration or fantasy and is perceived as grotesque. Satire aims at showing and correcting the shortcomings of individuals, groups, and society.[5]

There is no exact equivalent in Arabic for satire, especially if one refers to the genres of classical literature. Satire is rendered as *hijā'*, synonymous with *hajw*, which means invective and is normally restricted to poetry. As van Gelder notes,

> [m]uch invective poetry aims at ridicule, contempt and scorn, yet lacks a moral dimension which is the hallmark of true satire; conversely, there is a moralistic type of poetry that is called *hijā'* or *dhamm* ('blame') because it condemns or polemicizes, but which lacks the wit or sparkle usually associated with satire. (van Gelder 2010b: 693)

5 For a stylistic approach to satire, see: Simpson 2003.

Usually combined with vaunting (*fakhr*), invective was a central element of pre-Islamic poetry, in which poets of one tribe ridiculed the opposing tribe, at the same time reinforcing the ties within their own group. Moving from the scenario of nomadic life to the Umayyad court, poets like al-Akhṭal (d. *ca.* 710), al-Farazdaq (d. 728), and Jarīr (d. 729) were famous for exchanging flytings (*naqāʾiḍ*). In Abbasid poetry, *hijāʾ* could serve to exalt the qualities of the patron in face of the defects of his opponents. A genre considered particularly suitable for this mode was the epigram, effective for its brevity (van Gelder 1988, 2010a; Talib 2018). In pre-modern prose narratives, satire is found in anecdotes, *maqāmāt*, treatises, and catalogues listing bad manners and foibles; in performative arts, it was exploited in the language of mimes, live performances, and shadow theatre (*khayāl al-ẓill*). Both the narrative and dramatic traditions have provided material for the evolution of satire in the modern and contemporary context under different socio-political circumstances and modes of production.

Dark or black humour (*kūmīdyā sawdāʾ*) and its close relatives of absurdist humour and gallows humour derive from satire, although lacking its moralizing dimension. Dealing with subjects that are usually too serious to be funny, such as war, death, and disease, black humour bounces the readers back and forth between laughter and tears. Literary criticism traces black humour back to the feeling of helplessness expressed by some Western authors since the 1960s, linked to the philosophical concept of the absurd. This capacity to laugh in face of tragedies is found in folk humour about death and in several forms of creative resistance produced in times of wars, including conflicts in the Arab countries (Chiti 2016; Damir-Geilsdorf 2020; Monaco 2019).

1.2 Humour theories

1.2.1 Phylosophical aesthetic theories: an integrated model

Humour in Arabic culture abounds in proverbs, sayings, jokes, and anecdotes that have been collected by scholars. These collections usually adopt a descriptive approach, since they select, arrange, and translate humorous texts according to their subject or historical period (Branca, De Poli & Zanelli 2011; Rosenthal 2011; Schmidt 2013a, 2013b; Stewart 2015). By presenting humour as a key element in Arabic culture, they also question the common idea that Arabs or Muslims are devoid of sense of humour. Besides preserving a large number of anecdotes, they illustrate the classical thinkers' theories on the nature and acceptability of laughter.

While relying on Western humour theories only for general definitions, these collections overlook the analysis of humour-generating techniques in the texts. As Malti-Douglas (1980: 300) notes, they do not ask themselves which elements of the anecdotes make us laugh and why.[6] Malti-Douglas adopts a conscious theoretical approach for her textual analysis of jocular anecdotes revolving around avarice (*bukhl*), a favoured comical topic in pre-modern Arabic literature attested in two famous collections of anecdotes of this kind, *Kitāb al-bukhalāʾ* (1971; *The Book of Misers*, 1997) by al-Jāḥiẓ (d. 868–869) and al-Khaṭīb al-Baghdādī (d. 1071). Her study opens with an overview of the main humour theories elaborated between the end of the 19th and the first half of the 20th century and applied to literary humour. She focuses on Bergson's (1901), Freud's (1905), and Koestler's (1964) contributions for their cultural relevance and applicability to literary studies, placing them within the conventional classification schemes for humour theories.

Keith-Spiegel's classification scheme, mentioned by Malti-Douglas, lists eight categories that fall into three main classes of theories, *i.e.* hostility, incongruity, and release/relief theories (Keith-Spiegel 1972: 4–13).[7] Hostility theories are based on superiority, malice, aggression, and derision at the foolish actions of others. They argue that we laugh in the face of other people's deficiencies, particularly those of our enemies. Bergson's theory shares this attitude, as it views laughter as a humiliation directed against someone who does not elicit sympathy; laughter is intended as a social corrective. The concepts of superiority and hostility also emerge in biological theories, which see humour and laughter as built-in to human nature. Bergson and other critics remark that laughter is restricted to the realm of the human.

Incongruity theories argue that humour is caused by the incongruity in pairings of ideas or situations, as well as the perception of something outside the normal. Similarly, surprise theories insist on the surprise or shock in resolving such incongruity. Both Bergson and Koestler locate the stimulus for humour in incongruity. Bergson thinks that humour is produced by the insertion of the mechanical upon the living (*du mécanique plaqué sur du vivant*). A person that behaves in an automatic or rigid manner is laughable, whereas "a situation is

---

6 In note 1, Malti-Douglas (1980: 300) refers to studies conducted in the first half of the 20th century by Pellat, Margoliouth and Rosenthal.

7 The categories in Keith-Spiegel's classification scheme are: biological, instinct, and evolution; superiority; incongruity; surprise; ambivalence; release and relief; configurational; and psychoanalytic. For a historical overview and classification of humour theories, see: Carrell 2008; Ferroni 1974; Larkin-Galiñanes 2017. For a discussion of the main humour theories with many examples from literature, folklore, and social interaction, see: Propp 2009.

invariably comic when it belongs simultaneously to two altogether independent series of events and is capable of being interpreted in two entirely different meanings at the same time" (Bergson 1911: 96). Koestler coined the notion of bisociation of matrices of thought or behaviour, "that is, association at the same time of two elements not normally found together, generally because they belong to two different patterns of thought" (Koestler 1975: 33–34).

Release/relief theories perceive humour as a release of excess tension and a relief from social constraints. Freud's theory is usually framed within this class because it speaks of the release of comic pleasure that arises from the economy or condensation in the expenditure of psychic energy. Such condensation is achieved by juxtaposing and substituting words from different spheres, a mechanism that reminds of incongruity.

Malti-Douglas argues that the afore-mentioned conceptions are either too broad or too restrictive when applied to literature one by one. Considered together, instead, they offer a set of causes or influences eliciting humour. In her integrated model, she identifies two types of influences acting simultaneously from different directions, represented as a horizontal and vertical axis. The first type of influences are the mechanical techniques of joke formation, including Koestler's bisociation, Freud's condensation and substitution, Bergson's reversal of the interaction roles in a given situation, incongruity and its resolution, surprise and exaggeration. The second type of influences are the psychological or attitudinal states necessary for the mechanical techniques to produce humour, including superiority, aggression, *Schadenfreude*, Bergon's absence of sympathy with the subject, pleasure produced by the solution of ambiguity and by exerting power on the other, the appeal of subjects like the sexually or scatologically obscene. These psychological states, which are more subject to variation in different cultures, emerge in a dynamic interaction between the text and the reader. The focal points where the two axes encounter are the punch lines, which usually revolve around the main themes of the anecdote, thus providing thematic and organizational unit.

Malti-Douglas combines the afore-mentioned model with a structuralist approach to isolate micro-units within the broader text, in this case the stories revolving around avarice. The function-generating actions of the anecdotes are associated with morphological categories; "[p]articular morphological categories are, to a limited extent at least, related to particular humour-generating tendencies, which are derived directly or indirectly from the nature of the narrative" (Malti-Douglas 1980: 311).[8] The first level of analysis examines the anecdote's

8 The concepts of morphological categories and functions are taken from Propp, further elaborated by Greimas.

structure to see how the humour-generating tendencies related to morphology build the narrative. In other words, it finds where the expected tendencies manifest themselves in the story. The second level of analysis moves to the semantic, syntactic, and rhetorical level within each narrative phase to see how the two axes of influences interact to release tension and generate an explosion of humour. These two levels illustrate that the object of humour is not simply the subject of the text (a person in real life and a character in literary texts), but the text itself.

Malti-Douglas's theoretical framework proves that humour theories and narratological theories can be applied to multiple literary traditions, keeping in mind their cultural and linguistic specificities. This model integrates the main humour theories, combining the cognitive processing and the attitudinal positioning; both aspects influence the anecdote's structure and are visible in the semantic, syntactic, and rhetorical choices. This approach seems particularly effective with pre-modern Arabic prose, whose basic textual unit is *khabar*, a self-contained narrative account related by an eyewitness, often equipped with a chain of attribution (*isnād*). In a more recent narratological contribution discussed in the next section, Larkin-Galiñanes (2000, 2002) develops a similar approach for the study of humorous novels in contemporary American fiction. She draws from the three main classes of theory, as reformulated by linguistic studies of humour, to see how the cognitive processing and attitudinal positioning affect the textual structure:

> She draws on each of the groups to suggest how superiority is fuelled by readers' negative identification with particular characters, how sequences of events build up tension which is then released through humour, and how some character-related incongruity can be resolved with reference to the knowledge we already have about the character.
>
> (Marszalek 2020: 32)

1.2.2 Linguistic theories and narrative humour

Moving to the field of linguistics, the structuralist model – later called by Attardo isotopy-disjunction model – sees humour as the disjunction from one isotopy to another (Attardo 2008: 106–107). Isotopy is a concept associated with Greimas's semantics, that Attardo suggests interpreting essentially as a sense of the text. Thus, the isotopy-disjunction model formulates incongruity theory with more specific linguistic terminology; it also relies on narrative functions, introduced in humour studies by Morin (1966). Attardo considers it too loose since it does not apply exclusively to humorous narratives.

The linguistic study of humour initially focused on the taxonomy of puns, till Raskin marked an innovation with his Semantic Script Theory of Humour (SSTH). It is based on the concept of the script, defined as "an enriched, structured chunk of semantic information, associated with word meaning and evoked by specific words" (Raskin 1985: 99). In every joke two opposing scripts fully or partially overlap and the punch line triggers the switch from one script to the other. At that point, the reader resolves the script-opposition as an unexpected reversal that elicits humour. Scripts may be manifested as oppositions between actual/non-actual, expected/unexpected, possible/impossible situations. They usually involve binary categories essential to human life, such as real/unreal, true/false, good/bad, death/life, obscene/decent, rich/poor.

Attardo and Raskin (1991) expanded the Semantic Script Theory of Humour into the General Theory of Verbal Humour (GTVH), which identifies six hierarchically ordered dimensions in jokes, known as Knowledge Resources (KR): Script Opposition (SO); Logical Mechanism (LM) by which SO is resolved; Situation (SI) in which the joke is set; Target (TA), the butt of the joke, which is not always present; Narrative Strategy (NS), that is the rhetorical structure of the text or the joke's genre (for example, riddles, question and answer, and crossing jokes); Language (LA) or diction used to tell the joke, with its lexical, syntactic, and phonological choices.

Unlike the previous conceptualization, the General Theory of Verbal Humour has an interest for social and narratological issues illustrated by three KRs (Situation, Narrative Strategy, and Language). Since these dimensions are not restricted to jokes, some linguistically oriented studies have enquired the applicability of humour theories to longer narratives, such as short stories and novels.

The expansionist and the revisionist approach

Attardo (2020: 319–339) overviews the main contributions to the study of humour in literature.[9] He identifies two approaches within linguistics: the expansionist approach, which applies the analysis of jokes proposed by the Semantic Script Theory to longer humorous texts, and the revisionist approach, which revises the joke theory and builds a broader theory to deal with longer texts.

Within the first approach, Attardo mentions Chłopicki (1987) who discusses three major tendencies in humor development in short stories (escalation, variation, and accumulation); he introduces the notions of shadow opposition (an opposition between scripts underlying the entire text) and background or major scripts identifiable on the initial lines of the text and functioning as a frame throughout the reading process. This approach has been criticised for flattening the narrative onto a script opposition, missing the linear aspect of the text

9 For other overviews of these studies, see: Chłopicki (2017: 143–148); Ermida (2008: 99–110).

(Attardo 2020: 323) and not processing the macrostructures (Ermida 2008: 103). More recently Chłopicki has further elaborated the hierarchical organization of scripts and developed an approach based on character frames, mentioned in Attardo's overview and illustrated below.

Another script-based contribution is Halcomb's (1992) which attempts to connect the basic level oppositions into the network of oppositions structuring the text as a whole. To do so, Holcomb introduces the concept of nodal points, defined as: "locations in the narrative where humor is perceptibly more concentrated than in the immediately surrounding text. Although they can be isolated as funny instances in the story, the nodal points remain semantically tied to the entire narrative." (Holcomb 1992: 234 in Attardo 2020: 323) While this study is partly criticized for its vagueness, Attardo admits that nodal points anticipate the idea of jab lines developed in his own study of narrative humour which fits into the revisionist approach.

Revising the joke theory, Attardo (2001) presents an elaborated application of the General Theory of Verbal Humour for the analysis of longer humorous texts. This linear model distinguishes between punch lines and jab lines: punch lines are found at the end of the text and, revealing the presence of a second script, force the reinterpretation of the text itself; jab lines are in any other position and do not disrupt the overall interpretation. Charting these lines along the text, read as a vector, allows to identify the thematic or formal connections between them and graph their patterns of occurrence: a strand is a group of three or more jab lines related either thematically or formally; a stack is a group of strands which occurs in longer, intertextually related, textual corpora; a bridge is the occurrence of two related lines at a certain distance; a comb is the repetition of a certain feature or several lines in a restricted part of the text. All these patterns confirm that repetition, which is not so relevant in jokes, plays a bigger role in structuring longer humorous texts.

Humour enhancers

While it is true that the expansionist and revisionist approaches deal with the text as a whole, other contributions remark the need to focus on the peculiarities of the literary discourse. Triezenberg (2004, 2008: 537–539) argues that the General Theory of Verbal Humour and its expansion are necessary but not sufficient to describe humour in longer texts that are literary in the first place and, secondarily, funny. She suggests supplementing the linguistic method with a literary one that should include humour enhancers:

> A humor enhancer is a narrative technique that is not necessarily funny in and of itself, but that helps an audience to understand that the text is supposed to be funny, that

> warms them up to the author and to the text so that they will be more receptive to humor, and that magnifies their experience of humor in the text. (Triezenberg 2008: 538)

Humour enhancers are not humorous in themselves, since they do not contain any discernible script opposition, but increase the readers' experience of humour by adding pleasure to the reading experience, lowering their efforts and defences, and connecting them with the author. Triezenberg lists the following humour enhancers:

- Word choice or diction – One of the six KRs in the General Theory of Verbal Humour, it is considered a humour enhancer because words are carefully chosen to activate a script in the minds of the audience. For example, "a joke about lawyers will benefit from being prefaced by legal jargon, and a joke about farmers will benefit from being prefaced by rustic idioms" (Triezenberg 2008: 539).
- Shared stereotypes – These pieces of shared knowledge, or a known script, about the target make the joke less painstaking to understand, thus increasing the experience of humour. Stereotypes magnify some features that the reader half-consciously knows, while creating a normal/abnormal opposition. Furthermore, humourists should make sure of choosing stereotypes that are not likely to offend the audience, unless this is their aim. This strategy includes the use of stock characters, which are convenient for the author because the reader already knows them and feels a pleasant expectation of humour to come.
- Cultural factors – Stereotypes and stock characters are culturally bound. Successful humorous writers are well-versed in the prejudices, hang-ups, and taboos of the intended audience, as well as the history of humour in that audience's culture.
- Familiarity of the issues – It refers to issues that are close to the reader's experience and issues that have been tackled before but are presented in a fresh and original way. The reader recognizes humour with less effort and laughs along.
- Repetition and variation – It may be interpreted as an actual script opposition because normal language strives to avoid repetition. Furthermore, the same event happening over and over defies or exaggerates reality. Repetition influences the reader's expectations, while variation introduces something unexpected. Furthermore, humour is enhanced by the escalation of the situation and the admiration for the author's mastery at variation.

Narrative humour

Combining the linguistics of humour, discourse analysis, and narratology, Ermida (2008) suggests considering the comic narrative as a process in which interdependent meanings are built in partnership. Disregarding Attardo's and other linear models that, in her view, examine only the horizontal sequence of humorous instances, she argues that the comic narrative is a highly unified and interdependent whole to be examined in its structural and pragmatic dimensions. Her central hypothesis establishes five defining principles of humorous narratives (Ermida 2008: 172–173): opposition – each script processed in the text activates an opposite script; hierarchy – the scripts activated in the text are hierarchically organized in higher supra-scripts and lower infra-scripts; recurrence – the supra-scripts are recurrently activated by several infra-scripts throughout the text, which leads the receiver to make predictions and interpretive expectations; informativeness – these interpretive expectations are surprisingly broken when a supra-script inversion occurs; and cooperation – between the sender and the receiver in the interpreting process. As Chłopicki (2017: 147) and Attardo (2020: 329) remark, this hypothesis is both too broad, since it also applies to non-humorous texts, and too restrictive, since it excludes texts that are not entirely humorous; these principles seem to be satisfied only by the prototypical humorous story. Another issue raised by Chłopicki is that Ermida tends to consider oppositions as abstract notions, while they should be grounded in the text-specific narrative elements, such as characters, events, or objects.

Unlike Ermida, Chłopicki (2017: 148–151) remarks the centrality of the genre, or type of story, and agrees with those scholars who argue for a continuum of humorous genres ranging from the most prototypical ones to the least prototypical ones. Moreover, Chłopicki postulates the existence of humorous diversions as opposed to humorous lines: humorous diversions are non-essential for the development of the plot, which may be a relatively serious one, but amuse the readers by diverting their attention; humorous lines, instead, support the development of the narrative while providing entertainment. The study of humour in narratives implies dealing with some key dichotomies overlapping with each other: humorous vs serious, aesthetic vs entertaining, revealed vs concealed, linguistic vs humorous, text-specific vs stereotypical. The two latter dichotomies concern the cognitive aspect of humorous processing: Chłopicki remarks the centrality of perceptual imagery and introduces the notion of text-specific frames, such as character frames which are flexible structures to be filled with information about a character as the story evolves. The slots of the frame allow to incorporate humorous oppositions and humorous language, as well as the complex network of references with the other frames of the same text.

As Attardo (2020: 331) remarks, these complex character frames contrast with the construction of characters proposed by Larkin-Galiñanes who applies relevance theory to the study of humour in its narratological dimension (2000, 2002). She argues that humorous novels, unlike high literature, rely on strong implicatures creating predictable characters that function almost as stereotypes in jokes. Like stereotypes, they are readily available for the reader, which requires a minimum expenditure of mental efforts in the incongruity resolution; in terms of attitudinal positioning, the pleasure of the reader derives from the satisfaction of having his/her expectations confirmed, including the reader's positive or negative identification with the characters induced by the narrator's constant attitude toward them. Beside focusing on the reader's decodification and the textual features, this approach incorporates the main concepts of linguistic humour theories: "as the narrative develops, the very mention of a character's name will evoke for the reader a series of well-defined traits, together with specific expectations as to his behaviour and reactions – a specific script, in fact." (Larkin-Galiñanes 2002: 144) The overall humorous effect depends on the interplay of the internal level of the story (characters and their interaction) and the external level of the discourse (the communication between the narrator and the reader, and the appeal to the reader's encyclopaedic knowledge of the world outside the novel). While the internal level is characterized by coherence, it displays a high degree of incongruity with the external level, a sort of internal logic against the external illogicality.

Humour and stylistics

Another approach to humour in literary texts overviewed by Attardo (2020) is that of stylistics, a branch of research that explores literature using the models, methods, and techniques of contemporary linguistics. As Simpson and Bousfield (2017) clarify, stylistics focuses on the creative expression of the system of language, including literature. In this respect, stylistics combines the study of the formal properties of a text with the contextual analysis; it also takes into consideration the reader's response and may employ corpus-assisted analysis. These methodological stanpoints are applied to the stylistic study of verbal humour in literature, responding to two key theoretical principles:

> the first principle is that humor requires some form of stylistic incongruity. More narrowly, the incongruity can be engendered by any kind of stylistic twist in a pattern of language or any situation where there is a mismatch between what is asserted and what is meant. The second principle is that the incongruity can be situated in any layer of linguistic structure. That is to say, the humor mechanism can operate at any level of language and discourse, and, as we shall seek to demonstrate in our sample analyses, it can even play off one level against another. A large part of the stylistic analysis of humor therefore involves identifying an incongruity in a text and pinpointing where in the language system it occurs.
> (Simpson & Bousfield 2017: 159)

While the pun is a common stylistic device for creating humor in literary texts, recent scholarship has investigated other forms of linguistic manipulation, such as idiomaticity and coercion (Attardo 2020: 332–334). Moreover, Simpson and Bousfield (2017) apply stylistic research on the pragmatics of dialogues to humour, arguing that both impoliteness and humour break the norms of expectations; it is their compound effect that contributes to characterization. Stylistic has tackled parody and satire, which draw on echoic irony (the echoing of other utterances or forms of discourse) for achieving incongruity, and register humor (Attardo 2020: 334–336; Attardo 1994: 230–253 and Alexander 1997: 190–192 in Simpson & Bousfield 2017: 160–161), defined as follows:

> Whereas a dialect is a variety defined according to the user of language, a register, by contrast, is a variety defined according to the use to which language is being put. In other words, a register is characterized by a fixed (and recognizable) pattern in vocabulary and grammar [. . .]. Context, so most theories argue, is an important determinant of register, although this predictive aspect is more about likelihood or general tendencies than about absolutely fixed patterns in grammar and style. Where the humor mechanism comes into play is when, as Attardo points out (1994, p. 239), speakers subvert predictions about the appropriateness of certain registers in context, and the resulting mismatches lead to the type of incongruity we identified early on as being at the heart of humor.
> (Simpson & Bousfield 2017: 160–161)

In other words, there is an incongruity between the facts and the language used to describe them, between an expected register and an observed one, or the juxtaposition of different registers at the same time. Register humour develops over relatively large stretches of text and differs from the use of a dialect to achieve comic effects.

The analysis of the Egyptian novels conducted in this book will often refer to register humour, especially because the diglossic situation of the Arabic language further complicates this picture. While this analysis does not follow a rigorous stylistic or linguistic approach aimed at seeking the mechanisms of verbal humour in literary narratives, it employs humour as a lens to explore the formal and thematic features of the novels. To this aim, it draws on the previously illustrated studies of narrative humour for some key notions: a continuum of humorous genres, the emphasis on characterization, the appeal to the reader's encyclopaedic knowledge, repetition, and linguistic manipulation. Since humour enhancers highlight the culturally bound nature of this type of discourse, it is worth illustrating the Arab comic tradition that can be revived in contemporary humorous narratives.

1.3 Arab humorous tradition

This section overviews the literary forms, themes, and characters of humour in the Arab cultural heritage. Within recent scholarship, three collective volumes systematize the study of Arab humour, suggesting an increasing interest in this subject. *L'humour en Orient* edited by Fenoglio and Georgeon (1995) focuses on modern and contemporary cultural expressions of humour, such as the satirical press, cinema, cartoons, and jokes; it also illustrates the vitality of traditional humorous narratives and places the birth of modern satire in the late Ottoman Empire. *Humor in Arabic Culture* edited by Tamer (2009) covers a broad historical spectrum, from the early literary sources (the Qur'ān and *ḥadīth*) till contemporary fiction and drama. *Ruse and Wit* edited by Brookshaw (2012) deals with humour in classical Arabic and Persian literatures and, in the second part, looks at satire in the 19th and early 20th century in Iran, the Ottoman Empire, and cross-cultural contexts. All three volumes hihglight the cross-cultural nature of humour. Devoted to this specific subject, part 2 in *Humor in Arabic Culture* looks at the circulation of humorous traditions in the classical Mediterranean cultures and the interplay of oral and written materials. In *Ruse and Wit*, the cross-cultural dimension emerges from the comparison of three literary and cultural traditions of the Islamic world (Arabic, Persian, and Turkish) and their encounter with Europe. *L'humour en Orient* looks at the circulation of comic tropes across the Mediterranean through different media.

These collective volumes explore various manifestations of humour in premodern culture and identify the 19th century as a turning point for the birth of modern satire. As regards the first aspect, scholars agree that a wide variety of comical motifs are found across popular and high literature. Van Leeuwen (2005: 210–213) provides a useful schematization by identifying three main categories: 1) anecdotes in *adab* literature,[10] either incorporated in works tackling other issues or in specialized collections about comic types, whose humorous effect relies on linguistic puns, the author's artistry, and bizarre situations; 2) literature for entertainment comprising light verse and prose, tales of wonder, and love romances, achieving comic effects through the inversion of roles, disguise, magic, tricks, the grotesque, the heroes' cleverness or stupidity, and the subversion of power relations; 3) shadow theatre that expressed popular culture in the Mamluk period through obscene, invective, and subversive humour. Integrating this schematization with the three edited volumes and some

10 *Adab* literature was highly refined prose writing, insterpersed with verse and rhymed prose, containing the knowledge of the cultural elite.

seminal studies of humour in the Arab tradition, the next sections overview the main genres and turning points.

1.3.1 Jocular anecdotes

Jocular anecdotes (*nawādir*) are short humorous prose narratives incorporated in *adab* literature upon the principle of the mixture of jest and earnest (*al-jidd wa-l-hazl*). They provide a suitable perspective to look at Medieval Muslim thinkers' judgement on the legitimacy of humour in interpersonal communication and its inclusion into the narratives (Ammann 1993). Van Gelder suggests that the merits of jesting and earnestness were contrasted at once on moral and literary grounds, two almost inseparable dimensions in the concept of *adab*: just as the principle of measure should guide to the good Muslim in his approach to humour, a judicious mixture of jest and earnest was allowed or even demanded in works of literature.

Writers often justified this compositional principle in the prologues, supporting their view with some authoritative opinions about the social acceptability of jesting (Rundgren 1970–1971: 111–119).[11] The balanced mixture of jest and earnest was conceived for pedagogical purposes, such as instructing while entertaining and avoiding the reader's tedium that might be caused by hard-to-grasp subjects. Throughout the literary compositions, the two elements tend to appear neatly separated: amusing stories alternate with serious passages. Examining this distribution, Sadan "distinguishes between three levels of interaction: the balanced alternation in a work of *adab* as a whole, in a section or *faṣl*, and in one or a few sentences (*jumla* or *fiqra*)" (Sadan 1984 in van Gelder 1992a: 84).

One of the earliest proponents of the balance between jest and earnest was al-Jāḥiẓ (§1.2.1), considered the master of Abbasid prose and frequently associated to classical Arab humour. Montgomery (2009, 2013) argues that the author's reputation as a humourist leads to detect humour even in those works that do not present clear traces of it. Both Montgomery and van Gelder examine the works

11 Rundgren (1970–1971) collects prologues of prose writings where this literary *topos* is discussed, whereas Van Gelder (1992a) examines similar cases in poetry and literary criticism. While this section focuses on jocular anecdotes, humour in pre-modern poetry is usually associated to invective (*hijā'*) and wine poetry (*khamriyya*, whose most famous representative is Abū Nuwās, d. 814); it ranges from sophisticated puns to scabrous verse exploiting licentiousnees and obscenity (*mujūn* and *sukhf*) (Antoon 2014; Rowson 2010a, 2010b; Talib, Hammond & Schippers 2014). Two essays in *Humor in Arabic Culture* explore humour in the verse of the Umayyad love poet ʿUmar Ibn Abī Rabīʿa (d. *ca.* 712) and the Abbasid poet al-Ṣanawbarī (d. 945).

in which al-Jāḥiẓ discusses or applies the harmonious mixture of *al-jidd wa-l-hazl*. Interestingly enough, his *Risāla fī l-jidd wa-l-hazl* (An epistle on earnestness and levity) does not tackle this issue. In his *Kitāb al-bayān wa-l-tabyīn* (The book of eloquence and exposition), instead, al-Jāḥiẓ explains that the insertion of light passages serves to revive the reader's interest. Van Gelder (1992a: 101) suggests that such an overall variety fights monotony, whereas Montgomery (2009: 228) links the need to keep the reader's interest alive to the author's engagement with the theory of psychic capacity, which sees human capabilities (*wusʿ*) as limited.

In some passages of *Kitāb al-ḥayawān* (The treatise on living creatures) and *Kitāb al-bukhalāʾ* (*The Book of Misers*), al-Jāḥiẓ presents jesting as something serious and attributes positive moral qualities to laughter, probably to justify himself from some criticism. Moreover, the author recommends not to overlap jest and earnest but flouts this rule in some of his writings: van Gelder (1992a: 104) mentions *Kitāb al-tarbīʿ wa-l-tadwīr* (The treatise on quadrature and circumference), whereas Montgomery (2009: 229) looks at some minor debate treatises in which jocundity is inserted when debating the respective merits of two slightly ludicrous or uncustomary things.

Besides these examples taken from al-Jāḥiẓ's oeuvre, van Gelder notes that jest and earnest were not totally separated in the literary practice. A different pattern of interaction is found in collections that are primarily entertaining or anthological:

> [. . .] here jest and earnest are usually merely juxtaposed; if they interact at all it is only faintly. It is to be noted that the less serious sections of an anthology tend to come at the end, as e.g. in Ibn Qutayba's *ʿUyūn al-akhbār*, Ibn ʿAbd Rabbih's *al-ʿIqd al-farīd* or Abū Tammām's *Ḥamāsa* [. . .]. Conversely, anthologies that are devoted mainly to "unserious" themes may end on a sterner note. (van Gelder 1992a: 94)

These considerations are further developed by Lopez-Bernal (2015) who classifies the afore-mentioned *ʿUyūn al-akhbār* (Quintessential reports) by Ibn Qutayba (d. 889) and *al-ʿIqd al-farīd* (The unique necklace) by the Andalusian Ibn ʿAbd Rabbih (d. 940) as works conforming to the formal principle of alternating jest and earnest, with the addition of a section devoted almost exclusively to ludicrous accounts. Then, she identifies another group of works in which humorous accounts prime and end with a final sterner note, which might be interpreted as a formal convention. The second group includes *Akhbār al-aḥmqā wa-l-mughaffalīn* (1990, Fools and simpletons) by Ibn al-Jawzī (d. 1201) and *Ḥadāʾiq al-azāhir* (The gardens of flowers) by the Andalusian Ibn ʿĀṣim al-Gharnāṭī (d. 1426). In both works, anecdotes are arranged according to the comic types or the form used to express witticism (answers, jokes, tales).

With the passing of time, the concept of the balanced mixture became more flexible. For example, the afore-mentioned *Ḥadā'iq al-azāhir* aims openly at entertaining and contains an obscene tone, bawdy elements, and sexual jokes. In Ibn al-Jawzī's three collections respectively on witty, clever, and stupid people, the author still justifies the serious purport of entertainment; nevertheless, Marzolph (2010b) interprets "the justifying reference as a compulsory exercise, however all the more necessary to raise the traditionalistic author above all doubt of aiming to indulge in pure pleasure." Another way of blurring the boundaries between jest and earnest, according to van Gelder (1992a: 94), is the satirical mode both in poetry and prose: "If nonsense and jesting can serve to ridicule an opponent who is at the same time attacked on serious grounds, then the cooperation of jest and earnest may be rhetorically effective." Among the prose writing of this kind, van Gelder (1992b: 176) mentions some satirical treatises and the *maqāmāt*.

1.3.2 *Maqāmāt*

The *maqāmāt* are narratives written in elaborate rhymed and rhythmic prose (*saj'*) comprising several episodes, each set in a different city of the Islamic world, featuring the same narrator and protagonist.[12] The classical form of this genre developed between the 10th and 11th centuries (Brockelmann & Pellat *EI2*; Kilito 1983; Monroe 1983; Hämeen-Anttila 2002; Kennedy 2006; Pomerantz & Orfali 2013). Badīʿ al-Zamān al-Hamadhānī (d. 1008) wrote fifty-two *maqāmāt* with ʿĪsā b. Hishām as narrator and Abū l-Fatḥ al-Iskandarī as protagonist. His writings became popular and were imitated, among others, by al-Ḥarīrī (d. 1122), whose fifty *maqāmāt* feature al-Ḥārith b. Hammām as narrator and Abū Zayd al-Sarūjī as protagonist.[13] Originated in Iran and Iraq, this literary genre travelled to other languages and cultures in the East (in Persian, Syriac and Hebrew) and West (Andalusia and North Africa).

Like jocular anecdotes, the *maqāmāt* are structured as brief episodes with recognizable types of characters: "a clever and unscrupulous protagonist, disguised differently in each episode, succeeds, through a display of eloquence, in swindling money out of the gullible narrator [or a third part], who only realizes the identity of the protagonist when it is too late." (Stewart 2006: 145) Within a

12 The term *maqāma* is usually translated as assembly or session in English and *séance* in French.
13 For a recent translation of al-Ḥarīrī's *maqāmāt* into English, see: al-Ḥarīrī 2020.

frame narrative, the stories usually follow this scheme elaborated by Stewart (2006: 145) on the basis of Kilito's and Monroe's studies:

1. The transmitter arrives in a city;
2. Formation of an assembly or gathering for learned discussion;
3. The protagonist enters the assembly;
4. The protagonist undertakes an eloquent performance;
5. Rewarding of the protagonist by the transmitter or other character;
6. The protagonist leaves assembly, which breaks up;
7. The transmitter realizes the protagonist's true identity;
8. The transmitter follows the protagonist;
9. The transmitter accosts or reproaches the protagonist;
10. Justification by the protagonist;
11. Parting of the two;
12. Departure of the transmitter from the city (implicit).[14]

The plot can be divided into a public part (no. 1–6) and a private one (no. 8–12) after the moment of acknowledgement (no. 7). Considering the *maqāmāt* as a pre-modern dramatic genre, Neuwirth labels the two parts as drama and post-drama respectively (Neuwirth 2009: 242; Chenou 1995). The centrepiece of each story is the eloquent display (no. 4), which may consist of an invective, panegyric, sermon, eloquent description, literary criticism, prayer, or debate. The eloquent display and, in general, the style of the *maqāmāt* is extremely refined, embellished as it is by rare vocabulary and ornate rhetorical figures. Thus, this genre acquired the didactic purpose of teaching grammatical norms, obscure vocabulary, and rhetorical skills.

Besides this didactic purpose, scholars identify humour on several levels. Firstly, the structure exploits dramatic irony since the narrator is unaware of the protagonist's tricks, while the audience is totally aware. Due to the repetitive episodic structure, the audience is curious to know which ruse the rogue protagonist will employ in the next episode. Secondly, there is a game between the gullible narrator and the eloquent and clever, though dishonest, protagonist, who follows a materialistic philosophy. Kennedy (2006: 160) describes al-Hamadhānī's narrator as "half dupe, half savvy". Thirdly, the eloquent display parodies the conventions of a certain discoursive genre. Eloquence does not serve a laudable purpose and is sometimes presented as void or false.

14 Hämeen-Anttila (2002: 45) suggests another pattern for the structure: 1. *isnād*; 2. general introduction; [link]; 3. episode; 4. recognition scene *(anagnorisis)*; 5. envoi; 6. finale.

Hämeen-Anttila lists some partly overlapping sub-genres: picaresque and comic, beggar, philological and aesthetic, exhortatory, panegyrical, a group of uncategorizable *maqāmāt*. Within this list, he identifies the picaresque element as the most developed motif in al-Hamadhānī. The term picaresque is applied in a looser sense than the corresponding definition in European literature, "emphasizing the trickster nature of the main character (hero or antihero), in contrast to criminality (although in later maqamas we may see how the trickster sometimes becomes a rogue)." (Hämeen-Anttila 2002: 55–56) This type of character moves freely in the city, providing a lively portrait of urban life in the Abbasid period, as displayed by merchant and scholars in the markets, mosques, and caravansaries, but also by beggars and vagrants in the urban underworld.

The *maqāmāt* were revived in the 19th century when Arab intellectuals were elaborating new literary genres to express their concerns, drawing both from the Arab literary heritage and non-native narrative forms (short stories and novels) circulating in translation from European languages. The *maqāmāt* were chosen for their prestige and flexibility either to enhance stylistic refinement or to satirize the modern society. Their long-lasting resonance is recognizable in the structure of some modern and contemporary novels (§4.1.2).

1.3.3 Stock characters

With its balanced mixture of jest and earnest or more openly entertaining compilations, pre-modern Arabic literature gave form to a rich repertoire of jocular anecdotes revolving around some categories of people:

> Throughout the history of classical Arabic literature there is an abundance of nawādir that make fun of misers, spongers, schoolteachers, ḥadīth scholars, qāḍīs, physicians, bedouins, non-Arabs, poets, philologians, women, singing girls, simpletons, homosexuals, effeminate men, and many other categories: anecdotes that pretend to be based on actual fact but are often obviously fictional and, like most jokes, anonymous.
>
> (van Gelder 2010b: 694)

These anecdotes could be interspersed in *adab* literature or collected in compilations devoted to a single topic. For example, al-Jāḥiẓ and al-Khaṭīb al-Baghdādī compiled anecdotes about stingy people (§1.2.1). The latter, mainly known for a biographical dictionary of *ḥadīth* transmitters and Baghdadi scholars entitled *Tārīkh Baghdād* (The history of Baghdad), also composed a book on party-crashers or self-invited guests, *al-Taṭfīl wa-ḥikāyāt al-ṭufayliyyīn* (1983; *Selections from the Art of Party-Crashing in Medieval Iraq*, 2012). Ibn al-Jawzī's *Akhbār al-aḥmqā wa-l-mughaffalīn* (1990; Fools and simpletons) collected anecdotal material on fools and simpletons, exemplifying this concept in classical Arabic culture. Examining his work, Ghersetti (1993) notes that the fool (*aḥmaq* or *jāhil*) is somebody who lacks intellect (*ʿaql*) and acts improperly or incoherently, although his purpose might be correct. Paraphrasing the etymological meaning, he puts things in the wrong place. Because of this innate quality, the fool is usually vain, garrulous, cannot keep a secret, does not think about the consequences of his actions, has exaggerate reactions, and is driven by earthly appetites, and is vain.

Other social behaviours exposed by these anecdotes concern the religious sphere. As Tamer (2009: 3–28) remarks in his study of Islamic humour, these anecdotes do not ridicule the Qur'ān and the revelation but make fun of the way the religious practices are performed by some types of people; Qurʾānic quotations may be applied to alien contexts or intentionally misquoted to generate the comic effect. Humour is directed against false prophets, religious authorities such as incapable judges or mystics, the Bedouin who break the basic religious rules of praying and fasting, and stupid people who take the Qurʾānic verses literally.[15]

This anecdotal material tended to concentrate, both in the literary and folk tradition, around specific characters who became proverbial for representing a certain feature or social behaviour. Marzolph (1998: 123) defines as focusees those "individuals serving as a focus for the attribution of narratives."[16] The idea underlying this phenomenon was already expressed by al-Jāḥiẓ: an anecdote, even if boring, would be more effective if attributed to a well-known trickster, whereas a clever anecdote ascribed to an unknown protagonist would be boring and dull (Kishtainy 1985: x; Marzolph 1998: 124).

Marzolph (2010c: 295) lists the main focusees in Arabic jocular anecdotes: "Thus, in classical and post-classical sources, Ashʿab used to represent the stereotype greedy and stingy person, Bunān the sponger, Qarāqūsh the absurd judge,[17] or Buhlūl the wise fool. The most prominent of all is Juḥā." Other famous protagonists of jokes and buffoonery were Abū Dulāma, Abū l-ʿAynāʾ, Muzabbid, Abū l-Ḥārith Jummayn, and Habannaqa. These characters as well as their historical counterparts are briefly sketched out, before focusing on Juḥā, who has become the protagonist of Arabic jocular narratives and folklore over the centuries.

---

15 See also: Marzolph 2009. Tamer's and Marzoph's examples are taken from Marzolph 1992.

16 Marzolph explains that focusees is a transposition of the German word *Kristallisationsgestalten* used in folk narrative research.

17 Qarāqūsh appears as a fictional character based on his historical counterpart in Shalabī's *Time-Travels* (§4.3.3).

Ash'ab was a singer and entertainer who lived in Medina in the 8th century. Because of his profession, his anecdotes are included in the 10th-century *Kitāb al-aghānī* (The Book of Songs) by Abū l-Faraj al-Iṣfahānī (d. *ca.* 972). Rosenthal, who translated these anecdotes in his seminal study of classical Arab humour, argues that jokes attached to Ash'ab regarded initially the nobility in Mecca and Medina, then religion, and finally the urban middle-class. The latter were the most persistent and Ash'ab became proverbial for his greed and begging (Kilpatrick 1998; Rosenthal 2011). The mild mockery of the Islamic institutions and religious practice found in some jokes "is harmless because it is put into the mouth of a buffoon, someone who may say uncomfortable truths with impunity" (van Gelder in Rosenthal 2011: xvi).

Abū Dulāma was an early Abbasid black poet and wit of the 8th century. He was a court jester for the caliphs al-Saffāḥ (749–754), al-Manṣūr (754–775), and al-Mahdī (775–786). Other popular jesters were Abū l-Ḥārith Jummayn and Muzabbid at the time of the caliph al-Mahdī, and Abū l-'Ibār at the time of the caliph al-Mutawakkil (847–861). Muzabbid was still a popular character in the 17th century, as it can be inferred by his presence in two compilations of that period.

Buhlūl embodies a slightly different type and is still popular in the Persian and Turkish oral traditions (Marzolph 1983). This character is based on a contemporary of the caliph Hārūn al-Rashīd (786–809), a pious or even ascetic man linked to Shiism, who is believed to be buried in Baghdad. Marzolph (2010a: 160) describes him as "[s]ome kind of uncompromising, probably mentally deranged ascetic character, Buhlūl (by way of contamination with several other contemporaries) became the stereotype wise fool in the popular tradition of the Islamic world." Furthermore, he acted as "a mirroring reminder of the *vanitas mundi* (a function that, incidentally, corresponds to that of the court-fool in medieval Europe)" (Marzolph 1998: 123).

Juḥā

While the popularity of the afore-mentioned stock characters has decreased over the centuries, Juḥā is still popular in the folk tradition of several Mediterranean regions and beyond as the model of the trickster and fool. To give an example of his ability to travel and adapt in different contexts, he is known as Giufà in Sicily, Si Djeh'a in North-African Berber culture, Djoha in Jewish culture, Goḥa in Egypt, Jeḥa in Tunisia, Joḥi in Persian folklore, and is mixed with the Turkish Nasreddin Hoca. As is the case of other focusees, the fictional character has its starting point in a historical counterpart, identified with Dajīn ibn Thābit, known as Abū l-Ghuṣn, who lived in Baṣra and Kūfa in the 7th–8th century. A tradition established around the 14th century suggests that two different men who died in the same year inspired the fictional Juḥā, a pious man from Baṣra and a fool from Kūfa. This may explain the birth of a character who is sometimes capable of great intelligence and sometimes of utter foolishness (Corrao 1991: 21).

Juḥā is mentioned in the literary sources by the 7th-century poet ʿUmar ibn Abī Rabīʿa, as reported by Corrao. The first anecdote in which he appears as the protagonist is found in al-Jāḥiẓ, followed by his presence in various compilations. A booklet devoted entirely to him, *Kitāb nawādir Juḥā* (The book of Juḥā's anecdotes), was listed in the 10th-century *al-Fihrist* (The catalogue) by Ibn al-Nadīm (d. *ca.* 995) but did not survive. Marzolph (1998: 123) argues that his repertoire expanded considerably in the 15th/17th-century compilations, since this character combined a clear basic structure (the provocative half-wit) with a certain degree of openness. Thus, he was ascribed some anecdotes previously attributed to known or anonymous characters and new tales fitting his image, whose motifs are found in cross-cultural folklore. In this way, his popularity overshadowed that of other focusees.

With the printed editions of the 19th century, his tales started to merge with those originally attributed to the Turkish jester Nasreddin Hoca and the two characters started getting mistaken. Portrayed as either smart and wise or a fool with a great sense of humour, Nasreddin Hoca is the main protagonist of jocular anecdotes in the Turkish area of influence (from the Balkans to the Persian area). His supposed historical counterpart lived in the 13th–14th century and is often associated with Tamerlane's invasion of Anatolia. He is said to be born in a town near Eskişehir, whose natives were famous in folk stories for their strange behaviour and ingenuousness. A mausoleum attributed to him survives in Eskişehir (Marzolph *EI2*, 1996, 2002).

Marzolph suggests that Juḥā's repertoire has not just expanded but also developed. Early anecdotes contained some scatological and obscene material, whereas later compilations and printed editions domesticated this aspect, developing the image of the half-wit, philosopher, and social critic, sometimes harmless and sometimes provocative.

Juḥā is usually represented on his donkey, an animal associated with foolishness, but also with a great capacity of resistance and adaptability (Corrao 1991: 31). Across this rich tradition, his age varies: when he is young, he interacts with his father and mother; when he is old, he is accompanied by his son, who may be seen as his double. At the beginning of the anecdotes, the established order is usually disrupted either because Juḥā is victim of the situation or does not act according to the expectations. His own reaction or the external help from the members of his family function as magical tools restoring the order. In this process, Juḥā sometimes proves to be clever, sly, and to have a practical sense; sometimes his own foolishness solves the complicated situation, or he plays the fool to get out of troubles. His ruse often turns the situation against his opponents, who usually belong to a more powerful social group, thus challenging power relations. Furthermore, he often transgresses social and moral boundaries, even though not always consciously.

Language plays an important role in creating the humorous effect. For example, Juḥā takes idiomatic expressions literally or misunderstands some instructions. Some of his answers or key elements in the tales have crystallized in proverbs and sayings, such as Juḥā's nail (*mismār Juḥā*). In the story, the nail is a small clause that turns the contract in favour of Juḥā; in popular wisdom, it means a feeble excuse, but also a nuisance.

One of the reasons why Juḥā has become so popular is his ability to laugh at all aspects of everyday life and appeal to universal human experience. He is appreciated for his inclination to face all situations with a mixture of humour and wisdom, and his apparently candid way of exposing at people's faults. As Marzolph (2002: 767) puts it, "he would usually allow the audience to either share his delight in fooling his opponents and 'teaching them a lesson', of feel superior to his overt simplicity of mind." These features make him a dynamic character adaptable to the circumstances of modern life. He has abandoned his donkey and travels by train, bus, car, or plane; his opponents have become lawyers, politicians, and policemen; he tackles present day economic and political issues, such as unemployment, corruption, and inefficiency. Three essays collected in *L'humour en Orient* illustrate Juḥā's vitality in the modern Moroccan, Tunisian, and Jewish Ottoman traditions. This process of adaptation implies a partial overlapping with local folk characters and involves both the oral and written dimensions (El Hakim 1961; Fenoglio 1991; Fenoglio & Georgeon 1995).

1.3.4 *Arabian Nights*

Juḥā exemplifies how anecdotes are attached to certain characters and folktales migrate from one context to another. Such circulation of tales was central in the *Arabian Nights* (*Alf layla wa-layla*), a form of intermediate literature in which stories of multiple origins, originally performed orally as evening entertainment, were arranged in manuscripts.

Due to the entertaining purpose of this narrative, humour appears on various levels. In *Humor in Arabic Culture*, Ott suggests that laughter in the *Arabian Nights* carries the existential function of saving lives. To this purpose, the tales should be exciting and amusing, a combination expressed in Arabic by the notion of *ʿajīb wa-gharīb* (Ott 2009: 256). The variety of stories collected in the *Arabian Nights* paves the way for different types of humour covering the following functions: expressing human feelings, including *Schadenfreude* and a mocking attitude; driving the action; and sketching comic types, such as the court jester and characters pertaining to the lower strata of society. In this respect, *The Arabian Nights Encyclopedia* classifies the instances of humour into four main categories (Marzolph et al. 2004: 593–594): 1) anecdotes serving for entertainment at face value, usually related to sexuality and human weaknesses; 2) anecdotes integrated from works of *adab* literature, set in the court or among the Bedouin, serving as exemplary tales; 3) stories in which a rogue usually from pertaining to the lower class outsmarts a victim usually pertaining to the upper class; alcohol and hashish are prominent components in such stories; 4) comical effects caused by conflict or contrasts, such as the inversion of roles, opposition of roles (for example, the caliph and the vizier), disguises and mistaken identities, bawdy episodes and caricature eroticism, wordplay and general stereotypes.

The inversion of roles and integration of *adab* anecdotes are tackled by Larzul's essay in *L'humour en Orient* (1995), which examines the long tale of Abū l-Ḥasan the Wag (*al-khalīʿ*), known as *le dormeur éveillé* in Antoin Galland's French translation (1704). When Abū l-Ḥasan, the son of a merchant, dilapidates half of his fortune, he discovers that none of his friends is willing to help him. From here on, he invites a stranger into his house every night. One of his guests is the disguised caliph Ḥārūn al-Rashīd who makes him fall asleep and transports him to court making him believe that he is the caliph. In a subsequent encounter, Ḥārūn al-Rashīd reveals his trick and makes Abū l-Ḥasan his boon companion. The tale's epilogue contains Abū l-Ḥasan's revenge: the merchant and his wife play a trick on the caliph and his wife, using their false death to extort money. Having analysed the tale's structure, its interplay with *adab* sources, and main character, Larzul (1995) concludes that the *Arabian Nights* could create pieces of true humour without conforming to the balance of jest and earnest, due to their nature of entertaining intermediate literature. Furthermore, this literature was receptive of a non-orthodox way of thinking about gender relations and moral conduct, integrated through the lens of fiction and comedy.

Marzolph (2015) investigates the sources in which the same tale is attested for chronological purposes; his reconstruction illustrates that the story's epilogue was attributed to Abū Dulāma in several *adab* sources, whereas it was attached to other jocular characters of the Abbasid period, such as Abū Nuwās and Buhlūl, in 20th-century compilations.[18] Due to the popularity of these focusees, one might wonder if they appear in the *Arabian Nights*. However, their presence is very limited, as Marzolph explains:

> Besides the case of Juḥā in the Madrid manuscript, not one of the popular fools and tricksters of classical Arabic literature, such as Ash'ab, Buhlūl, Muzabbid, or Habannaqa play a prominent role as the protagonist of a story in an Arabic manuscript or edition of the *Arabian Nights*. In fact, the only prominent mention of such a character in the *Arabian Nights* is the chapter on Buhlūl the Jester in *The Diwan of Easy Jests and Laughing Wisdom*, once more added from extraneous material to the Mardrus edition. (Marzolph 2005: 322)

1.3.5 Shadow theatre and Ottoman *karagöz*

Another form of popular entertainment is shadow theatre (*khayāl al-ẓill*). Travelling from the Far East, mainly China and India, shadow theatre was attested in the Muslim world, from the Levant to Andalusia, since the 10th century. Due to the orality, the puppeteer's improvisation, and the crackdown of censorship, only few performances have been preserved.

The manuscripts of three shadow plays by Ibn Dāniyāl (d. 1311) have exceptionally survived.[19] They are characterized by their satirical depiction of the early Mamluk society and affinity with the classical *maqāmāt* (Corrao 1996; Dorigo Ceccato 1987–1988; Zargar 2006). With a focus on the lowest strata of the Cairene society, these plays rely extensively on licentiousness, obscenity, and scatology. Recent scholarship discusses the role of this indigenous dramatic tradition in modern Arabic theatre (Moreh 1992, 2010; Ruocco 2010).

These performances were imported from Egypt to Istanbul in the 16th century. According to some historical sources, the Ottoman Sultan Selim watched a shadow play by an Egyptian puppeteer re-enacting the hanging of the last Mamluk Sultan, which sealed the Ottoman conquest of Egypt in 1517. The play pleased the Sultan so much that he wanted this form of entertainment to be imported to Turkey. There, it developed as *karagöz* and spread to the regions controlled by the Empire, including Syria, Egypt, and North Africa.

In the same period, *Commedia dell'Arte* emerged in Western theatre. The two dramatic traditions have been paralleled for their structure, contents (including universal themes, such as food, love, and money), and characters (built

---

18 Marzolph classifies these narrative motifs: heritage squandered (Mot. W 131.1), the sleeper awakened (Aa.-Th. Type 1531), and the double pension – burial money (Aa.-Th. Type 1556). For motif classification, see: El-Shamy 1995, 2006; Thompson 1989.

19 For a recent critical edition and translation into English, see: Guo 2012.

mainly on geographical and professional stereotypes). The cast of characters in the Ottoman *karagöz* provides interesting insights on the mechanisms of humour and the audience it sought to entertain. As Stavrakopoulou (2012) notes, the cast usually discussed does not belong to the traditional repertoire (16th–17th century), but to the plays performed and written down in the 19th century. The two main characters are Karagöz and Hacivat: the former is an ordinary man, a kind of trickster who is wry and cunning; the latter is an opportunist who serves the wealthy and powerful. Around them gravitate characters of international folklore, such as the hunchback, the addicted, and the fool, as well as urban and female characters. Other types represent the different ethnic groups that lived under the Ottoman Empire, like the Albanian, the Jew, the Armenian, and the Arab. The parody of their accents and stereotypical attitudes produces a comic effect (Nicolas 1995). Furthermore, the political, military, and religious authorities were mocked, allowing a temporary disruption of the social and moral order, re-established by the end of the play. The *karagöz* adapted itself over the centuries and was able to target the shortcomings of society in the 19th and early 20th-century under the surface of a farcical show based on pranks, buffoonery, and obscenities.

This performance appealed to an audience that could recognize itself in the performance, as if it was a distorted mirror of reality. As Georgeon (1995: 92–94) suggests, the late Ottoman audience comprised mainly middle-class males belonging to different ethnic and religious groups. Originally the performances coincided with festive occasions, especially Ramaḍān nights, whereas at the turn of the century they were usually held in urban spaces like the cafés or trade centres (*khān*). The *karagöz* was similar to two other traditional forms of popular entertainment, *i.e.* improvisation theatre and professional storytelling. All three forms were affected by the introduction of modern media like the radio, translations and adaptations from Western comedies, and the decline of the Ottoman Empire. Their popularity rapidly declined between the beginning and the mid-20th century, but they survive as folkloric heritage (Georgeon 1995: 106).

1.3.6 Satirical press

The development of the printing press in the late Ottoman Empire favoured the birth of the satirical press, which flourished in periods of political change.[20]

20 To make a comparison, the satirical press in Iran flourished after the Constitutional Revolution (1906–1911) (Gheissari 2012).

The number of satirical magazines increased around the years of the Revolution of the Young Turks (1908) and also included Greek and Armenian contributions, as examined in *L'humour en Orient*. Needing a certain degree of freedom to be produced, the satirical magazines denounced the oppression caused by the indigenous and colonial political authorities, while depicting the local community with self-mockery. This portrait was particularly interesting in transitional periods, when the concept of nationalism was elaborated and the various communities negotiated their affiliation. Many of these publications were ephemeral because of censorship, changes in the political scenario, and circumstances affecting their main contributors (in some cases, their single contributor).

Kishtainy (1985: 69–99) makes similar considerations in his portrait of the pioneers of the Egyptian satirical press. The first magazines appeared in the late 19th century in the context of nationalistic struggles: Yaʿqūb Ṣanūʿ (also James Sanua, 1839–1912) launched *Abū naẓẓāra zarqāʾ* (est. 1877, The man with the blue spectacles), whereas ʿAbd Allāh al-Nadīm (1842–1896) created *al-Tankīt wa-l-tabkīt* (1881, Joking and censure) and *al-Ustādh* (1892–1893, The teacher). Their satire targeted the British colonial presence, the Egyptian royal family, despotic habits of the local authorities, and social behaviours of the Egyptians, including the backwardness of the peasants and the blind adoption of European customs by the bourgeoisie (De Angelis 2007; Ettmüller 2012b, 2013). Both authors supported the nationalist cause and were considered political agitators: Ṣanūʿ was exiled, whereas al-Nadīm, who had also been an orator for the 1881–1882 ʿUrābī revolt (Campanini 2005: 28–66; Daly 1998: 239–251), was chased by the authorities. The use of the Egyptian Colloquial Arabic, known for its immediacy and humorous effects, was part of their project to attract a wide audience to the nationalist cause.

Their satirical writings included colloquial poetry (*zajal*), dialogues, essays, and one-act plays (in the case of Ṣanūʿ), all of which has been recently reevaluated for its contribution to modern drama and fiction. *Zajal* refers to "rhymed strophic poems composed in non-classical Arabic and based rhythmically on metrical patterns adapted from the classical tradition" (Booth 1990: 10). Some decades later, the Egyptian satirical press hosted the literary compositions of another renowned humourist, Bayram al-Tūnisī (1893–1961). These literary figures will be further discussed in ch.2 to define the status of humorous writings in Egyptian literature. After the 1919 revolution against the British occupation, the publication of satirical magazines flourished again: *al-Kashkūl* was launched in 1921, whereas *Rūz al-Yūsif* was established in 1923. These magazines featured the first professional cartoons, after the early drawings by Ṣanūʿ (*Abou Naddara Collection* website; Booth 2013a, 2013b). Kazazian (1995) describes the Armenian Alexander Saroukhan (1898–1977) as the father of the Egyptian caricature.

Starting from this historical reconstruction, the study of satire and political humour also covers the contemporary period. For instance, Zanelli (2011) overviews Egyptian political humour, comprising satirical journalism, cartoons, and jokes till the 1990s. Other contributions look at satirical cartoons in North Africa, especially when contested by the religious and political authorities or even by religious extremism (De Poli 2011). Another type of political humour that has received great attention are jokes, as discussed in §1.4.

1.3.7 Contemporary literature

When it comes to the modern and contemporary period, the three edited volumes consulted for this overview pay large attention to humour and satire in social interactions, jokes, cartoons, and cinema. Besides this, *Humor in Arabic Culture* looks at a selection of contemporary authors from heterogeneous contexts: Driss Chraïbi (1926–2007), who wrote in French in post-colonial Morocco; Rashīd Ḍaʿīf (b. 1945), a contemporary Lebanese author invited to work with a German writer in the exchange programme *West-östlicher Diwan*; Zakariyyā Tāmir (b. 1931), a Syrian writer living in exile in London since 1981; and historical plays revisited in Egyptian drama. Each case study is analysed from a different perspective, according to its main stylistic features and the humorous aspects developed at most.

For instance, satire in Tāmir's short stories is crafted through the characters' caricature and parody of the literary heritage. These techniques generate a kind of black humour and a Kafkesque world view, which conveys the author's socio-political criticism (Dové 2009). The essay about the Egyptian drama considers satire on stage as a form of artistic resistance, particularly effective when kings or sultans interact with the ordinary people. In the two plays under scrutiny the counter-discourse of the oppressed is inserted through the popular oral tradition, including rhyming songs, jokes, and tunes. To circumvent censorship, old plays, foreign plays, and plays re-enacting historical episodes are usually staged (Abou El Naga 2009).

One of these foreign plays adapted to the Egyptian context is *al-Malik huwwa al-malik* (The King is the king) by the Syrian playwright Saʿd Allāh Wannūs (1941–1997), known alongside Muḥammad al-Māghūṭ (1934–2006) for his satirical criticism of the political scenario (Hamdan 2004; Milich & Tramontini 2018. Ruocco 1987). Egyptian playwrights, like Alfred Faraj (1929–2005), Yūsuf Idrīs (1927–1991), Najīb Surūr (1932–1978), and ʿAlī Sālim (1936–2015), have developed different aspects of humour and satire in their works. Besides his satirical plays, Sālim is famous for *Riḥla ilā Isrāʾīl* (A journey to Israel), the travelogue of his journey to Israel published in 1994 (Franke-Ziedan 2013; Ruocco 2010: 100–105, 173–174).

Another type of comedies in Egyptian theatre and cinema exploits funny characters, misunderstandings, absurd situations, and laughable sketches that usually lead to a happy ending. The popularity of these comedies is linked to some famous actors, for example ʿĀdil Imām (b. 1940). One essay in *L'Humour en Orient* examines two films of the 1990s starring Imām, in which different comic strategies allow to tackle the same political issue, *i.e.* the violence perpetrated by Islamic extremist groups which threatened social coexistence (Poulet 1995).[21]

The study of humour in contemporary fiction and drama focuses on single authors and satire, seen as a weapon of cultural resistance for its oblique socio-political criticism. Satire also characterizes other forms of cultural production circulating in the last decades and intensifying around the 2011 Revolution, such as cartoons, comics, graphic novels, satirical columns and fictionalized essays (often collected in books published under the label of *adab sākhir*), songs, blogs, TV programmes, jokes and memes circulating online. These forms of humour are closely intertwined with the current events and represent a cultural background shared among the intended audience of humorous writings. Political humour is one of the elements contributing to their success with the audience: starting from a classic study in this field by Kishtainy (1985, 2009), recent scholarship looks at different brands of political humour across the Arab world, exploring its relationship with the upheavals (crem 2019 website; Damir-Geilsdorf & Milich 2020; Fähndrich 2012).[22] Among the manyfold genres of political humour, the next section tackles Egyptian political jokes as part of popular culture.

1.4 Egyptian political jokes

> The desire to build and strengthen bridges led them to gradually explore the art of fine evening conversation. It fell upon El Shanqeety to take the initiative, for he had spent his military service training how to erect bridges, and one evening he accosted Abdel Maguid with that most common of Egyptian passwords: "Have you heard the latest joke?" Abdel Maguid pretended to be interested: "No, what?" El Shanqeety, with a slow deliberateness, that allowed him to remember the detail he had been struggling all day to memorize, related the joke: "This man's getting drunk and his friend asks him, 'Why do you drink?' So

21 For further reference on comedy in Arabic theatre, see: Kolk & Decreus 2005. For further reference on comedy in Arabic cinema, see: Devi & Rahman 2014.

22 For cartoons and caricatures, see: Ettmüller 2012a; Guyer 2015, *Oum Cartoon* (website). For comics, see: Jacob Høigilt 2019. The best-known satirical TV show launched after the 2011 revolution was *il-Barnāmag* by Bāsim Yūsuf (b. 1974).

> the man says, 'To forget.' His friend asks him, 'Forget what?' The man thinks for a minute then says, 'I can't remember.'"
>
> Abdel Maguid burst into laughter and came back from the bank the next day with a similar password. "This man called Ass gets fed up with his name so he changes it and goes to his friend. He's really happy: 'Guess what?' he says, 'I've changed my name.' His friend says: 'Congratulations. What did you change it to?' The man says: 'Fish.' His friend's surprised, he asks him: 'Can you swim?' He says: 'No.' His friend says: 'So you're still an ass.'"
>
> El Shanqeety burst into laughter. In fact, he slapped his thighs with the palms of his hand, initiating a period of thigh slapping that did not last for long, for the spring from which they had supped soon dried up. Indeed, the technological progress that the Egyptians had been achieving had led to a diminishing of their creative ability in the one field in which they had historically dominated all other nations, and their output declined, quantitively and qualitatively, until they had exhausted its limited themes: politics (the laughing cow, or *la vache qui rit*) and racism (the Upper Egyptians). (Ibrahim 2001: 76–77)

This passage from the novel *Dhāt* (1992; *Zaat*, 2001) by Ṣunʿallāh Ibrāhīm exemplifies the presence of political jokes in literature. By portraying two neighbours exchanging innocent jokes, the narrator mocks the Egyptian tradition of political humour and its diminishing effectiveness: now it seems confined to regional humour directed against the Upper Egyptians and political humour mocking president Mubarak, who was nicknamed *la vache qui rit*, from a cheese brand, to make fun of his supposed appreciation for joking. To be sure, the study of literary humour is not limited to instances of jokes in fiction, where the comic is rather developed in multiple strands and intertwined with formal techniques like parody, ambiguity, and linguistic variation. Nevertheless, political jokes illustrate what contemporary Egyptians laugh at and belong to a shared cultural background that can be appealed to in humorous narratives.

Jokes are a vital component of popular culture because they circulate from mouth to mouth reflecting common feelings about society, marriage, religion, and taboos. Among them, political jokes are a barometer of the situation. In his analysis of political jokes about the former presidents Nasser (1956–1970), Sadat (1970–1981), and Mubarak (1981–2011), Shehata (1992) shares this view and maintains that political jokes are more common and pervasive in authoritarian societies. When freedom of speech and political opposition suffer limitations, political jokes become an alternative form of criticism without fear of reprisal. They can elude censorship thanks to their oral collective circulation and the impersonal joke-teller can say something that, otherwise, would be unacceptable.[23]

23 For political jokes in authoritarian societies, see: Larsen 1980. Political jokes are also tackled in the collected volumes consulted in the overview: Binay 2009 in *Humor in Arabic Culture*; Helmy Ibrahim 1995 in *L'humour en Orient*.

Shehata relies on Freud's distinction between innocent jokes that do not have a purpose and tendentious jokes that have a purpose. The latter are divided into hostile jokes, serving the purpose of aggressiveness, and obscene jokes, serving the purpose of exposure. Shehata places all political jokes within the category of hostile jokes because their main function is ridiculing the leaders and regimes. This non-violent aggression triggers the mechanism described by Freud (1960: 103) as follows: "by making our enemy small, inferior, despicable or comic, we achieve in a roundabout way the enjoyment of overcoming him." Freud's classification is followed by many scholars, including Raskin (1985: 222–246). While political humour is often seen as a weapon of creative resistance, its practical effects in achieving change are still debated. The aggressive theory is, thus, complemented by the relief theory, which sees laughter as a discharge of nervous energy and temporary psychological relief. Transposed to the social level, political jokes function as a safety-valve (*tanfīs*) and coping mechanism for bearing the pressures of life.[24]

Another approach describing the collective and subversive nature of political jokes is the Bakhtinian concept of the carnivalesque. In their essay about translating jokes, Salem and Taira (2012) identify humour as a key element in the mass protests leading to the ouster of Mubarak. Among other definitions, these protests were labelled *al-thawra al-ḍāḥika* (the laughing revolution), because of the high number of jokes and their immediate dissemination. Humour allowed the demonstrators to break the fear barrier, incorporate the unfolding events, and mock the official discourse thanks to a collective counter-narrative. Salem and Taira frame this mockery, which suspends socio-political hierarchies and dethrones revered figures of power, into Bakhtin's conceptualization of the carnival:

> As the Russian cultural critic Mikhail Bakhtin succinctly put it "during carnival: what is suspended first of all is hierarchical structure and all the forms of terror, reverence, piety, and etiquette with it" and "mock crowning and subsequent decrowning of the carnival king." Finally, "his crown is removed, the other symbols of authority are taken away, he is ridiculed and beaten."[25] (Salem and Taira 2012: 185)

Moreover, they suggest two further functions of political humour: eliciting not only sympathy, but also solidarity amongst the people and performing a didactic function by communicating important demands in a simple way. Finally,

24 On the functions of political humour, especially discussing the notion of *tanfīs*, see: Mannone 2020.

25 Another essay that applies the carnivalesque to the study of Arab political humour is Badarneh (2011).

they underline the role of the new media in the dissemination of political jokes, which also affects their forms and themes.

As regards the analysis of forms and themes, political jokes have been tackled through an interdisciplinary approach. Shahata adopts a sociological perspective by examining how political humour changes together with the historical circumstances and a thematic/narratological perspective by illustrating the jokes' motives, structure, and characters.[26] This double approach reconstructs how the three former presidents were ridiculed:

> Under Nasser, Egyptians criticized the absence of freedom of expression, police methods, including torture, the Egyptian Army's performance in the 1967 War and the failure of (Nasser's) socialism in Egypt. During Sadat's presidency, Egyptians were highly critical of Jihan Al-Sadat's role in politics, Sadat's harsh relations with the Coptic Church and Pope Shenouda III, the corruption of the Sadat regime, and the facade of 'the religious president'. Finally, the criticisms of Mubarek have been quite personal and ridicule his intelligence, competence and worthiness as a leader. (Shehata 1992: 87–88)

Mubarak was ironically compared to the donkey, the monkey, and the laughing cow, as mentioned also in the passage from the novel *Dhāt* quoted above. His surname, literally meaning 'blessed', also led to wordplay. With Mubarak staying in power longer and longer, new topics were added: the repressive measures taken by a regime that presented itself as more liberal, violations of human rights, unemployment, corruption, government negligence determining absurd situations in daily life, Mubarak's age, and the possibility that his son would inherit the presidency.

This reconstruction, based mainly on content, does not overlook the culturally bound nature of humour and linguistic strategies, all of which is systematically analysed by the General Theory of Verbal Humour (§1.2.2). Hammoud (2014) slightly modifies this theory to study one-line Egyptian political jokes posted on Facebook from November 2011 till January 2012, with the aim of comparing spontaneous and professional jokes. She concludes that the two types of jokes are similar, except for some differences in Target (professional jokes are keener on introducing self-criticism) and Narrative Form (spontaneous jokes rely frequently on question-answer sequences). They are similar in Situation, since they are all set in Egypt and deal with its socio-political scenario. This setting leads to the inclusion of several "words or pieces of information that pertain only to Egyptian cultural elements that can hardly be understood outside their cultural-bound context" (Hammoud 2014: 24). These cultural elements pose a big challenge for translators, as Salem

26 The same double approach is found in Binay's study of Lebanese jokes (Binay 2009, 2013). For a content-based review of Egyptian political jokes, see: ʿĀdil Ḥamūda 1990.

and Taira (2012: 195–196) remark. The main challenge is transferring all these elements, as well as wordplay and rhetorical figures, in an effective way that renders the immediacy of the jokes. As regards Language, the jokes examined by Hammoud employ lexical ambiguity (paronymy and homonimy) to create wordplay, antonyms to juxtapose contradictory ideas, repetition to provide a rhythmic pattern that exaggerates the situation, figurative language, and satire. Hammoud's language-driven approach examines the jokes' content through the lens of semantic classes. For example, the opposition between 'we' and 'they' serves to criticize the rulers or expose the mishaps of the ordinary Egyptians.

The linguistic register of the analysed jokes reflects the diglossia (in some cases, polyglossia) existing in the Arabic-speaking communities, where two languages coexist and cover different functions (Bassiouney 2008; Haeri 2002; Kebede, Kindt & Høigilt 2013). Modern Standard Arabic (MSA) is the language of formal communication especially in written texts, such as textbooks, newspapers, magazines, fiction and nonfiction, and administration. The language of daily exchanges and nonprint media is Colloquial Arabic (CA), used in television, radio, theatre, and cinema. Even though it is not accepted as the written language in formal contexts, the colloquial is usually employed in captions and advertisement, and has influenced the style of the printed media. Since the colloquial expresses verbal humour in non-formal interactions, the spontaneous jokes of Hammoud's corpus are mainly in this linguistic variety, whereas professional jokes are written in Modern Standard Arabic with some colloquial words put into quotation marks. The juxtaposition of different linguistic registers produces a comic effect.

To sum up, an integrated content and language-driven perspective illustrates the strategies used to ridicule the rulers and expose the shortcomings of society in Egyptian political jokes. Translation studies remark the difficulty of balancing the jokes' brevity with the need to clarify the cultural references, while transferring wordplay and rhetorical figures often based on sound.

1.5 Literary and popular references

Keeping in mind the culturally bound nature of humour, which varies in different cultures and historical periods, the main aesthetic and linguistic theories explain the cross-cultural mechanisms underlying this phenomenon. This chapter has focused on the application of these theories to literary criticism. Malti-Douglas adopts a theoretical framework which goes beyond the descriptive study of humour instances to examine the narrative and rhetorical elements eliciting humour in pre-modern Arabic literary texts. In her study of American humorous novels, Larkin-Galiñanes integrates the main humour theories, linguistics, and narratology to see how the cognitive processing and attitudinal positioning affect the textual structure. The studies of humorous narratives provide useful notions such as register humour, cooperation between producers and receivers, and humour enhancers. Translation studies look at the transferability of humour despite the local cultural references and wordplay.

Triezenberg's humour enhancers will inform the analysis of the Egyptian novels that contain stereotypes, stock characters, and repetition/variation. Stock characters, in fact, are the protagonists of jocular anecdotes in the Arab literary tradition and folklore. Juḥā is the famous Arab trickster and wise fool, who travels across the Mediterranean acquiring different traits in each region. Furthermore, the master of pre-modern prose, al-Jāḥiẓ, suggested that anecdotes are more effective if ascribed to famous tricksters or historically recognizable characters. The analysis of the characters in the novels of the corpus will look at the revival of stock characters, their role in the contemporary context, and familiarity with the intended audience. In other words, are these comic characters the modern versions of Juḥā? Is al-Jāḥiẓ's rule still valid?

Humour in the Arab tradition is found in many literary and popular forms that have been collected and studied with a focus on the pre-modern period and late Ottoman Empire. Humour in contemporary literature, instead, has received only partial attention. It is usually examined alongside other forms of cultural production, such as satirical journalism, cartoons, jokes, and cinema, which suggests the relevance of socio-political satire and the constant exchange between literary and non-literary forms. Moreover, there is a focus on single authors, such as Zakariyyā Tāmir and Imīl Ḥabībī, who are considered masters of irony and satire in the Syrian and Palestinian literature respectively. These writers appear almost as exceptions.

Keeping this in mind, this book aims at looking at a recent period in Egyptian literature (from the 1980s onwards) to identify some representative authors of humorous novels, establish the connections between them and within the literary scene, and examine humour through a close textual analysis. The next chapter examines humour in the novelistic canon and illustrates the selected corpus and analytical framework.

2 Masters of humour

> It was a joke at the start. Perhaps it was a joke in the end too. Actually it was not a joke in the real sense, but an incident, rather, which happened to involve those fabricators of jokes who were past masters of the art. Y. Idris, Did You Have to Turn on the Light, Li-Li?, 2009: 109

The three Egyptian authors chosen for this study belong to two different generations. Muḥammad Mustajāb (1938–2005) and Khayrī Shalabī (1938–2011), whose career has spanned over several decades, belong to the so-called Generation of the Sixties. Ḥamdī Abū Julayyil (b. 1967) belongs to the so-called Generation of the Nineties and the group of authors who gained recognition at the beginning of the 2000s. Despite this generational gap, all three writers share many similarities in their lives, careers, and style.

This chapter outlines the selection criteria for the corpus and the research questions. It describes the analytical framework for the study of the four selected novels, which is conducted in ch.3–6. Then, it sets the selected authors against the background of the contemporary Egyptian literary scene, providing their biographical profiles and illustrating some features of their literary output relevant for the subsequent analysis.

2.1 Re-designing the canon

The study of humour in the contemporary Egyptian novel requires to consider the canon formation of modern fiction and the boundaries of the legitimate literary field (Casini, Paniconi & Sorbera 2012; Jacquemond 2008; Selim 2003, 2004). The realist novel was canonized as the main narrative form within the hegemonic liberal nationalist discourse of the early 20th century, responding to the needs of the reformist intellectuals and the taste of the emerging middle-class audience. Developing over the decades and taking an experimental turn since the 1960s, the novel has been considered by the literary establishment as a serious venue to define the cultural identity and negotiate modernity.

In his sociological study of modern Egyptian literature, Jacquemond (2008) draws from Bourdieu (1992) the concept of legitimate field: Bourdieu sees the cultural field as the site of a struggle for the monopoly of legitimacy, *i.e.* the monopoly of power to define who is a writer. Jacquemond argues that the legitimate field in Egyptian literature broadly coincides with engaged literature characterized by the fusion of creativity and commitment. The struggle over legitimization concerns both formal experimentations and those genres that are considered popular, such as romances, detective stories, and satirical writings. Jacquemond suggests that

https://doi.org/10.1515/9783110725414-003

satire and humour blur the boundaries between high and low literature, as categorized by literary criticism and cultural institutions, because they have been employed both in novels and other writings published in popular outlets in the early stages of the novelistic canonization and the following decades.

These writings published in the press or in book-length collections include columns, sketches, travelogues, autobiographical writings, and neo-*maqāmāt*. For example, Ibrāhīm ʿAbd al-Qādir al-Māzinī (1890–1949) was a poet, literary critic, and writer whose humour emerges both in his novels and series of vignettes later collected into volumes (Badawi 1973; Hutchins 2010; Kilpatrick 1993: 234–235).[27] Similarly, Mustajāb, one of the authors of this corpus, is famous for the devastating satire of both his fiction and columns.

This complementarity leads to reconsidering the contribution of satirical writings to Egyptian early modern fiction. Recent scholarship has re-evaluated some pioneers of the *nahḍa* such as Ṣanūʿ, al-Nadīm (§1.3.5) and Muḥammad al-Muwayliḥī (1858–1930, §4.1.1), whose writings aimed at the satirical dissection of the society.[28] They integrated a didactic purport with some fictional elements and gave a new form to pre-modern satire, especially the *maqāma* for prose and *zajal* for poetry. Adapted from the classical rhymed strophic poems composed in non-classical Arabic and based rhythmically on metrical patterns, modern *zajal* includes narrative ballads and other colloquial poetic compositions. In this respect, a seminal study is Booth's analysis of Bayram al-Tūnisī's output in the form of *zajal*, vernacular prose dialogues, and parodical neo-*maqāmāt*. Booth (1990) examines al-Tūnisī's satire in relation to the historical context, his political and cultural mission, and the publication venue. She argues that satire explodes at the intersection of the thematic focus, compositional form, diction, and intertextuality with the literary antecedents.

The attention to such writers leads to the second consideration about the boundaries of the legitimate field. Except for al-Muwayliḥī, the afore-mentioned

27 Al-Māzinī's novels are *Ibrāhīm al-kātib* (1931; *Ibrahim the Writer*, 1976) and *Ibrāhīm al-thānī* (1943, Ibrahim II). His vignettes, comic sketches, and essays were collected in *Ṣundūq al-dunyā* (1929, Peep show) and *Khuyūṭ al-ʿankabūt* (1935, Spider's webs).

28 *Nahḍa*, often translated as Arab Renaissance, was a period of cultural and socio-political development starting from the 19th century. It marks the beginning of modern Arabic literature with changes in the literary language and genres thanks to the rediscovery of the Arab cultural heritage and the influence of Western models. This re-evaluation also involves the Lebanese Aḥmad Fāris al-Shidyāq (1805–1887, §4.1.1), who developed satire and parody in his rich and varied literary output engaging with the European and Arab cultural traditions (Hamarneh 2010; Junge 2019).

authors made an extensive use of Egyptian Colloquial Arabic. Humorous and satirical writings have been placed on the margins of the legitimate field also because of their diction. Indeed, poetry and fiction written in the colloquial are popular among the audience and allow emotional identification but struggle for critical recognition (Booth 1992, 1993; Cachia 2011; De Angelis 2007: 53–78; Radwan 2012).

Yet, the exclusive correlation between the colloquial as a written language and non-serious topics has been challenged by recent scholarship. Booth (1993), Selim (2004), and De Angelis (2007) argue that the pioneers of the satirical press chose the colloquial to involve the broadest possible audience in their discussion of socio-political reforms. These pioneers are described as humorous reformers (*iṣlāḥī fukāhī*) (Booth 1993: 422; De Angelis 2007: 62). Furthermore, Selim (2004: 25–35) remarks that Ṣanūʿ and al-Nadīm anticipate the novel's dialogic dimension with multiple contrapuntal voices representing the society of the emerging nation. These voices include the hybrid colloquial voice of the peasants, both subaltern and rebellious, mocking the official discourse of the authorities, aristocracy, and new urban elite. Selim (2004: 119–126) finds this parodic colloquial voice also in a canonical novel known for its ironic representation of the Egyptian legal system: *Yawmiyyāt nāʾib fī l-aryāf* (1937; *Maze of Justice*, 1989) by Tawfīq al-Ḥakīm (1898–1987). She suggests that the villagers' colloquial language contrasts comically with the narrator's controlled Modern Standard Arabic and conveys a critique of the hegemonic discourse, including that of the realist bourgeois novel.

As Rosenbaum (2011) and De Angelis (2007: 187–193) note, Egyptian Coloquial Arabic as a literary language has significantly expanded and increased its recognition with the practice of some writers in the 1960s, the 1990s, and the beginning of the 21st century, when it has also been influenced by Internet communication. Some writers choose exclusively the colloquial, while many others mix the two varieties not simply for ideological purposes but also for aesthetic ones.[29]

Reflecting this negotiation of the boundaries of legitimate literature, humorous writings of the 2000s have attracted some critical attention because of their extensive use of the colloquial and re-definition of popular genres. Among several examples, it is worth mentioning at least three works: *An takūn*[a] *ʿAbbās al-ʿAbd* (2003; *Being Abbas el Abd*, 2009), a post-modern novel by Aḥmad al-ʿĀydī (b. 1974); *ʿAyza itgawwiz* (2008; *I Want to Get Married!*, 2010) by Ghāda ʿAbd al-ʿĀl (b. 1978), a blog turned into a book and TV comedy series, whose social satire revolves around marriage; and Khālid al-Khamīsī's (b. 1968) *Taksī. Ḥawādīt al-mashāwīr* (2006; *Taxi*, 2008), which merges a sociological portrait

29 For an anthology of Egyptian literature written in the colloquial, see: Dūss & Davies 2013.

and the episodic structure of the neo-*maqāma*. While it is true that the exensive presence of Egyptian Colloquial Arabic is a key factor in their success, the interest in these writing is not limited to the equation between this linguistic variety and humour. Their humorous style and thematic focus have been examined by looking at multiple linguistic registers, characters' construction, genre-crossing, and exploitation of the literary antecedents for comical purposes (Avallone 2011; El-Ariss 2013: 145–171; Pepe 2012).

Furthermore, *'Ayza itgawwiz* and *Taksī* share some features with the new wave of *adab sākhir* (satirical literature), a broad label including political columns, fictionalized essays, and humorous books published since the mid-2000s exposing the mishaps of Egyptian society in a humorous way. Reviving the tradition of socio-political satire of the Seventies and afterwards, this new wave develops some issues that are close to the Egyptian youth employing their slang and references to pop culture. Among satirical writers are Bilāl Faḍl (b. 1974), 'Umar Ṭāhir (b. 1973), Aḥmad al-'Usaylī (b. 1976), Haytham Dabbūr (b. 1986), Usāma Gharīb, and Īhāb Mu'awwaḍ (b. 1969). Satirical books soon became bestsellers due to a combination of marketing and linguistic strategies: serialisation and labelling makes these products recognisable on the one hand, while on the other, mixing Modern Standard Arabic and Egyptian Colloquial Arabic attracts many readers. As it happened to their antecedents, the literary status of these writings has been questioned because of their publication venue, the interplay of fiction and non-fiction, and the colloquial diction linked to a non-serious representation of everyday life (Dozio 2019: 292–294). Nevertheless, this new wave has attracted some critical attention for its ability to exemplify the changes in the book market and the evolution of code-mixing in the written language (§Introduction).

2.2 A canon of humour

Re-defining the status of humorous writings within the canon, with special reference to the *nahḍa* and the recent resurgence of satirical writings, allows to identify some masters of humour. This gallery of masters is complemented by some consecrated authors who employ humour as one of their stylistic tools.[30] They are usually presented as individual cases: al-Māzinī and al-Ḥakīm for the early modern novel; Najīb Maḥfūẓ (1911–2006) and Yūsuf Idrīs (1927–1991) for realist fiction (Allen 1994; Bayyūmī 1994).

30 In sociology of literature, consecration is the culmination of a legitimizing process which entitles the consecrated writer to confer a similarly privileged status on others.

A comparative approach, instead, is found in the study of the literary innovations introduced by the Generation of the Sixties, some of which are related to irony, parody, and satire. This literary avant-garde broke the mimetic approach in fiction by developing some experimental techniques, such as narrative fragmentation, fractured or cancelled time, antiheroes, unreliable narrators, and polyphony, including the voices inserted through intertextuality and metafiction. These formal innovations allowed to criticize, often indirectly, the oppressive regime as well as the alienation of the self and the intellectual in society (Casini 2003; Ramadan 2019). In his study of innovations in Arabic fiction from 1979 till 2002, Caiani remarks that:[31]

> Nonetheless, it is true that most of the texts under scrutiny in this study, though not devoid of humour, ironic asides and comic sketches, have a non-ironic purpose. [. . .]
>
> We often find the same serious approach to socio-political criticism and discourses on historiography, which in contemporary writers like Rushdie are mainly conveyed through irony and humour. Other contemporary Arab writers, like Ṣunʿallāh Ibrāhīm for example, use irony to convey their political criticism and Ḥanān al-Shaykh (b. 1945) is one of the few Arab writers who portrays serious themes (such as the life of Arab exiles in London in *Inna-hā Lundun yā ʿazīzī*, 2001; *Only in London*, 2001) in an often lighthearted and humorous style.
>
> (Caiani 2007: 129)

Ṣunʿallāh Ibrāhīm, mentioned in this quote, and Jamāl al-Ghīṭānī (1945–2015) are two writers of the Sixties whose experimental novels have received great critical attention for their ironic purpose and techniques. Kassem-Draz (1981, 1982), who examines al-Ghīṭānī and Ibrāhīm alongside Yaḥyā al-Ṭāhir ʿAbdallāh (1938–1981) and Majīd Ṭūbyā (1938), argues that the ironical ethos presides over the formal innovations of the Generation of the Sixties. A close textual analysis captures the strategies creating an ironic distance (*al-mufāraqa*) to break the mimetic approach and avoid censorship.

In his novel *al-Zaynī Barakāt* (1971; *Zayni Barakat*, 2006), al-Ghīṭānī plays an intertextual game with the chronicle of the Mamluk historiographer Ibn Iyās (d. 1522). The setting of the novel, Mamluk Egypt on the eve of the Ottoman conquest, is paralleled with Nasserist Egypt on the eve of the 1967 military defeat through parody, pastiche, and polyphony. Furthermore, as Kilpatrick (1993: 266) remaks, al-Ghīṭānī employs other humour-related techniques in his novel *Waqāʾiʿ ḥārat al-Zaʿfarānī* (1976; *The Zafarani Files*, 2009) to expose the mechanisms of

---

31 This study looks at Fuʾād al-Takarlī (1927–2008), Idwār al-Kharrāṭ (1926–2015), Ilyās Khūrī (b. 1948), and Muḥammad Barrāda (b. 1938). The comparative approach lies in the choice of authors from four Arab countries (Iraq, Egypt, Lebanon, and Morocco, respectively) and the reference to the notions elaborated in Western literary criticism (for example, post-modernism and Bakhtin's dialogic imagination).

coercion in society: the story opens with an epidemic of impotence in the alley and includes grotesque characters, doses of humour, and fantasy.

According to Kassem-Draz (1981) and subsequent studies, Ibrāhīm is a master of satire for his novels *Najmat Aghusṭus* (1974, The Star of August), *al-Lajna* (1981; *The Committee*, 2002), and *Dhāt* (1992; *Zaat*, 2001). His satirical tools are antiheroes, the narrator's detachment, ironic echoes of the official discourse, and intertextuality with non-fictional sources. These techniques mock the shortcomings of a rapidly changing society in the years of economic liberalization and global capitalism, while expressing the alienation of the self.

Kassem-Draz (1981) analyzes the mechanisms of ironic distance also in Yaḥyā al-Ṭāhir ʿAbdallāh and Majīd Ṭūbyā: the former employs the folktale as hypotext for parody,[32] whereas the latter inserts the fantastic into reality to create a sense of ambiguity. Storytelling and folk culture (in ʿAbdallāh), the magical and fantasy (in Ṭūbyā and al-Ghīṭānī), and the influence of Sufi language (in ʿAbd al-Ḥakīm Qāsim) are other facets of literary experimentation that have been recently studied.

Adopting Kassem-Draz's approach, Paniconi (2006a) employs narrative irony as the lens to examine some novels of the 1980s and early 1990s written by writers of the Sixties who had reached by then their maturity and recognition.[33] She suggests that irony is a critical distance that allows to represent reality with non-mimetic techniques and ultimately criticize it. Furthermore, she contrasts these literary innovations with those brought about by the Generation of the Nineties.

The Generation of the Nineties has taken the formal innovations of the previous decades to their extreme, elaborating a poetics of the self (*kitābat al-dhāt*) which shies away from big national and ideological issues (*ikhtifāʾ al-qaḍāyā al-kubrā*). The literary critic Sayid al-Baḥrāwī (2005) defines this poetics as "l'écriture pour la vie", whereas the novelist May al-Tilmisānī (b. 1965) calls it "writing on the margins of history" (*kitāba ʿalā hāmish al-tārīkh*) (Paniconi 2006b: 66). Speaking of "the novel of the closed horizon", Sabry Hafez (2001, 2010) suggests that these experimental narrative techniques reflect the recent urban transformations, in particular the haphazard development of informal settlements in Cairo (*al-madīna al-ʿaswāʾiyya* or third city). On this background, Paniconi (2006a, 2006b) argues that the new avant-garde does not aim at representing reality, not even

32 In semiotics and literary criticism, the term hypotext is defined in relation to hypertext. Gérard Genette (1982) used the term hypertext to designate those literary texts that allude, derive from, or relate to an earlier work or hypotext. The hypotext can be re-elaborated in a number of forms, such as imitation, parody, pastiche, transpositions, and continuations. The hypertext and its hypotext make up a multilayered palimpsest.

33 This study looks at Ibrāhīm Aṣlān (1935–2012), Salwā Bakr (b. 1949), Ibrāhīm ʿAbd al-Majīd (b. 1946), Ṣunʿallāh Ibrāhīm, and Yaḥyā Tāhir ʿAbdallāh.

through ironic distance. Instead, irony becomes a self-referential mechanism to explore the self's inner world and the writing process.

Egyptian fiction of the late 1970s and 1980s offers some interesting material for the study of humour and related phenomena. So far, it has been examined how ironic distance is intertwined with the narrative elements, leading to formal experimentation. This book, instead, looks at those novels that combine this experimentation and the amusing effects of comedy. These writings do not only use irony as a critical distance from reality and the established literary conventions but employ humour as their main compositional feature. Keeping in mind that the same years saw a significant production of satirical plays and journalism,[34] a comparative approach allows to explore a fictional trend in humorous writings and the network of relations between authors. This study aims at identifying some masters of humour who have received some critical recognition but are still understudied compared to the pioneers and other writers of the 1970s and 1980s (for example, al-Ghīṭānī and Ibrāhīm). Doing so, it aims at contributing to the study of experimental post-Mahfuzian literature by defining a humorous sub-genre in which it is possible to identify some recurrent humour-generating techniques and see how they evolve over the decades.

A criterion for the selection been Larkin-Galiñanes's definition of humorous novels: "those which maintain a constant and recurring effect of laughter caused by the adventures and mis-adventures of their characters, and the situations they get themselves into and create" (Larkin-Galiñanes 2002: 143). Besides this definition, the selection has been guided by Arab and Western reviews describing some novels as humorous and satirical; nevertheless, the aim is going beyond these labels to understand the mechanisms of humour. Another factor is the presence of humour on the level of the story, as it is performed in comical episodes and witty repartees by individual characters and groups, popular entertainers, and comedy actors. Finally, attention has been devoted to novels that discuss humour from a sociological perspective (what do Egyptian laugh at?) or metanarrative perspective (how to write in a playful way?). Indeed, these passages contain humour-related vocabulary describing the comical types (agents and victims), functions of humour, and degrees of laughter.

Among the writers of the Sixties, Khayrī Shalabī is usually associated with humour because of his vivid language and depiction of eccentric characters living on the margins. The Egyptian literary critic ʿAṣfūr (1999: 309–318) suggests that this writing from and about the margins reflects a carnivalesque joy subverting both the

34 For satirical drama, see the afore-mentioned ʿAlī Sālim, whereas popular satirical prose writers were Muḥammad ʿAfīfī (1922–1981), ʿĀṣim Ḥanafī, and Maḥmūd al-Saʿdanī (1927–2010).

social hierarchies and literary compositional principles. Because of this reception, Shalabī's works are suitable for exploring literary humour in contemporary Egyptian fiction. Moreover, the thematic focus on the margins and urban underworld has restricted the selection to a sub-group of novels that portray these communities with humour. Therefore, the selected corpus does not encompass all the major features and topics of humorous writing but is representative of a certain trend. Besides Shalabī, Muḥammad Mustajāb and Ḥamdī Abū Julayyil exemplify this trend over a time span of three decades. Shalabī and Mustajāb belong to the so-called Generation of the Sixties and reached their maturity in the 1980s. Both increased their critical recognition at the beginning of the 21st century and influenced younger writers. In particular, Shalabī published some popular novels in the 1990s and 2000s, which represent the link with younger authors like Abū Julayyil.

Applying these stylistic, thematic, and chronological criteria, four novels have been selected:

1. *The Secret History of Nu'man Abd al-Hafiz* (2008; *Min al-tārīkh al-sirrī li-Nu'mān 'Abd al-Ḥāfiẓ*, 1986 [1982]) by Mustajāb, the antiepic of a village boy told by a non-reliable historian.
2. *The Time-Travels of the Man Who Sold Pickles and Sweets* (2010; *Riḥlāt al-ṭurshajī al-ḥalwajī*, 1991a [1981/1983]) by Shalabī, which follows the narrator's time-travels in the Fatimid and Mamluk eras to portray what is authentically Egyptian;
3. *The Hashish Waiter* (2011; *Ṣāliḥ Hēṣa*, 2000) also by Shalabī, which depicts a community of hashish addicted intellectuals who are amused by the hashish waiter who gives the title to the novel.
4. *A Dog with No Tail* (2015; *al-Fā'il*, 2008) by Abū Julayyil, a short novel about construction work and literary aspirations from the perspective of a young Bedouin who moves to Cairo.

2.3 Analytical framework

The selected corpus consists of four novels published from the beginning of the 1980s till 2008 that are representative of a trend of humorous writing featuring the adventures of eccentric characters in marginal communities. The analysis aims at understanding how these novels fit into and contribute to contemporary Egyptian fiction through humour and illustrating the humour-generating strategies that determine their main thematic and stylistic features. Furthermore, it explores the literary and popular reference employed to elicit humour, comprising the partial disruption of literary models, the folk culture of laughter, jokelore, and socio-political satire. Comparing the three selected authors on these grounds allows to identify recurrent tropes and tracing a thematic and stylistic evolution.

To define the main humour-generating techniques, the analysis focuses on some narratological categories and textual strategies that have already been addressed in the studies devoted to the masters of humour. In his study of Ṣunʿallāh Ibrāhīm's literary output from 1966 till 2011, Starkey (2006b, 2016) argues that the author has developed a peculiar novelistic technique based on the extensive use of intertextuality and the deliberate patterning of different narrative modes. With the exception of *Warda* (2000, Warda/Rose), his novels revolve around antiheroes, defined as men or women given the vocation of failure. Starkey (2006b: 148) investigates the relation between the characters and narrative modes: "What, then, are some of the characteristics of the narrator/'anti-hero' and how do they relate to the narrative techniques that Ṣunʿallāh Ibrāhīm has employed in the work?" In this question, the narrator and the antihero coincide because Ibrāhīm privileges a first-person narrator with many autobiographical traits. Nevertheless, Starkey examines how this relation evolves in Ibrāhīm's novels told in the third-person, such as *Dhāt*.

Similarly, Booth focuses on these narratological elements for her analysis of Bayram al-Tūnisī's satire. She looks at the characters, focusing on their diction and the social identities and stereotypes they draw upon, the narrating voice and focalization, and intertextuality with the literary antecedents. She explains how these factors are intertwined in creating a satirical effect:

> The interplay of narrating voice and focalizing perspectives is integral to the construction of satire based on ironizing gaps which exploit and explode the initial presentation of characters. The relationship of narratorial structure to focalization is also a pivotal element in the way each set of texts exploits its particular textual model. This leads, in each case, to a discussion of the internal organization of the text and its relationship to both textual model and thematic presentation. (Booth 1990: 4–5)

With a focus on literary humour, the analysis of the novels looks at the three aspects mentioned by Starkey and Booth: the narrating voice, characters, and intertextuality. Firstly, it looks at the attitude of the narrating voice toward the characters and the story, if not the entire world crafted in fiction. The ironic distance from which the narrator looks at the story can be achieved through various techniques, such as a detached attitude, a sympathetic attitude, or the corrective look of the social critic. Moreover, the narrator may be a subject or agent of humour. In self-mockery, he/she adopts a debasing yet playful attitude toward himself/herself. When self-mockery targets both the narrator, the reader, and the group they belong to, it reinforces group affiliation and involves the audience in a shared intellectual game (Mizzau 1984: 104–106).

As regards the characters, Starkey's definition of antihero is related to incongruity and ultimately humour: the antihero is "incompetent, unlucky, tactless, clumsy, cack-handed, stupid [and] buffoonish" (Starkey 2006b: 154). The antihero is commonly defined as someone ordinary who does not do heroic deeds. This feature becomes humorous when the character's trivial deeds contrast with a high narrative register, for example that of the epics. Besides antiheroes, humour revolves around stock characters of the Arab popular and literary heritage. Stock characters include regional, professional, and social types, entertainers, wits, wise fools, village yokels, rogues, and picaresque figures. While they bear a cross-cultural dimension, the focus here is on their Egyptian connotations. Furthermore, the construction of characters belonging to the lowest strata of society, with their unconventional behaviour, hybrid language, and jargon, may elicit the carnivalesque side of buffoonery. The analysis of the novels explores the characters' physical description, behaviour (especially when breaking taboos or social hierarchies), geographical identity, and group affiliation. When they are presented as members of a community, it is worth enquiring whether this community ridicules other groups or is laughed at. Finally, the social functions of humour in these groups is taken into consideration.

When discussing intertextuality, Caiani remarks the complexity of al-Ghīṭānī's dialogue with the cultural heritage, which is not confined to parody for the purpose of political criticism:

> As far as the use of the *turāth* is concerned, we could say that Munif, al-Ghīṭānī and al-Kharrāṭ all see in formal innovation an aesthetic value *per se* and not a means to convey political ideas.[22]
>
> [[22]] Although Meyer seems to suggest that in Ḥabībī and al-Ghīṭānī the *turāth* is there mainly to provide a vehicle for the irony with which they comment in an indirect way on political matters (cf. Meyer 2001: 71–72). Such is the extent and the scope of these writers' use of *turāth*, however, that it would seem to point to wider artistic reasons (the whole of al-Ghīṭānī's impressive novelistic production relies on Arabic literary models of the past, including the *khiṭaṭ* genre and the mystical work of Ibn ʿArabī (cf. Allen 1995: 123).
>
> (Caiani 2007: 73, 150–151)

Similarly, Mustajāb, Shalabī, and Abū Julayyil are broadly interested in folk and popular culture and revisit the cultural heritage on many levels. The next chapters focus on those aspects of the cultural heritage that are related to humour, such as sayings, idiomatic expressions, songs, jokes, banters, and eccentric characters. References to local culture and jokelore make humour more effective for an audience that shares a common encyclopaedic knowledge. Indeed, Triezenberg includes cultural factors among the humour enhancers since the author of a humorous text should be well-versed in the comical tradition of the readers.

As regards the incorporation of the literary comic tradition, it is worth investigating whether the three novelists recall literary forms that traditionally contain a humorous dimension, like the *maqāmāt* and anecdotes. At the same time, the analysis measures to what extent they adopt or mock the conventions of some sub-genres of contemporary Egyptian fiction, such as the village novel, storytelling, social portrait, and migration tale. The parodic effect may target the canonical novelistic and cinematic representation, the dynamics of the intellectual community, and official historiography both in its classical and modern form. Some historical turning points linked to the social groups portrayed in their novels are going to be identified.

Each of the following chapters (ch.3–6) is devoted to a single case study. After summarizing the plot, it looks at the interplay of literary models, main narrative threads, and the attitude of the narrative voice. Then it examines how the main character revives the previous models and is constructed through comical episodes: as regards the action, it enquires whether humour derives from misunderstandings, inappropriate behaviour, or absurdity; as regards the language, it looks at the rhetorical tools and linguistic varieties that increase the humorous effect. Finally, it identifies the targets of comedy and satirical criticism taking into consideration also the functions of humour discussed on the metanarrative level. Before examining the novels, the next section introduces the selected writers remarking the similarities in their careers and writings.

2.4 Authors in their context

2.4.1 Origins

Mustajāb, Shalabī, and Abū Julayyil come from rural areas and humble social backgrounds. Since the 1960s, many Egyptian writers belong to the lower-middle class of the provinces and move to the city to complete their higher education or find work opportunities. Yet, the authors examined in this study do not simply come from the provinces but from the marginal areas they depict in their novels. However, this did not prevent them from joining the urban literary circles and institutions.

Mustajāb was born from a peasant family in the village of Dayrūṭ in the Governorate of Asyūṭ in Middle Upper Egypt (Mauritz 2009; Mehrez 1993: 175; M. M. Mustajāb 2016). When he was a child, he worked in the fields with his family. In the late 1950s, he went to Cairo for the first time but did not have a stable job. In the mid-1960s, he returned to Upper Egypt to work in the construction of the High Dam in Aswan. It is then that he started writing: he met Jean-Paul Sartre (1905–1980), who was travelling in Egypt in 1967, and took part in the Congress of Young Writers organized by the Arab Socialist Union's Youth Organization in al-Zaqāzīq in 1969. After spending some months in Iraq, he moved to Cairo where he enrolled in the Academy of Fine Arts but did not finish his studies.

While Mustajāb came from Upper Egypt, Shalabī was born in the Nile Delta, in the village of Shabbās ʿAmr in the Governorate of Kafr al-Shaykh (Bushnaq 2002: 495–499; Jacquemond 2008: 147; Mehrez 1993: 175). His family enjoyed some social and intellectual prestige, and his father was a political activist and one of the founders of the *Wafd* party. However, when the political scenario changed, he went through some financial difficulties, which made it hard to provide for his numerous children. Because of this, Shalabī started working when he was young, while struggling to continue his education: he worked as a cotton gatherer, tailor, carpenter, and street seller. In the mid-1950s, he enrolled in the teacher training college in Damanhūr, a medium-size city in the Delta. After being expelled, he made a living from various jobs and frequented the cafés where the local writers met. Later he moved to Alexandria, where he continued his training with university students and local writers. In the 1960s he went to Cairo and began to work in journalism: after an internship at *al-Jumhūriyya* newspaper, he worked for *Majallat al-masraḥ* (Theatre journal). He also attended the Academy for Scriptwriters and wrote some radio dramas. Afterwards, he obtained a post at *Majallat al-idhāʿa wa-l-talfizyūn*, the Radio and Television Weekly.

Abū Julayyil is an author of Bedouin origins. His family emigrated from Libya and settled in the Fayyūm region in northern Upper Egypt in the first half of the 19th century. They had enjoyed a certain prestige among the nomadic communities but faced some socio-economic difficulties when they became sedentary. Like his family, Abū Julayyil experienced migration when he moved to Cairo to work as a construction labourer. In the 1990s he lived in Manshiyyat Nāṣir, a neighbourhood established in the Nasserist era on the outskirts of the southern industrial district of Ḥulwān in Greater Cairo. Originally conceived to host the factory workers, it soon developed informally due to government negligence and overpopulation. His first novel is set there.

The three authors' humble origins, migration, and work experience prevented them to continue their formal education. In some interviews, Mustajāb and Shalabī proudly insist on being self-taught and appreciating folk culture. Shalabī recalls the rich cultural life of his village: in the houses of the learned middle-class, religious scholars discussed religion and literature; his father's friends debated politics and their libraries included political memoirs, sociological essays, and modern fiction; at the same time, he was fascinated by recorded music and storytelling, especially the recitation of the folk epics (*sīra shaʿbiyya*) (El-Assyouti 2000).

Another common trait is that they did manual labour while pursuing their literary aspirations. This experience made them familiar with some unprivileged communities of workers in the countryside and the city, whose routine, jargon, and displacement are depicted in their novels; Shalabī and Abū Julayyil portray the precarious living conditions of seasonal and daily hired labourers.

2.4.2 Career and recognition

When the three authors moved to Cairo, they gradually entered the literary circles and started their career. Mustajāb published his first short story, *al-Waṣiyya al-ḥādiyyat ʿashara* (1969, The eleventh testament) in *al-Hilāl* magazine and, thanks to ʿAlī Sālim, contributed to the satirical magazine *Ṣabāḥ al-khayr*. Meanwhile he published his short stories on several literary journals, attracting the attention of the critics. Soon afterwards, he was assigned a governmental post in the Academy of the Arabic Language and was later appointed director of the same institution.

His novella *Min al-tārīkh al-sirrī li-Nuʿmān ʿAbd al-Ḥāfiẓ* (*The Secret History of Nu'man Abd al-Hafiz*) was published in instalments in 1976–1977 in the magazine *al-Kātib* and released as a book in 1982. It was followed by the publication of the short story collection *Dayrūṭ al-sharīf* (Dayrut the noble; *Tales from Dayrut*). The two works may be seen as complementary and were published together in 1986. In the 1980s and 1990s Mustajāb published several collections of short stories written in those years and his early career. In the 2000s he published a family's genealogy using his family name, including the novels *Qiyām wa-inhiyār āl Mustajāb* (1998, Rise and fall of the Mustagabs), *Innahu al-rābiʿ min āl Mustajāb* (2003, Mustagab the Fourth), and *Kalb āl Mustajāb* (2004, The Dog of the Mustagabs). His last work, *al-Lahw al-khafī* (2005, Hidden amusement), was published a few months before he died.

Over his career, Mustajāb has developed his satirical vein both in fiction and newspaper columns published in *al-Sharq al-awsaṭ*, *al-Muṣawwar*, *al-Usbūʿ*, *al-ʿArabī*. His columns were later collected in anthologies, such as the popular *Nabsh al-ghurāb* (1999–, The crow digs up). Mustajāb confirms that satire crosses the boundaries between literature and journalism, fiction and non-fiction. In an interview about the decline of *adab sākhir* in the Egyptian cultural scene, he mentions himself alongside other popular satirical writers, such as al-Saʿdanī, Ḥanafī, and ʿAfīfī, as well as the pioneers of Egyptian fiction al-Māzinī and Tawfīq al-Ḥakīm (Darwīsh 2001).[35]

35 Shalabī is interviewed in the same article.

Shalabī was a very prolific writer. He is the author of almost seventy books including novels, short story collections, historical tales, and critical studies.[36] Meanwhile, he was employed in public institutions: he was editor-in-chief of *Majallat al-shiʿr* (Poetry journal) and the book series *Maktabat al-dirāsāt al-shaʿbiyya* (Library of popular studies), published by the General Organization of the Cultural Palaces (GOCP, *al-Hayʾa al-ʿāmma li-quṣūr al-thaqāfa*) attached to the Egyptian Ministry of Culture. His interest in folklore and storytelling informs both his editorial tasks and literary output, as exemplified by *Thulāthiyyat al-amālī* (2010b [1990–1995], The trilogy of hopes) which resembles the folk epics.

Thanks to his affiliation to the cultural institutions and the press, Shalabī knew the community of fellow journalists and writers very well. He mentions many colleagues in his novels *Time-Travels* and *The Hashish Waiter* and depicts the community of intellectuals in his non-fictional writings, such as a compilation of biographical portraits of Egyptian outstanding figures and an autobiography in the form of essays about his masters and friends, published in 2011, the year of his death.[37]

Journalism has played a significant role also in Abū Julayyil's career, providing him a publishing venue and the opportunity to enter a network of fellow intellectuals. He had Mustajāb among his mentors and worked with the consecrated novelist Ibrāhīm Aṣlān (1935–2012), who was a good friend of Shalabī's (Grīs 2011). He started publishing his short stories in the mid-1990s and has realised three collections: *Asrāb al-naml* (1997, Swarms of bees), *Ashyāʾ maṭwiyya bi-ʿināya fāʾiqa* (2000, Items folded with great care), *Ṭayy al-khiyām* (2010a, Folding the tents). He has published three novels: *Luṣūṣ mutaqāʿidūn* (2002; *Thieves in Retirement*, 2006), *al-Fāʿil* (2008; *A Dog With No Tail*, 2015), and *Qiyām wa-inhiyār al-ṣād shīn* (2018, Rise and fall of S.Sh.). He has authored two non-fictional books

36 His critical studies cover various topics: literary criticism in *Muḥākamat Tāhā Ḥussayn* (1972, Tāhā Hussein's trial); philology in *Fatḥ al-Andalus* (1973, The conquest of Andalusia), a recently discovered play by the Egyptian nationalist leader Muṣṭafā Kāmil (1874–1908); contemporary theatre in *Fī-l-masraḥ al-miṣrī al-muʿāṣir* (1981, Egyptian contemporary theatre) and *al-Shāʿir Najīb Surūr: masraḥ al-azma* (1989, Najīb Surūr: The theatre of crisis); vernacular poetry; and biography. Shalabī was a screenwriter for radio dramas and wrote some unpublished plays in the 1960s; he published a play entitled *Masraḥiyyat ṣuyyād al-lūlī: masraḥiyyatān ghināʾiyyatān* (1982, The pearl fisher: two musical plays).

37 *ʿAmāliqa ẓurafāʾ: siyar wa-tarājim* (1985, Refined people: biographies) and *Uns al-ḥabāyb: al-shukhūṣ fatrat al-takwīn* (2011, In company of the loved ones: people in my formative years).

that offer a historical guide of Cairo, a book about Islamic history, and a book for children.[38]

Like Shalabī, Abū Julayyil worked as editor for some book series attached to the General Organization of the Cultural Palaces, such as *Silsilat al-thaqāfa al-shaʿbiyya* (Folk and popular culture series) and *Āfāq al-kitāba* (Horizons of writing) directed by Aṣlān.[39] More recently, he has worked as a journalist for the Emirati daily newspaper *al-Ittiḥād* and the cultural page of the Lebanese daily *al-Safīr*; he currently writes for to the Egyptian newspaper *al-Maqāl*, whose editor in chief is Ibrāhīm ʿĪsā (b. 1965).

The careers of the three writers partially overlap in the 1990s and 2000s, when Shalabī and Mustajāb increased their recognition, while Abū Julayyil attracted a positive critical reception since his first publications. Shalabī and Mustajāb were awarded the *State Incentive Award* (*Jāʾizat al-dawla al-tashjīʿiyya*), respectively in 1980 for the travelogue *Fallāḥ miṣrī fī bilād al-faranja* (1978b, An Egyptian peasant in the land of the Franks) and 1984 for *The Secret History*. Almost two decades later, the *State Merit Award* (*Jāʾizat al-dawla al-taqdīriyya*), awarded to Shalabī in 2004 for *Wikālat ʿAṭiyya* (1991b; *The Lodging House*, 2006) and posthumously to Mustajāb in 2005, confirmed their national recognition and paved the way for their international reception. Even though some of Mustajāb's short stories had already appeared in translation before 2005, it was only after his death that *Dayrūṭ al-sharīf* and the novella were translated together into English as *Tales from Dayrut*. This was followed by the English translation of other short stories published in journals, anthologies, and blogs.

The case of Shalabī illustrates how international reception simoultaneously relies on and reinforces internal recognition: his afore-mentioned novel *Wikālat ʿAṭiyya* received the *Naguib Mahfouz Medal for Literature* in 2003, securing itself the English translation (Mehrez 2010a: 41–57). This was followed by the English translation of his two novels selected for the corpus, *Time-Travels* and *The Hashish Waiter*. His last novel *Isṭāsiyya* (2010a, Ecstasy) was longlisted for the *International Prize for Arabic Fiction (IPAF)* in 2011.

---

38 *al-Qāhira: shawāriʿ wa-ḥikāyāt* (2003, Cairo: streets and stories); *al-Qāhira: jawāmiʿ wa-ḥikāyāt* (2013, Cairo: mosques and stories); *Fursān zamān* (2012, Heroes of old days); *Naḥnu ḍaḥāyā ʿAkk* (2017, We are all victims of the ʿAkk tribe).

39 When Abū Julayyil and Aṣlān were working for *Āfāq al-kitāba*, they were involved in the controversy over the censorship of the novel *Walīma li-ashʿāb al-baḥr* (1983, Banquet for seaweed) by the Syrian Ḥaydar Ḥaydar (b. 1936). For an account of the Ḥaydar Ḥaydar affair, see: Hafez 2000; Mehrez 2010a: 18–21.

In the same years Abū Julayyil established himself as an emerging writer, whose short story collections were awarded with one international and two national prizes. His first novel was translated into English, French, and Spanish, whereas his second novel won the *Naguib Mahfouz Medal for Literature* in 2008 and was translated into English as *A Dog with No Tail.*[40]

2.4.3 Literary influences

"If I am stranded on a desert island for the rest of my life, the *Thousand and One Nights* will be quite enough" (El-Assyouti 2000). This sentence condenses Khayrī Shalabī's love for storytelling. Nonetheless, it simplifies the many aspects of popular culture that Shalabī, Mustajāb, and Abū Julayyil insert into their writings: folk epics, sayings, anecdotes, Bedouin and rural legends, cinema, and television.

Intertextuality with the literary heritage and popular culture are part of the experimentation conducted by the Generation of the Sixties. Mustajāb and Shalabī belong to this group in chronological terms but followed their own paths. Mustajāb shared with his peers some influential readings, for example existentialism, but had different political beliefs. Shalabī did not engage in politics and chose solitude for his writing, sometimes in Cairo's historical cemeteries. Shalabī's eccentricity in the relation with his peers coincides with his disaffection for modernist writers, like Idwār al-Kharrāṭ (1926–2015), who encouraged young authors of the Sixties to gather around the literary magazine *Jalīrī 68*. On the contrary, he appreciated realist novelists: "He considers Yehia Haqqi his literary father, Youssef Idris his older brother and Abdel-Rahman El-Sharqawi, Saad Mekkawi, Naguib Mahfouz, and Ihsan Abdel-Quddous his relatives" (El-Assyouti 2000).

Compared to their peers, Mustajāb and Shalabī are still understudied. One of the reasons may be the non-radical innovations in their writings, especially in the case of Shalabī, who often relies on mimetic representation, while deeply experimenting with the collective narrative voice and folk tradition. In particular, he chooses marginal characters and reproduces orality in its richness of registers, like the afore-mentioned Yaḥyā al-Ṭāhir ʿAbdallāh. Mustajāb's experimentation is

40 *Jā'izat al-majmūʿ al-qiṣaṣiyya* (Prize for best short story collection), awarded by the Ministry of Culture in 1997; *Jā'izat al-qiṣṣa* (Prize for best short story), awarded by the newspaper *Akhbār al-yawm* in 1999; and *Jā'izat al-ibdāʿ al-ʿarabī* (Prize for Arab creativity), awarded by the United Arab Emirates in 2000. The English translation of *Luṣūṣ mutaqāʿidūn* (*Thieves in Retirement*) is reviewed by Zaki 2007, whereas the Spanish translation (*Ladrones jubilados*) is reviewed by Gutiérrez de Terán 2009.

praised by Malti-Douglas (1993: 127–128) who suggests that metafiction and intertextuality in *The Secret History* exemplify post-Mahfouzian fiction, alongside other techniques employed by Jamāl al-Ghīṭānī and Yūsuf al-Qā'id (b. 1944). Furthermore, both authors insert fantastic elements into their writings: like the afore-mentioned Majīd Ṭūbyā, Mustajāb treats fantasy with a matter-of-fact tone, whereas Shalabī adds a magical atmosphere to the realistic description of space. Another reason may be that they were their less engaged in politics than was expected from the writers of their Generation. This apparent lack of engagement does not mean that their writings disregard social criticism or the search for justice. Like their peers, they were deeply concerned with crafting a counter-historiography (Allen 2007; Mehrez 1994).

Among the writers of the Sixties, an intimate friend of Shalabī was Aṣlān, who depicted some marginal urban communities with irony, especially in the popular Cairene neighbourhood of Imbāba where he lived (Heshmat 2004: 110–136; Paniconi 2006a: 15–52). Aṣlān was also a joining link with the younger generation of writers, including Ṭāriq Imām (b. 1977) and Abū Julayyil. The latter considers Ibrāhīm Manṣūr (1932–2004) a mentor,[41] while the literary critics indicate Mustajāb and Aṣlān as his masters. Lindsey points out some similarities and differences with Mustajāb's style:

> Abu Golayyel is a protégé of the late satirical master Mohamed Mustagab [. . .], and he shares his mentor's sweeping sarcasm [. . .] and talent for weaving the startling and the ridiculous into chronicles of the dispossessed. Where they differ is in their prose styles: Mustagab had a penchant for lyricism, and Abu Golayyel says his goal is "to make literary language reach the level of spoken language – in simplicity, lightness, and the power to convince". (Lindsey 2010a)

Badawī suggests that, in different moments, both authors had an influence on this emerging writer:

> Ḥamdī Abū Julayyil distanced himself from Mustajāb, maybe afraid to follow his path toward exemplary abstraction. Indeed, Mustajāb's prose became a kind of fortress, made of metaphors and symbols. The weight of reality was decreasing, while his characters almost lost their psychological and social characterization. Abū Julayyil became closer to Aṣlān, who has not forgotten Hemingway's suggestion of writing only about what the writer knows. In this sense, Ḥamdī is a "realist" writer, even if influenced by Milan Kundera's views of wandering about with his imagination. (Badawī 2008, my translation)

Within this network, Abū Julayyil has benefitted from the endorsement of consecrated novelists and the reputation of Dār Mīrīt as the leading private

---

41 *A Dog with No Tail* opens with two short quotations from Ibrāhīm Manṣūr and Marguerite Duras respectively. For a portrait of Manṣūr, see: Rakha 1999.

publisher of good-quality innovative literature. His prompt critical recognition is probably due to his ability to balance between the experimental narrative techniques of the Generation of the Nineties and a renewed concern for social issues that has emerged at the turn of the millennium. *Thieves in Retirement* and *A Dog with No Tail* experiment with structural and temporal fragmentation, repetitions, attention to minute details, multiple narrations of the same event, intertextual references to cinema, and metafiction. At the same time, these novels centred on the self portray the social reality in a vivid way thanks to the narrator's positioning as both an insider and outsider. This hints at the possibility of causing a rupture in the closed horizon by adopting the viewpoint of the marginalized, as suggested by Hafez (2010: 61).[42] Furthermore, Booth places Abū Julayyil among a new generation of authors who combine "attention to issues of socioeconomic right, gender politics, globalization (in all of its many forms), and dislocation with a profoundly introspective layering that eschews the navel-gazing of which some young writers over the past fifteen years have been accused, if not always with justification" (Booth 2006: xvii).

Because of the degree of violence and explicit language, humour in *Thieves in Retirement* is eminently dark; some episodes are so absurd that they provoke a bitter laughter. Brutality, slang, and coarse words as aesthetic tools have been further developed in Egyptian novels published after 2011, such as the afore-mentioned *Women of Karantina* by al-Ṭūkhī and *Istikhdām al-ḥayāh* (2014; *Using Life*, 2017) by Aḥmad Nājī (b. 1985), where humour takes mainly the form of sarcasm.

2.4.4 From the margins

After looking at the connections between Shalabī, Mustajāb, and Abū Julayyil, this section illustrates a common feature of their literary output, *i.e.* the representation of marginal communities. This overview includes some novels that are not examined as case studies in the next chapters but help framing the analysis of the corpus. In their works, the rural or urban space is not just a physical landscape but a network of social and ideological relations that are subject to change. To give access to these marginal places and communities, all three writers insert many autobiographical elements into their fiction.

Mustajāb and Shalabī give voice to the Egyptian countryside respectively of Upper Egypt and the Delta. In their village novels, they abandon the bourgeois urban perspective of the pioneers of Egyptian fiction (Elad 1994), such as

42 On the possibility of breaking the closed horizon, see also: El-Ariss 2013: 145–171.

Muḥammad Ḥussayn Haykal (1888–1956), Ṭāhā Ḥussayn (1889–1973), and Tawfīq al-Ḥakīm, or the external look of the committed realist novelist ʿAbd al-Raḥmān al-Sharqāwī (1920–1987). They adopt, instead, the perspective of the insider and the village's narrative modes. In this respect, they are paralleled to other authors of village novels in the 1970s and 1980s, such as ʿAbd al-Ḥakīm Qāsim (1935–1990) and Yaḥyā al-Ṭāhir ʿAbdallāh.

Mehrez argues that, instead of focusing on the story of an exceptional subject, the whole village emerges as hero or antihero. Because of this shift from the subject's (auto)biography to collective history, the story does not necessarily have a beginning, middle, and end contained within the boundaries of one novel; on the contrary, the interwoven stories of the village may expand over a short story collection, a novel with an episodic structure, or a series of novels. Furthermore, the collective narrating voice prevails over the individual one, with innovations in style, language, and type of realism (Mehrez 1993: 166–167).

As Mehrez (1993) notes, these changes are exemplified by *al-ʿArāwī* (1986, Buttonholes) by Shalabī and *Dayrūṭ al-sharīf* by Mustajāb. The former contains several tales about the hamlets of a Delta village told by a young boy who works in a tailor's workshop. As the metaphor of sewing suggests, these tales are woven together to map the geography and history of this place. *Dayrūṭ al-sharīf*, instead, collects thirteen short stories that appeared in 1970–1977 and a story published in 1983, which Mehrez suggests reading as episodes or chapters of the same narrative. Ch.3 will look at incongruity and fantasy in these short stories as a continuum with the novella *The Secret History*. On a broader level, Mehrez's considerations about the episodic structure apply to the analysis of the corpus; the insertion of anecdotes, folktales, and storytelling may elicit humour thanks to intertextuality and the brevity of the single textual unities.

In his village novels, Shalabī depicts the unprivileged and the exploitation of seasonal and daily hired workers (*ʿummāl tarāḥīl* and *anfār*). Shalabī, who was a daily worker in cotton collection, portrays this community in his novel *al-Awbāsh* (1978a, The riff raff) (Elad 1994: 169–170). Selim (2004: 156–158) argues that this novel challenges the nationalist image of the harmonious rural community by revealing its internal divisions, which are overcome through rebellion and a collective act of narration. Similarly, Shalabī's last novel, *Isṭāsiyya* (2010a), explores social injustice and sectarianism in the Egyptian countryside (Abū Julayyil 2010b; Heshmat 2012).

Some decades later, Abū Julayyil describes the precarious living and working conditions of construction labourers in the city in *A Dog with No Tail*, grounding his fictional account in his personal experience. Moreover, the novels of the corpus tackle other social issues mentioned here: while humour tackles sectarianism only tangentially, it mocks the religious authorities spreading superstition and corruption; it also challenges the idyllic picture of peaceful coexistence through crime and brutality. Portraying the margins from an unsual perspective, these novels reshape the boundaries of the national and local communities: while *The Secret History* is set in the countryside, the other three novels portray how the rural enters the urban due to migration; the traditional rivalry between the city and the countryside still shapes some comical characters and misunderstandings. Migration leads to reconsidering the history of the village and the city, which are both changing.

As he does in his village novels, Shalabī depicts some marginalized characters also in his fiction set in the city. His urban characters include the ordinary people, as well as the underworld of vagrants, rogues, drug dealers, and petty criminals (ʿAṣfūr 1999: 314; al-Fāris 1990). ʿAṣfūr gathers these types under the label of *shuṭṭār* (scoundrels, smart cunning people), which is also the title of one of Shalabī's novels. They roam the alleys, cafés, hash dens, and semi-legal shelter places of the popular districts, all of which the writer knows from his own experience as a young migrant who did not have a stable dwelling. They belong to the city's margins or neglected central districts. From this position, they coexist with or confront the ruling class as single individuals, small cliques, or the chaotic throng.

These types combine the resilience of the urban poor with a peculiar Egyptian identity emerging from their way of speaking and connection to the place they inhabit. The author plays with the stereotypical image of the authentic Egyptian (*al-miṣrī al-aṣlī* or *ibn al-balad*): he is an ordinary man who does not belong to the elite; lives in the city, especially in the popular neighbourhoods; may have received formal education but has learnt from life; is resourceful and sometimes opportunist; and has an innate sense of humour (Booth 1993: 438, fn. 26; De Angelis 2007: 35–51; el-Messiri 1978).

This urban underworld is central in *Time-Travels* and *The Hashish Waiter*, set in Cairo, and *Wikālat ʿAṭiyya*, set in a run-down caravanserai in the Delta city of Damanhūr (Tarbush 2007). Considering the *wikāla* a microcosm of the whole city, Booth (2011) parallels this enclosed location to the setting of Abū Julayyil's first novel: *Thieves in Retirement* revolves around a single apartment building in the informal neighbourhood of Manshiyyat Nāṣir on the southern edge of Cairo. This area is inhabited by people of rural origins who have adapted to the life in the urban fringes. Abū Julayyil's second novel, *A Dog with No Tail*, shapes another urban underworld made of labourers and fellow villagers. In Shalabī's and Abū Julayyil's novels the village enters the city since the migration waves and lack of urban planning have led to the creation of informal settlements where the urban and rural customs merge. Cairo is populated by outsiders who keep their accent and sense of humour alive.

This fictional representation of recent urban change revives the traditional opposition city/countryside and regional humour targeting the Bedouin and the peasants, especially from Upper Egypt. Both writers populate their urban underworld with picaresque figures that resort to creative, yet often illegal, survival strategies. Their adventures rely on incessant movement (the dimension of the journey is central, especially in Shalabī) and evening entertainment, such as hashish smoking sessions and storytelling.

Moreover, all three authors explore the relation between space and its inhabitants from a historical perspective and, like other modern Egyptian writers, remap space through their memories and historical documents. The characters' biography is as important as the genealogy of the place. In particular, Shalabī remarks the interplay of time and space through the subtitle *Riḥla fī l-zamakān* (A journey in space-and-time) affixed to *Time-Travels* and the label *jughriwāyya* (geo-novel) applied to *Baṭn al-baqara* (1996, The cow's belly). In the dedication of the latter novel, the author traces his interest back to *al-khiṭaṭ*, a topographical genre in Islamic historiography:

> To my cousin, the late Sheikh Ali Mohammed Okasha. . .
>
> I rummaged through his library as a young schoolboy and got my hands on the first volume of Al Maqrizi's *Plans*. I fell in love with it. It was without cover or title so I gave it a title of my own, inspired by its subject matter—*The History of Houses and Streets*—and I believe that the spontaneity of feeling embodied in that title still governs my view of this unique science: the study of street-plans; the history of place. (Shalabi 2012)

Ch.4 will illustrate how this historiographical genre was revisited by ʿAlī Mubārak (1824–1893) and later by al-Ghīṭānī. Al-Ghīṭānī and Shalabī, who shared a great interest for the city's history and landmarks, parody Mamluk historiography with different purposes.

The authors of the corpus insert many autobiographical elements into their writings. As illustrated above, Mustajāb depicts his native village and creates a semi-autobiographical family saga, whereas Shalabī draws inspiration from his work experience and wanderings in the city. To exemplify this, it is worth focusing on Abū Julayyil who employs autobiographical references to portray the self in post-national communities.

The first autobiographical element is the depiction of the Bedouin community whose identity is gradually fading.[43] In *Thieves in Retirement* and *A Dog with No Tail* the first-person narrator is a young Bedouin who transmits a repertoire of legends about his forefathers; alternative versions of the same tales

43 Other contemporary authors of Bedouin origins are the Libyan Ibrāhīm al-Kūnī (b. 1948) and the Egyptian Mīrāl al-Taḥāwī (b. 1968) whose novels are often read as semi-autobiographical.

appear in Abū Julayyil's short story collections, challenging the reliability of storytelling. Moreover, the negotiation of Bedouin moral codes in the city is embodied by complex gendered identities: El-Ariss (2013: 114–144) and El Sadda (2012: 190–201) investigate the representation of masculinity and queer identities in *Thieves in Retirement*, whereas *A Dog with No Tail* tackles romance and sex with self-irony.

The second autobiographical element is labour migration and life in the city's outskirts. Abū Julayyil draws inspiration from on his own experience but is aware of the fictional conventions, as he states in this interview:

> AFKAR/IDEES: Quelle est l'importance de l'expérience personnelle dans votre roman?
> HAMDI ABU GOLAYYEL: J'écris sur moi-même, mais on ne peut pas parler d'une autobiographie. Je pense que le transfert littéral de la réalité est impossible. Lorsqu'on écrit une lettre, les mots pensés et dits se transforment en quelque chose de différent au moment de les écrire. L'écriture présente des normes. J'aimerais écrire la réalité telle qu'elle se présente, car je crois que c'est là le plus bel art qui puisse exister, mais les règles de l'écriture obéissent à quelque chose de non naturel, elles sont différentes de la vie réelle. (Abou-Golayyel & Ciuccarelli 2010: 34–35)[44]

The city's outskirts are a common setting in the *oeuvre* of the Generation of the Nineties, to which Abū Julayyil is certainly related. In fact, the insertion of autobiographical elements and realistic details corresponds to the formal experimentation of Egyptian fiction in the 1990s, which focuses on the self's inner world and minute details of everyday life, while blurring the boundaries between reality and fiction through fragmentation, repetition, and metafiction. Besides the setting of Manshiyyat Nāṣir in *Thieves in Retirement*, the picture is further complicated in *A Dog with No Tail* whose first-person narrator is an aspiring writer who works as a labourer with the same name, surname, and date of birth of the real author.[45] In this respect, Muftī (2011) argues that the overlapping

---

44 AFKAR/IDEES: "Which role does your personal experience play in your novel?" HAMDI ABU GOLAYYEL: "I write about myself, but it cannot be defined as an autobiography. I think it is impossible to directly transpose reality. When we write, our thoughts and utterances become something else once they are on paper. Writing has its own rules. I would like to write reality as it is, since I consider it the most skillful art that might exist, but the rules of writing obey to something that is not natural, they differ from real life." This and the other translations from French are mine.

45 In *A Dog with No Tail* the narrator is anonymous until ch.4 when he reveals that his name is Ḥamdī, an information completed in ch.5: "my name in full: Hamdi Abu Hamed Eissa Saqr Abu Golayyel" (27/32). His date of birth is 16th August 1967 in *A Dog with No Tail* (not translated/96), whereas it is 16th August 1968 in *Thieves in Retirement* (53/56).

of the narrator and protagonist makes *A Dog with No Tail* close to a fictional autobiography (*al-sīra al-dhātiyya al-mutakhayyala*) or autofiction (*al-takhyīl al-dhātī*), whereas Badawī (2008) believes that Abū Julayyil writes about what he knows on the basis of his own experience.

Having illustrated different aspects of writing from the margins in parallel with the thematic evolution of the corpus, the first case study is *The Secret History* by Mustajāb which is the only novel of the corpus set in the countryside from the 1930s till 1956.

3 Reversed epics. Nuʿmān, the village antihero

> He proceeded to remind me of our days in Deirut, when we used to work together in the Legal Department. He then demanded a cigarette and began to smoke it saying 'Do you remember at Deirut – how we used to stand at the window looking over the roofs for a woman's chemise worked in lace – just to convince ourselves that women really existed in those parts.' That country was indeed primitive and barbarous. The southern part of Egypt is terrifying for the inhabitants of the Delta [. . .]
>
> He puffed smoke from his nose and mouth and continued: 'God confound that place! I bet if you opened the heads of nine-tenths of the people of Deirut you'd find them shaken up through being whacked with steel piping.'
>
> T. al-Hakim, *Maze of Justice: Diary of a Country Prosecutor*, 1989: 129

The Secret History of Nu'man Abd al-Hafiz by Muḥammad Mustajāb is a village novel, set in Dayrūṭ in Upper Egypt, which combines some elements of the folk epics and scholarly writing: an anonymous historian or biographer narrates the early life of a village boy turning him into a legendary figure. Humour emerges from the incongruity between the protagonist's trivial deeds on the one hand, and the narrator's great efforts to document his life on the other.

Nuʿmān was born in the 1930s from Umm Nuʿmān, a salted-fish seller, and ʿAbd al-Ḥāfiẓ Khamīs, who is extremely unpopular because of his awkward behaviour. Born right after his father's death, Nuʿmān lives in his mother's portable hut along the channel's banks and spends long hours in the fields. This formative period ends with an unknown disease cured by exorcism. Two main events mark his adolescence. A local wealthy woman, Madame Fawqiyya, wants to purchase him from his mother. The boy spends only one night at the lady's house for her pleasure and the guests' entertainment. What happens between the two of them is a mystery but Nuʿmān runs away terrified. The second significant event happens when the boy joins Ismāʿīl the Gravedigger. A possessed woman, who is undergoing a healing treatment at the cemetery, discovers that Nuʿmān is not circumcised; this makes the ritual impure and the woman runs off possessed by the devils. More adventures follow. Nuʿmān's belated circumcision must be performed on the threshold of a local saint's tomb, so the circumcision procession leaves Dayrūṭ for the neighbouring village of Amshūl. There ʿĪd the Barber starts his duty but is abruptly interrupted by the villagers. The boy, wounded and in pain, is carried back and forth between the two villages and treated with traditional but ineffective remedies. He heals only when Madame Fawqiyya sends him to the city's doctor. Once recovered, it is time to marry him off to one of the village girls. The choice of the bride and the wedding night close Nuʿmān's partial biography.

https://doi.org/10.1515/9783110725414-004

The story covers two decades, from the mid-1930s till the mid-1950s, during which Egypt takes part in World War II, becomes independent after the 1952 Free Officers' Revolution, and is involved in the 1956 Suez Crisis. These historical events are deliberately kept on the background, as if official history did not affect Nuʿmān's life and the mythical rhythms of the village.

Indeed, the village is the novella's real protagonist since the boy's adventures illustrate its traditions, beliefs, and socio-economic conditions. At the same time, the village contributes to the narration with gossip and accounts reported by the narrator-historian. The interplay of the protagonist, the village, and the narrator allows Mustajāb to portray a marginal rural world, barely affected by the Egyptian politics and modernization. Far from being nostalgic, this portrait tackles superstition, ignorance, poverty, violence, and the rural-urban conflict in a satirical vein.

The playwright Bahīj Ismāʿīl (b. 1939) adapted this novella into a play directed by Yāsīn al-Ḍawī in 2001.[46] This play presents some differences from the original text: the time of the story is longer, the narrator is less complex and resembles a storyteller, and its reading of the events is more political. Nuʿmān's story, in fact, becomes the history of Egypt from the perspective of the downtrodden. According to the Egyptian theatre critic Selaiha, these changes in the thematic focus on poverty and injustice are balanced by the playwright's ability to heighten the comic potential of some episodes through dramatic comedy:

> Ismail infused his script with a healthy dose of earthy jokes and bawdy humour, obliquely hinted at Fawqiya's morbid passion for the child No'man (which is all anyone could do given the watchful eye of the censor), and built up No'man's courting of his prospective, lisping bride into a delicious sequence of comical, rough-and-tumble flirtation, country-style. (Selaiha 2001)

Furthermore, Selaiha notes that the formal features and narrative voice shaping the novella's ironic tone are hard to transfer on stage. This confirms that it is the interplay of structure, narrative discourse, characters, and language which gives the novella its liveliness, involving the reader in the game of irony.

In her analysis of *The Secret History*, Malti-Douglas (1983) examines the formal level (structure and writing conventions), discoursive level (the narrator's language), and semantic level (the characters' interaction). The incongruities on all three levels concur to flout the rules of writing, language, and life, thus breaking the illusion of reality and bringing more attention to the writing process than to the story. As regards the formal level, Malti-Douglas argues that this novella exemplifies the 'suspense of form' theorized by Olson (1968), since

46 I have not seen the play and very few reviews are available. See, e.g., Bakīr 2001.

it oscillates between scholarly and fictional writing. Despite their apparent conformity, the elements borrowed from scholarly writing (footnotes, bulleted lists, the nearly absence of dialogues, and linguistic annotations) do not follow all the conventions of this genre and acquire an additional meaning in this fictional text. On the discoursive level, Malti-Douglas focuses on the narrator: his technique of reporting the events creates a distance between himself and the story, whereas some linguistic choices unmask his unreliability and the contradiction of the utterances. Finally, on the semantic level, she conducts a structuralist analysis of three episodes ascribable to the morphological category of the interrupted ritual (the father's burial, the therapeutic burial, and the protagonist's circumcision).

However, Malti-Douglas refers only partly to the novella's humorous effect: she illustrates that absurdity governs the combination of facts and utterances but does not fully explain the mechanisms producing a comic effect. The analysis conducted in this chapter adapts her analytical framework to explore how humour is produced in the text. The first section follows her analysis of the formal and discoursive level to describe the narrator as unreliable and full of contraddictions. While Malti-Douglas focuses on scholarly writing, it is worth giving more space to fictional writing since it is the disruption of both sets of writing conventions that determines the formal incongruity. Therefore, the first section opens with an exploration of the village novel in Mustajāb's writing, considering also the short story collection the novella is attached to. After defining the narrator as the vehicle of the discourse, the second section deals with his comic counterpart, Nuʿmān. Overcoming the clear-cut separation of the three levels of analysis on the assumption that humour depends on their interplay, this section examines how he is portrayed as a folk antihero through his partial biography and the three interrupted rituals. Finally, the third section illustrates how the protagonist is the vehicle of social satire targeting the village: the novella exposes the village's superstitions and stages the trope of rural-urban rivalry by turning Nuʿmān into a puppet entertaining the local elite.

3.1 Suspended form and unreliable narrator

3.1.1 Village novel

This section examines how *The Secret History* plays with the writing conventions of both genres underlying its formal composition: scholarly writing, thoroughly examined by Malti Douglas, and fictional writing, especially the village novel, an issue overlooked by previous studies. Mustajāb's novella and the short stories collected in *Dayrūṭ al-sharīf* belong to the village novel, a sub-genre that has developed since the beginning of modern Egyptian fiction. He is among the authors that have shifted from the traditional authoritative narrator to the village's collective voice. This innovation can be seen in the representation of time, space, storytelling techniques, fantasy and horror.

Mythical time

While historical and biographical accounts employ exact dates, *The Secret History* provides only approximate temporal references. For example, Nuʿmān was born between 1930 and 1938, on the eve of World War II. Another military event marks the end of the story, since the protagonist gets married just before 1956, as it can be inferred from this passage:

> And at the same time, an ambassador was on the move, approaching the Revolutionary Command Council to deliver to it a strongly worded warning requesting that Jamal Abdel Nasser either withdraw his army from the area around the Suez Canal or permit Britain and France to bomb the country's airports and houses. (203/254)

The novella provides only one date, the Coptic year 1668, mentioned twice in relation to Nuʿmān's circumcision. Significantly, it corresponds to 1952, when the Free Officers' revolution took place. The Coptic calendar is the main temporal reference, reproducing its usage in the countryside to keep track of the agricultural seasons and hinting at the coexistence of Copts and Muslims in Upper Egyptian villages, whereas the Islamic calendar marks the father's burial and the wedding's preparations.[47]

Another way to keep track of time are the rhythms of nature and agriculture, which emphasizes the village's internal perspective, as in this example:

> The business – the business, that is, of Nu'man – was taken care of in just the same manner as are those of the wind, of evil, of procreation, of clouds, of honor, of fear, of grace, of the sun, of good fortune, of the stars, of love, of the moon, of courage.
>
> Thus, at the beginning of the Bahr Yusuf flood,[2] [. . .] (137/170)
>
> [2] The first signs of the flood appear immediately following the wheat harvest and are themselves followed by the ripening of the dates, the spread of mange among the camels, a readiness to engage in the making of groats, the storing of straw, the manufacture of pots, the appearance of mendicant dill-sellers, and the leaping of the male farm animals onto the female. (144/179)

---

47 None of the main characters in the novella is a Copt, but Nuʿmān rides the jenny of Juljula, Tādrus's wife. Juljula and Tādrus are Coptic names. A priest who practices magic and an Italian monk are also mentioned.

Finally, one hundred and one thousand, used in storytelling to indicate a hyperbolic indefinite number, are found in two amusing anecdotes.

Magical nature

The attention to the rural rhythms goes hand in hand with the representation of nature as a semi-human creature with emotions and intellectual capacities. Such a depiction of nature characterizes magic realism, which transcends the boundaries of Latin American fiction and is discussed in Arabic fiction as well (Abdel Nasser 2011, 2015; Hart and Ouyang 2005). In *The Secret History*, the natural elements witness or take part in the events, as in these examples:

> That autumn dawn, the fields witnessed a painful exchange between Umm Nuʿman [. . .] and her son [. . .] (155/193)

> [. . .] and fear seized Nuʿman, Ismaʿil, the rocks, and the palm fronds. (167/209)

Moreover, the description of the pleasant natural scenery tinges with irony when the mechanisms of fiction are revealed. This can happen by juxtaposing animal and human elements in wordlists or when magic realism is brought down to earth.[48] For instance, when the narrator introduces Nuʿmān as the product of a noble lineage and a beautiful natural environment, he suggests adding further elements to the idyllic landscape, thus showing its artificial nature:

> All these roots combined to nourish Nuʿman's innermost being, as did the Bahr Yusuf, whose waters purled at the foot of the hut, and the towering trees rustling in the breeze, and a vast sweep of fields filled with green; and if we add to the scene a few birds in the air and a few lizards on the ground and mix all that with the tributary streams of Nuʿman's original parental heritage, things become clearer. (129/120–121)

48 This technique is also exploited in other short stories of the same collection with an estranging and sometimes humorous effect. For instance, "Kūbrī al-Bughaylī" (1975, "Bughayli Bridge" 24–34) opens with the juxtaposition of the human and animal worlds: "From the beginning – and even long before the beginning – we have had to put our faith in the fact that the fish dwell in water, bats in ruins, teachers in schools, peace of mind in death, foxes in fields, monks in monasteries, falsehood in books, seeds in cracks, poison in menstrual blood, and wisdom in the aftermath of events; and the best of you, good gentlemen, is the one who is spared either the wisdom or the events." (*Dayrūṭ* 24/32) Later in the story, magic realism is stripped of its fantastic dimension with an ironic effect: a dog is so expressive that he seems able to speak, but its earthly habits dispel the supernatural atmosphere: "Then a dog broke through the ring of onlookers and into the empty area, looking at the officer so hard that we were sure he was about to say something. He, however, (the dog, that is) made for the railing of the bridge, scratched his back, and raised his right hind leg." (*Dayrūṭ* 29/38)

In line with this magical representation of the nature, the village of Dayrūṭ is not described with precision: we only know that a canal separates the northern and the southern side and that there is a graveyard. The open nature of the countryside is opposed to Madame Fawqiyya's house and the city, presented as enclosed owe-inspiring places despite the lack of any detailed description:

> [. . .] until [Umm Nu'man] reached the government hospital building, with its cold cement touch [. . .] (132/164)

> It is most upsetting to have to lure Nu'man into abandoning the fields and the trees, the gushing of the water, and the pursuit of birds and lizards to go live in a village crowded with walls, contentiousness, gossip, deception, weddings, the distillation of grapes, and secret liaisons. (137/171)

This spatial representation introduces the traditional trope of rural-urban opposition, which is part of the novella's social satire (§3.3).

Storytelling

Besides experimenting with time and space, Mustajāb employs some storytelling techniques in the characters' construction. Nuʿmān's mother, Ismāʿīl the Gravedigger (*al-ḥaffār*), ʿĪd the Barber (*al-muzayyin*), and Madame Fawqiyya are presented for their role of helpers in the boy's life, while their psychological dimension is barely developed. Since the dialogues are reduced to the minimum, their feelings and thoughts are conveyed by their actions. For instance, Nuʿmān's mother oscillates between happiness and anger, protecting and rebuking her son. These feelings are expressed alternatively by her ululations of joy, tears, and quarrels with Nuʿmān. In one of their fights, the focus is on her actions, while the curse that she supposedly pronounces is reported by the narrator: "[she] could find nothing else to do than to smack the face of the bastard son of a bastard with a hefty lump of mud." (155/194)

Moreover, the villagers are named after their profession or religious title. In one case, the accumulation of similar names and professions has an ironic effect:

> In the end, Madame Fawqiya was moved to request everyone to desist, but no one could hear and the laughter, comments, and tossing continued until Sheikh Ali the Poultryman grew exhausted, followed by Mahmud, clerk of the market, than by another Mahmud, clerk of the slaughterhouse, followed by Abu Tis'a, followed by Sheikh Ahmad, the school principal,[5] followed by a third Muhammad, clerk of the community center, followed by Sheikh Rashid (who was blind), followed by the other Ahmad, broker of the sugar refinery. (142/177)

Other villagers are known with their nickname based on a physical defect: "Abd al-Wadud the Nasal, the longest established cloth merchant in the village and its most traditional" (171/213); "Abd Allah al-Ghashim – he of the huge head" (186/231); "Ibrahim Ghalla, of the coppery hair and dented face" (186/232).[49] Similarly, the candidates for marrying Nu'mān are examined on the basis of their physical or behavioural defects:

> At first, the daughter of the son of Abu Abd al-Mawla was proposed as a bride for Nu'man, but she was rejected because she spoke through her nose. Then it was the daughter of the son of Bayyumi al-Banna', but she was rejected because descended from the loins of women known for giving birth to few male children. Then it was the daughter of the sister of Abu al-Uyun, but confirmed reports indicated that she was a good-for-nothing who trembled in front of the baking oven, as a result of which her bread did not spread properly. Then it was one of the granddaughters of Kamila, the chicken seller, and Umm Nu'man was on the point of agreeing and would have done so were not for a rumor that she had bad breath. [. . .]
>
> Abu al-Uyun's sister's daughter began to rise once more to the head of the list; [. . .] All these were matters that had their weight and might compensate for the reported affliction of the voice of this proposed bride for Nu'man – the disdained nasality which, or so it was said, prevented her from pronouncing the letter *r* at all. (192–193/239–240)

Like in a fairy tale, Nu'mān marries "the most beautiful of all the beautiful girls in the village." (191/238) These scenes have a very local flavour and exploit the comic potential of quarrels among the ordinary members of a small community. In other Egyptian novels and short stories, similar fights involve the residents of an alley or apartment building.

Another storytelling technique is the formulaic repetition of the main characters' names, turning them into mythical figures who can easily be identified and remembered. Umm Nu'mān becomes "she over whom a question mark will forever hang" (155/194), due to her consent to sell her son to the lady. Fawqiyya is "the majestic, and also beautiful, lady" (*al-sayyida al-jalīla wa-l-jamīla ayḍan*), with two adjectives linked by assonance. Once, the epithet of the gravedigger is distorted by exchanging the order of the letters: Ismā'īl *ḥaffār – aw faḥḥār al-qubūr* ("Isma'il the digger – or delver – of graves", 162/202). The meaning does not change but the name is duplicated through wordplay. Some formulas have an estranging effect: one character corresponds to two villagers, "Abd al-Hamid Abd al-Aziz (or his brother Ahmad)", then a single option is given, "Abd al-Hamid the leader", and finally a footnote describes him as an opportunist. Other formulaic phrases concerning Nu'mān connect the episodes one with the other: "the forelock that was dedicated to Sheikh al-Farghal and could be removed only after the slaughter of a

49 In the original Arabic, their attributes are *al-akhnaf, dhū al-ra's al-ḍakhm*, and *dhū al-dimāgh al-munba'ja al-nuḥāsiyya*.

kid" and "the thing between his legs", referring to his circumcision, are repeated all throughout the novella.

Furthermore, sayings, insults, and songs insert orality in the writing. During the wedding celebration, the bride's and the groom's qualities are praised with several idiomatic expressions, reported by the narrator as if the village was speaking in one voice (201–202/251). Similarly, in the short story collection Mustajāb records the countryside forms of entertainment, such as dancing girls, theatrical performances, and the festivals of local saints. The power of storytelling and joking in a small rural community becomes the central topic of "al-Qurbān" (1973, "The Offering" 40–59).[50]

Fantasy and horror

Some fantastic elements in the novella and the short stories are borrowed from folklore. The supernatural manifests itself in devils and spirits, miracles and exorcism, usually linked to odd sexual practices. Among the village's legendary figures is *ḥājja* Fāṭima, who died twice. There is also a monk whose magic abilities have an influence on the majestic lady; he reminds of Rasputin, a figure of international folklore (145/181).

The supernatural also affects the representation of crime, which oscillates between crude details and fantasy. Crime is one of the central elements in the early Egyptian village novel, as exemplified by Tawfīq al-Ḥakīm's *Yawmiyyāt nā'ib fī l-aryāf* (§2.1): a prosecutor is sent to the Delta countryside to investigate petty crimes and a murder which remains unsolved; his struggle with the village's backwardness and the abstract nature of the Law are portrayed with irony. In Mustajāb's collection of short stories examined here, "Ightiyāl" (1972, "Assassination" 19–23) and "Kūbrī al-Bughaylī" (1975, "Bughayli Bridge" 24–34)

50 In this short story the villagers lose their ability to speak, so they resort to sign language and then become wedding entertainers thanks to their hand clapping performance. The following quote illustrates the social functions of storytelling and joking; the punch line subverts the conventional roles of agents and victims of mockery: "They busied themselves with the art of the sign, improving it and inventing new gestures, not just for rapid communication when haste was imperative, but also for the telling of stories. My village became capable, even, of recounting the tales of wonder, such as those of the Man with the Flayed Leg, the She-goul, Clever Hasan, and Thimble and the Moon of All Moons. Indeed, it reached a point where the two arms could reproduce, in miniature, all the effects of the tongue and even tell jokes, puzzles, riddles, and funny stories, and there came a time when my village used to tell – yes, tell – stories that included anecdotes about a man who could speak, just as nowadays we might tell an anecdote about a man who was dumb." (*Dayrūṭ* 49/63)

accumulate a high number of crimes caused by the village animosity which respond to an internal logic but cannot be understood by the official law.[51]

Similarly in *The Secret History*, the pervasive presence of violence described with hyper-realistic details diminishes its horrifying effect. Terror is often evoked but the episodes are not frightening, rather absurd. Horror ultimately becomes grotesque, as Tarbush (2009) puts it in her review: "The story lays bare the violent feud-ridden history of the village. It shows Mustagab's surreal imagination, forthright language and characteristic narrative style teeming with characters and incidents, by turns hilarious and horrifying."

To sum up, these narrative techniques break the conventions of realist fiction and revive the Arab tradition of the folktales and epics. Nevertheless, fiction and folklore are presented as facts since the novella is structured as a historical account or official biography. The next section examines the formal aspects borrowed from scholarly writing.

3.1.2 Scholarly writing

The Secret History adopts some conventions of scholarly writing, which have an impact on its structure and the reader's expectations, giving the impression that it is a manuscript whose subject is worthy of being investigated with objectivity and accuracy. Malti-Douglas notes that objectivity and accuracy are often flouted by incongruity. Furthermore, she remarks that applying these structural elements to a fictional text interrupts the flowing of the narrative and does not allow an immediate identification with the characters, creating a distance and making the reader aware of the mechanisms of fiction. Following Malti-Douglas, I shall examine footnotes, linguistic annotations, bulleted lists, and the absence of dialogues.

Footnotes and linguistic annotations

Metwally (2014: 166–196) explores the types and functions of footnotes and marginal annotations in a selection of contemporary Egyptian novels, including *The Secret History*. He suggests that scholarly footnotes draw attention to some words or concepts in the body of the text, providing a commentary, an explanation, or a reference to the sources. They engage with the text, because of their referential

51 "Ightiyāl" reminds of some popular crime films of the 1950s–1960s and the characters are known only by the initial of their names as in police reports; "Kūbrī al-Bughaylī" accumulates some many crimes that the bridge where the police and the villagers stand witnessing the discovery of corpses ultimately falls.

nature, and address the external context, because of their interpretive and critical nature. Adopted by modern fiction since the 19th century, they have also acquired creative functions. In this respect, Metwally recognizes that Egyptian fiction was influenced both by the European novel and the Arab literary heritage, whose historical, literary, and lexicographic texts included marginal or infratextual glosses. Early modern novelists, like Jurjī Zaydān (1861–1906), employed footnotes in their historical novels to reference the sources. Later, experimental novelists incorporated footnotes into the narrative, influenced also by the Nouveau Roman, which was among Mustajāb's readings.

Metwally suggests that footnotes in fiction are paratextual elements which expand the horizon of the text both in its structure and significance: they modify the novel's graphic, extend the story's boundaries, and offer alternative narrative threads.[52] Benstock argues that footnotes in literature belong entirely to the fictional universe since "[they] direct themselves toward the fiction and never toward an external construct, even when they cite 'real' works in the world outside the particular fiction" (Benstock 1983: 205 in Metwally 2014: 169).[53] This determines how the author and the reader look at the text, reflecting on the construction of the text itself.

It is worth outlining the types of footnotes found in all eleven chapters of *The Secret History*, except ch.6–7. Many of them are interpretive, *i.e.* they provide explanations about Islamic history, places, people, and technical or highly local terminology. Other footnotes cite the narrator's written sources, ranging from literature to historiography, such as verses from the Qur'ān, the village novel *al-Arḍ* (1954, *Egyptian Earth* 2005) by ʿAbd al-Raḥmān al-Sharqāwī, ʿAbd al-Raḥmān al-Rāfiʿ's essay about the 1919 revolution, Ṭāhā Ḥussayn's *al-Fitna al-kubrā* on Islamic history, and Miles Copeland's *The Game of Nations*. Explanatory and referential footnotes follow the conventions of scholarly writing in their form and meaning, thus reinforcing the image of the narrator as an authoritative source.

On the contrary, other footnotes do not clarify the element they are anchored to, rather increase its obscurity and suggest multiple possibilities, providing a counter-narrative to the one contained in the main text. For example, when the narrator introduces some villagers, he tells additional anecdotes in the footnotes to change their initial presentation and expose their defects. When investigating some events, he reports multiple versions and later dismisses them; yet he raises doubts about which version is truthful.

52 For the footnotes as elements of the paratext, see: Genette 1987.

53 Benstock looks at the fictional footnotes in works by Fielding, Sterne, and Joyce.

Linguistic annotations can be seen as explanatory footnotes inserted in the main text. They do not add any relevant information but reinforce the narrator's image as a scholar. In addition, these meta-linguistic commentaries drive the reader's attention to the linguistic register of the learned narrator, contrasting with that of the ignorant villagers. An alert reader knows that Mustajāb was a member of the Academy of the Arabic language.

Malti-Douglas finds an example of linguistic explanation in the spelling of a name, "my paternal uncle Mihimmad (so pronounced)" (117/146, *ʿammī Miḥimmad bi-kasr al-mīm al-ūlā wa-l-ḥāʾ*). The narrator could have indicated the local pronunciation by writing the word with the short vowels. This expanded version of vocalization, instead, highlights the name and is a technique borrowed from pre-modern historiography and lexicography. Besides this example in the body of the text, some linguistic explanations are found in the footnotes of ch.10 (fn. 4–7, 197/246). These footnotes provide the word's etymology, the local usage, and the reference sources, building the image of a nitpicking narrator who enjoys minute details.

Bulleted lists and dialogues

Like footnotes, bulleted lists have an impact on the graphic of the text. They enumerate the offenses inflicted upon Nuʿmān's father (ch.1), the topics of the conversation at the lady's house (ch.3), the rules for the therapeutic burial of the possessed woman (ch.6), and the composition of the dowry and bridal attire (ch.10).

Malti-Douglas notes that these lists juxtapose inconsequential issues without any clear connection. Mentioning inconsequential events also characterizes the narrator's discourse, an aspect of the discoursive level that should be anticipated here. When providing the context of a specific event, he employs the bulleted lists or reinterprets the historical genre of the annals. For exemple, in the long opening sequence of ch.9, he lists several accounts about the village, the nearby town, and Cairo. However, each piece of information is very short and does not indicate the exact date. The events are extremely varied: political measures, prices, deaths, murders, miracles, the pilgrimage to Mecca, and entertainment. Like in the bulleted lists, they are incoherent and inconsequential.

In addition, Malti-Douglas remarks that the bulleted lists substitute the narrative modes: enumerating events serves to summarize them, while listing topics of conversation substitutes dialogues. To this, it is worth adding that listing the rules of a ritual highlights their fixity and anticipates that they will be disrupted. These considerations are intertwined with the absence of dialogues, which strips the characters of their own voice. Everything is filtered through the narrator's reported speech, evoking one of the formal conventions of premodern historical writing. Reported speech as a discoursive strategy wil be examined in the next section.

Besides this, it should be noted that the bulleted lists are often followed by humorous episodes, developing one or more enumerated elements. For instance, the list of offenses inflicted upon Nuʿmān's father is followed by a narrative sequence in which the father is publicly ridiculed with a shift from physical to verbal aggression. The apex of verbal aggression is a satirical poem composed by some religious men, even though the few lines quoted in the text are not aggressive and sound like a childish song. It is only through a footnote that the poem's authors are mocked for using their wisdom for purposes in contrast with their spiritual role:[54]

> Abu Nuʿman remained patient and silent until his enemies exceeded the bounds of honour by proclaiming in the middle of the village that his stock of manhood was meagre and that the reason his children had died before they had been weaned was that they had been conceived by methods repugnant to God. From then on things got more unpleasant until the sheikhs composed a poem against him that went:
>
> | | |
> |---|---|
> | *Abd al-Hafiz, Abd al-Hafiz,* | عبد الحافظ يا خميس |
> | *You whose ways are the ways of Iblis.* | يا اللي فعلك فعل إبليس |
> | *Go your way and leave us in peace!* | هاجر وامش |
>
> and so on to the end of the poem,[6] which also contained an open threat to tie him onto a donkey back to front with his head covered in mud. Regrettably, the poem exceeded its duties as a warning and became mangled on the tongues of children and hooligans, who became addicted to greeting him or bidding him farewell with it, accompanied on occasion by rocks and brickbats. (122/152)
>
> [6] The poem is forty-nine lines long, and it is said that Sheikh Rashid, though a well-known chanter of the Qur'an, permitted himself the indulgence of writing secular verses that he recited on numerous occasions, and some of these in fact came to be regarded in many of the neighboring settlements as containing semi-divine wisdom. (126–127/158)

Finally, a formal aspect overlooked by Malti-Douglas is the chapters' structure. Most of them open with a quotation or preamble discussing a hypothesis. Then, the events of the previous chapter are recapped by formulaic phrases as in storytelling. At this point, the narration continues, and a key word of the preamble acquires a new meaning in the story. The conventions of scholarly writing tend

54 The original Arabic is not found in the English translation and is added here to give an idea of the poem's structure, length of the lines, and assonance.

to order the chapters according to their topic, whereas the conventions of storytelling tie them together.

To sum up, this section examined the creative function of the elements borrowed from academic writing: to paraphrase Benstock (1983), how do they shape the interplay between author, reader, and text? The implied author places the fictional biographical account in dialogue within a rich tradition, whose conventions are alternatively respected and subverted by the narrator.

3.1.3 Discoursive strategies

The first-person narrator is a local scholar who reconstructs the partial biography of an ordinary village boy or countryside folk hero. His attitude toward the subject and the incongruities in his discourse turn him into a humorous character who attracts the reader's ridicule and sympathy. This section examines his discoursive modes against the background of scholarly writing.

Firstly, the narrator's sources are the villagers' sayings and accounts (*maqūlāt wa-riwāyāt*). To guarantee their authenticity, he reports the chain of transmission (*isnād*). He often admits the sources' unreliability, as in these formulas found in ch.1:

> in an account attributed to Sheikh Abd al-Aziz Khalil which we are disposed to trust [fī riwāya namīlu ilā l-wuthūq bihā li-l-shaykh ʿAbd al-ʿAzīz Khalīl]; (118/147)
>
> And this in itself causes us to regard as unlikely other, highly dubious, accounts [wa-hādhā nafsuhu mā yajʿalunā nastabʿidu riwāyāt ukhrā yarqā ilayhā al-shakk]; (118/147)
>
> Further accounts with weak chain of transmission include. . . [wa-min al-riwāyāt al-ḍaʿīfa ayḍ^{an}]; (118/147)
>
> The weak point in this story lies in the fact that the report of it only appeared in recent years [Wa-nuqṭat al-ḍaʿf fī l-riwāya tarjaʿu ilā anna hādhihi al-maqūla lam taẓhar illā fī l-sanawāt al-akhīra]. (122/153)

Since the sources are often collective, the main reporting technique consists of impersonal formulas and passive verbs: "this gave rise to rumours that" (*ḥattā uthīra ḥawlahu kalām^{un} ʿan*); "it was said that" (*qīla inna*); "it was reported that" (*ruwiya anna*); "news went around that" (*tarāmat akhbār anna*); "it is certain that" (*min al-muʾakkad anna*); "it is believed" (*fīmā yuʿtaqadu*).

As Malti-Douglas notes, this reporting technique provided objectivity in premodern writings where the compiler's opinion emerged from his arrangement of the material. She argues that in *The Secret History* this objectivity gives the impression of distance between the narrator and the anecdotes' content, as though he was not responsible for what the villagers say. Since the reports are dubious, the implied reader doubts of the narrator. To this, it is worth adding that this traditional technique allows to reproduce the village's polyphony in a modern novel, depicting the village from an internal perspective.

Malti-Douglas identifies another discoursive strategy which challenges the authoritative image the narrator crafts of himself: he is not reliable because he accepts the paradox in facts and utterances. He often uses the particle "or" (*aw*) to present two incongruous elements as simultaneously possible: for instance, he gives two options to identify characters, time, and action. This opens the story to multiple options and suggest the nonsense (*al-lā maʿqūl*) of the whole account. This technique is so recurrent in the novella that it almost becomes a void formula; the reader does not focus on the two incongruous elements but rather on the narrator's image and language.

These discoursive techniques lead to consider other peculiarities of the narrator. If the narrator reports and rejects the village's gossip, who is the author of the story? At a certain point, in fact, the story slips through the narrator's fingers because of his lack of sources. He stops being almost omniscient and it is unclear if he relates past or contemporary events. He admits being deceived by the events and the characters in two metanarrative passages commenting on scholarly writing, at the beginning of ch.6 and 10. Irony emerges from the narrator's elaborate style as he comments on two ordinary events that have disrupted his theory, *i.e.* Nuʿmān's belated circumcision and his wedding.

Moreover, his apparent detachment contrasts with his role as a witness since his family comes from the same village. He mentions his paternal uncle Mihimmad (117/146), his grandfather *ḥājj* Mustajāb, and a villager called Muḥammad Mustajāb (185/230). The family name involves the author in a metanarrative game, since the Mustajābs and the protagonist are compared for their dumbness: the narrator reports some gossip about the hereditary lack of discernment in Nuʿmān's family, which causes Umm Nuʿmān's harsh reaction when her son abandons the luxury of the lady's house to go back home empty-handed:

> To be even-handed, I have to declare my reservations about accepting the disturbing statement made by a certain scoundrel against the Khamis lineage, among whom Nuʿman is to be numbered, to the effect, apparently, that they are a people lacking in discernment: *when they come across a purse full of gold, they undo the cloth purse, filch it, and leave the gold,*[1] and if one of them in those days had recourse to a moneylender to buy a sack of chemical fertilizer, he would pay the price of it many times over, and in installments, and sell the sack immediately for half its real value in order to buy tea and tobacco. [. . .]
>
> That autumn dawn, the fields witnessed a painful exchange between Umm Nuʿman, who had wished to introduce her only son into the circle of the majestic lady's entourage so that he might strut in the glory of the incandescent lamps, the meats, the rice, the tea,

> and the potatoes, and her son, the destroyer of her dreams, that idiotic boy who had insisted on *leaving the gold while not even filching the purse.*
>
> (154–155/192–193, emphasis added)

This punch line is effective because the narrator's words translate the mother's practical mentality. The related footnote (fn. 1) illustrates that attributing silliness to a whole family is part of popular jokelore. This feature characterizes the al-Khamīs, the Mustajābs, and could be extended to other families. Similarly, the Palestinian writer Imīl Ḥabībī revives this trope in his *al-Waqāʾiʿ al-gharība fī ikhtifāʾ Saʿīd Abī l-Naḥs al-Mutashāʾil* (1974; *The Secret Life of Saeed: The Pessoptimist* 2002). The protagonist of this tragicomic novel, characterized by an episodic structure, is a wise fool who inherits his dumbness and awkwardness from his ancestors (Camera D'Afflitto 2007: 135–140).

The overall impression is that of a narrator full of contradictions, who does not discern the relevant from the irrelevant, is extremely accurate and pedantic where is not needed, is dead-pan and at the same time intrusive. Selaiha (2001) considers him the real butt of satire for "his miserable failure to deliver a coherent reading of history despite his scrupulous research". Thus, he attests the failure of official historiography and big narratives. The next section examines the narrator's counterpart, Nuʿmān, looking at his presentation, the semantics of his actions, and some stylistic peculiarities.

3.2 The puppet

3.2.1 A folk antihero

The protagonists of biographies and folk epics are expected to have exceptional qualities that make them stand out and, at the same time, be representative of a group. Nuʿmān is rather an ordinary boy and the product of the Egyptian rural environment he lives in. His humble birth and dubious genealogy do not confer upon him any social prestige, while his life as a vagabond does not prospect a bright future. His trivial deeds (semantic level) contrast with the narrator's apparent accuracy and the epic tone of some episodes (discoursive level). The inadequate high register emphasizes the protagonist's defects and his antiheroic nature. Nevertheless, Nuʿmān arises the reader's sympathy because he is the victim of events bigger than him.

Besides this incongruity, two main strategies generate humour: repetition and digression. As regards repetition, all adventures follow a similar scheme since they start with great expectations and end into banal accounts. Once the readers are familiar with this framework, they expect something ridiculous to happen to Nuʿmān. As regards the second strategy, digressions illustrate the narrator's artistry and provide more prestigious terms of comparison, distracting from the main topic. These strategies induce the readers to take Nuʿmān's story not very seriously: the issue does not require a great mental effort, so the audience is relaxed and ready to perceive humour. As illustrated below, these strategies are employed at the beginning of the novella to shape a certain image of the main character.

Birth and lineage

Nuʿmān's story echoes the structure of the classical biography, which provides information about the subject's birth, lineage, education, field of specialization, and patronage, while inserting some amusing anecdotes to exemplify his qualities. Some of these anecdotes mention renowned political events to provide the temporal setting for the personal events (Osti 2013). However, *The Secret History* is a partial biography, so it does not include material about maturity, death, and legacy.

The first episode under scrutiny is the reconstruction of Nuʿmān's birth in ch.1. While heroes usually boast a noble lineage and a memorable birth, the boy's genealogy does not respond to these canons. It may be compared to the opening of *al-Waqāʾiʿ al-gharība*, in which the first-person narrator and protagonist Saʿīd parodies the style of the epics and admits that he was born again when a donkey saved his life during the 1948 defeat (*nakba*). In *The Secret History*, the narrator illustrates his findings about Nuʿmān's birth three times, repeating the same scheme based on digressions: I) relevant international or national events, II) reports about local events, III) a footnote expanding one of the above-mentioned reports, IV) conclusion.

The first attempt to establish Nuʿmān's date of birth is the opening of the novella, which is quoted below and marked according to the above-mentioned scheme:

> [I] No one in this world can pinpoint the year in which Nuʿman was born. It is certain that Germany's Reichstag had been burned down as Adolf prepared to rid himself of the opponents of the Third Reich, and that Lenin had died and handed socialist Russia over to his obdurate successor. On the other hand, we find it difficult to credit that Chamberlain had yet taken over the reins of power in Britain, Greatest of them all, [II] and it cannot be confirmed that my paternal uncle Mihimmad (so pronounced) had yet left the prison where he had been incarcerated for sowing poppies amid the cotton, which happened in parallel with the story of my grandfather, Hajj Mustajab, and the watch.[1] [III] [IV] Thus we may close the parentheses around an approximate date for Nuʿman's birth (and in doing so slap the hands of certain opinions that have sought to detract from our hero's standing), since it appears to be established that Nuʿman was born in one of those days of intense heat when the summer corn is starting to ripen. (117/146)

> [1] It is related of Hajj Mustajab that on his way back from the fields at noon on a Friday in summer he came across a round piece of shiny metal, which he then picked up, thanking God for His kindness. However, this piece of metal had two thin wires that jumped about beneath its glass covering and this dismayed the heart of the pious believer, which heart increased in dread when he brought the piece of metal close to his ear, for the satanic thing was ticking. He therefore threw the metal demon to the ground, uttered prayers for God's protection, and then pounded it with his crutch until he was certain that it was completely destroyed. This is a recent tale, not to be confused with the one about Charlemagne's clock and Harun al-Rashid. (125–126/156–157)

This passage is a single long sentence juxtaposing events of different relevance with the same tone. The biographer cannot reach a definitive conclusion: he uses the impersonal form of the reported speech and provides an approximate date calculated according to the agricultural rhythms. The footnote narrates an anecdote about the grandfather and introduces another account without telling it in full, probably because it belongs to common knowledge. In fact, both historiography and popular tales report that Charlemagne and Hārūn al-Rashīd exchanged embassies. Among the gifts sent by the Abbasid caliph was a brass water clock, which chimed the hours by dropping bronze balls into a bowl, while twelve mechanical knights – one for each hour – emerged from little windows (Musca 1996; Truitt 2015: 20).

As regards this clock, Metwally (2014: 173) adds, without mentioning his source, that "the monks of the king believed it was inhabited by a demon responsible for its strange movements. In night they destroyed it with the axes." This additional information establishes a clear parallelism with the grandfather's anecdotes. Metwally interprets this footnote as a satirical commentary about the stagnation of the East after a golden age of cultural and scientific advancement. In my view, the footnote juxtaposes two anecdotes of different import concerning the same issue: the confusion between science and marvel, technology and superstition. The anecdote about the grandfather features a traditional character in jokelore, *i.e.* the village yokel shocked by modernity and technology. A similar scene, including the physical reaction, appears in Abū Julayyil's *A Dog with No Tail* (§6.2.2).

The second attempt to establish Nuʿmān's birthday is found after two paragraphs. It mentions some Egyptian political events [I]: the resignation of the Prime Minister Muṣṭafā al-Naḥḥās (1879–1965)[55] and 'the Troubles' (*al-hawja*), which may refer to the ʿUrabī uprising, the 1919 revolution, or a local dispute.

55 Al-Naḥḥās was exiled with Saʿad Zaghlūl in 1921–1923 and was Prime Minister in 1928, 1930, 1936–1937, 1942–1944, 1950–1952. The novella reports that the British tanks surrounded ʿAbdīn palace at the time of his resignation, probably referring to 1944.

The latter hypothesis introduces facts of local interest [II]. Two footnotes [III] indicate the sources used to check both the national and local accounts. The narrator resorts to the birth registers and the military service board's reports, where more than one Nuʿmān appear because Umm Nuʿmān had three children bearing the same name who died young. Even these sad circumstances are absurd because two brothers named Nuʿmān lived together until one of them died: "However, these two Nuʿmans survived for a period before one of them died, though we have failed to identify which of the two was." (126/157) The narrator is totally detached and continues to enumerate his evidence. He concludes that Nuʿmān was born between 1930 and 1938: "It has thus become virtually certain that Nuʿman first saw this world on the bank of the Bahr Yusuf in the period extending up to eight years after 1930, according to the strictest suppositions." (119/148)

The third and final version interprets some natural elements as the warning signs of World War II:

> However, Sheikh Abd al-Hafiz's miracle did not survive for more than a few days, and consequently when [Nuʿman] entered this world he did so on an eroded bank, in a hut made of straw where the winds howled, tracing for the newborn a new and different world, while the waters of the Bahr Yusuf, carrying the good news to the land and the fields, billowed on without attention to those dark clouds that were gathering over the world as it pondered the first signs of the Second World War (for it is said that, at precisely the same time, Mussolini's warship began to pound the shores of Abyssinia). (125/156)

Education

The second episode of interest is Nuʿmān's education. Even though he does not receive any formal education, the narrator follows his achievements year after year. While playing in the fields, Nuʿmān interacts with modernity by stoning a few passing cars and chasing an aircraft to insult its pilot. Explaining this behaviour in a footnote, the narrator indirectly compares the boy to a famous genius with a ridiculous effect:

> Also, when he was eight, he struck two birds with one stone, messed about with an irrigation channel outlet and flooded twenty feddans and five qirats of land, [. . .] had stoned all the (few) cars that passed along the nearby highway, and had pursued a hovering aircraft, maintaining, in a loud voice, a flow of insults against its pilot till he (Nuʿman) fell into a fissure in some unflooded land.[1] (130/162)
>
> [1] There is a trustworthy account of the reason for Nuʿman's habit of chasing aircraft, which is that a kite snatched Nuʿman in his first year, while he was lying quietly in his swaddling bands at the bottom of a dry canal; that the kite, scared off by the terrible scream released by Umm Nuʿman, was unable to complete its mission; and that Nuʿman suffered from bloody wounds to his right temple and left arm that did not heal for many

> long months thereafter. We have deliberately overlooked this incident, as it occurs in similar form in Dr. Ahmad Ukasha's book on Leonardo Da Vinci. (135/167–168)

Once again, the digression blurs the boundaries between an authentic anecdote and a piece of shared knowledge. In his notebooks, Leonardo said that a kite inserted its tail in his mouth, when he was a child. Freud (1995 [1910]) interpreted this episode as the manifestation of adult fantasies in his one of his essays translated into Arabic by ʿUkāsha.[56] Metwally (2014: 176) notes that both in biographies and folktales "[t]he fantasy about an incident of childhood as an omen of adult fortune or genius is an established literary pattern". An alert reader may have recognized this pattern since the beginning of the footnote; when the narrator confirms the reader's impression, he/she feels involved in an intellectual game. Furthermore, the parallelism between Nuʿmān's miserable situation and Da Vinci's great achievements turn the first into an antihero: foreseeing a bright future for him is only an artificial story and this causes a sudden collapse into the ordinary.

A similar strategy is employed to portray Nuʿmān's fatherlessness. At the beginning of ch.3, the narrator argues against a fictional opponent who believes that the boy's fatherlessness is just a literary convention. This convention would allow to compare him with "prodigy performers and miracle workers", in particular "a certain person who didn't even have a father to begin with." (136/169) This is a reference to Jesus and, according to Malti-Douglas, to Prophet Muḥammad. Even though the narrator refutes this argument, the imbalanced comparison reveals that the quarrel is artificial and pompous. Another Biblical reference is found in the comparison between Nuʿmān's painful journey after the circumcision and the flight of the holy family into Egypt (178/221).

3.2.2 Interrupted rituals

After looking at the way the protagonist is introduced, this section examines three key episodes in which he is involved: the father's burial (ch.1), the therapeutic burial (ch.6), and Nuʿmān's circumcision (ch.7). Even though Nuʿmān is not directly involved in the first episode, it negatively affects his reputation. Relating them to the morphological category of the interrupted ritual, Malti-Douglas identifies three phases in their structure: I) the ritual begins, II) an external factor intervenes, III) the ritual remains unaccomplished. She concludes that these episodes

56 For a study of Freud's essay, see: Schapiro 1956. Schapiro explains that Freud's interpretation was based on the assumption that the bird was a vulture, due to a wrong translation.

break the rules of life and social expectations. It is possible to remark that subverting the order of things reveals the liberating power of humour, a central aspect in Bakhtin's theory of the carnivalesque. While Malti-Douglas conducts a structuralist analysis, this section also looks at the stylistic choices reinforcing the comic effect.

The father's burial

Nuʿmān's father, ʿAbd al-Ḥāfiẓ Khamīs, dies on the last Friday of Ramaḍān. Since those buried on this day are believed to be blessed, the village changes its mind about him, who had previously been considered an outlaw and is now turned into a revered figure. Their opinion is confirmed by the miracle that happens during his funeral, when the bier does not want to be buried and drags the mourners behind it:

> The strange thing is that the village that declared him an outlaw was the very same village that went out as one man to walk his funeral procession, for the day of his burial happened to be the last Friday of Ramadan, and there is a belief among the common people that anyone who goes to meet his Maker on such a day is, without doubt or exception, blessed. They therefore said the prayers over Abd al-Hafiz Khamis at noon of the last Friday of Ramadan in the mosque of Amir Sinan, built by the Sharif Hisn ibn Thaʿlab, a companion of Amr ibn al-ʿAs, and it is said that the bier went round and round from place to place in the village and refused to head for the burial ground, and that the sheikhs pleaded with it to make its way to the grave but were compelled to bring it drums and pipes to make it happy, and that the women started ululating, so that it became a noted day, for the bier dragged the mourners along in its wake not just within Dayrut al-Sharif but to the neighboring villages, the men panting after it and pouring sweat, and people of consequence got in touch with the district chief, who brought his soldiers in an attempt to bury the noble body by force, but the bier continued to resist, dragging the chanting, praying, drumming, and ululating masses along behind it. (123–124/154)

This scene is amusing because fantasy and reality, science and superstition overlap. An inanimate object is attributed a human or even supernatural will, as expressed by the verbs "refused", "pleaded", and "resist". On a semantic level, the inability of the religious authorities and the soldiers to restore the order indicates that the power relations are subverted. Furthermore, the bier ridicules those who had despised ʿAbd al-Ḥāfiẓ Khamīs and changed their mind after his death out of a spiritual afflatus or interest. The targets of satire are summarized in the closing sentence, in which juxtaposition and repetition emphasize this episode's absurdity.

This scene marks the beginning of the ritual. The bier is buried in an ordinary tomb, waiting to be moved to a holy shrine that is being built. However, the ritual is interrupted by some wild animals that open the first tomb tearing the corpse apart, a scene described with macabre images which tend to be grotesque. As a consequence, both the first tomb and the holy shrine are left empty and the initial situation is reinstated: ʿAbd al-Ḥāfiẓ Khamīs's prestige is dispelled and he is again a troublemaker and the object of mockery.

Therapeutic burial

The continuity between the first and the second ritual is indicated by the same location, since Nuʿmān settles in an empty tomb that probably coincides with his father's shrine. A woman goes to the graveyard to cure a skin irritation in her private parts caused by the demons. Once again, the bodily and the spiritual dimensions are intertwined. The ritual begins according to the prescriptions enumerated in the bulleted list; one rule forbids uncircumcised men to take part into the burial. When the woman is buried in the sand with only her head left outside, the external factor intervenes since she realizes that the boy is not circumcised:

> The woman felt she was being throttled, and Nu'man realized that the devils were trying frantically to get out. Then the woman sneezed, and it became clear that the treatment was working according to the plan. Next, Isma'il the Gravedigger ordered Nu'man to level the ground around the tomb so that the angels should not be harmed. Nu'man took off his jellabiya so it wouldn't get in his way as he carried out the leveling. His body was pouring sweat and he bent over with the remains of a palm branch to tidy the place as the woman's *constricted head* beseeched God to grant her recovery. Stillness and a whispering silence buried in the shuddering end of the humid night reigned over the place. Finally, Nu'man sat down next to the woman's *head.*
>
> The most distressing thing is that the cry from the woman's *constricted head* did not arise as the result of the bite of a snake or scorpion, or the sudden onslaught of a devil, or a poke from an angel. It was the result of a sharp glance of the *eyes* at Nu'man's body, the result of which was that the accursed woman awoke to the presence of the topknot rising like a mushroom above Nu'man's *head.* She asked him – in the midst of her entreaties – about his mother, about his father, and about the sheikh to whom the shaving of his topknot was dedicated. Then, in terrified silence, she turned *her head* till *her weary eyes* were able to take in, in the weary dark, Nu'man's *thighs,* and she whispered, "God forbid, my son, that you be not circumcised!"
>
> [. . .] The woman's *head* continued to shiver and shake above the sand, refusing to submit to all the recitations of Isma'il the Gravedigger and his entreaties to the jinn. Then the shuddering overwhelmed the rest of the thrashing *body* [. . .] but the devils had opened a fissure in the calm and her *body* was drawn up put of the enfolding hole – strong, hard, naked, bloody bottomed, and screaming – and the woman, raging, set off immediately along the road. (166–168/208–210, emphasis added)

The focus is on the parts of the body that are a metonymy for the whole subject: Nuʿmān's thighs and topknot reveal that he is not circumcised, while the woman's head is constricted by the treatment and her mobility is limited to her eyes. At the same time, these parts are described as autonomous items subject to mechanical movements. This mechanical appearance and extremely objective description of physical details are ludicrous.

The external event is introduced by the woman's exclamation in Egyptian Colloquial Arabic, which is one of the few dialogues in the novella. Nuʿmān unintentionally breaks a rule due to his ignorance; conversely, the other characters and the narrator know this rule but ignore the meaning of the boy's topknot. The reader has probably guessed its meaning, or at least its relevance, due to the several repetitions. His/her knowledge determine a feeling of superiority toward the gullible characters and narrator.

The ritual is unaccomplished: the woman remains possessed by the demons, emerges from the sand as a monstrous creature, and runs away. The focus shifts from the head to her whole body, with a final sentence summarizing her features. This monstrous creature is not dreadful: it terrifies the dead and the angels but does not bother the village which sleeps undisturbed.

Nuʿmān's circumcision

The previous incident leads to Nuʿmān's circumcision, which had been delayed due to his mother's straitened circumstances. The ritual begins in the village of Amshūl where the barber shaves the topknot and cuts the tip of the foreskin. However, the festive atmosphere is interrupted by an inhabitant of Amshūl who asks to respect an agreement, according to which barbers should perform the circumcision only in their villages; this short dialogue is in Egyptian Colloquial Arabic. Unlike the previous episode, which employs the imagery of horror, this scene parodies tragedy. Firstly, the characters' reactions are exaggerated by the parallel structure of the sentences (triplets and anaphora) conveying a feeling of immobility, as in these examples:

> Nu'man, therefore, had his circumcision, Umm Nu'man her dancing, and Isma'il the Gravedigger his straining on Nu'man's shoulders halted. (174/218)

> It appeared, at this point, that things would be difficult to fix. Eid the Barber was furious but powerless to act. Umm Nu'man wavered back and forth between curses and entreaties. Isma'il the Gravedigger tried to calm the man down while other individuals tried to stir him up. Nu'man tried to stand, but felt another savage and powerful flood of pain, and he wept. (175/218)

Secondly, the dramatic tension focuses on a single part of the body, the tip of the prepuce, which is almost reified. At the beginning, Umm Nuʿmān places it over her head and dances with it; when the rite is interrupted, she clutches it in her hand; at the end, it is the symbol of the whole tragedy: "On the site of the tragedy they left a palm branch with plaited fronds, the skin of a rabbit of large size, broken biscuits, a great deal of blood, and a prepuce wallowing in blood and dust." (176/219). The final description evokes the crime scene in a detective story, oscillating between the epic tone of tragedy and scientific precision.

As Malti-Douglas notes, the following chapter does not provide the ritual's conclusion despite its title ('On How the Circumcision Was Completed'). While she does not analyse this episode, I have identified some humour-generating strategies establishing a continuity between the two chapters. The circumcision becomes tragicomic and involves the whole village. When Nuʿmān, his mother, the Barber, and the Gravedigger return to the village riding their donkeys, they are accosted by ʿAbd al-Ḥāmīd ʿAbd al-ʿAzīz (or his brother Aḥmad), who seeks revenge for the village's offended pride. The village organizes an expedition described with military and religious terms.[57] The project's magnitude is conveyed by metaphors referring to the human body (the village is a single body raising its head) and the parody of the military discourse. In this passage, the narrator adopts the perspective of a military chief who incites its army:

> We had never realized that our village loved Nu'man so much. We had never imagined for an instant that his love could be translated, and with such a speed, into this host, armed with rifles, sickles, and knives. It was up to Amshul to rethink what it had done. Nu'man was an orphan, true enough; yet Dayrut al-Sharif was his village, his home, and his father. Nu'man was poor, true enough; yet Dayrut al-Sharif was his lineage, his strength, and his wealth, and though faced by a thousand villages and a thousand armies, Nu'man's forces would defeat them all. (181/225)

The exaggeration between the military discourse and Nuʿmān's circumcision is conveyed by some dramatic images, hyperbole, and comical counterpoints. The village intervenes because it sees its pride haemorrhaging from Nuʿmān's wound, with blood breaking through "the dams of coffee grounds and dirt" (179/223). Coffee grounds and dirt are traditional remedies, not so effective as to be compared to dams. Moreover, the village gathers an army of a thousand, or two thousand, or three thousand men who march with military discipline behind a donkey, an iconic animal in the humorous tradition. However, the armed expedition fails and Nuʿmān is brought back to Dayrūṭ:

57 The expedition is described as "a blessed procession" [al-masīra al-mubāraka]; "the expeditionary force" [al-ḥamla al-musallaḥa]; "the march of zeal and determination" [riḥlat ḥamiyya wa-iṣrār]; "this doomsday procession" [yawm al-ḥashr]; "army" [jaysh] and "forces" [ḥamla] (180–181/224–225).

> At this point, Abd al-Hamid the leader shouted his apology to the people, proclaiming his utter gratitude to Amshul and the men of Amshul, and swore on the divorce of his wife that there would be no circumcision for Nu'man anywhere but in Dayrut al-Sharif, their mighty village.
>
> The two jennies [bowed] their heads and the army followed behind them. Nu'man fainted, throbbing with pain, silence, and shock. Eid the Barber hurried, between each leg of the journey, to uncover the swelling wound between Nu'man's thighs and bank up the blood with dirt. And Abd al-Hamid, the leader, proceeded at the front of his people, his head held high. (182/226–227)

This closing passage subverts all the elements of this chapter. Firstly, ʿAbd al-Ḥāmīd, who had sworn to divorce his wife if the boy was not circumcised in Amshūl, swears to divorce if the boy is not circumcised in Dayrūṭ. His vow is exaggerated and nonsensical. Secondly, he keeps his head held right but is described as an opportunist in a footnote (fn. 4, 183/228). Thirdly, the donkeys bow their heads, whereas the village had raised it before. The donkeys ride back and forth on a bumpy road in an aimless and repetitive way, which increases the humorous effect. Finally, the Barber's action is repeated four times. In one of these occurrences, he checks "the mess between his thighs" (178/221). In the original Arabic, the mess is *al-mahzala*, meaning a farcical or comical situation.

The desecrating effect of the three interrupted rituals lies both in their content and form. On a semantic level, they are religious rites concerning central aspects of one's public life, *i.e.* death, disease, and masculinity. The ritual's spiritual meaning and codified rules are disrupted by a minor external factor which intervenes unexpectedly. Thus, prescriptions are subverted and social expectations are disregarded. On a formal level, the absurdity of the situation is conveyed by the summarizing final sentence, parallelism, and parody of the military, horror, and tragic discourses. Since the body is at the centre of these rituals, irony is achieved through its objectification. The repetition of the same structural pattern in all three rituals prepares the reader to something unconventional and ultimately hilarious. Malti-Douglas applies this pattern to the novella's title, which announces a partial account of an interrupted biography. I suggest extending this pattern to the final episode, leading to opposite results.

Like the circumcision, the wedding night concerns the social dimension of sexuality. Continuity is symbolized by the Ursa Major and Ursa Minor appearing in the sky, like in the therapeutic burial. In Arabic, these stars are called *banāt al-naʿsh*, literally the daughters of the bier, probably implying a reference to the first ritual. The wedding ritual starts with the village's celebrations. Then, the bride is carried into the groom's room, where the midwife helps Nuʿmān to deflorate her with his finger. The first attempt is only partially successful, but the midwife supervises the ritual and, after cursing Nuʿmān, helps him to accomplish his duty. In this case, the accomplished ritual responds to the social expectations: it marks the end of Nuʿmān's early life and gives the story its happy ending.

3.3 Social satire: the village

3.3.1 Ignorance and superstition

As illustrated above, Nuʿmān is the protagonist of absurd situations that reveal his antiheroic nature. In these episodes, his village either witnesses the scene or intervenes. The boy is the butt of humour for his mishaps and, at the same time, the vehicle of the author's social satire toward the village's mentality. The main aspects criticized by the implied author are ignorance and superstition, as can be seen in two episodes revolving around medical treatments without scientific basis.

In the first episode, examined also by Metwally, ʿĪd the Barber uses coffee grounds and smooth dirt to stop Nuʿmān's bleeding after the circumcision. The Barber, the Gravedigger, and Umm Nuʿmān tell some stories to confirm the efficacy of these traditional remedies. However, the only two accounts narrated in full contradict one another. In the main text, the narrator reports that the Barber says that his niece "had been saved by coffee grounds and only died after envious and ignorant people had misled her family into taking her to the hospital." (178/221) The footnote, instead, reports the incident of a pregnant young girl whose bleeding was treated with dirt, straw, and scraps of clothes; when she was brought to the hospital, it was too late. Criticism is strengthened by the fact that the relative responsible for her was a former school principal, thus an educated person. The two stories are told with the same detached attitude, but the former has a defensive aim, while the latter denounces the inhuman treatments and discredits the previous one. Similarly, Nuʿmān's inflammation is cured with traditional methods whose non-scientific basis is revealed in the footnotes.[58] Only the majestic lady can solve this problem: when she sees the wound, she curses ignorance and sends the boy to the city's doctor.

---

58 "Spinal-cord cauterizers" are defined in fn. 3, 189/236; *al-rāsakht*, a powder, is defined in fn. 4, 189/236; *zār*, the practice of exorcising the spirits from possessed individuals, is mentioned in the main text; in the next chapter, fn. 2, p. 196/245 describes how the village people used penicillin, sprinkling it onto the wound instead of doing an injection, to avoid the sting of the needle.

In an earlier episode, Nuʿmān falls ill when he is still a child. After performing a ritual against the evil eye, Umm Nuʿmān carries her son to the far-away government hospital. To comment on her prompt decision, the narrator mentions Camus: "Albert Camus, or one of those people, says that if you die this year, death will avoid you the next. Umm Nuʻman, not being concerned with the sayings of Albert Camus, wasted no time [. . .]" (132/164). This is ironic because Camus is totally alien from the woman's environment and his existentialist philosophy is summarized in a maxim that sounds like dark humour.

When Umm Nuʿmān reaches the hospital, she fights with the doorkeeper, losing her chance to see the doctor. Finally, she returns to the village and entrusts her son to the cures of a local *shaykh*, who mixes religious formulas and magical rituals against the spirits. The incongruity emerges from the *shaykh*'s quotations of the Qurʾān followed by his abrupt request of being paid twenty piasters for the treatment. The spiritual content and the solemn language of the Qurʾān, with footnotes indicating the precise reference, contrast with the direct language of the material request.

Both episodes raise the question of who is responsible for the villagers' ignorance. The educational institutions are criticized in the first anecdote, whereas in the second one the religious authorities are blamed for their greed and lack of real knowledge, reviving a long tradition in Arab humour. Another common feature is the journey from the village to the town. When Nuʿmān and his mother reach the small city in the second episode, they are stopped by a policeman and then by a crowd of political supporters who mistake the young boy for a great guest and involve him in the celebrations. A picture of his mother appearing on the newspapers highlights the non-sense of this scene, with ordinary people turned into heroes in the least appropriate moment. The quarrel between the mother and the hospital's doorkeeper, instead, reveals the mutual hostility between the city and the countryside. This hostility is confirmed by urban architecture enclosing the open nature and the comparison between formal and infomal education.

The implied author criticizes ignorance, superstition, and opportunism in an indirect way, through the narrator's matter-of-fact style, the footnotes providing counter-information, jibes directed at minor characters, and the contrast between the city and the village.

3.3.2 Entertainment for the elite

The city and the village are also contrasted for their values and forms of entertainment in the night that Nuʿmān spends at the lady's house. She hosts night gatherings with some local middle-class men who enjoy drinking, chatting, and joking. This section explores how Nuʿmān contributes to their merriment and which stylistic elements convey the situation's absurdity.

The entertainment at the lady's house revolves around her guests' witty talk, whose topics are juxtaposed in a sentence and later in a bulleted list of eleven elements:

> Madame Fawqiya had not become disheartened, but had opened her luxurious hose at night to people of standing, excellence, and eminence, there to quaff draughts of scholarship, conversation, ease, food, and literature and to discuss such topics as al-Naʿisa, Diyab, Abu Nuwas, the Constitution, the British, Imam al-Shafiʿi, Makram Ebeid, and Najib al-Rihani. (138/171)

> while conversation continued among the assembled persons on the following topics:[. . .]
> j. Extensive and impolite discourse on the subject of Abu Nuwas and the slave girl Jinan.
>
> k. The tale of how a ruler of olden times had been castrated at the hands of his slaves. (140–141/175–176)

Both lists include the following topics: contemporary Egyptian politics; Islamic history and jurisprudence; topics of local interest, such as crimes, prices, and business; oddities, with a focus on sexual perversion; and various literary genres. Al-Nāʿisa and Diyāb are characters from *al-sīra al-hilāliyya*, a famous folk epic (§6.2.2), whereas Abū Nuwās is the epitome of court wine poetry, and Najīb al-Rīḥānī (1892–1949) was one of the major Egyptian comedians of the first half of the 20th century (§4.3.3). The tale of the castrated ruler mentioned above (k) revolves around the subversion of sexual hierarchies through storytelling. These literary references, which draw on the Arab cultural heritage, anticipate the delightful atmosphere: the tales suggest the participants' taste for the odd, whereas the sexual allusions place pleasure at the centre of entertainment. Abū Nuwās is the literary counterpart of the guests, who enjoy wine and bawdiness. In other words, their conversation anticipates their actions.

The first hilarious moment portrays *shaykh* ʿAlī ridiculing *shaykh* Abū Tisʿa in a witty repartee. The latter falls into the trap of explaining the meaning of his nickname, literally 'He of the Nines', with great eloquence: he mentions some verses from the Qurʾān containing the number nine, then pleads God to grant him a numerous offspring based on the multiples of nine. His antagonist turns the religious knowledge and rhetoric against him, quoting a verse in which the number nine has a negative meaning:

> To this, Sheikh Abu Tis'a added that his father had nine boy children and nine girls, that he himself had fathered seven, and that he prayed to God to extend His blessings so far as to allow him to follow the example of His Miraculous Verses and father nine, or, if He were not feeling stingy, nineteen, or even, were He feeling expansive, ninety-nine.
>
> At this, Sheikh Ali cried out in challenge to Sheikh Abu Tis'a, "If that is the case, O Sheikh of the Devils, why do you flee God's words in Surat al-Naml?" at which Madame Fawqiya asked delightedly, for the millionth time, "And what does it say in Surat al-Naml, Sheikh Ali?" and Sheikh Ali stood up (the seat pad of the chair falling as a result between his feet) and recited, "There were nine men in the city who spread corruption in the land!"
>
> At this exquisite moment, when the audience had been won over to Sheikh Ali's side and were displaying their unbounded admiration for his cleverness, Madame Fawqiyya caught sight of Nu'man and his mother in the entrance to the salon and beckoned them into her presence. (139–140/172–174)

This anecdote revives the Arab humorous tradition of poking fun at futile jurisprudential disputes. Yet, the winner is appreciated for his cleverness. In addition, it evokes the classical trope of scholarly competition and debate (*munāẓara*). Premodern sources often illustrate methodological differences though accounts of discussions between two or more scholars (Osti 2006). These stories, featuring teachers, students, and patrons, provide a physical context to a scholarly debate, linking it to personal concrete situations. The above-mentioned passage can be compared to a *majlis* (session) with two local scholars wrangling in front of the audience; the female patron invites them to discuss for the guests' pleasure.

The second funny episode in this chapter moves to the level of action. One of the drunken guests lifts Nuʿmān up to the ceiling, the guests form a circle and toss the little boy in the air. Nuʿmān is an inanimate object, a puppet, providing merriment (*al-maraḥ*) and pleasure (*al-mutʿa*), released through their laughter (*al-ḍaḥkāt*), cheerful uproar (*al-ḍajja al-saʿīda*), and ribald talk (*al-kalām al-badhīʿ*, 142/177). The contrast between their excitement and Umm Nuʿmān's fear makes this scene even funnier. Furthermore, the narrator partly adopts the internal perspective of the young boy, who does not fully understand the situation. While the boy is the object of fun, his reification during the game corresponds to lady's intention to purchase him. This extravagant form of entertainment hints at Madame Fawqiya's weird habits and possible paedophilia. It establishes a hierarchy between the two characters and evokes the magic atmosphere lingering in her house.

The next chapter, in fact, moves to the lady's private apartments. Both chapters employ the main stylistic features enhancing humour in the whole novella. Repetitions convey the idea of the mechanical in the actions and narration: the verb 'to laugh'; the lady's name; the formulaic phrase about Nuʿmān's topknot, repeated with a magical effect when Madame Fawqiya caresses his head; the lady opening and closing the doors. Moreover, the physical description focuses on single parts of the body, as in the almost scientific description of the majestic lady's beauty:

> The majestic, and also beautiful lady, who had decided to acquire Nuʻman Abd al-Hafiz for her magnificent house was composed of a nose, two lips, two eyes, two eyebrows, two cheeks, and a neck, followed by a chest, two breasts, a navel, and two thighs, which were components rarely found gathered together, and complete, in the women of our village, whose particulars hung loosely by reason of the constant changes in the climate and such factors as erosion, heat, children, mud, dung, cold, and men. (145/181)

In another passage, she is described with a list of her possessions. Both descriptions are followed by an accumulation of mysterious stories including murder and superstition. As usual, these anecdotes are not told in full and contradictory information is provided in the footnotes. The horror stories become grotesque because of the matter-of-fact narration, which does not attempt to provide any explanation nor moral evaluation.

3.4 Conclusion: a tale of incongruities

In *The Secret History*, humour is based on several of patent incongruities. The margins become a central element both in the structure, marked by the footnotes, and the action, revolving around an antihero. The first section of this chapter explores how the oscillation between two distant writing conventions places the story into a disorienting frame (suspense of form), paving the way for further incongruities, such as the narrator's manipulation of the village's gossip and his attitude toward the main character.

The narrator-historian and Nuʿmān are the novella's two comical characters. Adapting and expanding Malti-Douglas's analytical framework, this chapter argues that they are involved in situations that are not funny *per se*. While the narrator struggles with his own creation, the boy lives some dreadful experiences which may end in tragedy. What makes them humorous is the complex interplay of the three examined levels (form, discourse, and action), enriched by abundant intertextual references and a great mastery at linguistic manipulation. In the biography of this antihero, two episodes are overtly funny thanks to their dramatic construction featuring some popular characters: the father's bier dragging the mourners behind it and the choice of Nuʿmān's wife. Another key scene portrays the boy as a puppet for the lady and her guests' entertainment, mixing fun and mystery to obtain a grotesque effect; furthermore, this episode allows a satirical comparison of the lower and higher classes in an enclosed social environment.

In the passages analyzed in the second and third sections, some recurring stylistic features contribute to the humorous effect, such as repetition, parallelism, hyperbole, lists, and accumulation of stories of different import or containing contradictory information. As regards the physical descriptions, there is a focus on the single parts of the body, as if they were reified, and some hints at sexual taboos. In terms of linguistic registers, it is significant that the narrator's flowery Arabic is interrupted by some brief dialogues in Egyptian Colloquial Arabic in the rituals' key moments. These elements are combined with some features of the village novel that overtly clash with scholarly writing and are reminiscent of folktales, such as the magical representation of nature, storytelling techniques, fantasy, and horror.

To sum up, Mustajāb exploits the collective dimension of the village, with its multiple characters and antihero, not only to criticize the shortcomings of the Egyptian society but also to unmask the absurdity of life. In this respect, I agree with Malti-Douglas who insists on the nonsense in the actions and utterances, and Selaiha (2001) who remarks the author's cynicism in his lack of moralistic evaluation and modernist critique of realist mimetic art:

> using the narrative strategies characteristic of a lot of postmodernist fiction, [the novella] recklessly carries the essential ironic nature of the novel as a genre to its extreme outward limits, threatening to destroy it altogether. [. . .]
>
> Mustagab's irony is morally nihilistic, devastating and thorough, levelling everything on its way.

Moving to the urban underworld, the next chapter examines *Time-Travels* by Khayrī Shalabī whose picaresque protagonist, far from being the butt of humour, embodies some proverbial comic agents. Mustajāb's sharp irony leaves place for a light kind of humour, still based on the complex intertextuality with historiography and literary sources.

4 Ibn Shalabī, a (pre-)modern trickster

> 'Why did you return, Ram?'
>
> I lit another cigarette and stood by the window once more.
>
> 'You told me so many times you love Egyptians. I, too, Edna, but unconsciously, not like you. Egypt to me is so many different things. Playing snooker with Doromian and Varenian the Armenians, is Egypt to me. Sarcastic remarks are Egypt to me – not only the fellah and his plight. Riding the tram is Egypt. Do you know my friend Fawzi? He can never give an answer that isn't witty. . . and yet he isn't renowned for it. He's an ordinary Egyptian. Last week I was riding the tram with him when a man stepped on his foot. "Excuse me," said the man, "for stepping on your foot." – "Not at all," said Fawzi, "I've been stepping on it myself for the last twenty-seven years". . . How can I explain to you that Egypt to me is something unconscious, is nothing particularly political, or. . . or. . . oh, never mind,' I said.'
>
> W. Ghali, *Beer in the Snooker Club*, 1964: 190

Like Mustajāb's novella examined in ch.3, *The Time-Travels of the Man Who Sold Pickles and Sweets* by Khayrī Shalabī has an episodic structure and revolves around an antihero: Ibn Shalabī, an ordinary Egyptian and first-person narrator, who travels through time.[59] He moves back and forth between the present (1979) and different periods in the past, while remaining fixed in space since all events take place in the historic heart of Cairo. He cannot control his movements but only check the date on his wristwatch which follows the Islamic calendar. Travelling to the Fatimid (969–1171), Ayyubid (1171–1260), and Bahri Mamluk (1250–1390) eras, he witnesses some relevant events in the Egyptian history, often related to the construction of monuments which have later become the symbols of the urban landscape.

Invited by the Fatimid Caliph al-Muʿizz li-Dīn Allāh (953–975) to a banquet for the first Ramaḍān celebrations in Cairo (973), Ibn Shalabī arrives early and witnesses the foundation of the city by General Jawhar al-Ṣiqillī (969). The Fatimids build al-Azhar Mosque and the Great Eastern Palace before being expelled by the Ayyubids. In his time-travels set in the Ayyubid period, the protagonist is summoned by Ṣalāḥ al-Dīn (1174–1193), makes fun of the awe-inspiring viceroy of Egypt Qarāqūsh, and witnesses the construction of the Citadel.

59 It was originally published in instalments in *Majallat al-idhāʿa wa-l-talfizyūn* in 1980. Bushnaq (2002: 500) reconstructs its multiple editions in book form: a shortened version (eight chapters out of twenty-four) was published by *Kitāb Akhbār al-yawm* in 1981 and later by Madbūlī in Lebanon. In library catalogues, 1983 usually appears as the year of the first edition, while many reviews indicate 1991. This latter reprint was probably more popular, which may suggest the novel's double reception over the 1980s and 1990s.

https://doi.org/10.1515/9783110725414-005

Jumping back in time, Ibn Shalabī wants to find a job at the Fatimid chancery. Although he is sponsored by the historian Ibn al-Ṭuwayr (d. 1220), he fails to get this job and is arrested. To get out of prison, he tries to impress the Fatimid Caliph Manṣūr al-Āmir bi-Aḥkām Allāh (1101–1130) with a 20th-century cassette recorder. However, this technological device does not work and Ibn Shalabī is sent to the Storehouse of Banners (*khizānat al-bunūd*), the prison where high officers are jailed. He cannot escape from this place but finds himself in another time: when the Mamluk Sultan al-Malik al-Nāṣir Muḥammad b. Qalāwūn (1293–1294, 1299–1309, 1309–1340) comes back from his campaign against the Mongols, the Storehouse of Banners is used to detain the war prisoners, including the powerful Emir Khazʿal who establishes a state within the state.

This episode marks the beginning of the second part of the novel, set in the Mamluk period with a few visits to contemporary Cairo. This dynasty receives more attention because, as the author stated in an interview, the Mamluk period was the one that influenced most the Egyptian people in terms of social system, manners and customs, traditions and way of living (Schalabi & Bushnaq 2006: 17). In this temporal setting, Ibn Shalabī is a double agent in the Storehouse and the Citadel, working for Khazʿal and at the same time being a *mamlūk*, intended here as a slave at court.[60] He witnesses the intrigues of court involving Emir Qawṣūn, Tashtamur al-Sāqī known as Green Garbanzo, and Quṭlūbughā al-Fakhrī, until al-Malik al-Nāṣir Shihāb al-Dīn Aḥmad (1342) is summoned from al-Karak in Jordan to reign over the land of Egypt. Given as a present to Sultan Aḥmad, the protagonist becomes a court jester. When the Sultan leaves Cairo, the emirs depose him and choose his brother Sultan al-Ṣāliḥ (1342–1345). Ibn Shalabī becomes his confident and later the press secretary of the newly appointed viceroy of Egypt, the Polo Master (*al-ḥājj* Āl-malik al-Jūkandār).[61] An old enemy of the Storehouse, the Polo Master condemns its immoral conduct and finally destroys it. The protagonist should join the Storehouse's prisoners but has a weapon of last resort: time-travelling. He finds himself at the bus stop in Citadel Square, just in time to catch the bus to go back home.

60 The term literally means "thing possessed", hence "slave". It refers to military slaves mainly from Central Asia who were part of the Islamic armies, until they seized power in Egypt and Syria from 1250.

61 The English translator Micheal Cooperson explains that the nickname Green Garbanzo refers to his fondness for the popular dish made of green chickpeas (*ḥummuṣ akhḍar*), whereas *jūkandār* was a title originally attributed to the official responsible for the sultan's polo equipment and the conduct of games (Glossary, 'Tashtamur the Cupbearer, called Green Garbanzo' 258 and 'The Emir Polo Master' 256).

Time-travelling generates a humorous effect on various levels in this novel. Firstly, all journeys are placed within a frame narrative, in which the narrator tells the odd incidents triggering his displacements. Thus, each journey is a window opening on the past and a brief episode in a repetitive structure. Secondly, the cultural distance between the past and present leads to funny misunderstandings allowing a critical view of both societies. In particular, the narrator reconstructs Egyptian history mixing the historical sources and his fictional interaction with them to convey a sense of continuity in power relations between the authority and the ordinary people, the rich and the poor, which allows him to mock some stereotypes usually attached to the Egyptians. Finally, the protagonist's identity is always changing in these journeys, either because he is mistaken for somebody else or because he plays a role. Like picaresque characters, he sets out of intricate situations thanks to his eloquence and good sense.

The first section of this chapter places time-travelling and the protagonist against the background of previous literary models, such as the early modern travelogue (*riḥla*), *maqāma*, and historiography. Reviving the past, the interplay with these literary sources allows to craft an unusual historical novel and to root the main character's comic potential in the humorous tradition at the crossroads between high literature and popular culture. After illustrating these literary antecedents, the second section describes the main features of Ibn Shalabī as a narrator, trickster, and time-traveller. Finally, the third section examines some types of humour (verbal, situational, self-mocking, carnivalesque) found in *Time-Travels*, which is extremely rich in wordplay, linguistic variation, and comic sketches.

4.1 Reviving the past

4.1.1 Travelogue

Time-travelling conveying both social criticism and comic effects is not new in modern Egyptian literature. The most famous antecedent is a marterpiece of the *nahḍa*, *Ḥadīth ʿĪsā b. Hishām, aw Fatra min al-zaman* (1907; *What ʿĪsā Ibn Hisham Told Us*, 2015) by Muḥammad al-Muwayliḥī (§2.1), which is in turn indebted to the pre-modern narrative genre of the *maqāma* (§1.3.2).[62] The narrator ʿĪsā b. Hishām

62 *Ḥadīth* was published in instalments since 1898 in *Miṣbāḥ al-Sharq* (Light of the East), the magazine created by Muḥammad al-Muwayliḥī and his father Ibrāhīm (*ca.* 1844–1906), and later in a book form, a common practice in those times. It was adopted as a school text in secondary schools in Egypt in 1927, in its fourth edition which includes *al-Riḥla al-thāniyya*, *i.e.* the episodes reporting the visit of the *Exposition Universelle* in Paris in 1900.

accompanies the Pasha Aḥmad Bāshā al-Maniklī along the streets of Cairo. Appointed Minister of War in 1862, the Pasha comes back to life after some two decades in which relevant socio-political changes have occurred, not least the ʿUrābī revolt (§1.3.6). Therefore, he cannot recognize the city where he used to live: his encounter with this new, yet familiar, reality triggers some funny episodes and satirical commentaries on various aspects of society, based on a comparison of past and present.

While *Ḥadīth* is often dubbed as neo-*maqāma* or proto-novel, Allen balances the work's literary and historical merits by defining it as "a bridge work between the classical narrative prose genres and the emergence of a tradition of modern Arabic fiction", and an accurate source for reconstructing the social condition of Egypt at the turn of the century (Allen 1992: xii–xiv). Then Allen illustrates *Ḥadīth*'s intellectual references and literary models in the context of the *nahḍa* (Allen 1992: 15–31):

1. the classical *maqāma* and its re-elaboration over the *nahḍa*, for instance by Nāṣīf al-Yāzijī (1800–1871) in *Majmaʿ al-baḥrayn* (1856; The meeting-point of the two seas) and Aḥmad Fāris al-Shidyāq (1805–1887), who parodied the *maqāma* style in *al-Sāq ʿalā al-sāq fīmā huwa al-Fāryāq* (1855; *Leg over Leg*, 2013–2014);
2. travelogues activating social criticism through the description of a different society, such as *Takhlīṣ al-ibrīz fī talkhīṣ Bārīz* (1834; *An Imam in Paris*, 2002) by al-Ṭahṭāwī (1801–1873) and *ʿAlam al-dīn* (1882; The sign of religion) by ʿAlī Mubārak (§4.1.3);
3. fictionalized essays by Ṣanūʿ and al-Nadīm satirizing the political institutions and social attitudes;
4. sociological essays about education and progress in Egypt reflecting the contemporary intellectual debates;
5. the fictional device of resurrection, as in *Les ruines ou Méditations sur les révolutions des empires* (1791) by Constantin-François Volney (1757–1820) and *L'homme à l'oreille cassée* (1862) by Edmond About (1828–1885).

Moreover, Cooperson (2008) places *Ḥadīth* within the Arab and Western time-travel literature to examine some recurrent tropes of displacement, providing some useful insights to read also *Time-Travels*, which employs a similar narrative device almost eighty years later.[63] Cooperson examines these time-travel

63 In this essay, Cooperson reviews previous studies exploring the antecedents of *Ḥadīth*: Allen 1992; Bencheneb 1944; Pérès 1944. On Arabic time-travel literature, see: Bushnaq 2002: 490–494; Cooperson 1998. Bushnaq also mentions literary texts in which historians travel to the future.

stories: *L'An 2440* (1788) by Mercier (1740–1814), *El Anacronópete* (1887) by Gaspar (1842–1902), *The Chronic Argonauts* (1888) by Wells (1866–1946), *Les ruins* (1791) by Volney, *Takhlīṣ* by al-Ṭahṭāwī, *Lumen* (1865) by Flammarion (1842–1925), *A Connecticut Yankee in King Arthur's Court* (1889) by Twain (1835–1910), and *Jadis chez aujourd'hui* (1892) by the French illustrator Robida (1848–1926).

Before proper time-machines inserted into fiction by Gaspar and Wells, displacement was achieved through other strategies, such as the narrator's protracted sleep in Mercier and the spectre in Volney. *Les ruins* was translated into Arabic as *Āthār al-umam* by Shākir Shuqayr only one year after its publication; it is likely that al-Muwayliḥī read the original French or the Arabic translation. Among the ruins of Palmyra, a pensive narrator meets a spectre called the Genius. Prompted by the narrator's questions, the Genius expresses his meditations on history and, almost as a time-machine, leads the narrator to a congress of nations taking place in the future. As noted both by Allen (1992: 29–30) and Cooperson (2008: 422), al-Muwayliḥī exploits the opening resurrection scene and two characters discussing different aspects of life with a certain didactic and satirical intent. Moreover, Cooperson remarks that the Genius is disembodied and omniscient, while the Pasha is resurrected and unaware of the changes. The Pasha is not a mere expository device explaining history but wanders with the narrator, his double, through a multifaceted social world: his misadventures are the pretext for satirizing the institutions and society. When action gradually decreases in the second part of *Ḥadīth*, the Pasha almost becomes a voice commenting on social issues, while displacement is achieved through al-ʿUmda, who is the representative of the countryside in contrast with the city.

Cooperson examines the tropes of the double and displacement in another antecedent mentioned by Allen, *i.e.* al-Ṭahṭāwī's *Takhlīṣ*. Even though this is not a time-travel story, al-Ṭahṭāwī experiences a "*décalage*, that is, a gap between where (or when) he is and where (or when) he is supposed to be" (Cooperson 2008: 435). He is the representative of a civilization whose glory lies in the past and a trans-historical observer of the spectacle of history embodied by modern France. Beneath the main character are both the young al-Ṭahṭāwī who travelled to Paris and the experienced al-Ṭahṭāwī who wrote the travelogue.

Another common feature of these antecedents is the interplay between the displaced subject and history. For instance, Flammarion's *Lumen* is a dead scientist who repeatedly arrives on the Earth from a distant planet to visit different periods in the past with his disembodied soul. In one of his journeys, Lumen (the spectral self outside history) sees himself as a child (his double, the non-spectral self participating in history) and is discomforted by the wretched status of his childhood's days. Cooperson's considerations about the relation with history are valid both for *Ḥadīth* and *Time-Travels*:

> In other words, the specter is a metaphor for that sense of history whereby one has a sense not only of the present as history but also of oneself as present *in* history. In a proper time-travel novel, one can achieve this effect simply by moving the protagonist physically to another time. The multiplication of selves, and the realizations that follow from it, can thus be achieved without the use of specters and apparitions. Certainly, being pulled out of one's native time makes one more representative of one's native time than one can ever be while one is in it. (Cooperson 2008: 432)

Once the conventions of time-travelling literature were established by the end of the 19th century, some authors exploited its humorous potential in terms of structure, characters, and anachronism. Cooperson exemplifies this turn with Twain's *A Connecticut Yankee in King Arthur's Court* and Robida's sketch *Jadis chez Aujourd'hui*. The protagonist of *Jadis* transports Louis XIV and his court into the present with a time-machine. These rulers, who travel with their bodies and are a relic of their time, like al-Muwayliḥī's Pasha, explain everything in anachronistic terms with comic effects. The court of Versailles had already appeared in *L'An 2440* (1788) by Mercier, whose narrator travels to a better future society (uchronia) and visits the ruins of Versaille with an old Louis XIV denouncing the follies of his own time. Published nineteen years before the French revolution, this work was considered prophetic in its representation of historical change.

To sum up, Cooperson argues that al-Muwayliḥī's *Ḥadīth* combines some literary tropes in an unanticipated way: the spectre (resurrected with his body and soul), the double, ruins, temporal displacement to de-familiarize the present and show its absurdities, and one historical order used as the basis for criticizing another. This allows a two-folded criticism of past and present:

> At first glance, [the Bāshā] might be read as a metaphor for the Egypt of 1898: a bumbling relic bewildered by modernity. But the story already contains many Egyptians native to 1898, including the narrator. Therefore, the Bāshā must serve another (not necessarily exclusive) purpose. One might then guess that he represents Egypt's recent and relatively glorious past and that his misadventures in the 1890's are meant as a critique of that period, not his own.
>
> As it happens, both readings can be sustained. Unlike any of its French predecessors, the *Ḥadīth* places the past and the present in a relationship of dialogue that valorizes neither, at least not for long. (Cooperson 2008: 443)

Shalabī's *Time-Travels* is not the direct descendent of *Ḥadīth* since it incorporates multiple literary conventions enumerated by Bushnaq (2002: 494) in her study of the historical novel: the picaresque story, travelogue, utopia, mirror for princes, fantasy, and science-fiction.[64] However, *Ḥadīth* remarks the existence of time-travel stories in Arabic literature to keep in mind in the analysis. The

64 On Arabic science-fiction, see: Barbaro 2013; Campbell 2018.

link between *Time-Travels* and *Ḥadīth* is also suggested by an anthology of Cairo's literary representations in modern Egyptian fiction edited by Mehrez. In the anthology's "Prelude", *Ḥadīth*, *Time-Travels*, and Najīb Maḥfūẓ's *Awlād ḥāratinā* (1959, *Children of the Alley*) guide the reader across the gates of Cairo. Mehrez (2010b: 13–15) argues that these novels fictionalize a similar relation between the writers and urban space: all narrators are rogue-like characters who introduce themselves as writers but are not recognized as such; they map the city's transformations from their marginal status, thus becoming underground historians and geographers. These features (mobility, representation of urban society, and rogue-like characters) can be traced back to the *maqāma*, a pre-modern narrative re-elaborated by modern Arabic literature including *Ḥadīth*.

4.1.2 *Maqāmāt* across time

As illustrated in the overview of the Arab humorous tradition (§1.3.2), the *maqāmāt* are pre-modern narratives comprising several episodes, each set in a different city of the Islamic world, featuring the same narrator and protagonist. This section focuses on the notion of mobility in this genre and illustrates its impact on early modern and modern writings.

The classical *maqāmāt* are set in different cities without following any route or chronological order. The urban reality is always changing, yet still familiar. Neuwirth (2009: 241) suggests that the *maqāma* exploits the trope of mobility on many levels: geographically, the protagonists are constantly travelling, not in search of established knowledge (*riḥla fī ṭalab al-ʿilm*), rather in search of the extraordinary and the miraculous (*riḥla fī ṭalab al-istiṭrāf*); artistically, the text transcends the borders between different genres; conceptually, the anecdotes express unconventional ideas, sometimes breaking the social norms and giving an innovative representation of gender relations.

To examine some of these transgressions, Neuwirth (2009: 250) refers to Bakhtin's carnivalesque laughter which underlies the aesthetics of the grotesque. Despite its heterogeneous manifestations, the imagery of the carnivalesque laughter is grounded in what Bakhtin calls grotesque realism: "The essential principle of grotesque realism is degradation, that is, the lowering of all that is high, spiritual, ideal, abstract; it is a transfer to the material level, to the sphere of earth and body in their indissoluble unity" (Bakhtin 1984: 19–20). Bringing everything down to earth, the grotesque style employs exaggeration, hyperbolism, excessiveness; insisting on the materiality of the body, there is an emphasis on the apertures and convexities to indicate its unfinished transformation, while food, drinks, and bodily fluids flow in great quantity. Far from being a destructive force, this degradation has a universal and creative nature because it links life and death, the old and the new, in an eternal transformation (Bakhtin 1984: 18–34, 303–367).

Literary critics claim the *maqāma*'s influence on many literary genres which developed over the *nahḍa*, such as drama, novels, short stories, and even newspaper articles. While some intellectuals aimed at preserving these stories' eloquent style,[65] other authors developed their dramatic and parodic features. Al-Muwayliḥī, for instance, drew on this prestigious tradition for his modern concerns. *Ḥadīth* reproduces some formal elements of al-Hamadhānī's *maqāmāt*: the narrator's name; the opening formula *ʿĪsā ibn Hishām ḥaddathanā* (ʿĪsā ibn Hishām told us); rhymed prose only at the beginning of each chapter; sophisticated vocabulary, leading to the inclusion of a glossary after the text; a participating narrator who enjoys little narrative distance from the implied author. It recalls the *maqāma* also for its episodic structure: while this fragmentation is due mainly to the serial publication, Allen (1992: 41) argues that this feature was not totally eradicated from the thoroughly revised book form in order to preserve the work's factual nature.

Furthermore, *Ḥadīth* develops the trope of mobility and the picaresque character. The two protagonists, in fact, walk in various neighbourhoods in Cairo and visit Alexandria, even though they do not delve in the urban underworld nor portray the lower strata. In this respect, Ouyang (2013: 86–97) notes that these characters move from one public space to another on a journey of negotiations of power and identity in the first decades of the British occupation of Egypt: the narrator is an apparent insider but has a marginal position in the network of power relations, whereas the Pasha loses his privileges, and the ʿUmda seeks social recognition among the elite. Ouyang concludes that:

> *Ḥadīth ʿĪsā ibn Hishām* can thus unproblematically inherit the *Maqāmāt*'s freedom of mobility. The geographical, historical and intellectual wanderings of the narrator and protagonist are an expression of relative marginalisation not complete powerlessness. Where powerlessness is complete, freedom of mobility is lost too.[66] (Ouyang 2013: 97)

65 Hämeen-Anttila (2002: 351–357) rejects the idea that modern intellectuals resurrected a forgotten genre, since copies of the manuscripts continued to circulate and *maqāmāt* were also written in the previous centuries. In the 19th century, al-Yāzijī was the most prominent author of this genre, but other authors composed *maqāmāt* in the earlier part of the century: al-Rāfiʿī, al-Barbīr, al-Tirmānīnī, and Ḥasan al-ʿAṭṭār who was al-Ṭahṭāwī's mentor.

66 The last sentence of this quotation introduces the analysis of Ḥabībī's *al-Waqāʾiʿ al-gharība* (*The Pessoptimist*, §3.1.3 and 3.2.1), whose protagonist is often described as a *maqāma*-like picaresque figure. Ouyang notes that he does not enjoy mobility since he is imprisoned in his own country.

Al-Muwayliḥī's and other contributions to this genre inspired some Arab authors to write what have been called neo-*maqāmāt* till the mid-20th century: Ḥāfiẓ Ibrāhīm (1871–1932), Bayram al-Tūnisī, Najīb Ḥankash (d. 1977; *al-Maqāmāt al-ḥankashiyya*, 1964), and ʿAbbās al-Aswānī (1925–1977; *al-Maqāmāt al-aswāniyya*, 1970). In the development of the Egyptian novel at the crossroads between the Western influence and Arab literary heritage, the *maqāma* was revived for its prestige as the only recognized native novel-like genre. With the canonization of the social-realist novel, the neo-*maqāma* often lost its fictional dimension to concentrate on socio-political satire, as Jacquemond (2008: 155) notes.

Jacquemond (2013: 152–157) suggests that *Ḥadīth* contained the ingredients for the development of both the social-realist novel and satirical writing. The continuity of this literary model is confirmed by the trends of bestselling books in contemporary Egypt, which often belong to the two afore-mentioned genres. Contemporary satirical literature draws from *Ḥadīth* the picaresque element and all-encompassing social criticism. For instance, the afore-mentioned *Taksī* by Khālid al-Khamīsī (2006, §2.1) is a fictional sociological reportage collecting a series of conversations between the first-person narrator – and writer's *alter ego* – and Cairo's taxi drivers. The novel's subtitle was supposed to be *maqāma ḥadītha* (modern *maqāma*) but was reformulated as *Ḥawādīt al-mashāwīr* (oral stories collected going around), anticipating the book's content and use of Egyptian Colloquial Arabic (Jacquemond 2013: 154).

To sum up, *Time-Travels* does not incorporate all the elements of *maqāmāt* or neo-*maqāmāt* but fits into an Egyptian literary tradition which has developed the comic potential of episodic narratives featuring picaresque characters who introduce some physical transgressions in the urban landscape and some linguistic transgressions. One of these linguistic transgressions in *Time-Travels* is the choice of pre-modern historical sources as hypotext to re-write Egyptian history.

4.1.3 Historiography

The urban dimension and a refined style also characterize the novel's choice of pre-modern historical sources, all focusing on Egypt. On a thematic level, these sources shape the novel's setting providing information about the ruling dynasties and the mark they left on the urban landscape. On a formal level, their manipulation blurs the boundaries between fact and fiction causing some incongruities that contribute to crafting a humorous historical novel. Since *Time-Travels* is set mostly in the Mamluk period, the main references are prominent historians of that time, such as Ibn Khallikān (d. 1282), Ibn ʿAbd al-Ẓāhir (d. 1293), al-Maqrīzī (d.

1442), and Ibn Taghrībirdī (d. 1469/70). Besides them, the novel mentions Ibn al-Ṭuwayr from the late Fatimid period, al-Jabartī from the Ottoman period, and Stanley Lane-Poole from the era of the British protectorate.[67] When Ibn Shalabī meets them as fictional characters, he provides only a few biographical details about the real-existing historians; in some passages he quotes from the sources, especially al-Maqrīzī and Ibn Taghrībirdī, without giving full bibliographic references. What matters is making these historians recognizable for the Egyptian readers, who may at least have heard of them at school, and using their writings as time-machines both for their content and style. Their profiles are outlined here to understand which historiographical genres are revived in *Time-Travels*.

Historical writing flourished under the Mamluks (Irwin 2006; *Mamluk Bibliography Online* website; *Mamluk Studies Resources* website). Born in Iraq and trained as a jurist, Ibn Khallikān employed the obituary pattern in his *Wafayāt al-aʿyān wa-anbāʾ abnāʾ al-zamān* (1968–1972, Obituaries of celebrities and news about the author's contemporaries), an alphabetically arranged bibliographical dictionary of notable people (Wedel *EI3*). Ibn ʿAbd al-Ẓāhir, instead, was the head of the chancery (*kātib al-sirr*) and a court historian who compiled the histories of Baybars (1260–1277), Qalāwūn, and Ashraf (1341–1342). His *al-Rawḍa al-bahiyya al-ẓāhira fī khiṭaṭ al-muʿizziyya al-Qāhira* (The magnificent garden in the topography of al-Muʿizz's Cairo) was a topography taken as a reference by the later historians al-Maqrīzī and Ibn Taghrībirdī, especially for the time of the Fatimids (Bauden *EI3*; Irwin 2006: 162–163).

Al-Maqrīzī started his career in the state chancery and later occupied administrative and religious posts. He lost court patronage and by contrast developed an interest in the Fatimids (Bauden 2010; Craig et al. 2003; Perho 2001; Rosenthal *EI2*). He was among the disciples of Ibn Khaldūn (d. 1406), born in Tunisia and settled in Egypt, who enquired socio-economic issues and the cyclical rise and fall of dynasties (Broadbridge 2003). His contemporaries, including Ibn Taghrībirdī, accused him of not stating his sources clearly, if not of plagiarism. Modern scholarship, instead, gives al-Maqrīzī the merit of saving some of

67 A high-ranking Fatimid and ayyubid official, Ibn al-Ṭuwayr (d. 1220) compiled *Nuzhat al-muqlatayn fī akhbār al-dawlatayn* (History of the two dynasties) during the reign of Salāḥ al-Dīn; although this work went lost, it influenced to the work of later historians (Bora *EI3*). Al-Jabartī (d. 1825/6) is the most prominent historian of Ottoman Egypt, known for his chronicle *ʿAjāʾib al-āthār fī l-tarājim wa-l-akhbār* (The marvelous chronicles: biographies and events); his largely traditional approach was influenced by the French expedition to Egypt in 1798 (Ayalon *EI2*; Winter 2006). A British orientalist and archaeologist, Stanley Lane-Poole (1854–1931) completed the *Arabic-English Lexicon* by his uncle E.W. Lane (1801–1876) and wrote books about Salāḥ al-Dīn and the history of Egypt (Lane-Poole 1898, 1901, 1906).

his contemporary sources from oblivion. His history of Egypt since the Muslim conquest included three works, the latter being *al-Sulūk li-maʿrifat duwal al-mulūk* (1934–1973, The path to knowledge of dynasties and kings), a history of the Ayyubids and Mamluks updated until 1441. Besides *al-Sulūk*, al-Maqrīzī is renowned for his topography of Cairo, *al-Mawāʿiẓ wa-l-iʿtibār fī dhikr al-khiṭaṭ wa-l-āthār* (2002–2004, Admonitions and reflections on the quarters and monuments), whose contents are arranged according to the types of buildings

Almost contemporary of al-Maqrīzī, Ibn Taghrībirdī succeeded al-ʿAyni (d. 1451) as court historian. Many contemporaries accused him of partiality to the Mamluks, but he criticized the dynasty's corruption and factionalism (Popper *EI2*). Irwin (2006: 168) argues that, like other historians of the 15th century, he was critical of his own time and looked back at the early Mamluk period with nostalgia. Despite his criticism of al-Maqrīzī, Ibn Taghrībirdī is known for two chronicles which are a continuation of *al-Sulūk*: *al-Nujūm al-ẓāhira fī mulūk Miṣr wa-l-Qāhirah* (1929–1972, The flowing stars, on the kings of Egypt and Cairo) and *Ḥawādith al-duhūr fī maḍā al-ayyām wa-l-shuhūr* (Episodes of the epochs which pass in the days and months).

As regards the historiographical genres, the court chronicle provides information about the political events, while the topography (*al-khiṭaṭ*) reconstructs urban social history. The term *khiṭaṭ* originally refers to the plotted quarters of the newly founded early Islamic towns laid out (root *kh-ṭ-ṭ*) by the Arab-Islamic chiefs. Thus, this historiographical genre developed out of the administrative concern of keeping records of the newly established towns of the expanding empire. Developed especially in Egypt by the late 10th century, it combined the topography of a specific place with the urban sociology recording the evolution of the customs. Due to its administrative concerns, the *khiṭaṭ* needed to be rewritten under new dynasties, often conveying a sense of nostalgia. For instance, al-Maqrīzī focused on the lost palaces of the Fatimids (Rabbat *EI3*)

Some centuries later, ʿAlī Mubārak revived this genre in *al-Khiṭaṭ al-tawfīqiyya al-jadīda* (1888, The new topography of the reign of Tawfiq) to map Cairo under khedive Tawfīq (1879–1892) who made radical urban transformations on the model of modern European cities. A contemporary re-elaboration of this genre is *Khiṭaṭ al-Ghīṭānī* (1981, al-Ghīṭānī's topography) by Jamāl al-Ghīṭānī, in which Cairo is unidentified but recognizable though some symbolic sites. As Mehrez notes, like in the traditional *khiṭaṭ*, the city's architecture embodies its economic, political, and social relations. Unlike its antecedents, this novel blurs the boundaries between fact and fiction writing an alternative history: it focuses on the city's collapse rather than its expansion, and criticizes the oppressive alliance between the police and the media (Mehrez 1994: 58–77; Starkey 2001). As illustrated in ch.2 (§2.2), al-Ghīṭānī uses the past as a mirror of the present also in other novels, to express criticism while avoiding censorship. Overall, this intertextuality with historical sources is complex and experimental. In *Time-Travels*, instead, the fictional topography illustrates the continuity of the past in the present, insisting on the homology between space and its residents. On a formal level, it provides the spatial organization connecting the multiple episodes of *Time-Travels*. It portrays urban decline, as in *Khiṭaṭ al-Ghīṭānī*, but also expresses some nostalgia for a glorious past.

To sum up, this section has overviewed the main literary references that lie beneath Shalabī's humorous historical novel, illustrating their multi-layered influence across time and their Egyptianization for the author's purposes. The early modern travelogue portrays socio-cultural change with a satirical vein; in the masterpiece *Ḥadīth* by al-Muwayliḥī this satirical portrait is achieved through anachronism and the trope of the double. The travelogue and other modern narratives are influenced by the episodic structure of the *maqāmāt*. In their classical and modern form, they elicit humour through the mobility and eloquence of a picaresque character in the urban underworld. While these two genres belong to the comic tradition, Mamluk historiography (especially the court chronicle and topography) is inserted in *Time-Travels* both to provide accurate information and to be parodied. These literary antecedents work as a time-machine that transports the protagonist across different eras enriching his features as a comic type, as will be outlined in the next section.

4.2 The trickster

4.2.1 Ibn Shalabī and his doubles

The first element recalling the above-mentioned literary models is the frame narrative, especially in the first part of *Time-Travels* (ch.1–7), which includes several temporal jumps from the present into the Fatimid and Ayyubid eras without following a clear chronological order. The second part (ch.8–24) also includes time-travelling but is more linear and focuses only on some years of the Bahri Mamluk dynasty. Marking the beginning and the end of each journey, the narrator tells the odd incidents causing his displacement, such as running out of a café without paying the check, climbing up the steps to a pedestrian overpass, contemplating a monument, and hitting his head. These incidents elicit humour for their apparent irrelevance (an irrelevant cause leading to a disproportionate effect), their ability to point at the fantastic in everyday life, and their focus on the body. Through the mechanism of repetition/variation, this episodic structure makes the reader familiar with the literary device of time-travelling and eager to know what happens in the next adventure. This episodic narrative structure challenges the conventions of the modern progressive novel, reviving the *maqāma* and neo-*maqāma*, as illustrated above, as well as popular storytelling inserted in Egyptian experimental novels since the 1970s. While there is little plot progression, the episodes are kept together by the protagonist who is characterized by some clearly defined features throughout the novel and recalls some proverbial humorous characters.

"Ibn Shalaby, a Hanafi, an Egyptian, a seller of pickles and sweets, and a writer." (55/66)[68] With this presentation, the main character and narrator reveals his duplicity: on the one hand, he is a journalist, a writer who instructs his public, and a social observer; on the other hand, he is the representative of the ordinary Egyptians and a naïve participant, whose weapon of last resort is entertainment. The name by which he is known (*shuhra*) combines the patronymic (*nasab*), by which pre-modern writers were usually identified, with the real writer's surname. Since his name is extended to the rest of the population, collectively called Sons of Shalaby (*banū Shalabī*), it encourages identification with the ordinary Egyptians. Through this identification, his name becomes almost a synonym for the stereotypical Egyptian who is labelled in the urban context as *ibn al-balad* (§2.4). As a genuine representative of the flaws and virtues of the ordinary Egyptians, Ibn Shalabī praises their generosity and resilience, while mildly criticizing their opportunism and inclination to side with the strong against the weak. He is witty, but sometimes plays the fool or is labelled as a fool. For example, a woman in the Storehouse tells him:

> "You are *such* an Egyptian," she said, smiling. "You're a big idiot." ["Miṣrī anta ḥattā l-nukhā' ayy annaka 'abīṭ kabīr"]
>
> "And a Son of Shalaby, too!"
>
> "You are so stupid," she said, "that you help your enemies and treat them with respect because you consider them guests in your country. You've played host to your enemies for a long, long time, Ibn Shalaby." (89/ 99)

Moreover, Ibn Shalabī seeks identification with the ordinary people through his humble profession (a seller of pickles and sweets), which epitomizes the combination of sweet and sour moments in everyday life: "Having been a pickle-seller for a long time, I've come around to selling sweets: that is, I drank enough brine to cure myself of being a sourpuss, and now I'm a total sweetie. Rather than believe anyone or anything, I put absolute trust in reality." (170/186)

68 He claims his double nature also in the novel's prologue, which echoes the style of pre-modern literature: "By the Pen of God's Neediest Creature / The Knowing but Unlearned / The Tutored but Unwise / Ibn Shalaby, the Hanafi and Egyptian / The Seller of Pickles and Sweets / May God Guard Us from His Ignorance, Amen!"

However, he does not belong to the underworld, even though he is sympathetic with the urban poor, vagrants, and petty criminals. Neither does he belong to the crowd and fears its rebellion, even though he is attracted by its culture of laughter. He is a trickster, rather than a *ḥarfūsh* or one of the rabble.[69]

On the opposite pole, Ibn Shalabī boasts about his superiority as a writer who has a better understanding of the society. As the writer's *alter ego*, he meets Khayrī Shalabī's colleagues and friends, depicting the intellectual community with a certain degree of self-mockery. For instance, his Samsonite briefcase ridicules consumerism and westernization when it loses its practical function to become a magical device to set out of troubles, as in this passage:

> I heaved my Samsonite briefcase into his range of vision. That briefcase, as far as I'm concerned, is worth its weight in gold. If I wave it at taxi drivers, they always stop. If I snap it open and shut, salesman and petty brokers treat me with respect. But the Persian guardsman, far from deferring to my briefcase, regarded it with contemptuous disdain. Surprised that American industry had lost its magic touch, I made a mental note to report the incident to the Arab oppositional paper so they could use it as an example of the disappointing performance of foreign imports. (42/53)

In another passage, Ibn Shalabī talks to the Fatimid historian Ibn al-Ṭuwayr, who rewards him with a job in the chancery for his eloquent display about swindling the gullible writers:

> "I work as an editor at a newspaper," I said. "I own a famous pickling plant and a confectionery, too. And I'm thinking of opening a broad-based literary agency."
>
> "What's a 'literary agency'?"
>
> "I'd bring in writers, editors, and artists from around the world and sponsor them to work in different countries, all in return for a hefty commission from both parties. I'd also collect essays, short stories, and investigative pieces written by people who don't like to travel. I'd sell them to more than one paper, and use the proceeds to expand the pickling plant and the confectionery. If the authors insist on being paid, I would claim that the piece never sold and give them ten pounds to keep them from bothering me. No one would ever find out because I would only sell to newspapers, magazines, and journals that aren't distributed here."
>
> "I don't know what you mean by 'magazines' and 'newspapers,'" he said, "but I think you're qualified to work in the chancery." (48/59)

69 *Al-ḥarfūsh* is a vagabond, but also a ruffian or rascal. This word appeared in Mamluk chronicles to indicate the lowest strata of society, forming groups of professional beggars, entertainers, and looters in the urban centres. They belonged to a guild-like organization and allied themselves with various elements in the government. See: Guo *EI3* and Glossary in *Time-Travels*, 'harfush', 256. In modern fiction, this term can combine the negative connotation with a positive one. See: Cobham 2006.

This passage exemplifies the protagonist's picaresque nature. Like other tricksters and the *maqāma*'s protagonist, in each episode Ibn Shalabī disguises himself or is mistaken for somebody else.[70] Sometimes taking on a false identity serves to get out of trouble: for example, the protagonist enters the Fatimid palace without authorization during the Ayyubid pillage, yet he can move around freely claiming that he is a member of the inventory committee. Due to the repetitive structure, the reader is curious to know which identity he will take on and which ruse he will employ to fool his antagonists or simply to survive. According to the situation, Ibn Shalabī plays clever tricks or plays the fool; acting like a wise fool is a survival strategy attributed to the ordinary Egyptians. For example, in this passage he pretends to be unable to write although he is a writer:

> "All you interrogators are the same," I answered "You put us in a delicate situation and then you trap us. What do you want from Ibn Shalaby?"
>
> "Write down exactly what you just said and hand it to me."
>
> "Write?" I shrieked in alarm. "You've got to be kidding. So forced confession dates back to you guys? Anyway, I don't know how to write." (58/69)

Furthermore, the protagonist revives the stock character of the court jester (*muharrij al-malik*) or clown (*bahlawān*), when he entertains (*tasliyya, musāmara*) to the merry and jolly Sultan Aḥmad (*al-sulṭān al-mariḥ*). For the Sultan and the court, fun means laughing and teasing (*mudāʿaba*) the performer. Ibn Shalabī fills this traditional figure with the popular entertainment of his time, performing like contemporary comedy actors and singers. His repertoire includes the imitation of waiters serving the coffee in popular cafés, funny gaits, obscene gestures, bizarre antics, and lunacy (*junūn*). He tells jokes circulating among students or crafted by professional comedians, such as Sulṭān al-Jazzār, Ḥusayn al-Fār, and Ḥamāda Sulṭān, but these jokes fall flat (179/195). This is because the members of the court appreciate the novelty of his show, but do not get the contemporary cultural references. Yet, these references are shared by the implied reader, increasing his/her appreciation of humour. Another example illustrating the juxtaposition of different timeframes and sources to elicit humour is found in this passage:

---

70 Ibn Shalabī is a slave preparing a banquet for the Caliph, an official in charge of the Storehouse window, a secret agent, a *mamlūk*, a court jester, the Sultan's counsellor and confident, and the viceroy's press sectary. He is mistaken for a Crusader, a Turk, a Daylami, a servant, a spirit, devil, genie, the agent of Baldwin the Frank, a sorcerer, an impostor (when the cassette recorder does not work), and a tourist.

> I found myself saying to the Sultan, "Listen, chief! You want to know my advice? Two wrongs don't make a right, so kill 'em with kindness!"
>
> The Sultan laughed so hard he fell backward in his seat. [fa-ḍaḥaka al-sulṭān ḥattā istalqā ʿalā qafāhu] "You sit down with sultans and the best you can do is cite the wisdom of the rabble in the street? That's all well and good if you're hungry and weak, but you're sitting with the fat cats now!" (183/199)

When the Sultan asks Ibn Shalabī for advice, he resorts to popular wisdom and answers with a proverb. This reply, which is incongruous with the court etiquette, makes the Sultan bursts laughing. The formula used to describe his laughter, found in pre-modern anecdotes and the *Arabian Nights* (Müller 1993), exemplifies a technique in pre-modern writing which consists in expressing emotions in a physical way; despite this refined intertextual reference, the Sultan himself responds with a vivid conversational language.

While being rooted in contemporary Cairo, Ibn Shalabī travels back in time thanks to his appropriation of stock characters and literary conventions. The next sections provides more details about time-travelling, illustrating the way he embodies history and his interplay with the historical sources.

4.2.2 Out of time

Time-Travels contains twenty-four chapters, which Bushnaq (2002: 527) relates to the twenty-four hours of the day. To indicate the temporal setting of each episode, the protagonist reads the date on his wristwatch according to the Islamic calendar. Some of these dates, especially round numbers, are significant: Ibn Shalabī comes from the 14th century and once he mentions the year 1400 AH (1979 AD); at the end of the novel, his watch stops on "Friday, the fifth of Safar, AH 1500: 1 January, AD 2077" (247/267). In this closing passage, the protagonist gets on a bus, which may be seen as a kind of time-machine. A crowded bus, the typical Cairene means of public transport, is a good image for the experience of urban (post-)modernity, as the train and tramway represented the trajectory of the self in the modern nation-state in the early Egyptian novels (Casini, Paniconi & Sorbera 2012: 23).[71]

71 In another passage, Ibn Shalabī realizes he is in the wrong time and tells al-Maqrīzī that he will take the direct bus to reach the correct time destination (14/22). The image of the crowded bus or mini-bus in is found two Egyptian novels that rely on dark humour: *al-Lajna* (Ibrāhīm 1981) and *An takūn^{a} ʿAbbās al-ʿAbd* (al-ʿĀydī 2003). Other means of transportation give the title to two recent Egyptian popular books with a satirical touch: the afore-mentioned *Tāksī* and the graphic novel *Mītrū* by Majdī al-Shāfiʿī (2008; *Metro: A Story of Cairo*, 2012).

As regards the mechanism of displacement, Ibn Shalabī travels with his body and soul, like the Pasha in *Ḥadīth*. Since he partly ignores the customs of the past and applies his modern way of thinking and speaking, anachronism has a comic effect. Yet, he does not find the past society totally unfamiliar, because he travels in Cairo usually in the holy month of Ramaḍān, learns from his previous journeys, and carries his historical knowledge with him. In fact, the first-person narrator adopts the attitude of the participant observer: he is both a naïve eyewitness, who experiences the past with curiosity and needs explanations to understand it, and a knowledgeable observer, who compares the two eras thanks to his command of history. He is able to laugh at this double positioning: "The Son of Shalaby who had asked the question said that the Son of Shalaby who had answered it was harebrained and shortsighted. But the Son of Shalaby who was both of them – that is, me – laughed at them both." (127/140)

His historical knowledge turns him into an acute social observer. Both past and present are subject to criticism, but *Time-Travels* points at continuity rather than change: the narrator provides a simplified, but never idealized, reconstruction of the past in search of the causes of the contemporary social attitudes. Like Flammarion's *Lumen*, Ibn Shalabī makes multiple journeys and sees himself as present *in* history. Pulled out of his native time and surrounded by several doubles, he becomes the best representative of his own society. Cooperson notes that travelogues originally served the purpose of reporting back from other lands, while early modern time-travel literature, including *Ḥadīth*, narrated the experience of modernity and expressed the need for social reform. In this respect, it is worth remarking that Ibn Shalabī lives in a post-modern society, where there is little room for change. Bitterly disillusioned, he says: "In short, I had assumed the role of the observer, though without seeing anything" (204/221).

The protagonist's displacement allows him to meet the rulers in their own time and observe them from his modern perspective. As seen above (§4.1.1), Cooperson (2008: 439) examines the rulers' displacement in some time-travel stories: usually moving from the past to the present, they are ridiculed for their excesses and sometimes raise a feeling of nostalgia. In *Time-Travels*, Ibn Shalabī adds some ridiculous details to the historiographical portrait of the rulers, heightening their stereotypical traits. Turning these historical figures into laughable characters plays with the conventions of historical writing and refers to a shared encyclopaedic knowledge, since depicting power relations is a way of portraying society at large.

Besides the protagonist, pre-modern chroniclers and contemporary intellectuals can travel. These displacements and the encounter of people of different eras are presented as ordinary issues. When the narrator introduces the characters based on the historians for the first time, he provides their full names and a feature characterizing them to make them recognizable, as in these examples:

> 1) We passed an old man with a long beard. He was carrying a reed pen, a calamus, an inkpot, and a sheaf of papers. [. . .] I recognized him: it was Maqrizi, the author of the still-famous Topography. Wanting to show my companion that I knew people in high places, I called out without breaking my stride, "Hey, Maqrizi! How are ya?" (3/9)

> 2) At the same moment there emerged a laughing head, one I recognized as belonging to my friend Ibn Abdel Zahir. "Hey there, big guy!" he said. "Think you can get away from me so easily?"
>
> "Unbelievable!" I said. "Is that really you?"
>
> "The judge, scholar, and secretary Muhyi al-Din Abd Allah ibn Abdel Zahir Rawhi at your service."
>
> [. . .] I pulled him back a little, but then, quickly as a *ghost*, he vanished.
>
> (22/31; emphasis added)

> 3) In the middle of all this I saw a tall, cruel-featured man who was doing his best to pretend he hadn't seen me. So I went up to him and extended my hand in a friendly greeting. "How are you, old fellow?"
>
> "Hello," he responded courtly.
>
> Somewhat at a loss, I asked, "You are Murtada Abu Muhammad Abdel Salam, right?"
>
> "Yes," he said, as coldly as before.
>
> "Son of Muhammad, son of Abdel Salam, son of Tuwayr?"
>
> He nodded.
>
> "Of Cairo and Caesarea, scribe in Egypt?"
>
> "Yes," he said, exasperated.
>
> "Do you remember the day you got me in trouble by sending me in to see the Ornament of the Treasurers?"
>
> He smiled. "But you handled yourself, didn't you?"
>
> How can you show up in my day and age and walk around the streets *as if you were still alive*?"
>
> "The same way you show up in our times," he said. (47/58–59; emphasis added)

In these presentations there are two canonical images of time-travelling, *i.e* the ghost (2) and the living creature travelling with his body and soul (3). Pre-modern historians become familiar because they experience the same mechanisms of displacement, such as anachronism generating funny effects and question-and-answer between a guide and a learner to contrast the two societies. They give Ibn Shalabī some historical explanations mainly through the dialogues, but they also play tricks on him embodying a playful idea of history. These characters are brought close to the contemporary reality, therefore they are juxtaposed to some contemporary intellectuals who can also travel through time:

> Meanwhile, a crowd of distinguished-looking people were pouring into the forecourt and lining up to sign what must have been the guestbook. I recognized the historian Ibn

> Taghribirdi, the biographer Ibn Khallikan, the chronicler Ibn Abdel Hakam, Maqrizi, the historian Abdel Rahman Zaki, the Fatimid scholar Hasan Ibrahim Hasan, the architect Hassan Fathy, the novelist Naguib Mahfouz, the critic Husayn Fawzi, the architectural historian Souad Mahir, and many other friends and acquaintances [. . .].[72] (7/15)

In another passage, there is a one list of incongruous elements comprising the real names of historians and invented names, based on assonance and word-play with the *shuhra*: "There I spotted all my important friends: Ibn Abdel Hakam, Ibn Abdel Barr, Ibn Abdel Zahir, Ibn Taghribirdi, Ibn Iyas, Ibn So-and-So, Ibn Whoever, and Ibn What's-His-Face" (76/86).[73] These encounters give the pre-modern chroniclers a certain vitality, while the juxtaposition of high and popular culture brings them closer to the audience.

Intertextuality with historiography is achieved in two ways, by turning the pre-modern chroniclers into fictional characters and by quoting the sources out of their context, in the dialogues and sequences summarizing the events, sometimes interrupting them. Ibn Shalabī's familiarity with these characters and his wanderings around the city make him experiences history from the inside, suggesting the importance of rediscovering the past to understand the present. He conceives history as cumulative (the image of many layers one on the top of the other) and repetitive (especially as regards power relations). On a metanarrative level, the narrator reflects on the challenge of writing historical novels, first admitting the difficulty of this subject, and then mocking the previous attempts in this sub-genre:

> Lighting a cigarette, I lapsed into a meditation on the authors and novelists I had read, both Western and Eastern. I was trying to capture a thought that kept flitting away, to the effect that the history of Egypt poses a real challenge to the talents of her citizens. One of those citizens, admittedly, was the artist hardly bigger than his own chisel who carved out the statue of Ramses, not to mention tens of thousands of other colossal images. But would the country ever produce a novelist whose imagination could grapple with a history that overwhelmed all powers of perspective, creativity, and organization? It's a good thing that the novelists who've already made a name for themselves have never read any

---

72 In the original Arabic the historians are mentioned only by their proper names and the contemporary intellectuals bear the title *al-duktūr*, while the English translation adds their fields of expertise. Among the contemporary intellectuals and popular icons of the 1970s that Ibn Shalabī meets or evokes in his journeys, there are singers (Umm Kulthūm, Muḥammad ʿAbd al-Wahāb, Muḥammad Qandīl), journalists (Ibrāhīm Manṣūr, Muḥammad Barakāt), TV icons and religious preachers (*al-shaykh* al-Shaʿrāwī), novelists and literary critics (Maḥfūẓ disguised as a tomato vendor, al-Sharqāwī, ʿAbd al-Fattāḥ al-Bārūdī).

73 In the original Arabic their names are: *Ibn al-farṭūs* which is an insult deriving from the word meaning 'sow'; *Ibn al-markūb*, an mild insult for a scoundrel; and *Ibn al-maḍrūb* which means 'you son of an old boot'.

> Egyptian history. If they did, they would be mortified by their amateurish attempts to depict it. (56–57/68)

This passage goes back till the Pharaohs and their monuments, an established trope in Egyptian fiction. The Pyramids are the antecedents of Medieval monuments since they immortalize the achievements of the ruling elite. The narrator reflects on the need of immortalizing history through the word of two rulers, Khazʿal and Sultan Aḥmad respectively, who express their cynical considerations employing the Pyramids as symbols:

> "We don't need a history lesson," said Khazaal. [. . .] Once, he explained, the Egyptians had been divided into pyramid builders on the one hand and serfs on the other. To hide the light of knowledge and civilization from the serfs, the builders preserved it in a language that only they knew [. . .] When the builders died, they were buried in magnificent tombs. For their part, the serfs were buried under monumental ignorance; and from the caverns of ignorance their children have come marching in long lines, like rats, and spread throughout the Fertile Crescent. Civilization, he went on, has vanished, along with everything else except the genius of the land itself. Given the ignorance of the serfs, the genius of the land requires that someone come and rule it. (108/119)

> Do you know why I agreed to take you on a Sultan's Mamluk? In a word, so I could watch you – to see for myself that there really are people out there so backward that they still concern themselves with philosophies and values and glorious achievements and matters of historic importance and all kinds of meaningless delusions! Look behind you at the Pyramids. They're like corpses practically screaming at you to live your life as you want to live it, and with passion. (183–184/200)

The latter passage reminds us of the total disbelief in official history expressed with sarcasm in *An takūn*[a] *ʿAbbās al-ʿAbd* by al-ʿĀydī (§2.1):

> 'You want us to progress??
> So burn the history books and forget your precious civilization.
> Stop trying to squeeze the juice from the past.
> Destroy your pharaonic history. [. . .]
> We will only succeed when we turn our museums into public lavatories.'
> (Alaidy 2009: 34)

Despite these considerations, the narrator provides his historical account focusing on Cairo's monuments, which are the emblem of power over subsequent dynasties and are also appropriated by collective memory. The next section looks at spatial representation, keeping in mind the centrality of topography among the historical sources and urban mobility as a key feature of the *maqāma* and *Ḥadīth*.

4.2.3 Out of place

Among his multiple identities, Ibn Shalabī describes himself as *ḥawārjī* (147/161, pavement-pounder), a neologism coined by adding the suffix denoting a profession *-jī* to *ḥawārī*, an occasional plural of *ḥāra* (alley). This word expresses the protagonist's passion for wandering in the alleys of Old Cairo. His favourite neighbourhood is *ḥayyī al-Ṣalība* and his literary guides are the realist writers Maḥfūẓ and Yaḥyā Ḥaqqī (1905–1992).

While walking in the streets, Ibn Shalabī reconstructs the history of the districts and monuments. The novel opens with the foundation of Cairo by the Fatimids, when planet Mars, the Conqueror (*al-qāhir*), was rising; this astrological coincidence gave the name to the city (*al-Qāhira*).[74] The narrator does not recount the foundation myth in full as reported by the sources, but tells the unfolding events he witnesses, disrupting the sacrality of the myth and highlighting the comic sides of this story.

When the protagonist stands in front of a monument, he digs beneath its modern appearance to reveal its history under subsequent dynasties: the Storehouse of Banners partly coincides with al-Ḥusayn Mosque; the gates and canals were the boundaries of the gradually expanding Cairo; the area of Bayna al-Qaṣrayn, with the Mamluk mansions and mausoleums, is named after the Fatimid Eastern and Western Palaces. Only once, he tells the full story of a monument in chronological order (ch.19): al-Ḥākim Mosque was built by the Fatimids, damaged by an earthquake (1303), and partly restored by the Mamluks. The building was in pitiful conditions until the 1980s, when a Pakistani sect named Bohra volunteered to restore it at its own expenses. In the fictional account, the protagonist meets the Pakistani volunteers and begins his reconstruction: like them, he saves the mosque from the carelessness of the contemporary Egyptians, bringing it back to its splendour with a feeling of nostalgia. While Ibn Shalabī is never tired of time-travelling, at the end of this journey he feels exhausted.

In the open-air museum of Old Cairo, monuments are not only the symbols of power but also the sites of collective memory. Once again, this topic is rendered with humorous images taken from everyday life, merging the figurative and literal meaning: "Time sticks to the edges of human memory like honey, or germs, or glue, or an infection. There are times when memory cannot easily be

74 On the founding myth of Cairo, see: *Kitāb al-ṭughrā* by Yūsuf Rakhā (b. 1976) (2011; *The Book of the Sultan's Seal*, 2015). This contemporary Egyptian novel, constructed around journeys in Cairo, also opens with the foundation of Cairo and mentions historical sources.

disentangled from the stickiness, and times when it searches for the stickiness but cannot find it." (199/216)

Finally, exploring the city becomes a humorous subject when the narrator tackles tourism, a key sector in the Egyptian economy. He remarks that tourists often know the history of the main landmarks, such as Khān al-Khalīlī bazar and al-Fīshāwī Café, while Egyptians ignore it. When he is mistaken for a tourist, he comments: "Laughing, I told him that the tourists [al-khawāja] knew what it was; but I, being an Egyptian, probably didn't." (190/207) He also mocks the habit of swindling tourists by placing modern tourism in an incongruous time: when the members of the Fatimid royal family are expelled from their palace, the protagonist compares them to a group of tourists waiting for their tour bus, introduces himself as an expert tour guide, and asks them for a tip.

To sum up, Ibn Shalabī is an ordinary Egyptian, picaresque character, wise fool, and court jester. In addition, he has a close relation with the city of Cairo: he loves walking in its streets (participant) and reconstructs its history (observer), revealing the homology between the urban space and its residents. Some comic passages revolving around his figure are based on the incongruity between serious/non-serious and ordinary/fantastic. The next section focuses on some humour-generating techniques and the main functions of comedy in this novel.

4.3 Humour in the urban world

Although indirectly, *Time-Travels* revives both *adab* literature in its purpose of edifying while entertaining and early modern satirical prose in its didactic intent. Its edifying goal is achieved by exploring the Egyptian past to find the origins of contemporary social behaviours, and wandering around the streets of Cairo to learn the history of the city. At the same time, this novel aims at amusing the reader.

Keeping in mind the narrative devices discussed above (episodic structure, time-travelling, picaresque character), humour relies on the clear-cut opposition of two groups: *al-awā'il wa-l-awākhir*, the rulers and the people. The social barriers are blurred by wordplay and a mixture of high and low registers. As Mehrez (2010b: 15) notes, Shalabī employs "daring narrative strategies that draw on the oral tradition as well as popular storytelling strategies, deliberately using everyday spoken dialect and idiom as an integral part of the literary text." This section identifies some types of humour in *Time-Travels*: verbal, situational, and social criticism mainly with a comforting function and sometimes with a subversive function. In all examples, the use of Egyptian Colloquial Arabic makes the puns more immediate and effective.

4.3.1 Verbal and situational humour

In *Time-Travels* language is manipulated to create puns and jokes. The first type of verbal humour is the definition of the same object with two juxtaposed terms, one taken from the common use and the other more suitable for the historical context. The comic effect is generated by the narrator correcting himself or intentionally degrading the object, as in these examples:

> a personal invitation to break the Ramadan fast at his table – or his dining carpet, as the invitation put it. (1/7)

> But there was nothing wrong with having [Saladin] wait for me in a hall, or even in a coffeehouse. (31/41)

The second type of verbal humour points at the narrator's difficulty to communicate with creatures of the past, due to cultural distance and linguistic change. For instance, Ibn Shalabī uses highly local idioms that require an explanation, making the dialogues almost surreal:

> "[. . .] when I put my mind to a problem [. . .] I bust it wide open."
> "What does 'bust it wide open' mean?"
> "It means I clean its clock."
> "What does 'clean its clock' mean?"
> "It means I make it comprehensible and clear."
> "Why didn't you say so right away?"
> "The Arabic language, may God preserve and enrich it," I replied, "contains expressions of every kind and species. [. . .]"
> "[. . .] If it's a matter of property, I'll put my neck on the line for it; and if it's action you need . . . "
> "What does 'put my neck on the line for it' mean?" he interrupted. (37–38/47–48)

Other techniques for verbal humour are wordplay, hyperbole, word lists, assonance, similes (including similes with animals), metaphors, and colloquial forms of address.

Situational humour happens when Ibn Shalabī does something inappropriate for the circumstances. Some recurrent scenes concern money, such as not paying the check at the café and not paying back the money to the person who lends it. Another recurrent situation is kissing the Sultan's foot in sign of deference: in the first occurrence, Ibn Shalabī does not want to conform to this obligation (72/83), while in the second occurrence, Green Garbanzo kisses by mistake the foot of a page boy between the Sultan's feet (165/170).

Another amusing episode portrays Ibn Shalabī like an expert rider and a knight on his mount. The clichés of Western films and epic tones contrasts with his inability to ride, making him the object of scorn:

> The horse stumbled and Ibn Shalaby was nearly hurled to the ground. [. . .] In any event, it was only thanks to the skill of the horse that Ibn Shalaby was spared a fall.
>
> Honor intact, he crossed the threshold of the storehouse. There he was welcomed by a crowd of whooping children, some of whom followed him in at a run. Led by Khazaal, a group of men, including some of the emirs appeared in the doorway, laughing, cheering, and clapping sarcastically as I rode toward them at a stately pace like a cowboy in a movie. All I needed to complete the thrilling scene was a torrential rainstorm.
>
> I dismounted with an athletic leap that stirred the envy of most of the onlookers. (127/140)

4.3.2 Egyptian idiosyncrasies

Humourists usually do not tell anything new to their audience; on the contrary, jokes are funnier when they are based on a shared cultural background. In *Time-Travels*, the narrator's travelogue covers several socio-political issues in contemporary Egypt, activating satire through the anachronistic comparison with the past. For example, to solve the housing crisis in his own time, the narrator suggests building skyscrapers in the past.[75] The absurdity of his idea is revealed by wordplay, in which the compound noun 'skyscraper' is split into the literal meaning of its two elements, 'scrape the sky':

> In front of us was the Storehouse of Banners, and I was able to see what the place really looked like. It was enormous: the space it occupied was enough to accommodate several giant skyscrapers (even if the sky, in those days, was too high for anyone to scrape). Hoping to get back into the sipahsalar's good graces, I said, "I know some foreign firms that could take that lot and fill it with skyscrapers."
>
> "We have no plans to scrape the sky," he replied scornfully. "Why should we?"
>
> "You'd solve the housing crisis!"
>
> "The only crisis we're facing at the moment is what to do with you." (75/85)

Referring to a shared cultural background and familiar issues, humour has an affiliative function: it strengthens the sense of belonging to a group, opposed to the Other. *Time-Travels* constructs a fixed image for each social group to represent

75 Other socio-political issues tackled in this way are traffic, migration, poverty, corruption, negligence, lack of morality.

the opposition between the rich and the poor, the rulers and the ordinary people. The rulers are accused of robbing the country for their own interests, causing poverty and social injustice. However, they are never safe and may be defeated by their rivals. In fact, as a series of doubles, they are criticized for their inclination to make the same mistakes. By depicting the repetitive nature of history, humour has a comforting effect on the reader.

At the same time, group affiliation allows a certain degree of self-mockery. Ibn Shalabī makes fun of his own category by using stereotypes and commenting on the social functions of comedy. For instance, at the beginning of ch.19, the narrator mocks the love-cum-hatred attitude of the ordinary Egyptians toward the rulers:

> Crying When It's Time to Laugh: A Genuine Egyptian Talent
>
> There's no doubt about it: Egyptians weep easily. When saying goodbye, especially, they'll cry a river, even when the person leaving is a debauched louse like the merry Sultan Ahmad ibn Qalawun. What I had really wanted to say to him by way of farewell was, "Good riddance, and may God never bring you this way again, or debase the Land of Egypt with anyone like you!" Instead of saying that, though, I embraced him; and even worse, I cried. Was I really sad to see him go? Or was it the instinct for flattery, so deeply ingrained in the poor and miserable Sons of Shalaby? The fact of the matter is that we Sons of Shalaby of the Egyptian branch laugh and distract ourselves with jokes even as the boot-heels of our oppressors grind us down. Then, when the bad times are over, we weep, as if our love for good company were stronger than the need for revenge. Our servile ancestors used to say, "Put up with a bad neighbor and wait for some calamity to carry him off, or for him to leave on his own." (188/194)

Crying at the oppressor's departure refers to the protagonist bidding farewell to Sultan Aḥmad, while evoking the grieving crowds at President Nasser's funeral (§5.3.1). This passage describes humour as a safety-valve to endure oppression, while mildly criticizing the political passivity of the Egyptians, as if it were an innate quality: as they accepted foreign domination in the past, nowadays they are too preoccupied with making ends meet for making a change. However, in other passages, Ibn Shalabī admits that the circumstances make it hard to revolt.

Moreover, humour allows to tackle political issue avoiding the traps of censorship. The protagonist criticizes surveillance, for instance in the episode of the cassette recorder, and political imprisonment. When he is imprisoned in the past, he thinks of prison in his time: "On the basis of things I had read and the testimonies of people imprisoned under Nasser, the mere sound of the word "prison" was enough to give me goose bumps." (52/63) The same topic serves to comment ironically on the relation between power and intellectuals, since political imprisonment reinforces one's a reputation as independent thinker: "'In my time,' I told him, 'people used to brag constantly about being in prison.

Anyone who came out of it was treated like a hero with medals tattooed onto his body. Go figure!'" (76/86) The narrator, close to the implied author, mocks the intellectual circles and the conventions of Egyptian literature, since prison literature (*adab al-sujūn*) became an established sub-genre in the late 1960s (Benigni 2009). Finally, prison is employed as a metaphor for the whole country, whose citizens have been trapped for thousands of years.

4.3.3 Comic subversion

To escape from this prison, in some episodes humour has a subversive function. In ch.3, Ibn Shalabī meets Bahā' al-Dīn Qarāqūsh (d. 1201), viceroy of Egypt during the reign of Ṣalāḥ al-Dīn. Based on this historical figure, Qarāqūsh is a stock character representing whimsical foreign rule and unfair justice. Highlighting the vitality of this character in Egyptian political humour, Kishtainy (1985: 54) mentions the idiom *ḥukm Qarāqūsh* (Qarāqūsh's justice) and a collection of anecdotes attributed to the Ayyubid official Ibn Mammātī (d. 1209) ('Abd al-Laṭīf 2015; Ḍayf 1999). The negative image of Qarāqūsh in folk humour overshadowed his positive portrait available in other historical sources, such as Ibn Khallikān (1968–1972: vol. 4, 91–92 mentioned in al-Musawy 2006).

In *Time-Travels*, the protagonist belittles this awe-inspiring ruler by playing with his double nature, as a historical figure and stock character. Humour is generated by the double meaning of the verb 'to see', meaning to meet someone (a real person) and to watch someone (a fictional character) on the stage:

> Gaping, I asked, "*That*'s Qaraqush?"
>
> "What do you mean?" asked the boy. "You've *never* seen him before?"
>
> "Just once."
>
> "Where?"
>
> "At the Rihani Theater," I said.
>
> [. . .] Feeling only half courageous, I pushed my way into the palace. All at once I found myself face to face with none other than Qaraqush himself. Marching along with a crisp regimental gait, he spotted me and assumed an expression of arrogant contempt, as if all he needed to do to crush me was to thrust out a foot. So I put on my own expression of arrogant contempt – the one I had picked up from the pictures of American politicians I saw in the papers every day. With my left hand in my pocket and my right brandishing the Samsonite briefcase, I addressed him as if he were nobody and I the celebrity. "Excuse me! Where can I find the tawashi Baha al-Din Qaraqush?"
>
> He stopped with a jolt. To be honest, I thought he was going to fall over. Something about the way I sounded or the way I looked must have frightened him. Whatever the reason, he answered in a deferential tone: "That's me, sir."

> Switching the briefcase to my left hand, I stuck out my right and said in a friendly bellow, "Hi there, tawashi! How's it going? Long time no see! It seems like forever since I saw them play you at the Rihani Theater."
>
> [. . .] "So where is my lord from? he asked.
>
> "Your lord is from a time that will see you without understanding you – a time that loves to hate you and greets you in the hope of wiping you out!"
>
> You're speaking in riddles, you – that is, my lord," he said, catching himself.
>
> "In the time I come from," I told him, "people will see you as a strong man and a force for justice, even if it's a dimwitted sort of justice. But they won't remember you the way you dream of being remembered. They'll love you for the charming way you have of crushing and smashing everything in your path, which at least kept the country quiet long enough for Saladin to liberate Jerusalem from the Crusaders, for which he honored you in his inimitable manner. They'll make you a character in books and plays and movies just to make sure no one tries to follow your example."
>
> Hearing this little speech, the eunuch looked as if he were going to faint.
>
> (26–27/35–36)

At the beginning of this scene, Ibn Shalabī talks to a child of the Fatimid family who experiences Qarāqūsh's brutality. Before meeting Qarāqūsh, he tries to gain self-confidence with some non-serious strategies, such as parodying his rival's attitude, ridiculing mediatic culture, and brandishing his Samsonite briefcase. Then he addresses Qarāqūsh in a very informal way Egyptian Colloquial Arabic, causing his bewilderment. Moreover, the protagonist mentions an anachronistic element, the Rihani Theater, before explaining its role in the comic subversion. This theatre exemplifies modern Egyptian comedy, since Najīb al-Rīḥānī was a popular comedian and playwright in the first half of the 20th century (Abou Saif 1973). It is also a way to map Cairo, since this theatre is located in ʿImād al-Dīn Street, once the heart of Downtown's entertainment, housing most of the vaudeville theatres and cafés where the artists met (Fahmy 2011: 132, 171; Helmy 2011). Starting from this reference, Ibn Shalabī tells Qarāqūsh that popular humour will exaggerate his defects to dispel the fear of being governed by despotic leaders. To sum up, at the beginning the victims fear Qarāqūsh; then popular humour is recalled and the situation, as well as historical narration, is subverted, with the leader being afraid.

The second example challenges the conventions of historical writing. In ch.13, Khazʿal, who is not a chronicler, provides an unsusual portrait of Emir Qawṣūn: he mentions an undefined date ("In the year seven-hundred-something") and only a few lines later the exact year (727); since it is a dialogue, he makes sure to be clear ("Makes sense so far?"); his interlocutor, Ibn Shalabī, also interrupts him with some commentary in Modern Standard Arabic and Egyptian Colloquial Arabic, mocking his narrative mode ("You know the date, too, Emir? You're as good as any historian!") or the historical content ("Wow! When it rains, it pours."). Finally, the narrator reveals that Ibn Taghrībirdī is the source of Khazʿal's account and the hypotext of the whole novel:

> Those words sounded familiar and I said so.
> "Everyone knows the story of Qawsun," said Khazaal.
> I told him that I heard the same story word for word from my friend Ibn Taghribirdi.
> "What age is this Birdi from?" he asked.
> "He's after your time," I replied.
> "Then he got the story from us." (131/144)

In this episode, pre-modern historiographers are both admired and ridiculed, since their official task of recording events is compared to the collective act of narration, which weaves together history, legends, and rumours. After the above-mentioned dialogue, a long passage continues the story of Qawṣūn parodying the style of the chronicles with many pieces of information coming from several cities, introduced by the formula "*qudima alaynā khabar min*" (news arrive from . . .). This historical reconstruction, based on *verbatim* quotations from the sources, is a parenthesis in the fictional narrative since it summarizes the events and leads to the following episode.

Besides the historical sources, this novel plays an intertextual game with popular culture and literary genres. Fantasy is exemplified by the Storehouse's guardians, tattooed cannibals whose appearance should be terrifying, but is so exaggerated that it elicits mirth. To use Bakhtin's concepts, they are comic scarecrows: "It transforms cosmic terror into a gay carnival monster" (Bakhtin 1984: 335). Furthermore, some dramatic scenes evoke the tradition of improvised comic sketches (*al-faṣl al-muḍḥik*), including beating and slapstick. These sketches stage a topsy-turvy world, in which the riffraff temporarily win and subvert power relations. For instance, this type of comedy is found in the episode of the judge, a religious and political authority, assaulted by a group of cooks who want to take revenge. Their aggression is a farce because their only weapons are their cooking tools and shoes:

> The moment he set foot outside the door of the mosque, the kitchen help and a crowd of chef's apprentices and general riffraff, armed with forks, spoons, knives, pot lids, ladles, and tureens, not to mention the sticks and clubs, set upon him. [. . .] But they did manage to pull his turban down around his neck and set it on fire and rid up his clothing. Then they began beating him with shoes, shouting, "You're with Qawsun, you infidel, you sinner!" (162/177)

Talking about revolts, the Storehouse of Banners is an alternative site of power, opposed to the Citadel from which the sultan rules. When the two authorities clash, the Storehouse's prisoners and the underprivileged Cairene population exploit the chaos to take to the streets pillaging the buildings. Like the carnival, which unites the opposing poles of life/death and up/down, the depiction of the streets combines destruction with vital creativity. In the final confrontation in the last chapter, the wine stored in the Storehouse invades the streets, creating an upside-down world:

> I saw men emerging from the storehouse carrying limp and battered corpses, as well as casks of wine. They poured the wine out, flooding the streets in all directions. The wine was mixed with dirt, blood, animal droppings, but the nasty mixture had its takers: men of all ages were coming out with pots and pans and covertly scooping up what they could. [. . .] As in my Cairo of the fifteenth century ah, when a little rain or a burst sewer pipe can turn the streets into a sea for human microorganisms to swim through, the torrent of wine made it impossible for the people to walk. Even so, the harafish in all their motley dress were smiling as they rolled up their pants and performed acrobatically impossible tricks to get around the puddles and the mud, all the while making fun of themselves, mocking their lot, and jeering at everything in existence. The earth was feeling no pain, said one. It didn't even mind being stepped on, said another. "The fun should last until dawn," said a third, "and that's a long way off. It might not come at all!"
>
> "It's already here," said a fourth. "It started when we began knocking down the storehouse and pouring out the wine."
>
> "True," said a fifth, "but we don't recognize dawn as observed by the government."
>
> "We don't recognize it because it's cracked," said another.
>
> "So the dawn's cracked too?" called another from the end of the street. "I thought we were the only ones who were cracked."
>
> "Wise-cracked, maybe," said another from atop a little hill he had managed to reach.
>
> "Or just wiseass," retorted another through an open window.
>
> Thus did the Egyptians chew up the tragedy and spit it out as if nothing had happened. (241–242/261–262)

Firstly, the sea of wine breaks the religious prohibition of not drinking alcohol, while the reference to the bodily fluids ("dirt, blood, animal droppings") increases the grotesque effect. Secondly, the narrator compares these extraordinary circumstances with an ordinary situation in his times ("As in my Cairo of the fifteenth century"), encouraging laughter through a familiar element. Thirdly, the mob has no limits in its behaviour and humour. This corresponds to Bakhtin's conception of laughter, which "is directed not at one part only, but at the whole. One might say that it builds its own world versus the official world, its own church versus the official church, its own state versus the official state" (Bakhtin 1984: 88). Finally, the distinction between performers and spectators is blurred, since they collectively craft a joke about the possibility of fooling the government all night long until dawn. Told in Egyptian Colloquial Arabic, this joke revolves around the double meaning of *bahīm* as 'livestock' and 'dark colour', while the English translator has re-created its effect playing with the words 'cracked' and 'wise'. Once again, this scene ends with the wise narrator remarking the continuity of a supposed Egyptianness across history.

To sum up, these episodes subvert the power relations by staging the carnivalesque culture of laughter and mixing multiple linguistic registers. The fictional world stages a rebellion that is only imagined in real life.

4.4 Conclusion: a very Egyptian story

Shalabī's novel could be labelled as "a very Egyptian story", echoing the title of a short story by Yūsuf Idrīs (§2.2). With his great mastery at this literary genre and linguistic variation, Idrīs (1980) stages the encounter between a taxi driver and a beggar who has turned his disability into a resource to make money at the traffic lights but is running away from the police, as if he were in danger. Through a lively dialogue, the beggar reveals that it is one of his clever ruses to avoid paying the bribe to the policemen and offers the taxi drivers to become his accomplice. This short story plays on some stereotypes attached to the ordinary Egyptians and portrays the victory of a victim who fools the system. The characterization and the resolution of multiple incongruities with a surprise effect open the possibility to laugh at the circumstances of Egyptian life as they are inscribed in the readers' shared knowledge. Exploiting similar techniques, *Time-Travel* by Shalabī multiplies the humorous stories and enriches them with intertextuality to craft an unconventional image of what is authentically Egyptian.

This image is embdodied by the protagonist, Ibn Shalabī, who revives the comic tradition at the crossroads between refined literature and populare references. The first section of this chapter argues that *Time-Travels* exploits some literary tropes of the travelogues and *maqāmāt* that are already part of the humorous tradition, while it selects some specific genres of pre-modern historiography (court-chronicle and topography) as hypotext to write an alternative Egyptian history. As happens in the travelogues and *maqāmāt*, mobility enables the satirical portait of various segments of society and favours the character's transgression of all norms. The humorous potential of displacement is reinforced by the fictional device of time-travelling encapsulated in a frame narrative: anachronism leads to funny misunderstandings expressed by wordplay and eccentric behaviours, while the frame narrative increases the perception of humour thanks to brevity and repetition.

Repetition also characterizes the main character who appears again and again over his adventures with a set of clearly defined traits and reminds of some proverbial comic types. The second section examines Ibn Shalabī's duplicity as a knowledgeable first-person narrator and an ordinary Egyptian who plays the fool. He can be considered a picaresque character because of his fluid identity and his capacity to turn the situation to his own advantage. He seeks identification with the readers by tackling some familiar issues, embodying some stereotypes, and using a streetwise language. Given this background, the third section overviews some types of humour and their function: verbal and situational humour provide a safty-valve from everyday life and attest the richness of linguistic creativity; tackling Egyptian idiosyncrasies through the stock characters of the wise fool, court jester, and whimsical ruler, all revived with references to popular culture, has a conforting and affiliative function; subversion, instead, is found in some episodes of rebellion ascribable to carnivalesque laughter and in interrupting the style of historiography with puns in Egyptian Colloquial Arabic.

As the novel's subtitle *Riḥla fī l-zamakān* (A journey in space-and-time) suggests, time and space are intertwined to depict the contemporary Egyptian society: since the author was fascinated by Mamluk historiography and architecture, his fictional alter-ego roots the social behaviours in a reimagined past, while preserving the Cairene monuments as the symbol of a shared memory. One of the social phenomena which, according to this fictional reconstruction, originated at the times of the Mamluks is smoking hashish: "It's the smoke from a period of time not too far off," he said, "a place like a little town, where the Egyptian habit of smoking different herbs and spices first began." (22/31) The next chapter looks at the interplay of drugs and humour in *Ṣāliḥ Hēṣa* also by Shalabī.

5 Laughing together at the hash den

> There is always a huge crowd on al-Tarikh Bridge every Wednesday. Young and old men and children in rags and bare feet start to arrive in the early morning and line up on the bridge with their faces toward the port, their gazes fixed on the empty space. The tram stops at its station behind them, and no one leaves his spot until evening.
>
> A long time after this started happening, the people realized that there was an incinerator at the port where the police burned drugs they had confiscated after stopping smuggling attempts or raiding dealers' storage places. Wednesday was the day on which the burning took place, and the sea breeze blowing at the bridge always passed the incinerator and, carrying the smoke of burning hashish, brought the people on the bridge pleasure and comfort free of charge. Now many vehicles besides the tram loiter on the bridge on Wednesdays.
>
> I. Abdel Meguid, *The House of Jasmine*, 2012: ch.8, location n. 1031

The main character of *Time-Travels*, Ibn Shalabī, epitomizes the flaws and virtues of the Egyptians in everyday life and in their relationship with the authorities. He is a wise fool who combines the double perspective of the ordinary man and the wise intellectual as a survival strategy. Temporal distance is the lens through which he looks at the contemporary society, revealing its shortcomings. This chapter completes the previous analysis of humour in Khayrī Shalabī's writings by looking at *The Hashish Waiter*, a novel published almost twenty years after *Time-Travels*. Both novels develop the stock character of the wise fool: while the protagonist of *Time-Travels* is presented as an eccentric individual, always out of place, the main character in *The Hashish Waiter* is immersed in a community of peers who share the same type of entertainment. Together, they witness the socio-political change of the 1960s and 1970s and try to resist their disillusionment. In *Time-Travels* the 1970s are the present from which Ibn Shalabī travels back to the past, whereas *The Hashish Waiter* re-reads this period as a golden age through the filter of nostalgia.

At the centre of *The Hashish Waiter* is the representation of the sub-culture of hashish smokers, which is a vital component of Cairene popular culture and a semi-legal activity in the urban underworld. The novel follows a group of young intellectuals who meet at Ḥakīm's hash den to smoke, talk about their lives, discuss political and cultural issues, and laugh. The den is in the Maʿrūf quarter, a run-down neighbourhood in Downtown Cairo. Its relaxed atmosphere is provided by the owner Ḥakīm, the hashish waiter Ṣāliḥ Hēṣa, and the den's boys, including the not-so-young Ṣābir. The protagonist, Ṣāliḥ Hēṣa, is the symbol of this place and life on the margins. His job consists in cleaning out thousands of bowls for the bong water pipes and refilling them with tobacco molasses. When he finishes this repetitive task, he mixes denatured alcohol and coke to get drunk; then

https://doi.org/10.1515/9783110725414-006

he starts talking freely and becomes almost aggressive. After sleeping soundly, he forgets everything and is as polite as usual.

The clique of friends gradually discovers his adventurous life story in a flashback. Over the British occupation, Ṣāliḥ's father is a sergeant in the Camel Corps, the division entrusted with sedating the protests. However, he cannot provide for his many children and his wife starts to work for a lawyer attached to the *Wafd* party who becomes a mentor for Ṣāliḥ. When the boy sees his father hitting the lawyer with the whip during a demonstration, he rebels and starts his life as an independent young man. After the military service, he remains in the army as a volunteer and is sent to Sudan, where he takes up boxing and meets his wife Wahība. However, their marriage is cursed because Wahība is his aunt. So Ṣāliḥ leaves the army and returns to Cairo, where he joins the Police, continues his boxing training at the Police Club, and takes part in the Olympics. When the Minister of Labour he works for tries to take advantage of him, he rebels and gets rowdy for the first time.

The group of young intellectuals is deeply influenced by Ṣāliḥ's philosophy and way of talking; in fact, they go to the hash den to spend time together and meet him. Their perception of having fun together is increased by intoxication, be it drinking or smoking hashish, and reaches its peak in a status called *hēṣa*, rowdiness. Hēṣa is the protagonist's nickname which gives the title to the book. It means noise and cheerful uproar in Egyptian Colloquial Arabic and acquires two meanings in the story: at the beginning, it indicates pure fun, laughter, escapism, and a status of ecstasy; later, it hints at political chaos and disrupting the order for one's own interests.

Over the 1970s the group gradually disperses but reunites at the den to watch the TV live coverage of President Sadat's visit to Jerusalem (1977). Ṣāliḥ Hēṣa is the only one who takes to the streets and speaks out what he thinks. Because of his vibrant protest, he is taken away by the police and is later found dead. His death marks the end of an era since the government cracks down on the hash dens, while local and international politics bring about a new vision of the world. One day, the narrator believes he sees Ṣāliḥ in flesh and bones, but it is Zakī, the actor of the clique, who turns the hashish waiter into a successful comedy character.

This novel has received some critical attention for its depiction of socio-political change and its representation of liminal characters and places (Lynx Qualey 2011c; Rakha 2000; Tarbush 2012). In her study of Downtown Cairo as a contested space in contemporary Egyptian fiction, Naaman (2011: 71–104) examines the interplay of space, characters, and language in *The Hashish Waiter* to argue that its representation of the hashish café culture in the 1960s–1970s negotiates alternative forms of modernity and fulfils the writer's political and aesthetic project of recovering the folk cultural heritage. Similarly, Lagrange (2015) argues that space, characters, and language blur the boundaries between the conventional notions of central and marginal. He focuses on the use of the vernacular and the translation's challenges, since he has translated the novel into French.[76]

Following Naaman's and Langrange's approach, this chapter looks at the liminality of space, characters, and language to understand which type of humour is performed at the hash den and how it portrays a specific segment of Egyptian society. The first section illustrates that the homology between the group of friends and the place where they meet is achieved by combining realist and post-modern narrative techniques. Within this collective biography, the hashish waiter Ṣāliḥ emerges as the group's leader. The second section describes him as a wise fool and investigates the role of popular culture in the collective experience of humour at the hash den. After examining the cheerful side of *hēṣa*, the third section follows the novel's development by exploring its gradual shift to political satire. It also looks at comedy theatre as a distorted mirror of society to exemplify how humour is both performed in the novel and discussed in some metanarrative passages.

5.1 Social biography of the coterie

5.1.1 The hash den

As in many modern and contemporary Egyptian novels, the events gravitate around one single building: Ḥakīm's hash den (*al-ghurza*) in the Maʿrūf quarter near Downtown. According to Naaman's historical reconstruction, this neighbourhood was not involved in the city centre's urbanistic renovation started by Khedive Ismāʿīl (1863–1879), so its villas and apartment buildings started to coexist with informal housing. After World War II, it received a wave of rural migrants mainly from Upper Egypt and Nubia who joined their relatives and fellow villagers, appropriating the district for their housing needs (Naaman 2011: 73–75; Abu-Lughod 1961). Despite its central location, it foreshadows the sprout of shantytowns in the urban fringes, where new waves of migrants arrived since the 1970s, as discussed in the next chapter (§6.1.2).

---

76 The challenges of translating Shalabī's works are also discussed in two interviews with the English translators, Talib and Cooperson (Lynx Qualey 2011a, 2011b).

Shalabī portrays this urban underworld facing poverty, overpopulation, and government negligence. The residents live in dilapidated houses at risk of collapse, which the authorities have ordered to evacuate. Therefore, the buildings and the population become invisible and their activities are semi-legal. Besides the run-down houses, another place that escapes the authorities' control is "Hakeem's cherished, magical, sleepless hash den" (18/21), an Upper Egyptian-style country house built over the rubble of a demolished urban building. This duplicity reconciles the rural-urban opposition since the the Upper Egyptian owner encourages friendship and solidarity among the young intellectuals hailing from the countryside and meeting there in the heart of the city. The hash den epitomizes the homology between the buildings and the residents since Ṣāliḥ's life coincides with the place's existence: he was born, lived, worked, and died there; soon after his death, the police shut down several dens in the city centre.

While the Maʿrūf quarter is considered a traditional popular (*shaʿbī*) neighbourhood, it is located behind Talʿat Ḥarb Street, the core of the modernization project of Downtown. Naaman argues that Shalabī's literary representation blurs the polarization between a modern europeanized and a premodern indigenous space in Cairo by portraying an in-between zone, whose community seeks an alternative way of dwelling in modernity. In this respect, the aspiring intellectuals meeting there develop a culture of laughter and free discussion, appreciate popular wisdom, mock the commodification of goods and the prestige attributed to some professions, establishing an alternative to the official intellectual circles meeting in the neighbouring cafés (such as Groppi, Café Riche, and Grillon).[77] However, despite their partial isolation, they move back and forth in the city and aspire to enter the cultural circles.

Furthermore, this interaction between the two districts appears in the first five chapters describing the Maʿrūf quarter and four different ways to access it. As Naaman remarks, it seems an enclosed world hidden from the view, yet it is accessible from the neighbouring Downtown: while Downtown is famous for its commercial establishments and official cultural institutions, the Maʿrūf quarter has a vital market and night life. Naaman notes that the crossing over from one district to the next has a bewitching quality and antropomorphizing images are employed in the vivid description of the street. Moreover, the narrator depicts human types, wares, colours, and sounds shaping a big carnival or festival (*mahrajān*), an image found also in *Time-Travels*. Examining the same chapters, Lagrange (2015) argues that this post-modern writing technique multiplies the narrative possibilities and expresses

77 For the role of cafés in the intellectual circles, see: Jacquemond 2008: 174–178. For Shalabī's extensive knowledge of the Cairen café culture, see: *Uns al-ḥabāyb* (§2.4.2).

the author's attempts to approach his subject; at the same time, this detour allows a vivid description of the hidden side-alleys populated by poor children, drug dealers, and local thugs. In this respect, it is worth noting that the picturesque details are combined with a mocking attitude toward a supposed Egyptian authenticity attached to the place and its residents, as in these two examples:

> And yet, because Egyptians are so generous – and because of that alone – everything had to be allowed to reach its destination. Cars passed through the eye of a needle [. . .] (2/9)

> Another man who'd made his bed in the street, slept deeply, looking to all the world like a mummy escaped from the Egyptian Museum just a few steps away. (11/15)

The quarter and the den's magical depiction conveys a feeling of nostalgia for a lost (under)world. Namaan (2011: 78) argues that this nostalgic depiction merges with a deeply critical one since the narrator also exposes the neighbourhood's unresolved problems. Moreover, it can be said that this critical attitude is strenghtened in the last three chapters, where the change in spatial representation corresponds to the novel's tragic denouement. Ch.21 describes the Maʿrūf quarter from the top floor of the Hilton Hotel, where the friends usually meeting at the hash den are invited to a wedding party:

> We were all shocked when one day we were invited to the Thousand and One Nights Ballroom at the Nile Hilton, which was just on the border of the Marouf Quarter. From their rooms on the top floors, tourists could see all the Marouf Quarter laid out like a large wound in the belly of the indigestion-plagued city as it constantly vomited up residents, whether in the cemeteries packed full of the living or in the streets teeming with the walking dead, that tumultuous stifling mass: houses – some crumbling, others ancient and about to collapse – adorned with laundry basins, dogs, hens, workshops, hash dens, shacks, coops, and mountains of rotting, putrid garbage. We left these shacks like worms exuding from pus-filled sores [. . .] (212/236–237)

Merging their view from below with the view from above, this description employs the metaphor of disease and illustrates how the cheerful mob becomes a suffocating throng, turning its original vitality into death. This imagery of death is repeated in the descriptions at the end of ch.22–23, thus the novel ends with darkness covering the world that the narrative was able to illuminate:

> Even when we left the hash den, we could only wave to each other as we parted, each of us heading down his own distant alleyway leading to two different paths beneath the same screeching, cloudy sky of the same city that was so crowded it was beginning to feel like a graveyard. (234/261)

> Suddenly all the lights went out and the city was plunged into a pitch-black darkness. Slowly we began bumping into one another like bodies turning in a grave even narrower than al-Hagg Gamal Farhan's bathroom. (243/271)

5.1.2 The narrator as a guide

As it emerges from the description of the four paths leading to the Maʿrūf quarter, the narrator has a key role in guiding the reader into the underworld of hashish smokers, which would otherwise be inaccessible. The anonymous first-person narrator is a member of the coterie meeting at the hash den. At the beginning, he employs the first-person plural (we) and addresses the second-person singular (you) to convey his internal perspective coinciding with that of his group, with the aim of involving the reader. Then he gradually moves to the first-person singular (I), focusing on his own opinions and wanderings in the city. This change is clear in ch.14, when he goes to the den to pay Ṣāliḥ a solo visit and declares his intentions: so far he has observed the group, but now he becomes a participant in the experiment (96/109).

This narrating voice leaves the floor to a third-person narrator in the flashbacks that reconstruct Ṣāliḥ's childhood and youth and the biography of some members of the clique. This may be seen an evolution of the first-person narrator: after collecting all the information, he assigns the account to an omniscient voice. Sometimes the sources of the accounts are some secondary characters, but the third-person narrator knows more than them. For example, Ṣāliḥ was the boxing trainer of Ibrāhīm al-Qammāḥ, a shop-window designer, who promises to tell Ṣāliḥ's life story when they have clear minds:

> Ibrahim said he was sorry, but the story was longer than the Epic of Ban[u] Hilal, and maybe even more important. It needed time and clear heads, not simply because so much happens in it, but also because the person telling it has to enjoy the telling, has to be able to hear himself telling it so he can learn the things he'd failed to learn from Rowdy Salih the first time around. [. . .]
>
> If we met back up again at night, he said, we could all watch the film of Rowdy Salih together without having to worry about any bastard censors cutting even a single scene. (68/77–78)

Ibrāhīm compares the waiters's life to the most popular Arab folk epics and a film, rooting the main character in Egyptian culture; furthermore, cinema and theatre are recurrent images throughout the novel. His story is actually narrated in ch.13 and 15 from the omniscient narrator's perspective in a linear chronological order. It includes some canonical motifs of the bildungs-narrative in Egyptian realist fiction, such as the father-and-son conflict, education to liberal values, political engagement for the nationalistic cause, and a troubled romance (Casini, Paniconi & Sorbera 2012: 37–152). In addition, it portrays the hard life of the downtrodden in the poor urban districts. Ṣāliḥ's formative years end with his rebellion, which leads him to the hash den; at this point, the flash back ends, and the first-person narrator goes back to the den's routine.

Comparing the two narrative voices, Lagrange argues that the homodiegetic narrator reproduces the hallucinatory effect of hashish through loosely tied episodes and evocative descriptions:

> Le haschich est le trait d'union entre ces deux groupes, et c'est lui aussi qui suscite la progression serpentine de la narration (les associations d'idées, les digressions de contour, les vignettes pittoresque), comme il inspire les métaphores filées dans les descriptions physiques des personnages, et enfin la virtuosité de l'auteur dans le jeu des registres et variétés de la langue, celle des fumeurs venant habiter celle des intellectuels.[78] (Lagrange 2015: 573)

Therefore, the opening chapters are told in an eternal present tense, as if time was arrested; times starts to flow when the heterodiegetic narrator relates the previous events in the flashback (Lagrange 2015: 576). Lagrange also notes that a key element of the narrating voice is linguistic variation, mixing refined literary Arabic, the jargon of hashish smokers, a local form of vernacular, idioms, proverbs, and storytelling techniques. In this respect, it is worth adding that the narrator mediates other voices through dialogue, free indirect speech, and the description of the characters' way of talking. For example, in this passage he assumes Ḥakīm's perspective and language:

> Whenever you showed up at the den on your own, Hakeem would put on a grave voice and tell you so-and-so was in here asking for you, that he was dying to talk to you. The thing was that the whole time we were sitting there, he'd never stop telling us – in brief snippets between long bouts of silence – a long list that you – as a friend – surely wanted to know: so-and-so's coming tonight at such-and-such a time; so-and-so wants you to come to his birthday party tomorrow night; [. . .] so-and-so. . . so-and-so. . . so-and-so. (27–28/30–31)

While the narrator portrays the members of the group in full details, information about him is scarce: he is a journalist and aspiring novelist who writes radio dramas and short stories. At the end of the novel, he gets married, but does not change his lifestyle: his modest apartment and economy car illustrate that he still refuses consumerism. Several autobiographical elements are found in this character, to the point that Rakha (2000) describes him as "a younger version of Shalabi himself". When the narrator introduces himself to a fellow smoker, his origins coincide with those of the author: "I told him about my family

78 "Hashish is the linking chain between the two groups and the element that determines the serpentine progression of the narration (association of ideas, digressions, picturesque vignettes). Moreover, it inspires the metaphors inserted into the characters' physical description and the writer's virtuosity at playing with the registers and linguistic varieties, especially the language of the smokers permeating that of the intellectuals."

in the countryside around Fouadiya and about my political, poet father, who was burdened with his many children, old age, and poor eyesight." (103/116–117). Another parallelism is that they both start their career in journalism as apprentices at *al-Jumhūriyya* newspaper: "In return, [Qamar] learned that I'd recently been attached to the Court of her Majesty the Press but that I hadn't been hired anywhere yet" (102/112). The narrator's extensive knowledge of the media, intellectual circles, and entertainment establishments derives from the author's own experience, as happens in *Time-Travels*. He often mirrors Shalabī's literary taste and his opinions on other intellectuals. For instance, Ibrāhīm Manṣūr (§2.4.4.3) is mentioned with admiration in the novel, whereas modernist writers are not appreciated.[79]

5.1.3 Aspiring intellectuals

The novel portrays a circle of aspiring intellectuals in their late twenties who regularly meet at Ḥakīm's den, described as follows:

> The group he [Hakeem] considered his best friends – our group – was made up of around thirty people with similar dispositions and the same taste in hash and drinks. We had a professor, writer, poet, artist, actor, journalist, antique-shop owner, composer, street magician, singer, songwriter, theatre director, manager of a firm that sold Egyptian products, accountant at the National Bank, novice lawyer, clerk in the public prosecutor's office, secretary at the government grocery co-op, and a chronic university student who was addicted to student union elections. We'd all gone to Hakeem's den solo at first [. . .]
>
> Thanks to Hakeem, we became an affectionate, amicable crew. (25–26/28–29)

Within the bigger crew, there is a core group of friends (*al-shilla, al-jamāʿa*), almost a family. They are put together by Ḥakīm's ability to turn customers into friends and create a network of support. Their conversation ranges from serious topics – such as philosophy, literary criticism, art, and politics – to pop culture, music, cinema, and football. They hail from low or middle-class families, mainly from the provinces. As mentioned above, they negotiate an alternative to urban modernity and official intellectual circles. For instance, they joined the Marxist cause at university, but are now less involved and more critical.

As regards their professions, they embody some innovative artistic and intellectual trends: the narrator writes radio and TV dramas; Ṭalʿat al-Imbābī is a lecturer of history at Cairo University, interested in political and social psychology;

79 In the novel, Manṣūr is one of the intellectuals arrested for their reaction to the news of President Sadat's visit to Jerusalem (221/246).

Muṣṭafā Lamʿī is a sculptor and illustrator of children's books; al-ʿUqla is a caricaturist; Fārūq al-Jamal is a vernacular poet who gets his verse published in the magazine *Ṣabāḥ al-khayr*; Ibrāhīm al-Qammāḥ is a shop-window designer; Qamar al-Maḥrūqī is a graduate of College of Applied Arts. Qamar's trajectory is particularly interesting: he introduces himself as an engineer but works in a ceramic workshop; he later becomes a research assistant for the Egyptian Arabic-English dictionary project conducted by the American University. As Lagrange (2015: 574) notes, his name is a play on ʿUmar al-Fārūqī, who collaborated with el-Said Badawi (al-Sayyd Badawī) for the realization of *A Dictionary of Egyptian Arabic*. In the novel, the project's supervisor is called Dr. al-Nabawī Sharīf al-Nabawī, with a clear homology to al-Sayyd Badawī. Naaman (2011: 81) argues that Qamar mocks the cult for engineers in the Nasserist era, whereas the shop window designer Ibrāhīm and the salesman Wajdī mock consumerism.

The crew shares and interest for literature and cinema. Two members work in cinema: Aḥmad ʿĀṣim is a director and Zakī Ḥāmid is an aspiring actor, whose name evokes the Egyptian star Aḥmad Zakī (1949–2005) (Lagrange 2015: 575; Naaman 2011: 82). The group interacts with some characters who embody the sociopolitical changes of the 1970s. Qamar invites to the den three well-off friends who have gained their fortune with the economic liberalization, the so-called *infitāḥ* promoted by President Sadat. Another enigmatic character is Wajīh Farḥān, an aspiring poet and journalist, and a sponger. When he reappears many years later as a member of the Israeli delegation, the clique condemns him as a traitor. His story resembles that of the Egyptian journalist Nabīh Sarḥān, who fled to Israel became an Israeli citizen in the late 1960s (Bashandī 2016).

The members of the coterie are tied by special bonds. For instance, Aḥmad ʿĀṣim is married to the Italian leftist activist Matilde; when they divorce, she marries Aḥmad's friend Ṭalʿat, without harming their friendship. Aḥmad's sister, Maḥāsin, is married to Qamar. Ṭalʿat and Qamar are almost doubles for their appearance, way of talking and laughing:

> Qamar al-Mahruqi let out a throaty laugh; as did Talat al-Imbabi, with the same sounds and rhythms – they were a lot alike. Most of the time we couldn't figure out who'd influenced whom. They both had the same skinny body-type, too, although Qamar was slightly taller and slimmer. (50/54–55)

They are also similar in their special bond with Ṣāliḥ:

> Qamar al-Mahruqi said, in an affectionate shout – he was the only one who had a special bond with Rowdy Salih that allowed him to talk to him however he pleased – (51/56)

> He [Talat] was always the most devoted, most affected, the closest of us all to Rowdy Salih, so it never occurred to me that he could ever turn his back on Salih until I bumped into Ibrahim al-Qammah the next evening when I was at the den by myself. (148/165)

Each member of the crew has a special relation with Ṣāliḥ, ranging from enthusiasm to devotion. The next section examines why they choose the hashish waiter as their leader and representative of their collective local identity.

5.2 Ṣāliḥ, the wise fool

5.2.1 Appearance

Ṣāliḥ is about forty-five years old. His family of Nubian origins comes from Upper Egypt, but he was born in the Maʿrūf quarter. Both places embody a kind of Egyptian indigenousness (*aṣāla*) that enshrines traditional values and folk culture. The main character does not have an identity card, so he does not exist for the authorities, except for the diploma he got from the local Elementary School. Despite his marginality in society, he becomes the leader (*al-zaʿīm*, as the title of ch.8) of the community of hashish smokers, chosen by the whole group, rather than by single individuals:

> He certainly was a fixture in the den, but back when we were going there as mere individuals, sporadically, each of us going when he could, with no set time for friends, he was always hidden away. There was no doubt that we'd each seen him working inconspicuously in the den more than once; you couldn't help but notice him. But then after we'd become a friendly group who got together every night to get high, after everyone's passions, jobs, and traits mingled, our viewpoints converged, our eyes learned to communicate with mere looks, after we got to be like that, that was when Rowdy Salih really came on to the scene. It wasn't simply because we'd started fixating on him, because he'd become our amusement, our topic of conversation, the star of our jokes and stories; rather it was because – in addition to being all that – he also possessed something of each of us, more than just one thing. He'd often act as if he were all of us and we'd often act as we were him. The truth was that he'd become – though we didn't know for how long – the main attraction for all the den's customers because he brought a certain virile, mischievous, warm and brotherly, attractive lunatic ecstasy to the place. Everything he did and said made us laugh because we thought it was a slice of utter insanity, but we soon realized that it invigorated us; it was everything we wished we could do or say. We obsessively repeated the things he said no matter what they were and claimed them as treasures of a living heritage. We started citing things he'd say in conversation about every aspect of life; we even used them as authentic examples of the vernacular language to which we could apply our artistic and literary theories and we discovered a depth of eloquence and innate wisdom in them. We occasionally got the feeling that Rowdy Salih

> had actually studied art and literature, had, in fact, actively participated in every single movement, but that history had passed silently over his involvement just as it passes silently over so many things. (30–31/33–34)

As it emerges from this passage, they choose him because they identify with him and he stimulates their amusement. Ṣāliḥ is both the subject and object of humour: his lunacy makes them laugh and, at the same time, he is the topic of their jokes and amusing stories. Moreover, he is the product of a collective narrative and becomes a cult figure, like folk heroes or film stars. As his description continues, the group's imitation anticipates a central humour-generating technique in this novel; they also adopt his way of speaking made of his vernacular language, expressing his ancestral wisdom, and refined Arabic. The last sentence of this passage describes him as one of those ordinary men and legendary characters forgotten by official history, to whom the narrator and implied author want to give voice.

This presentation suggests that the protagonist is a sage in a fool's clothing. This duplicity emerges from his physical description: behind his dirty clothes and humble job, the group sees his dignity and noble soul. Their impression is conveyed by similes and metaphors: he is compared to a disgraced nobleman, a heavenly creature, a giant, and an elegant swan (31–34/34–37). He is nicknamed *al-gentleman* (39/42) for his aristocratic but humble attitude, and compared to Tiresias, the blind prophet of Greek mythology, for his insight (147/164). As regards his attitude, he is polite and shy (36/39), but can speak daring words and insults, especially when he is drunk. The protagonist seems illiterate, but possesses an ancestral wisdom expressed by his very local vernacular. This duplicity is maintained until the end of the novel, when the neighbourhood pays tribute to him at his funeral: "The neighbourhood was shrouded in a dignified silence; it was so dignified it seemed slightly comic, just like Rowdy Salih himself, who combined a special balance in dignity and comedy [al-waqār wa-l-hazl] that rarely succeeded in others." (238/266)[80]

The hashish waiter's double nature emerges by comparing him to his friend Ṣābir on the one hand, and Oscar Wilde on the other. Born and raised in the same environment, Ṣābir works as a den's boy, the one who sits in front of the customers holding the bong for them and changing the bowls. Even though Ṣāliḥ and Ṣābir belong to the same underworld, the former has a certain gravity, whereas the latter epitomizes the street rascal:

---

80 In *A Dog with No Tail*, there is a humorous episode in which dignity (*al-waqār*) turns into comedy because of incongruity and a sudden fall into the ordinary (§6.1.3).

> The difference between them was in the person itself. Rowdy Salih – despite his ratty clothes and generally repugnant appearance – had this inborn gravitas that compelled your respect, maybe because, to you, he was the living embodiment of the phrase, 'fallen on hard times', whereas Sabir was the consummate sarcastic smart ass always sneakily laying malicious traps to catch out any silly idiot dumb enough to fall into one. (71/81)

The parallelism with Oscar Wilde, instead, is suggested by the juxtaposition of two quotations at the beginning of the novel:

> Humanity takes itself too seriously. It is the world's original sin. If the caveman had known how to laugh, History would have been different. Seriousness is the only refuge of the shallow. (Oscar Wilde)
>
> ***
>
> God made the world a rowdy place and then filled it with rowdy people. Everybody here's rowdy. They're all rowdy 'cause all they want to do is get rowdy and they either get to or they don't. And everybody here's run-down. But they're all run-down in their own way. And me, I'm the king of the run-down 'cause I'm run-down in every which way.
> (Rowdy Salih)

The reader, who does not know Ṣāliḥ yet but knows Wilde as a novelist, author of comedies, dandy, and wit, is induced to compare the two maxims: refined wit and popular wisdom, a master of comedy and an unknown character. As Lagrange (2015: 577) notes, the hashish waiter is the marginal counterpart of Oscar Wilde. Ṣāliḥ's motto, repeated three times in the book (37/40, 98/111–112, 243/271), is the starting point to examine his philosophy as a wise fool.

5.2.2 Philosophy

Besides the duplicity of his appearance, the main reason to classify Ṣāliḥ as a wise fool is the content of his utterances. These are often unintelligible and playful, yet they reveal a deep truth to a careful listener. The first part of the novel exemplifies his playful attitude, whereas the second part portrays him speaking the truth.

His philosophy is summarized by rowdiness, *i.e.* a status of elation causing a temporary subversion of power relations. In this parallel world, the hashish waiter becomes the leader and king of the run-down, as he defines himself in his motto. On the contrary, respectable men are turned into the butt of his sarcasm. Since rowdiness is caused by alcohol abuse, one might think that Ṣāliḥ speaks freely because of this drug, but intoxication only amplifies his philosophy based on freedom and dignity. He follows these principles over the course of his life and rebels many times, including in the final confrontation with the police. Besides enhancing subversion and freedom, his words contain a deep meaning; even though he speaks like a lunatic or madman, the coterie acknowledges that he is more balanced than the rest of society:

> In point of fact, Rowdy Salih had a completely balanced personality: he did everything he wanted to – whether he was drunk or sober – and with absolute freedom. It was just that he chose to do some things subconsciously, without really knowing it. But then why did he do those things at all? Obviously he had rational motivations that grew out of his conscious awareness. Talat al-Imbabi, perceiving the crux of the puzzle like a scientist, went on to explain that Rowdy Salih was actually more balanced than any of us, that he was different because he didn't suffer from any of the psychological complexes the rest of us did because he always did what he wanted to do without any hesitation. He'd chosen to live this way: Rowdy Salih wasn't obliged to do anything, he wasn't coerced, he wasn't faced with exigent circumstances. (40–41/43–44)

In the process of getting rowdy, humour functions as relief and satirical criticism. Ṣāliḥ is very methodical, as described in ch.7: after long hours of work, he goes to his shack, mixes half-litre of denatured alcohol with a bottle of Pepsi, drinks, and eats. In the first phase, he conveys his rage through insults; people laugh at his speech because of its indirect, yet effective, social criticism and the incongruity between its obscurity and its gravity:

> When he erupted and began shouting insults and curses, his booming voice brought people from nearby streets, people who came to double their pleasure by watching as well as listening to an interlude of creative, clever insults, which painted a surreal portrait that won bursts of frantic laughter. The first reason they were so funny was that they could only be partially understood because of all the foreign phrases in English, Italian, Turkish, and Nubian they included, and which were shouted at the tops of his lungs, his voice adding an air of gravity and dignity. It carried the seal and sign of greatness and the rhythms of gentlemen who, when they spoke, found people listened. He had that gentlemanly ability to mock with pitch and reproach with tone so he didn't even have to use words with clear social referents to get his point across. [. . .] Their ears knew for sure that they were hearing an aristocrat, but their eyes tried to convince them that it was only a beggar suffering from an alcoholic's delusions of grandeur. If, at a moment like that, he happened to call to a friend to ask for a friendly favor, and even though he sincerely wanted to put as much good feeling into his voice as he could when calling to his buddy so-and-so, when he shouted, "How's it going, Ace [yā fulān]," he couldn't help but making it sound like, "Hey, fuckface! [yā ḥayawān]"
>
> These kinds of discordances [al-mufāraqāt] came out one after the other, causing laughter to erupt all around him, but in hushed voices for fear of upsetting him.
> (36/38–39)

Ṣāliḥ's coarse words subvert the rules of linguistic courtesy, while his attacks subvert the social hierarchies. He is disrespectful but wants to be respected by those who are considered better than him in society. Nevertheless, getting rowdy is not totally liberating because the protagonist is afraid of being mocked. Therefore, in the second phase, he responds in a playful tone to those who might have ridiculed him:

> We all went off to see our affairs, promising to meet up again at night when Rowdy Salih would have entered phase two of his mirthful hellfire, when all that remained was his hilarious and constant laughter of the highest degree of purity, vigor, and brilliance. [. . .] It was true that – just like any drunk – he liked to tell himself he wasn't drunk even when he was totally smashed, but this was the only time he liked to make it obvious that he was drunk so he could take advantage of the fact that drunks have no shame. As soon as he heard the voice of someone he'd had stored in his mind, he'd fire back a flaming, spot-on retort, and he'd be the first to bust up with a carnivalesque laugh [ḍaḥkat mahrajān], filled with unbridled, gleeful, maniacal sounds, so that nobody could tell whether they were laughing at the brilliant snap or laughing at him for being so completely absorbed by his own laughter, at that horrible racket. (38/41)

In this oblique form of aggression, the protagonist targets some well-off customers who embody consumerism and social inequality. Humour serves to level off the social differences and restore humanity as a common value. Like the wise fools and court jesters, Ṣāliḥ takes advantage of his status to speak the truth with no fear of being punished. Moreover, his carnivalesque laughter smoothens the ridiculing effect and includes him in the collective funny game: as happens with self-mockery, laughing together reinforces the sense of belonging to a group.

Later in the novel, Ṣāliḥ enumerates the benefits of playing the fool: "You should know, by the way, that playing the fool [istilwāḥ]– no offense – is an art." (120/134) According to him, playing the fool is a defensive strategy from evil in society. Considered harmful, a clever fool (*al-lōḥ al-dhakī*, 120/135) gains the confidence of other people discovering their secrets and hidden nature; he can use this weapon to protect himself in hard times, either if he rebels or is submissive like the stereotypical Egyptian.

5.2.3 Intoxication and collective creativity

Developing as a series of gatherings at the hash den, this novel revives the anecdotic tradition about intoxication induced by wine or drugs, which may lead to a euphoric mood. The link between hashish and humour, well-established in classical and Mamluk literature (Marino 2016; Rosenthal 1971), is still alive in Egyptian popular culture. In his sociological study of the hashish sub-culture in the late 1980s, Hussein (1990: 35) finds that this drug is usually consumed in collective sessions (*il-'aʿdat*) in hash dens or private houses. These sessions are enjoyable because they are filled with jokelore and humorous conversations, while a certain degree of egalitarianism allows to overcome differences in age, class, and religion. What counts is the relaxed atmosphere, the smokers' generosity, and their experience in the consumption of hashish. These ideas are found also in Shalabī's literary representation:

> See, if a hash smoker can't get comfortable in a place, can't make the kinds of friendships that are necessary to maintain his dignity and sense of self in that strange, stoned world where one bong is shared between a philosopher and a man in the street, an intellectual and a thug, a ministry official and an office boy, a bey and a shoeshiner, his spirit will inevitably sink and be crushed. (24/27)

This novel re-creates this social practice and its subsequent containment by government institutions by focusing on the collective experience of humour. The members of the clique enjoy humour together: each of them contributes to crafting jokes and tries to emulate Ṣāliḥ's way of thinking and talking. Laughter is stimulated by hashish and alcohol, which are not deemed as deviant forms of addiction isolating the coterie from the rest of the society; on the contrary, they heighten their understanding and have a relief, if not resisting function. Moreover, humour and self-mockery have an affiliative function, reinforcing the group's identity and contrasting it to the external world. This section examines the discoursive techniques that convey the group's entertainment and self-representation.

Wordplay

The first episode revolves around Aḥmad ʿĀṣim, the film director, invited by the group of friends at the den as a new guest. Ḥakīm and Ṣāliḥ have the feeling that they have seen him before, but do not know exactly who he is. The coterie's deeper knowledge on this subject serves to play a verbal trick at Ṣāliḥ's expenses, who is confounded and looks like a fool.

When Aḥmad is introduced, Ḥakīm thinks that he is a tour guide (*murshid siyyāḥī*). Ṭalʿat corrects him by saying that he is a cinema guide (*murshid sīnamā'ī*). Ṣāliḥ picks only the last part of the sentence and, ignoring the full picture, understands the word *murshid* for its literal meaning: it indicates the usher in Downtown cinemas. So he addresses Aḥmad as a cinema usher, while the rest of the crew enjoys the show and bursts out laughing. Finally, Qamar tells him the truth by comparing the literal and metaphorical meaning of the word *murshid*: the cinema guide is not simply the usher, but the one who releases the movie and drives the audience to the cinema. The proper word for film director, *mukhrij*, reveals that the wordplay is also based on the assonance between the two terms.

The confusion of sound and meaning justifies Ṣāliḥ's unintentional misunderstanding, while the final remark dispels any possible tension:

> "Hey, buddy, get it through your head: Mr. Asim's a film director [mukhrij sīnamāʾī]. He's the one who makes the films, he doesn't show people to their seats!"
>
> Rowdy Salih's face flushed; bronze turning to the color of a child's face when he's made a terrible mistake. He pointed toward Tala al-Imbabi and stuttered, "No offense, sir. It's just he said you were a cinema guy. [murshid salmāʾī]"
>
> "I meant he guides the ideas, like an artist. [Murshid bi-l-fikr, yaʿnī! Bi-l-fann!] Now do you get it?"
>
> Rowdy Salih nodded and his apologetic expression meda it clear that he'd indeed understood.
>
> "Between me and you, there isn't a big difference. The guy who makes the film is the one who puts people in the seats, not anybody else," Mustafa Lami said under his breath.
>
> "You've got it right, Moos," said Ahmad Asim. (51/56)

Nonsense

The second episode is found in the same chapter. Ṭalʿat invites Ṣāliḥ to spend some days at his place, where he will be his guest and will not have to work. Before accepting, the waiter reverses the common ideas of work and laziness, since being an honoured guest would require him more efforts than doing his tough job. The humorous effect is conveyed by his convoluted arguments about social constraints such as playing the role of the guest and respectable man:

> [Salih] "No, but I'm going to be a guest. My whole job will just be to eat, drink, get high, get drunk, go to sleep, wake up, eat, drink, get high, get rowdy, go to bed. Honestly, now, what job could be harder than that? I'm not even sure I could last a whole day."
>
> The waves of a sea of laughter swirled and eddied. [. . .]
>
> "Well, if I want to do a good job of it, I'll be exhausted. For starters, I don't even know how to act. And secondly, a role like that needs practice. Practice I should've started on thirty or forty years ago so that when I get myself into a jam like this it'll be obvious that I really am the kind of respectable guest who deserves an invitation like this."
>
> (54–55/60–62)

The hashish waiter claims his right to be himself, without being forced to play a social role. A simple invitation turns into a complex meditation about freedom and social conventions, including a reference to acting as in the first example (§5.3.2). However, his philosophical aphorisms remain obscure to the rest of the coterie, who cannot discern if he is speaking seriously or in jest. Finally, Qamar puts an end to the nonsensical discussion, defined as a headache and rowdiness (55/62). Ṣāliḥ adds some unintelligible words, but admits he is unable to convey his thoughts.

Invective

The third episode revolves around the relationship between Ḥakīm, Ṣāliḥ, and Ṣābir. The two employees were raised in the run-down house that later became the hash den. With the excuse of saving them from a house on the verge of collapse, Ḥakīm took advantage of their poverty to buy their share of inheritance for little money. In this sharp-tongued dialogue, the three characters negotiate their self-representation and their opponent's image, discussing the limits between being gullible or the victim of misfortune, being smart or a ruthless opportunist. Their mutual invectives are smoothened by their sense of humour.

Taking part in this debate, the group of friends sarcastically labels Ḥakīm as a devil, a comparison he accepts with a certain degree of self-mockery. For example, when they ask him what would happen if the previous landlord of the building now hosting the hash den claimed his own rights, they are ridiculing his ruthlessness through exaggeration and dark humour:

> "But how'd you know the landlord's dead? Couldn't he just turn up here some day?" asked Qamar al-Mahruqi. [. . .]
>
> "You know who the landlord was? He was from our village and I used to come here to visit him when I was a kid. I heard all the news about this place as soon as it happened so I came and I brought cash. If he's a real man, he can climb out of his grave and come find me!"
>
> "Surely, he can't though," said Mustafa Lami. "He's scared of you."
>
> "Wait, you used to be young, Hakeem? You know, like, you were a baby once?" Faruq al-Gamal asked.
>
> "Hakeem's always been a devil just like he is now," Talat al-Imbabi interjected.
>
> (73–74/84–85)

All over the long dialogue which reveals the characters' past, humour is reinforced by the recurrent description of Ḥakīm's smile, which is antrophomized and compared to a prisoner who tries to escape. Similarly, the narrator inserts some picturesque details in the descriptive and biographical sequences, distorting the characters' features to elicit the reader's sympathy for their poor conditions, rather than ridicule them. The best example in this sense is the description of Ṣāliḥ's sisters, who are as ugly as monkeys (81/93). In the subsequent chapter, this animalesque comparison leads to a verbal skirmish at the hash den: the narrator describes Ḥakīm's monkey-esque mouth (107/121), then following the loose connections of idle talk, the conversation moves to the evolutionary theory, discussed in a simplistic way for the purpose of mockery:

> Out of the blue, Salih said that the scientists these days who claim that man originated as a primate were one hundred percent correct and if you wanted prof, you just had to look at Hakeem's face. Hakeem just looked at him and gave him a shit-eating wink, then he

> pointed backward and said, "God have mercy!" We all understood he was making a joke at the expense of Salih's fathers and sisters, who all looked like gorillas with the gift of speech. (108/121–122)

Ḥakīm's joke is extremely condensed, but the members of the clique laugh at it thanks to their shared knowledge. The reader, who has learned about Ṣāliḥ's sisters in the previous chapter, is involved in this game.

Colloquial poetry

While the previous examples illustrate how the members of the coterie contribute to crafting jokes, the fourth example portrays how they collectively compose a satirical poem criticizing the political scenario and praising Ṣāliḥ for his attitude toward society. The vernacular poet al-Jamal improvises the first three lines, then Ibrāhīm adds the fourth one, Qamar suggests a variation which is rejected, and Muṣṭafā adds the final line (177/198–199):[81]

Rowdy Salih went charging into history	صالح هيصة دخل التاريخ يجري!
On a horse without reins or saddle	راكب حصان من غير لجان ولا سرج!
He prods the joyful people in the castle	بيمد إيده يزغد المبسوطين في البرج...
And their cash drawers he swindles, */ And their saddlebag he swindles,*	ويخطف منهم الدُرج / ويخطف منهم الخُرج!
handing out what's in them to the disabled.	ويوزع اللى فيه ع العُرج!

The poem praises Ṣāliḥ for fighting injustice by comparing him to a folk hero or knight who steals from the rich and gives the poor. The legendary or historical setting serves to denounce the abuse of the contemporary ruling class. Arabic poetry has a long tradition of invective against the excesses of the rulers, both in the colloquial and Modern Standard Arabic; this poem achieves this effect through its short length, assonance, and fast rhythm. The use of Egyptian Colloquial Arabic in this composition reflects the preference for this linguistic variety in modern satirical poems and songs, while pointing at the broader development of vernacular poetry in Egyptian literature since the late 1950s (Radwan 2012). This poetic trend revived the richness of the vernacular language and folk heritage to express its socio-

81 Instead of reporting the whole dialogue containing the poem's collective creation, this quotation selects only the poem's lines to visualize the final version in the original Arabic and English translation. The original Arabic is not found in the English translation and is added here to give an idea of the poem's structure, length of the lines, and assonance.

political criticism and concern for the life of the ordinary people. Its main representatives (Ṣalāḥ Ǧāhīn, Sayyid Ḥiǧāb, Fu'ād Qā'ūd, and 'Abd al-Raḥmān al-Abnūdī) were known both for their nationalist poems and criticism, expressed with touching or satirical images. Shalabī, who studied this current in his poetry review, expresses his appreciation also in other passages of this novel.

5.2.4 Language and identity

As illustrated above, entertainment at the hash den relies on witty repartees, anecdotes, and jokes based on language manipulation. This section explores how the use of language in *The Hashish Waiter* generates a type of humour reflecting the group's identity; the interconnection of language and identity is expressed through metalinguistic considerations and mirrored in the linguistic hybridity of the narrating voice.

Ṣāliḥ is appreciated for his mastery at crafting new expressions that enter the vocabulary of the clique. Sometimes he plays with words even unintentionally, as in the example illustrated above (§5.2.2) in which the assonance *yā fulān / yā ḥayawān* risults in a mild insult when he gets rowdy. Sometimes he employs wordplay intentionally to make his message even more expressive. For instance, when he recalls that his brothers died of cholera, he remarks that Ḥakīm was tougher than the disease:

> '[. . .] My dad left home and ran away to Sudan, but my brothers were even bigger jerks than he was. They waited right up until I went to do my military service and then chol'ra wiped them all out. Well how come that son-of-a-whore chol'ra [il-kōrīrā bint l-'aḥba dī] didn't take Hakeem out? I'll tell you why: because he's just like chol'ra himself, only he's more choleric!' ['ashān howa nafsoh kōrīrā akrar minhā!] (75/86)

The Modern Standard Arabic word for this disease is *al-kūlīrā*, but Ṣāliḥ resorts to the colloquial pronunciation *il-kōrīrā*; therefore, the translator drops a vowel in the corresponding English word (chol'ra). Furthermore, the wordplay results from the alliteration of the sound 'r' and the manipulation of the Arabic grammar rule for the comparative grade of the adjective (*kōrīrā akrar minhā*). In the English translation, the wordplay is extended to the semantic level since choleric means hot-tempered and irritable. Finally, a coarse word, feminine in Arabic and masculine in English (*il-kōrīrā bint l-'aḥba dī* / that son-of-a-whore chol'ra), conveys the speaker's attitude.

The elative in the previous example may be classified as a neologism. Most of the neologisms in the novel are related to the sphere of rowdiness, defined as an action (*biye'mil hēṣa* = to do), a status (*fī l-hēṣa* = to be), and a change of status (*yelḥa' l-hēṣa* = getting rowdy). The latter is perceived by the coterie as a neologism with an obscure meaning, yet it is appropriated in their usage, as in this passage in which Qamar imitates Ṣāliḥ's laughter:

> My attention was drawn to a looming shadow on the ground and I looked up to see my good friend Qamar al-Mahruqi standing before me, laughing that clarion laugh almost exactly like Rowdy Salih, with its succession of interrupted *ahs* and ending with a drawn-out, blissful cry, which rested on individual letters to sound them out and give a joyful melody: *G. . .e. . .t I. . ..n!* Nobody actually knew what 'Get In!' meant. Rowdy Salih was the one who'd come up with it. Did it mean 'Get in on the rowdiness?' Or was it just a stand-in for 'Heads Up!'? Whatever it was, the thrill of imitating his laugh and shout took our minds off the search for its intended meaning. (98–99/112)

Another neologism, *al-ṣāliḥiyya al-hēṣiyya* (the *nisba* of the protagonist's name and nickname), describes the customers' devotion to the hashish waiter and their ability to imitate him.

Moreover, the circle of friends employs the jargon of hashish smokers. At the end of his sociological study, Hussain (1990: 66–70) provides a glossary of technical terms referring to the ritual of smoking and its effects. Many of them appear frequently in this novel: *il-mazāg* or *il-taḥshīsh* (getting high), *mazāgī* or *maṣṭūl* (stoned), *il-ta'mīra* (hashish), *il-nār* (coal), *il-ḥagar* (clay head, pottery bowl). As regards the specificity of this argot, Hussain (1990: 39) argues that there is no "special language or dialect" used by the larger community of hashish smokers, rather "certain words, expressions and symbols which are specific to a number of users in relation to their profession, ages, status, etc." Applying these considerations to the novel, a small group with a high level of interaction tends to craft its peculiar slang, which is almost unintelligible to the outsiders and reinforces their sense of belonging. This slang includes some expressions related to drugs, developed because of the illegality of this activity, and expressions related to the group's interactions, reflecting their view of the society. The clique adopts Ṣāliḥ's recurrent expressions, such as 'no offence' (*la-mu'ākhdha* or *min ghēr mu'ākhdha*), 'twenty-four carat' (*arba'a w-'ashrīn qīrāṭ*, meaning 'the best'), 'get out' (*inzil*).

The interplay of language and humour is also expressed by the narrator's precision at describing the way people talk and laugh.[82] In this way, laughter

82 The narrator also captures plurilinguism at the den: Ṣāliḥ has a good command of English because he received his education during the British mandate and the foreigners living in Cairo, like the Italian Matilde, speak Egyptian Arabic with an attractive accent. An interesting case is that of the shop window designer Ibrāhīm who cannot read and write but speaks the same language of his fellow intellectuals, mixing Egyptian Colloquial Arabic and eloquence.

becomes a language of its own, sometimes more meaningful than words. Each character has his own peculiar sense of humour: for example, al-Jamal laughs "with that Alexandrian lunacy of his" (59/66); Muṣṭafā clenches his molars and, when the laughter is particularly hearty, shakes his head in the same rhythm (50/54–55); Zakī rarely smiles; Ṭalʿat is sarcastic; Ibrāhīm is witty and has a playful sardonic spirit (62/70). In these examples, the parallelism between the two languages is explicit:

> We all shared in his [Ṣāliḥ's] raucous laughter, adding the words 'get out!' at the end, which was how he liked to cap things off; like a full stop at the end of a sentence. (144/161)

> Quick to smile, quick to grimace, as if with those two signals alone he [Aḥmad] could join in any conversation going on around him; he only used words when either smile or grimace required clarification. (50/54)

Within this rich linguistic landscape, Ṣāliḥ is praised as the living repository of Egyptian diction and wisdom, thus imitated to preserve a local sense of identity that might go lost. In his respect, Lagrange (2015) examines the interplay of language and identity in the novel on two levels. On the thematic level, Qamar is an assistant researcher for a dictionary project at the American University, corresponding to a real project undertaken in the 1970s which resulted in the publication of Badawi-Hinds's *A Dictionary of Egyptian Arabic* (1986). Qamar collects old expressions circulating in popular neighbourhoods, markets, coffeehouses, and hash dens (39/42 and 187/209). Ṣāliḥ is one of his sources, but one day he is denied access to the University building because he does not have any identity card. After a quarrel, Qamar leaves the project blaming it for foregrounding American neo-colonialism in Egypt:

> This whole dictionary's a conspiracy! The rowdy Americans are the ones behind all this rowdiness 'cause they're planning to invade and occupy Egypt! They want to know the meaning of every single word Egyptians say on the streets so they can know how to control us! I refuse to continue helping you all with this crime! I'd rather [do] with ten pounds from an honest job than all your rowdiness! (188/210)

This episode reflects the author's concern for the vernacular, which is able to convey the ordinary people's needs and cultural indigenousness but is silenced or appropriated by the cultural institutions. While the characters claim to preserve this language, it is appropriated and exposed by the novel itself.

On the stylistic level, the hybridization of the literary language does not reproduce but rather recreates orality, reinforcing the group's identity and the reader's involvement. Lagrange notes that the dialogues are in Egyptian Colloquial Arabic, whereas the narrative parts in Modern Standard Arabic accommodate lexical, idiomatic, stylistic, and less frequently syntactic elements of a very local vernacular

(Lagrange 2015: 583–585; Somekh 1993). As regards its functions, the narrator integrates the colloquial to cover some gaps in the standard language or for its richer connotations; moreover, the hybridity of multiple registers and the appreciation for the language of the margins is a linguistic transgression which parallels the transgression of hashish smoking. Lagrange remarks that "le narrateur concoctant son savant dosage de lexique du kif, de prise à partie dialectalisante du lecteur-type installant confiance et connivance, et de vocabulaire précieux dont le voisinage avec le haschich provoque le sourire" (Lagrange 2015: 572).[83] In other words, the coterie laughs thanks to its shared language and encyclopaedic knowledge; this jargon is made accessible to the readers who smile in recognition and complicity.

Thanks to his personality, language, and humour, the hashish waiter is a vessel of Egyptian folk culture, resulting in the possibility of laughing together and writing the biography of a whole generation. After examining the bright side of *hēṣa*, the next section looks at its dark side and metanarrative discourse.

5.3 What is *hēṣa*?

5.3.1 From pure fun to political satire

In the second part of the novel, the coterie experiences political disillusionment and increasing social pressure brought about by the political and cultural change in the Sadat era. Its collective humour turns into dark comedy and political satire, developing the second meaning of *hēṣa*, *i.e.* political chaos and disrupting the order for one's own interests. The three main targets of political satire are national politics after President Nasser, international politics, and the Egyptian-Israeli peace agreement.

As regards the national scenario, Ṣāliḥ has a different attitude toward the two post-revolutionary presidents: he jokes about Nasser, whereas he is sarcastic about Sadat. Recalling the iconic moment of the massive participation to Nasser's funeral, the hashish waiter mentions, half-seriously and half-ironically, the stereotypical Egyptian grandeur and devotion to the leaders:

> Salih smiled: "This last friend of ours, here, asked me, 'Why were Egyptians so sad when Nasser died?'" [. . .]

---

83 "With his clever mix of *kif*-related lexicon, dialect involving the ideal reader and infusing trust and connivance, refined vocabulary juxtaposed with the jargon of hashish, the narrator is able to get a smile."

> Salih laughed. "I told him that Egyptians are a great people. 'Great at what?' he says to me. So I tell him, 'At everything.' Great in age, great in rank, in intellect, understanding. 'What does that have to do with being sad about Nasser's death?' he asked. So I said to him, 'Think about it, Whitey! If we're great at everything, we're going to be great at grief as well! The thing is, we loved Nasser because Nasser, my western friend, was as great as the Egyptian people. He was on our scale. He was great in every way just like us. Egypt, we put our trust in him so he became Egypt and Egypt became him. The foreigner didn't know what to say to that. . . ha ha ha! Get out!" (144/160–161)

Since Ṣāliḥ talks with a foreign customer in a very relaxed atmosphere, interrupted by smiles and laughs, politics is not a serious topic of conversation but a way to understand Egyptian society from the perspective of the ordinary people. This episode reminds of a passage from *Time-Travels* analysed above (§4.3.2) in which Ibn Shalabī explains why Egyptians cry a river when their leaders die, with an implicit reference to Nasser. While *Time-Travels* frequently portrays Egyptian society and power relations through self-mockery and stereotypes, *The Hashish Waiter* employs occasionally this technique.[84]

Before and after mentioning Nasser, Ṣāliḥ openly criticizes Sadat for the war of attrition with Israel and the socio-economic liberalizations. In their political tirades, the hashish waiter and his friends attack those who profit from the deregulated economic situation, such as corrupted government employees, black market dealers, currency traders, and the so-called fat cats. These illegal activities are tolerated by the authorities, while the rest of the population suffers from the increase in prices, including that of hashish. Economic change is linked to authoritarianism and the international political and economic influence. Nasser's policies, instead, are not discussed thoroughly.

During Sadat's presidency, Egypt loses its leading role in the Arab world. The fight for hegemony is the second target of political satire, especially the interconnection of power and culture, which involves directly the aspiring intellectuals. The coterie criticizes those intellectuals who sell themselves to the new regimes, including their friend Ṭalʿat who gets a job in Saddam Hussein's Iraq.[85] Ṭalʿat's

84 See, e.g., this passage about Egyptian grandeur, pan-Arabism, and pharaonic heritage: [Ibrahim speaking] "[. . .] I mean, come on, guys, we're Egyptians. Sons of the pharaohs. If the leader of the Arab nation isn't Egyptian, it isn't just going to work. Trust me. Do they think being a leader is a game? It takes a man whose grandfather was Ramses the Second, and whose uncle was Khufu, for example, and whose mother was Hatshepsut, and whose cousin was Ahmose. You can call Ahmose Ahmad for all I care so long as it helps the Arabs." We enjoyed many pleasant evenings just like that one. (177–178/199)

85 Another member of the coterie, Muṣṭafā, takes the opposite path. He refuses to work for a Libyan newspaper called the *Revolution*. Its is ironically remarked that there is a *Revolution* newspaper in every country, so the word itself has lost its meaning (174/195 and 176/197).

ambition is a light topic of conversation, until he becomes the grotesque version of the emerging political leaders. The first quotation, in which the narrator and Ibrāhīm try to understand why Ṭalʿat and Ṣāliḥ's had a fight, employs political vocabulary to create a playful tone, whereas the second quotation explains what happened through the concept of rowdiness, meaning chaos:

> "Maybe. . . But I know Talat. He's got big ambitions, and people who've got big ambitions are fast talkers. I bet you he's planning to become *a minister* some day."
>
> "No, no, Talat al-Imbabi would never settle for anything less than *the presidency* of a large country like the Soviet Union or something."
>
> We giggled hysterically. Ibrahim said that perhaps that was the source of the disagreement: Talat was worried that Rowdy Salih would try to take *the presidency* away from him." (149/166, emphasis added)

> [Salih] "I'm getting there. Talat's finished *getting rowdy* here about now and he wants to *get in on the rowdiness* in Iraq. Wasn't Mr. Talat – no offense – a member of that group called the 'Vanguard'? Saddam's guys picked some of those guys to go work for Saddam. Journalists, broadcasters, professors, and people no one cares what it is they do so long as they sing the praises of Saddam and get down with his *rowdiness*.
> (167/187–188, emphasis added)

The international and national political scenarios are brought together by Sadat's visit to Jerusalem in 1977. After being scattered, the friends meet again at the den to watch the live broadcast because only good company and hashish can make the news bearable. At the beginning, they cannot believe what they see and explain the tragic situation with the stereotypical Egyptian love for comedy: "We were lulled into a sedate calm, convinced that President Sadat was merely trying to pull off the ultimate Egyptian joke" (215/240). When they realize the seriousness of the issue, they feel the volcano of rage burning inside them and the rest of the population but are metaphorically paralyzed by the calming effects of hashish. Ṣāliḥ is the only one who reacts condemning Sadat and his delegation of journalists:

> Rowdy Salih pointed at some of the famous journalists there with him and shouted, laughing, but nothing like his usual happy, unadulterated, unbridled laughter; this laughter seemed more like the rhythms of a volcanic, violent anxiety: "Ha ha ha! Look! He took all the rowdies with him! Every last one of them's rowdy. Getting rowdy. 'Cause what they want is to get in on the rowdiness and they're going to pay the price of admission with our children's blood. Come on, you bums, you sons of bitches! You've been screwing us for twenty-five years talking about the Revolution, liberating our land, the Crisis in Palestine. Ha ha ha! Get in! They think we're going to buy it. Get in! How are we supposed to believe all that war that just happened? Get in! People's kid died for what? For nothing! Just so a few chair-crazies get to play musical chairs? Ha ha ha! Get in!" (216/240)

While the wise fool is usually tolerated because he speaks in jest, Ṣāliḥ is harshly beaten and made disappear. Even though he is considered a lunatic, he is silenced. At the end of the novel, the narrator summarizes the events of the following years, such as the Camp David agreement (1978), the peace treaty (1979), Sadat's assassination (1981), the break-up of the Soviet Union, and the Gulf War (1990–1991), through the novel's key concept: "Rowdiness reached the peak of absurdity." (241/269)

5.3.2 From comedy theatre to farce

A similar development is found in the appropriation of popular culture for comic purposes in the crew's interaction and dramatic performance. Besides being among the clique's interests, theatre and cinema are used to describe the interactions at the den on the metanarrative level. Some of the guests sit on the ground level, while others sit on the top of a hill made of rubble, interacting respectively as the actors on the stage and the audience, exchanging jabs and banters in a cheerful atmosphere (21/24). When Ṣāliḥ gets rowdy, he takes parts in this game, usually subverting the roles of actors and audience (38/41).

The second type of performance consists in the members of the coterie imitating the hashish waiter for his Egyptian authenticity and longing for freedom. It is initially liberating, but later the doubles multiply and acquire an artificial nature. Even Ḥayāt, the only female regular, imitates him:

> None of the members of our circle had any problem acknowledging that there was something of Rowdy Salih about them anymore. At first, we teased one another when somebody did something that we realized – whether right then or only later – was a distorted imitation [ṣūra mamsūkha] of Rowdy Salih. It got us laughing no matter how distorted an imitation it was. Then we began cheering on the people who were the most proficiently Rowdy Salih-ish like Qamar al-Mahruqi and Talat al-Imbabi, who were the real pioneers. Even Hayat al-Barri had become one of the strongest devotees in the cult of Rowdy Salih with a passion equal to that of her naïve youthful exuberance for Marxist thought. [. . .]
>
> She, too, had become Rowdy Salih-ish, inside and out, repeating his phrases passionately and affectionately, she copied his free-flying, stuttering laughter and she called him by his name without any formality at all. (202/226)

In this passage, the distorted imitation is still enjoyable. The narrator exposes the mechanisms of reproduction through the neologism 'Rowdy Salih-ish' (*al-ṣāliḥiyya al-hēṣiyya*) and some rhetorical figures of sound.[86] His irony targets the confusion between reality and reproduction, since Zakī the actor is so talented that the copy is more amusing than the original. When Ḥayāt, who was attracted by Ṣāliḥ, marries Zakī, the narrator comments that she "had actually gone and married Rowdy Salih!" (214/238–239)

Zakī is the linking chain between this spontaneous performance and the professional one made by comedy actors who draw inspiration from popular culture. When Ḥayāt goes to the theatre to watch *Madrasat al-mushāghibīn* (The School for Troublemakers), a successful play which launched the career of many Egyptian comedy stars,[87] she notices their appropriation of popular humour, especially the stock character of the simpleton:

> They strolled around backstage, saying hello to Adel Imam, Saeed Sal[i]h, Younis Shalaby, Ahmad Zaki, Suhair al-Babili, Hassan Mustafa, and Hadi al-Gayyar. [. . .] she discovered something very peculiar, something she'd never noticed before: Saeed Salih and Adel Imam – in particular – had a certain air about them, which, granted, was only fleeting, but was clearly modelled on Rowdy Salih, whom she was pleased to have got to know very well. So it wasn't only Qamar al-Mahruqi who'd been influenced by Rowdy Salih's personality. As a matter of fact, she simply couldn't tell whether it was Rowdy Salih himself who was this new, widespread, highly influential trend that had an entire generation in its throes or whether it was the people he'd influenced who'd gone out and created this trend, especially as every single comedian in the country played the part of the idiot, or the fool, or the guy who acts an idiotic fool [shakhṣiyyat al-ʿabīṭ aw al-mustaʿbiṭ aw alladhī biysūʾ ʿalā al-habāla] so that he can get out of following any rules. They talked like Rowdy Salih, repeated some of his funny expressions, they thought like him when they were up on stage. There was no doubting that they'd all gone and smoked hash at Rowdy Salih's, but all they'd taken from him was an attitude and some cutting remarks, which they dropped into serious contexts to cause hilarious dissonances, but to Hayat, Rowdy Salih the man was himself a great deal more valuable than that when looked from a certain angle. (186/207–208)

Ḥayāt's opinion, and indirectly that of the implied author, is not totally negative: comedy absorbs popular culture to encourage the audience's identification and voice what cannot be said in real life. Only when its source of inspiration in

---

86 The rhetorical figures of sound in this passage are: *qalb*^{an} *wa-qālab*^{an}, an idiom meaning 'inside and out, with heart and soul'; *taḍḥak*^{u} *ḍaḥkatahu al-munqaṭiʿa al-munṭaliqat l-nabra*, with the alliteration of 'q' and 'ṭ'.

87 *Madrasat al-mushāghibīn* (1973) was written by ʿAlī Sālim, produced by Samīr Khafājī (in this novel, Khafāja, b. 1930), and performed by the Troupe Artists United (*firqat al-fannānīn al-muttaḥidīn*). It starred ʿĀdil Imām, Saʿīd Ṣāliḥ (1938–2014), and Aḥmad Zakī.

real life is silenced, comedy becomes a farce. When Zakī becomes a star, he turns the hashish waiter into the character of a film and during the shooting the narrator is confused by this mediated performance:

> Rowdy Salih was standing right there in the flesh. [. . .]
>
> I pushed through the crowd; I wanted to throw myself in Rowdy Salih's arms. But then I was stopped by huge hands right at the moment when the truth hit me. Now that I was closer, I could see that the Rowdy Salih standing before me was actually Zaki Hamid the actor filming a scene for a movie. [. . .]
>
> His voice – the same cherished, familiar voice – began to unfurl with threats of looming disaster like Tiresias in a Greek tragedy: "God made the world a rowdy place and then filled it with rowdy people. Everybody here's rowdy. They're all rowdy 'cause all they want to do is get rowdy and they either get to or they don't. And everybody here's rundown. But they're all run-down in their own way. And me, I'm the king of the run-down 'cause I'm run-down in every which way." (242–243/260–261)

The mechanical nature of the double invites to reflect on one's own condition: in this case, the evolution of the comic character embodies the loss of freedom. As Lynx Qualey (2011c) notes in her review, "Salih becomes just an echo of himself, a part played by an actor representing Salih on TV. There is no more freedom, or even proper escape – just the televised illusion of freedom."

5.4 Conclusion: hashish as a metaphor

The Hashish Waiter is constructed on the parallelism between humour and hashish. Both of them are part of the Egyptian culture and offer an alternative form of sociability. Even though they are accessible to several types of people in the city, this novel focuses on a specific neighbourhood and a coterie of aspiring intellectuals. As illustrated in the first section of this chapter, space and characters are intertwined due to their liminal nature: they are marginal but take part in all the major national events; they have a very local identity but are the quintessence of the nation; they practice some semi-legal activities which are largely tolerated but still controlled by the authorities through crackdown or censorship. Moreover, humour and hashish have similar effects in this literary representation since they work as a social glue within the community, provide some relief from everyday life and social constraints, and sometimes represent a form of resistance. Being outside officialdom and part of popular culture, they allow a temporary subversion in which producers/consumers can speak freely.

This ability to speak the truth with an irreverent language is attributed to the hashish waiter Ṣāliḥ, who is described as a wise fool and repository of popular culture in the second section. He stimulates the group of friends to craft they own way of joking through collective creativity, the euphoric mood induced by intoxication, and the juxtaposition of refined language and the smoker's jargon. The third section follows the evolution of humour and its artistic appropriation according to the changes in the political scenario. In this respect, humour and hashish are metaphors to measure the degree of freedom in the Egyptian society.

In *The Hashish Waiter*, humour is performed mainly through the dialogues. At the beginning of the novel, the group exchanges some witty repartees that turn into dark ironies and satirical attacks because of their political disillusionment. Similarly, there is an evolution of the humour-related images, such as the carnival describing the underworld's vitality, stereotypes mocking the notion of authentic Egyptianness, and the doubles within the coterie all imitating Ṣāliḥ (Ṭalʿat / Qamar, Ṭalʿat / Muṣṭafā, Qamar /Ḥayāt). Imitation is amusing because it gives a distorted image of the original, until it becomes a sterile caricature. Staging the interplay of popular culture and comedy theatre and cinema, *The Hashish Waiter* is a humorous novel about how comedy circulates and is crafted in an artistic way.

The next chapter examines another aspiring intellectual who negotiates his identity within his marginal community through self-mockery. Employing construction work as a metaphor, Abū Julayyil explores internal migration, completing the journey from the countryside to the city and what is in-between.

6 Laughing together at migration

> When asked about it, he would laugh and say: "Wells are like udders. They fill up and they dry up, each at its own time." Their mouths gaped in astonishment. Had he really explored the whole desert and knew which wells were full and which were empty? Had he lived long enough to learn all this?
>
> When Musallam went off this time, he didn't come back. The sandstorm was a swirl of dust. He disappeared from in front of his tent. They searched everywhere and asked every traveler they saw. Accounts of his disappearance varied, as did accounts of his life.
>
> M. al-Tahawy, *The Tent*, 1998: 87

A Dog with No Tail by Ḥamdī Abū Julayyil is a tale of internal migration which portrays two distant worlds coexisting within the same country and undergoing big change. It follows the story of a young Bedouin who leaves his village in Fayyūm to go to Cairo, where he works as a labourer with other construction workers hailing from the same region.[88] The protagonist, Ḥamdī, tells in the first person several episodes of his migration tale over the 1980s and 1990s, while reconstructing the story of his family which had abandoned nomadic life and settled down. He also leafs through the memories of his childhood and college years, tells his co-workers' adventures, and confesses his lack of success with women. In his Cairene exile, he dreams of becoming a successful writer: he publishes some short stories on newspapers and magazines and attempts to write a novel.

Ḥamdī's displacement resembles the author's own experience, which allows him to depict both communities with realistic details from the perspective of an insider. Nevertheless, the illusion of reality is broken through some experimental writing techniques, such as metafiction, intertextuality, multiple narrations, and repetitions. In fact, the novel does not follow a linear plot but juxtaposes several anecdotes kept together by the same narrating voice and by reappearing characters. In the opening chapter, this fragmentation is illustrated by the narrator saying that he sees his life as files stored in his head, unfolding one by one or simultaneously. The book has a circular structure, as it opens and closes with Ḥamdī thinking about his writing projects in his room: in the opening scene, he is working on a novel, one of his unfinished writing attempts; in the last chapter, he moves into an apartment where he gets a room of his own, which might give him a chance to finish his novel(s). These and other episodes portray the narrator in the act of writing, making *A Dog with No Tail* a novel about writing a novel. Moreover, these writing techniques based on ambiguity help exposing the contradictions of society and life.

88 The title of the original Arabic is *al-Fāʿil*, which literally means 'the labourer'.

https://doi.org/10.1515/9783110725414-007

This fictional biography does not portray the subject's evolution but follows the association of ideas and memories. In the novel's last pages, the narrator tells an anecdote about his grandfather Awla and then comments: "But I've stumbled. Enthusiasm drives me on, and I stumble. I can't find the words, and when I do they seem heavy, awkward, and somber. I like to write with humor. I like to joke, but I always find I've been too serious." (149/158) This metanarrative commentary summarizes the overall narrative tone, combining seriousness and jest and revealing the incongruity even in serious passages. Bearing in mind the interplay of writing and identity in *A Dog with No Tail*, this passage also depicts the narrator's attitude toward reality: it is an invitation to take life not too seriously. Placed in a key position, this commentary invites to explore humour in this work.

This chapter examines how humor is intertwined with the two main narrative threads underpinning this migration novel, *i.e.* rural-urban work migration and Bedouin identity. Unlike in ch. 3–4, no specific literary antecedents are mentioned, but the novel's peculiar way of addressing these themes emerges against the background of the literary representation of displacement in contemporary Egyptian fiction. Arguing that displacement triggers the protagonist's quest for identity, the first and the second sections reconstruct his trajectory in the city and the village respectively, remarking his double alienation. Then, both sections illustrate how the narrator fills these marginal communities with eccentric characters, almost outcasts. These anecdotes about his co-workers and ancestors exploit some recurrent humour-generating techniques and convey the narrator's self-mocking attitude. In doing so, migration and identity negotiation are brought from the individual to the collective dimension. The third section further investigates the collective experience of humour in other marginal communities in which Ḥamdī seeks a new sense of belonging (at college and in prison), wondering if it is a survival strategy to face migration.

Before starting the analysis, it is worth introducing the author's first novel, *Thieves in Retirement*, which also crafts some liminal identities through the literary representation of urban change, clash of different linguistic registers, and sarcasm. Without providing a comparison of the two works, some stylistic remarks about *Thieves in Retirement* might enrich the discussion of humour in *A Dog with No Tale.*

Thieves in retirement

Set in the informal neighbourhood of Manshiyyat Nāṣir, where the author himself lived, the novel gravitates around Abū Jamāl's apartment building where his family and some tenants live. Among them is the anonymous first-person narrator, a Bedouin who sometimes works in construction; he keeps a close eye on his neighbours for fear that they might unite against him. As Booth (2006), El Sadda (2012), and Mehrez (2010a) note, all residents are migrants from Upper Egypt who adjust to the neighbourhood's liminal nature, bringing their countryside's lifestyle inside the unplanned urban fringes.

The novel has received some critical attention for the following aspects: the representation of marginal urban space and Bedouin identity, which are also at the core of *A Dog with No Tail*; the construction of complex gendered identities, which is less central in the second novel, despite an interest for masculinity and gender relations; linguistic variation and bitter satire as stylistic features. As regards spatial representation, Abū Jamāl's life is paralleled with that of the neighbourhood, established by President Nasser in the Sixties to host the factory workers in the southern industrial area of Ḥulwān in Greater Cairo. As a worker, Abū Jamāl embodied the revolutionary project, until he was forced to retire early because of privatization. The parody of the revolutionary discourse is a first line of satire in this novel. Within this context, social conflicts move inside the apartment's building and the family: the father decides who stays and who leaves, manages a network of petty crimes, and exerts his patriarchal authority over his sons. In particular, he fights with Jamāl, his bully eldest son, over how to deal with the queer behaviour of the youngest son, Sayf.

As El Sadda (2012: 196) remarks, "[t]he narrator's depiction of the inhabitants of the building is satirical, teasing out the incongruities, the affectations, and the ridiculous in various situations." Nevertheless, in an interview mentioned by El Sadda (2012: 196), the author refuses the role of *iṣlāḥī lādhiʿ* (sharp-tongued reformist), as he does not seek social reform but exposing contradictions in all their objectivity. This satirical posture also targets the conventions of realist fiction and the official discourse about the represented communities, as clarified by Booth:

> Equally, the juxtaposition of different levels of language collapses official narratives into vernacular ones. Told in a voice of ironic detachment yet also of affection, the novel explodes narrative conventions as the narrator chooses at various points whether to "act" as a character within the novel or to take the easier path of remaining at a circumspect narratorial distance, thereby satirizing the conventions of realist fiction that have governed fictional representation in Arabic literature until very recently. There is much humor in this novel, but much darkness as well; (Booth 2006: xv–xvi)

This bitter humour exploits the juxtaposition of different registers: an amalgam of different linguistic variaties (Modern Standard Arabic, Egyptian Colloquial Arabic, and Bedouin dialect), coarse words juxtaposed to refined literary language and echoes of the Nasserist ideology, double meanings, and puns.[89] Comparing Abū Julayyil's two novels, Badawī (2008) points out the aggressive dimension of the ludicrous in *Thieves in Retirement*, whose satire (*sukhriyya*) reveals the gaps or paradoxes (*mufāraqāt*) through the characters' fear and rage. *A Dog with No Tail*, instead, makes these gaps respond to a playful logic. These considerations about humour-related phenomena (satire and dark humour) and humour-generating techniques (ironic detachment, parody, and linguistic variation) are useful for the analysis of *A Dog with No Tail.*

6.1 The labourers

6.1.1 Constructing identity

A Dog with No Tail enriches a traditional motif in Egyptian literature, *i.e.* rural-urban migration, since Ḥamdī migrates from the Bedouin settlement to Cairo to find a job. As in other contemporary migration novels, the protagonist's displacement triggers a process of self-discovery. Despite the novel's fragmentation, this section reconstructs the protagonist's migratory trajectory in chronological order providing a double reading of episodes related to construction work. As Lindsey (2010b) points out in her review, *A Dog with No Tail* is "a clever and complex meditation on the shaky edifice that is identity and the 'construction work' that is writing".

Ḥamdī travels to Cairo for the first time at the end of middle school. He joins some fellow villagers and works for two weeks to earn enough money to buy a bike. For him and the village boys, migration is a rite of passage:

> Over the course of successive generations, the young men of our village have, without exception, made their way to Shubra. More than mere job hunting, it's something like a local tradition, a first step that every man must take at the start of his life: independence, self-reliance, and returning to the village with a few hard-earned pennies. (10–11/17)

Over the following years, Ḥamdī is a commuting worker (*ʿāmil tarāḥīl*) who spends a couple of weeks in Cairo, working for the contractor *miʿallim* Bakr, and then returns to the village or to college in Banī Suwayf. After a period of work in Libya (*riḥlat ʿamal*), he settles in Cairo working for *miʿallim* Maṭar in Shubrā. Many episodes of the novel depict the routine of construction work (*al-fāʿil* or *al-miʿmār*), which consists in tearing down tottering buildings, renovating or expanding them, digging the foundations, preparing the material for

89 Hayam Abdou Mohamed (2015) examines the translation strategies of the Spanish version, especially how to render Egyptian Colloquial Arabic, idioms, slang, and coarse words.

craftsmen, lugging sacks of cement, and removing the rubble. This job requires physical strength and endurance but does not get any social recognition. Thus, it shapes a self-contained marginal urban underworld.

On a first level, these episodes portray with technical details and jargon the precarious living and working conditions of urban migrants: they are hired on a daily basis by the contractors or the apartment's owners for private jobs; they sleep in the buildings they are renovating or in the contractor's pickup, waking up early to reach the construction sites. They are *anfār*, a term originally used in the military context, which was later applied to daily labourers in agriculture and construction. On another level, these episodes work as a metaphor for the protagonist's quest for identity. In this passage Ḥamdī introduces himself simultaneously as a laborer and aspiring writer:

> I was working for a demolition contractor. No, not demolition: demolition and construction.
>
> He only worked with houses on the verge of collapse. The places sealed up with red wax, directives issued to tear them down: these were his bread and butter. Peeling back the wax with a delicacy befitting its official status he would slip into the house with his men: one team to dig out the foundations and another to smash the walls. A few days later and the miracle is complete: the decaying pile has become a lofty, freshly painted tower. Most of the houses in Shubra and the surrounding neighborhoods owed their continued existence to him. [. . .]
>
> In 1992, as the earthquake struck Cairo, I was digging at the bottom of a foundation trench beneath a three-story house, but everyone, even the closest to me, were left in no doubt that I was first and foremost a journalist. The stories I'd had published were enlisted to support my claims that I was, in fact, an editor for the *al-Ahrar* newspaper, which, I reckoned, was just about credible for someone in my position.
>
> Sometimes I'd say I was continuing my studies. If anyone asked what I was studying I'd panic. Then I learned of something called The Institute of Literary Criticism, and struck by the grandeur of the name I started claiming that I studied there. All the while I was hunting for a job, any job: reputable employment, starting at eight in the morning and finishing at two in the afternoon. (2–3/8–9)

Construction work acquires a symbolic meaning since it is described with life-related images (miracle, existence). In a city with no clear official urban planning, buildings on the verge of collapse are demolished and rebuilt, hence brought back to life. Construction workers redesign Cairo's geography, yet informally, almost illegally.[90] While families of residents benefit from their work, they do not have a stable dwelling of their own and their family is composed of

90 Some sentences from the excerpt quoted above are echoed in ch.30, where the narrator describes how construction crews work. In particular, the phrase "Peeling back the wax with a delicacy befitting its official status" is repeated on p. 131/138. It refers to the semi-legal way of doing renovation jobs.

their co-workers. This partial detachment from society is exemplified by Ḥamdī digging the foundations of a building during Cairo's 1992 earthquake. From inside the pitch, he does not feel the earth shacking and does not realize what is going on around him. His work protects him from danger but at the same time isolates him from other people, providing him with an unusual perspective on this event.

Like the buildings, the protagonist undergoes a process of demolition and construction: he is a Bedouin, whose ancestors were accustomed to nomadic life, who tries to settle down in the city; he is a labourer who wants to be considered as a writer. Therefore, he shows off his publications on newspapers and magazines when he is on the construction sites. To sum up, Ḥamdī's identity is constructed through negation. Moving between the city and the village, he experiences a double alienation and links space with his writing possibilities, as illustrated in the next section.

6.1.2 The city: working sites and accommodation

In her review, Lindsey (2010a) describes *A Dog with No Tail* as "another chronicle of the author's double alienation – as a member of a community still at odds with the state, and as a new urban migrant." Looking at Ḥamdī's alienation in the city, Cairo's map is restricted within the boundaries of working sites, such as Aḥmad Ḥilmī Square, a transit area where laborers are hired, or Salīm's café in Shubrā where the protagonist and his co-workers meet the contractor *mi'allim* Maṭar. Shubrā is described as a good work location, in comparison to the narrator's experience in the neighbourhood of Fayṣal, because the labourers meet nice residents who offer them food and tea: "Shubra is better by far; Shubra is life. There we work with people, in the midst of stable, happy families. Shubra is work and play." (119/127)

These buildings, almost an enclosed world, are opposed to an apartment building in Heliopolis (*Miṣr al-jadīda*) where a fellow villager and friend nicknamed the Doctor (*al-duktūr*) works as doorkeeper. In the chapter entitled 'A Visit' (*Ziyāra*), the narrator describes the building's well-off unscrupulous residents, exposing their hidden habits and revealing how they achieved their high social standing. They cohabit with an underworld of prostitution managed by drivers and doorkeepers, which they are physically and morally close to.

This place reminds of Abū Jamāl's building in *Thieves in Retirement*, since they both rely on the "house narrative" for spatial representation, with characters and actions revolving around a single building (Booth 2011). Mehrez (2010a: 144–147) includes *Thieves in Retirement* among contemporary Egyptian novels employing the apartment building (*ʿimāra*) as a literary metaphor for the whole city of Cairo and its social fabric. Replacing the metaphor of the alley (*ḥāra*), it renders recent urban change, spatial fragmentation, and rupture of social relations. Applying the house narrative to *Thieves in Retirement*, Booth (2006) argues that the proximity of characters of different origins and tempers in an enclosed place questions the naturalness of social coexistence (starting from the family itself) and the possibility of communication. Moreover, these living conditions generate a feeling of "crowded alienation", since the self is surrounded by many people but lacks any sense of belonging. This feeling applies to Ḥamdī's first accommodation in Cairo in *A Dog with No Tail*.

At the beginning of the novel, he and some co-workers rent a small room in a building in ʿAyn Shams owned by Abū ʿAntar. Considered as a temporary accommodation, this room is furnished only with some basic equipment: "it wasn't a permanent home. It was a limbo, a station platform that would either take us on to the life we dreamed of in the capital or return to the village." (129/137). The room is so crowded that it does not provide a suitable environment for Ḥamdī to write but just some space to display his books. This haphazard accommodation affects the narrator's writing possibilities: as crowded as it is, this room does not provide Ḥamdī enough space to write, hence meditations are rendered with fragmentation and repetitions.

These precarious living conditions resemble those of crowded marginal *ʿashwāʾiyyāt, i.e.* informal settlements or shantytowns that have sprouted in Cairo since the late 1970s and early 1980s to house new waves of rural migrants and the urban poor. I shall adopt El Sadda's definition of *ʿashwāʾiyyāt* as "liminal space [s], on the outskirts of the city but still part of it, in fact encroaching on its center" (El Sadda 2012: 200). Elements of originally separated spaces, such as the countryside and the city, merge in a continuum in these liminal spaces inhabited by marginalized communities emerging from the fragmentation of the national state into non-national spaces. Their haphazard nature finds a literary representation in the characters' complex identity (including gender identity) and experimental narrative techniques.[91]

As mentioned before, *Thieves in Retirement* is set in one of these informal neighbourhoods, Manshiyyat Nāṣir. In her reading of the novel, Heshmat (2004: 137–175) describes this setting as a ghettoized space that is almost isolated from the rest of the city and functions according to a counter value system; Abū Julayyil describes this world through satire, but does not judge it on moral grounds.

91 For a review of the studies about *ʿashwāʾiyyāt* and the connection between urban change and its literary representation, see: Dozio 2018: 77–82.

Mehrez, instead, insists on the homology between space, residents, and non-regulated policies. The novel is a "bitterly humorous testimony" from the underworld of the urban poor, which counters the official discourse about this space and its community (Mehrez 2010a: 152–160). While this apartment building is in the city's outskirts, the shared room in *A Dog with No Tail* is almost in a central area. This is not an open contradiction since informal housing and haphazard living conditions are also found in neglected central or semi-central neighbourhoods. Similarly, the Maʿrūf quarter in Shalabī's *The Hashish Waiter* (§5.1.1) exemplifies the multiplication of centres and peripheries.

The link between space and writing is made explicit in the description of Ḥamdī's second accommodation. At the end of the novel, he moves with some co-workers into a full apartment, in a dilapidated house they are rebuilding in Shubrā. Once again, it is pure coincidence that determines where they live and it is not clear how long they will stay there. The protagonist finds a box full of books, including the biography of an unnamed foreign writer who did manual jobs before winning the Nobel Prize, and gets a room of his own that might provide space and stability needed to write:

> This room was mine. When they saw the desk they acknowledged there could be no debate. I was on the lookout for an appropriate setting in which to write a novel. I wrote in the room, the one in Ain Shams, squatting on a box of books and scribbling anything that came to mind, but it seemed to me that a novel needed something else: a desk; wood and iron. A desk, at any rate, and a bed nearby. The desk for writing and the bed for pondering the results. The room promised a resounding beginning.
>
> What am I talking about? What novel? Enough of these questions. They only lead to frustration (147/155)

This description is found at the end of the novel, leaving many possibilities open: this might be the right opportunity for the protagonist to become a writer; otherwise, it might be just one of the many beginnings of his story. As has been seen, the book has a circular structure, since it opens and closes with the narrator in his room thinking about his writing projects, that is what he wants to accomplish with his migration trajectory.

6.1.3 Tales of labour migration

While reconstructing his own migratory experience, the narrator portrays some odd characters, almost outcasts, who gravitate around the urban underworld of construction workers. As Temlali (2008) puts it in his review, "[l]e roman de Hamdi Abou Golayel est une description décapante de l'univers sous-terrain du «faîl». Il tire des portraits touchants de ces paysans ou bédouins déracinés, pour qui la survie parmi les citadins, est une question de débrouille et, surtout, de capacité d'ironie."[92] This section examines three characters who function as doubles of the narrator, focusing on the narrative and linguistic strategies that make them humorous.

Three Ḥamdīs

In ch.4, the narrator describes a craftsman who is lazy and messy at doing his job. His defects make it a fun to work with him: "It was a pleasure to work with him, something between a holiday and a comedy." (21/27) What draws the narrator's attention toward his co-worker is his name, Ḥamdī, which reminds him of two funny characters from his village: Ḥamdī *muṭarraf* (Hung Hamdi) and Ḥamdī *al-ʿabīṭ* (Hamdi the Fool). In this short chapter, almost a self-enclosed anecdote, the narrator sketches out their odd behaviour to introduce Ḥamdī the craftsman as a funny character:

> The first thing that drew me to him was his name. A strange name; obscure and unintelligible. I once expressed how I felt about it in a short story. It wasn't Hamad or Haamed or Hamid, but Hamdi. You didn't know whether it referred to you or the person you were talking to. Most of the Hamdis I've known have either been crackpots or idiots of some kind. Hamdi our neighbor in the village was a freak. He had a huge penis. They said he could rest its tip on the ground when he pissed. Now, it's a matter of common knowledge that the well-endowed are prone to mental instability. It's not so clear, however, if this claim is motivated by spite or revenge or possibly a desire to affirm that a shortness of appendage (a problem that has haunted men down the ages) is in fact a natural state, or whether the long-dongs really are insane or at least soft in the head. The other Hamdi I knew from primary and secondary school was definitely crazy. He was called Hamdi the Fool and used to admit it of himself. This one time he stopped me on the street, put his hand on my shoulder and, with spittle flecking my face, declared, "Hamdi the Fool says to you, 'Your mother's cunt.'"
>
> He terrified me. This was in the fifties. He would dribble in his beard and ride around on a stalk of wheat or a sunflower like it was a car, honking his horn, swerving, and hitting the brakes to save people and passing sheep.
>
> At first, when I'd see Hamdi Shadid at the café I'd think of Hung Hamdi and Hamdi the Fool and make a quick comparison. He was closer to Hamdi the Fool in shape: his bulk, his stammer, and his unkempt beard. It wasn't long or short, just the beard of someone who wasn't doing so well. But his reserve and contentment with his lot reminded me of Hung Hamdi. (22–23/28–29)

---

92 "Abou Golayel's novel is a caustic description of the underworld of construction workers. It offers some touching portraits of these displaced villagers or Bedouin for whom surviving among the urban dwellers is a matter of resourfulness and, above all, of being ironic."

To reinforce the comic potential of the urban character, the narrator establishes a parallelism with eccentric individuals from the countryside. They are outcasts because of their crazy (*majnūn*) and idiotic (*maʿtūh*) behaviour: Hung Hamdi is indirectly associated with madness through gossip, while Hamdi the Fool is officially labelled as the village fool, a status that he internalizes by adopting this nickname to talk about himself. Their portrait reproduces the village's gossip: "Hamdi our neighbor in the village was [known to be] a freak" (*yashtahiru bi-annahu*); "They said" (*qīla innahu*); and "Now, it's a matter of common knowledge that" (*wa-maʿrūf ṭabʿan anna*). At the same time, this kind of discourse is mocked through a higher register in the aside exposing the villagers' concern about their masculinity. The characters' weird behaviour goes hand in hand with their odd physical appearance: the unkempt beard and the huge penis, which is a grotesque element. Their physical and behavioural traits merge into Ḥamdī the craftsman's final description. Furthermore, the light tone of this anecdote is reinforced by the sexual references to Hung Hamdi's body and Hamdi the Fool's vulgar language.

These funny anecdotes connected to the name Ḥamdī are also a self-mocking strategy: the author puts an ironic distance between himself and the text, while playing with the reader, who knows that Ḥamdī is his name; the narrator, who has been anonymous so far, reveals that his name is Ḥamdī in the following chapter.

The Doctor

Another way of portraying the labourers' urban underworld is following the adventures of the Doctor. His real name is Shinhābī and his nickname comes from his neat appearance. After leaving the village, he joins the construction contractors and tries various job to improve his condition but shortly after he quits. Indeed, his adventures revolve around his work experience: he is a lazy worker who pursues his own interests and tries to fools his employers, even if he fails most of the time. For example, when he gets a job as night guard for trucks in a garage, he devises a clever plan to sleep during his working hours: every time he hears a noise, he shakes a bunch of chicken legs to wake up some wild dogs that start barking (13/20).

The Doctor recalls the figure of the trickster who lives in the urban underworld, dodging and hustling. His interaction with his gullible employers in his humble jobs reminds of picaresque characters, even though the Doctor is a man, whereas *picaros* are usually young boys. Almost a double of the protagonist, he is more experienced and does not take the identity issue too seriously. When he accompanies Ḥamdī in his first trip to Cairo, the experienced Doctor wears casual clothes, while the young boy wears the traditional Bedouin garb as a sign of belonging. At the end of the novel, the Doctor is fired from his job as doorkeeper for threatening the prostitution business run in the building. Because of this, he leaves Cairo and goes back to the village, where he quickly adapts to the new lifestyle, as suggested by the description of his clothes:

> He had eventually settled in the village and quickly acclimatized, transforming into a bona fide peasant: a Bedouin gallabiyah with braiding on the neck and sleeves, a cashmere shawl, a white woolen headscarf, broad shoulders, and great rough hands from scything grass and dragging animals around by their halters. (136/143)

The Doctor can adjust to every situation thanks to his fluid identity and carelessness.

Abū ʿAntar, the landlord

The Doctor and the narrator share the same feelings toward Abū ʿAntar, the owner of the building in ʿAyn Shams where they rent a room. Their relationship is illustrated in a funny anecdote, in which some awkward details prepare the ground for mocking the landlord. The story opens with a descriptive sequence:

> Abu Antar, the owner of my building in Ain Shams was originally from Upper Egypt, from Qena, I think. He traveled to Saudi Arabia and lived like a monk for ten years until he had saved enough to buy a house. He was extremely tall. You don't see many that tall in a lifetime. He usually wore a gallabiyah on bare skin and wrapped his head in a turban that was sometimes gleaming white and sometimes filthy. He suffered from a speech impediment and hated talking. When he spoke it was like he was swallowing or vomiting. His Adam's apple would get into difficulties, rising and falling with astonishing speed, and he would fall back on gesticulation. When he growled, threw up his hands, and shook them, we would know that he was angry. He was always angry. Our loitering by the window, our many visitors, our incessant laughter: all were met by his flapping hands. We would see him on the stairs in a state of never-endind labor, carrying things upstairs and down. (107/115)

As already noted in the episode revolving around the three Ḥamdīs, the characters' brief physical description gives them a certain fixity and points out the ridiculous. In this case, the narrator exaggerates Abū ʿAntar's physical appearance, focusing on his tallness and Adam's apple. Because of the speech impediment, he communicates with agitated gestures and animal-like sounds. This language, echoed by the tenants, dehumanizes the landlord and anticipates the communication difficulties that will cause the incident. This description also reports the landlord's odd habits: he wears a *gallabiya* on bare skin, but the dress is too long and sweeps the stairs; moreover, he walks up and down the stairs carrying heavy things, in a repetitive mechanical way.

The second sequence reconstructs what had happened before, focusing on the hostile relationship between the landlord and the tenants. Abū ʿAntar gets angry because of their incessant laughter and tries to control them by eavesdropping at their doors. Trying to exert his patriarchal yet precarious rule, he looks ridiculous: eavesdropping compensates his lack of speech; he is hunched over the keyholes, in an unnatural position; when the tenants open the door and catch him red-handed, he falls into their room. The hostile relationship is the background for the key incident. In the third sequence, the Doctor and the narrator see Abū ʿAntar carrying a heavy sack upstairs and help him but something unexpected happens:

> Suddenly, his trousers fell down. They were white and baggy and from Saudi Arabia where he'd bought them back in the days of scrimp and save. One of us must have trodden on them, or maybe the elastic gave away. One moment they were round his buttocks and the next they were trailing between his feet. His bottom, perhaps from shame, was tightly clenched and looked like a mouth that had lost its teeth. I would never have guessed he had such a delightful bottom. Not skin on bone, but skin stretched across two hard muscles.
>
> The Doctor tried to cover him up. He growled a warning to the old man and tried repeatedly to lift the trousers, but Abu Antar climbed grimly until we reached the roof. [. . .] [we] waited for him to go off and cover himself up, but he just stood there naked, his penis a monkey crouched in a jungle. Before we could put the sack down he growled and muttered to himself.
>
> "We're filthy," said his wife. (109/117)

This scene is made ludicrous by the insistence on the physical details, in particular the lower parts of the body, which are usually linked to sexuality and humour. The focus on the body is accentuated by two similes (a mouth, a monkey). Another humour enhancer is repetition. For example, the verb 'to growl' (*zāma, yazūmu*), repeated six times in the whole chapter, dehumanizes the protagonist and conveys the absurdity due to lack of communication. The phrase "in the days of scrimp and save" (*ayyām al-rabṭ ʿalā al-baṭn*) is found in the above-mentioned passage as well as at the beginning of the chapter to describe Abū ʿAntar's migration to Saudi Arabia.[93] This migration provided him the money to build the house but did not change his status nor improve his behaviour.

This episode is funny because it narrates an embarrassing situation, combined with a disparaging attitude toward a patriarchal figure who embodies social authority.

93 Other references to transnational migration are a letter explaining how to move to Bahrein and the district Jazīrat Badrān, inhabited by a community of Syrians, whose main street is thus labelled Palaces of the Syrians (*quṣūr al-shawām*, 18/24).

Self-mockery of the aspiring writer

In the episodes examined above, humour is a survival strategy to endure the hardship of life and work; it renders both the vitality and the contradictions of the characters who inhabit the urban underworld. This segment of society is depicted from the perspective of the narrator, who is an aspiring writer. For him, construction work is a source of inspiration and a site where he can promote himself as an intellectual by showing his published stories to his co-workers and local families.

Nevertheless, the narrator insists on his failures as a writer and adopts a detached attitude toward his literary endeavours. The ironic distance with which he sees himself as a character results in a self-disparaging tone: when the narrator does not take himself too seriously, he can better express his in-between condition. As Temlali (2008) puts it in his review, "L'autodérision est le défouloir qui lui permet de supporter cette entreprise de dédoublement permanent. Et le lieu de cette autodérision est un roman qu'il écrit à ses heures perdues".[94] Similarly, Lindsey (2010a) notes that the narrator mentions his literary aspirations "sometimes as a form of redemption [. . .] but mostly as an occasion for self-deprecation."

For example, Ḥamdī presents his first writing attempts with self-mockery. He writes a short story about the plasterer Khalaf who suffers from a pain in his back. However, the story is completely misunderstood (116/124). On one level, the original title *Qīthārat Khalaf al-bannāʾ* (The guitar of Khalaf the builder) is misspelled and published as *Qīthāra khalfa l-bināʾ* (A guitar behind the building). Irony targets the young writer, who has great aspirations but stumbles on the complexities of the literary language; indirectly, it mocks the literary establishment that tends to romanticize even mundane stories. On another level, Khalaf intends the literary piece as a formal complaint for his medical treatment. Thus, the young writer does not obtain recognition in the audience that he wants to impress, an audience that is probably not familiar with reading literature.

In another episode, the narrator goes to a group job interview for a position as cultural attaché. The awe-inspiring examiner takes Ḥamdī by surprise with his first question: he quotes a popular song and asks who the composer is. The protagonist's reaction is inadequate to the situation, as he bursts out laughing:

> Before this could sink in, he snapped,
>
> "Whose words are those?"
>
> I burst out laughing. I had heard this song a number of times – I even hummed it to myself on occasion – but I never expected to hear it from the mouth of so exalted a

94 "Self-mockery is a safety-valve that allows him to bear the condition of always feeling split into two. And it takes place in a novel that he writes in his spare time."

> personage. The way he drew out the song in a brutal warble then suddenly whirled around to surprise, or rather assault, me with his question was something I was unable to let pass in silence. I tried to apologize. I almost kissed his hands. I told him I was from the countryside, that I had just remembered something funny, but he insisted on canceling the meeting. My interview, and with it those of my friend and the other applicants, was at an end.
>
> But for that fatuous cackle I would've become a distinguished cultural official. I was the best candidate: I had brought a file of my published work. Let's have no regrets. It had nothing to [do] with laughter. (4/10–11)

First of all, in this passage the narrator explains the mechanism of humour: laughter is caused by surprise, perceived as an assault, and incongruity between the popular song and the examiner's high status (*rajul bi-hādhā al-waqār*). Secondly, Ḥamdī justifies himself by resorting to the image of the peasant, who is likely to act like a yokel or a fool. Thirdly, the final commentary exemplifies the narrator's detached attitude toward his own attempts to be considered an intellectual.

6.2 Negotiating Bedouin identity

6.2.1 The village: a historical reconstruction

In *A Dog with No Tail*, the city is the place to improve one's economic condition and fulfil one's aspirations, but it is perceived as an alien place where the only community is the small group of fellow villagers and co-workers: "We would walk the streets of Cairo but as sons of another, distant country, to which we awaited the chance to return. And now, when I make the journey to the village, I say, 'I'm going home': returning to my homeland." (114/122)

While the protagonist's alienation in the city is expressed clearly, his alienation in his homeland is revealed only gradually through a historical reconstruction. Homeland is a tiny settlement of agricultural land on the edge of the desert, called Abū Ṭāḥūn, officially named Dānyāl after prophet Daniel's tomb. It is located in Iṭsā municipality, about forty kilometres south of Fayyūm City. In the novel, it is called *naj*ʿ (hamlet, small village), *ʿizba* (country estate, farm, rural settlement) or simply *balad* (a place that can range from a rural village to a town or a city, according to what the local reality is). In ch.26, two narratives about this place coexist:

> Our village is always on my mind. From my very first day in Shubra I thought of it as my true home, the only place where I move free from fear, a citizen with rights and obligations. I place it before me and leaf through its memories, those histories of a wounded homeland. Why I always associate homelands with injury I could not say. They seem somehow more impressive, more authentic when debilitated by wounds. And our village

> is wounded: poor and tiny, set far from the highway and the market and fresh water, and surrounded on every side by the desert. There's an old legend about the place that its nighbors like to tell, which goes something like this.
>
> Moses asked his Lord, "Lord, is there anywhere poorer than al-Abaaj?" "Come now, Moses," replied the Lord in a mournful yet heavenly timbre, "Abu Tahoun is poorer still . . ." [. . .]
>
> Its inhabitants are Bedouin tribesmen and peasants, its produce the crops and animals we tend. It has scant agricultural land: strips of green stretching serpent-like into the wastes. It was granted to our grandparents by Mohamed Ali Pasha in the days of forced settlement [ayyām al-tawṭīn]. Early on, the Pasha realized that there was no chance of founding a modern state with the Mamluks and Bedouin around. The Mamluks he slaughtered. The Bedouin he settled . . . and slaughtered [wa-l-badw waṭṭanahum. . . wa-dhabbaḥahum ayḍ^{an}]. Let's just say he settled the Bedouin who were willing to be settled and slaughtered those willing to be slaughtered.[95] (111–112/118–119)

The first part of the description combines homesickness (*al-ḥanīn ilā l-awṭān*) with a vocabulary traditionally associated to nationhood: Abū Ṭāḥūn is homeland (*waṭan al-umm*), or better said a homeland wounded by poverty (*waṭan jarīḥ*), where one feels like a citizen with rights and obligations (*bi-iʿtibārī muwāṭin^{an} lī ḥuqūq wa-ʿalaī wājibāt*) who lives in exile (*ghurba*) when he is far from it. Nevertheless, cracks in this nostalgic narrative appear on various levels: the narrator admits that he chooses the definition of wounded land because it sounds more impressive, more authentic; in the following passages it is said that the neighbours make fun of the village's reputation, while its official name is questioned since the tomb might belong either to a Muslim or a Christian prophet.

This disenchantment leads to reconstructing the village's history, revealing that had become a homeland due to forced displacement. Ḥamdī's family, which had lived alongside other Bedouin tribes in Libya, the Maṭrūḥ Desert, and the Nile Delta, was displaced to southern Fayyūm at the beginning of the 19th century by Muḥammad ʿAlī Bāshā, *wālī* of Egypt (1805–1848). This was part of the project of building a modern nation state, from which Bedouin peregrinations (*tanaqqulāt, ḥayāt tarḥāl*) and raids (*ghazw, hujūm, nahb*) had to be excluded. Homeland (*waṭan*) was basically imposed, as the causative form of the verb *waṭṭana* suggests. Since the Bedouin hardly adjusted to the new circumstances and were not able to exploit the poor natural resources, their nomadic peregrinations became labour migrations to the neighbouring cities and later to Cairo.

95 The expression "where I move free from fear, a citizen with rights and obligations" is repeated at 113/121. Highlighting that the narrative is based on memory associations, this repetition creates a parallelism inside the chapter: the first occurrence of this phrase is followed by a description of what homeland means for the Bedouin community, whereas its second occurrence is followed by what homeland means for the narrator as an individual.

Given this historical reconstruction, in the same chapter the narrator revisits his homecoming. Ḥamdī goes back to the village as a different character, an urban dweller and writer who struggles to transfer intellectual prestige into traditional social prestige. He hides his true profession, which might debase the family's prestige, and plays the role of the respected intellectual:

> It seems that I have lost my way again. I should be talking about my homeland. Now Abu Tahoun is small, and perhaps insignificant compared to a proper homeland, but it's the only place where I move free from fear, a citizen with rights and obligations. Whenever I visit, even now, I try to make them understand how successful I've been, to make crystal clear that I have achieved a degree of leverage in the city, in the enemy's back yard. (113/121)

Nevertheless, in the following chapter the narrator's self-mocking attitude reveals how feeble this constructed identity is. For example, Ḥamdī's pensive attitude is just an excuse to be lazy, and ironically the symbols of urban civilization are not books, but toothbrush and toothpaste. He is convincing only because of the physical and cultural distance that separates the city and the village:

> Every now and then, every fortnight or so, I'd take a nice little sum back to the village. I'd rub oil and white spirit into my neck and hands to wipe away the last traces of plaster and cement, put on a clean, pressed gallabiyah, and spend the holiday at home posing as a man of importance, playing the village intellectual to a tee. Rising late, towel slung over my shoulder I would make my way down the canal bank, toothbrush and toothpaste held aloft, then sit all day on the bench leafing through books and reading not a word.[96] (117–118/126)

In the city and the village, the narrator adopts the same mocking attitude toward his literary endavours, questioning self-acceptance and social acceptance. By looking at the village from an individual and collective perspective, he reveals that he is just the last ring in a chain of rural-urban migrations characterizing his family's history. These family memories allow him to cope with his own displacement and craft an alternative history of the Bedouin community, far from the straightforward official narrative and any attempt to cling to a glorious past.

6.2.2 Tales of Bedouin migration

Ḥamdī's ancestors migrate from the desert to the countryside and then to the city, negotiating their Bedouin identity. Since they cannot adjust to the new lifestyle and values, they are the protagonists of some amusing anecdotes based on

96 A similar passage is found at 11/17.

the incongruity between expectations and actual behaviour, as well as the traditional opposition between villagers and citizens.

Awla, the grandfather

In the first witty remark, Ḥamdī imagines his ancestors' possible reaction when they were first displaced to Abū Ṭāḥūn. He suggests that they did not immediately grasp the meaning of settling down (*al-iqāma al-dāʾima*) since they were nomads who used to stop in a site to rest just for a short time. The light tone contradicts Abū Ṭāḥūn's image as an attracting settlement, revealing that it is exactly the opposite, a place to flee from (*al-firār*):

> Having thought about it, I figure it's a place you flee from, or at best a stopover, a staging post for passing travelers. I'm pretty sure that when my forebears dismounted here they were intending to stretch their legs, not to stay forever. (113/120)

The second anecdote features the narrator's grandfather, Awla, who lived until the 1950s and was among the first tribesmen to gradually settle down. Nevertheless, he could not completely abandon the raids and tried to convert them into a modern business. He built a room on the edge of the desert, almost an office, where he worked as an agent: stolen livestock was hidden there, then the livestock owners came, paid a commission to Awla, and got their property back. This clever ruse allowed him to take advantage of a non-regulated situation. In this adventure, his antagonist was one of his cousins, depicted as the stereotypical cultivated citizen:

> One night, thieves made off with sheep belonging to Abdullah Abu Mansour, my grandfather's cousin, one of the first people from the area to have attended a government school, and a lawyer. He was renowned for his sharp tongue and bizarre appearance, entering the village wearing a suit and riding a bicycle. He spoke with a city accent and treated his relatives and neighbors like wild animals. (5–6/12)

The cousin took legal measures to frame Awla, who sorted out the situation thanks to his informal local network. In this quarrel, the sly Bedouin ridicules the cultivated citizen.

The father

The third anecdote features the following generation, that of the narrator's father. In his times, Bedouin migrated to Fayyūm City to work as doorkeepers, guards, and labourers.[97] Portrayed as the ignorant villager and aggressive Bedouin at

97 The narrator describes urban changes in Fayyūm City. He mentions personal memories about public places (cinema, restaurants, train station), as well as a construction project that

loss in the urban reality, Ḥamdī's father becomes the butt of humour. For example, when he and his wife saw electricity for the first time in the hospital, they misunderstood the electric cable for a snake and the socket for a rock. The father started beating the cable with his stick, as he would have done in the countryside or the desert. He understood the situation only when a passer-by, probably a citizen, explained it to him.[98] The juxtaposition of language registers renders the gap between what the parents know and what everybody else knows: while the dialogue between the parents is in Bedouin dialect, the closing remark in Standard Arabic establishes an ironic distance upon the way the mother reported her experience to the other villagers:

> My mother associates Fayoum with snakebites. [. . .] She screamed at the top of her voice, "Abu Hamid! A snake!"
>
> "Where? Where is it?" gasped my father, and she pointed toward the socket. "In that rock," she said and gave the violent shudder of the authentic snakebite victim. Abu Hamid vengefully raised his staff and would have set about pulverizing the snake's lair had not a passing citizen explained to him that it was in fact electricity and not a snake. My mother saw her first television on the same trip and conveyed news of these two miracles back to the village. She told our goggled-eyed neighbors about the electric demon that stings like a snake and the black box full of tiny people who accost you and speak to you. (123–124/131)

Compared to the times of grandfather Awla, the villager/citizen relation is reversed, as to suggest that Bedouin identity was fading or limited only to external traits, as in the following episode. When the popular singer Ṣabāḥ (1927–2014) went to Fayyūm City, she saw the narrator's father and was attracted by his unusual appearance. His identity is reduced to mere symbols, such as his traditional clothes and his dialect, and he is ironically compared to a specimen of an extinct species:

> Sabah was clearly taken with his appearance, awestruck by this living dinosaur with his shanna and Bedouin dialect. [. . .] When he remained motionless she offered to let him ride with her to the Auberge and take whatever he wanted in return. She would put a word in with the mayor to transfer him to a better job. He declined with maximal disdain and from that day forward was celebrated in Abu Tahoun and the surrounding villages as the man who turned down Sabah when she offered herself to him. (125–126/133–134)

This anecdote mocks traditional Bedouin masculinity based on disdain (*ibāʾ*) and praise (*fakhr*). The Bedouin disdainfully refused Ṣabāḥ's friendly offers; when

covered some archaeological ruins. He also reconstructs the Bedouin participation in the 1919 revolution, remarking how distant it was from the image of the same events in Cairo as depicted in canonical literature and cinema.

98 In the original Arabic, the person giving the explanation is *aḥad al-mārra*, which means 'a passer-by'; the English translator renders it with "a passing citizen".

this encounter was turned into village gossip, the father's refusal became a reason to brag in the male Bedouin community. The narrator unmasks the exaggeration in this collective narrative, thus questioning the veracity of the story itself.

Al-sīra al-hilāliyya

Another reference to the Bedouin heritage is *al-sīra al-hilāliyya*, the lengthy prosimetric folk epic about the deeds of the Banū Hilāl tribe, from its migration from the Arabian Peninsula, to the conquest of North Africa, and its eventual annihilation. It celebrates the heroes, who are not devoid of weaknesses, for the bravery they show in battles, journeys, and romance. Like other Arabic folk epics, *al-sīra al-hilāliyya* has developed interrelated oral and written traditions in the post-classical period. It remains a key element of popular culture: for example, professional poets in Egypt sing it in verse accompanied by music. The appearance of new forms of entertainment has reduced the number of master poets but the epic tradition is kept alive in social gatherings and through cassette recordings (Reynolds 2006).

In *A Dog with No Tail*, *al-sīra al-hilāliyya* is as an intertextual reference in two passages. In ch.5, the narrator reports that his family claims to descend from the Hilāl tribe, in order to link themselves to the positive image of the brave and generous Bedouin. However, the narrator insists only on the negative sides of this reference that, according to him and his mother, better suit his family's real attitude:

> The Abu Golayyel family are al-Rimah Bedouin, and it's claimed that they are descended from al-Fawayid Bedouin such as Judge Badir of the Sira Hilaliya, the epic saga of the Hilal tribe. Interestingly, some of them resemble old Badir, especially when it comes to meanness, cowardice, and shiftiness. My mother describes one of my uncles as a catfish. "He's slippery," she says. "You can't get a hold on him." (26/31)

In ch.27, instead, *al-sīra al-hilāliyya* is a form of entertainment for the group of construction workers:

> If we were working two week-long shifts in a row he [miʿallim Bakr]'d buy a kilo of meat from a famous butcher in Doqqi, I'd cook it with rice or pasta, and we'd spend our Thursday and Friday listening to the Sira Hilaliya, the epic of the Hilal tribe. He lived for the Sira, and through the long night he would vie with the tape recorder for the honor of narrating it to me. (116/124)

These nocturnal gatherings of urban migrants are a modern version of the reciting sessions that have given form to the epics: the tape recorder competes with the storyteller and contemporary urban migrants enjoy listening to the deeds of nomadic wanderers and warriors. This reference brings together the Egyptian folk heritage, nomadism, and storytelling as a narrative technique. The narrator, who praises *miʿallim* Bakr for his ability to narrate the *sīra*, indirectly refers to his own narrative technique: weaving together anecdotes of his life story (*al-sīra al-dhātiyya*), he enriches the history of the Bedouin community with a plurality of voices that speak through legends and sayings.

6.3 Which community?

Compared to *The Hashish Waiter*, the communities in *A Dog with No Tail* are provisional and lack a clearly defined leader; what prevails is the need to be accepted. Following the two main narrative threads, it has been seen that the protagonist's identity is fluid and multi-layered: he tries to balance his Bedouin identity, based on nomadic life, with his will to settle in the city, his job in construction with his dream of becoming a writer. He belongs to more than one community at a time and connects with these environments through funny anecdotes and a self-mocking attitude: this shift from the individual to the collective level allows him to challenge the narrative about both places and displacement itself. Both places are marginal and partly escape the control of the authorities but seen from Ḥamdī's in-between perspective they are lively, full of contraddictions, sometimes irriverent. Since displacement is not an exceptional condition, looking at other migratory trajectories with ironic distance provides some psychological relief and creates a sense of group affiliation.

Humour is also a common ground used by Ḥamdī to feel at home and construct his own community. Far away from the community of origins, he reconstructs a small group of friends who share the same geographical and social background, dialect, and sense of humour. This is exemplified by his flatmates whose incessant laughter irritates the landlord. Another example is the clique of friends (*shilla*) in his college years and the subsequent experience in prison.

The protagonist studies in the not well reputed Umm Ḥassan College in Banī Suwayf, where students from provincial cities, the countryside, and Bedouin villages meet. When he befriends two Bedouin from the Fayyūm and two Bedouin from al-Minyā (Upper Egypt), he becomes more confident about his Bedouin identity that he had previously tried to hide. In their company, he wears traditional clothes and is proud of his accent. Their dialect is almost a code language, unintelligible to the outsiders, used to make fun of other male students and harass female students. The Bedouin invective tradition is transferred into a contemporary context, with a shift from poetic flyting (*naqāʾid*) to direct insults (*shatāʾim*). While the young protagonist relies on this language to assert his masculinity, the experienced narrator reveals that it is a failure, as proved by the episode which gives the title to the novel's English translation.[99] The protagonist teases a girl by insulting her, but she picks up his Bedouin accent and answers in the same vein: "'You look like a duck coming back from market.' It was all the rage at the time. But she replied, with a disdain I'm all too familiar with, 'And you're a dog with no tail.'" (103/112)

At college, Ḥamdī takes part into in a students' demonstration. While university protests are often depicted as a key formative episode in modern Egyptian novels, Ḥamdī has a non-active role and focuses on marginal unusual details. He ends up being arrested and is transferred with the other students to the Directorate of State Security on a Central Security truck. During the journey they start laughing to express solidarity and spell the fear of being tortured:

> The central security truck was as packed as a public bus. Fifty students hale and hearty, a disabled student, and a student who turned out to be the son of a police officer and got out before we started to move. As I got in I saw a student I recognized. We'd never had much to do with each other but the moment we saw each other we shrieked and embraced in an ecstasy of relief. Staggering about, we both spoke simultaneously, "Did you see? Did you see what happened?" then burst into an uncontrollable torrent of giggles. I tried to pull myself together, reminding myself of the slaps and kicks to come, but it was no good. We were past caring, every one of us, and then it was all playful punches and slaps on shoulders, buttocks, and the backs of our necks. Even the soldiers were laughing. They took us from the college to the Beni Suef Directorate of State Security, and the entire journey was spent doubled up with laughter. Had you seen us in our security truck you would've thought we were on a school trip or off to a wedding. (77/82)

Contagious laughter flows among the students as "an uncontrollable torrent" also involving the soldiers. It is a physical reaction, a release of physical and psychological energy between the two tense moments of arrest and torture. In this carnivalesque scene, the rules and hierarchies between the protesters and the authority are temporarily suspended. The students' odd behaviour is emphasized by two similes (a public bus, a school trip or a wedding) that hint at ordinary situations that have nothing to do with political arrest.

Later the students are transferred to the general prison. At the beginning Ḥamdī avoids any social relation, until a lifer starts taking care of him because they come from the same region. The protagonist joins a community of fellow villagers, whose gatherings reproduce the social habits of the countryside and whose humour makes prison life lighter. One of them is known for his sense of humour. When they first met, Ḥamdī thought he was a dangerous criminal who might rape him, because of a rumor spread by the prison's director to frighten

---

99 In her review of the novel, Lynx-Qualey (2010a) reports that the English title was chosen by the author.

the young prisoners. When they meet again, in company of their mutual friends, humour reveals the misunderstanding and dispels the negative image:

> The man with the oranges came in and said to me, "Scared of me, you idiot? Believe me, I'd fuck the blanket I sleep on it if started twitching, but you? Never." We all laughed and made up. He was a born comedian; he could get a laugh from a lump of stone. He worked as a burglar and spent his life either sitting in jail or breaking into apartments.
>
> We would perform a little pantomime together that for some reason used to make me howl with laughter. Each time I met him I would say hello, and just as he was about to walk on I'd say, "Wait a moment, Amm Shehata," and carefully count my fingers, checking over and over again that they were all there. "Go ahead, Amm Shehata," I'd say, and we'd roar.
>
> So: I never left his side – meaning, of course, my upstanding fellow countryman and his band of killers and pickpockets. (87/92–93)

In this passage, a person with great sense of humour is defined as "*shakhṣ ẓarīf maraḥ qādir ʿalā iḍḥāk ṭūb al-arḍ*" (a witty hilarious person who can make everybody laugh).[100] In the first lines, the man eases tension by making fun of his own sexual desire in a colloquial and vulgar register, for example "you idiot" and "I'd fuck". This episode is followed by a gag (*masraḥiyya*) performed by Ḥamdī and the convict: every time they meet, they laugh about his past as a robber; since he can no longer commit this crime, in prison it turns into something harmless, an innocent joke. This playful atmosphere is dispelled when the narrator's mother visits him, which makes him cry out of shame.

The centrality of laughter in these episodes provides an original account of imprisonment re-elaborating the conventions of prison writing, as Shalabī had already done by employing a different kind of irony (§4.3.2). From a sociological perspective, humour strengthens the sense of community and is a resistance tool toward the authorities. Another example of confrontation with the security forces is provided by the references to religious political dissent, a central issue in contemporary Egyptian politics only hinted at in this novel.[101] Besides the

---

100 The idiomatic expression *yuḍḥiku ṭūb al-arḍ* appears in the Egyptian press to describe renowned humourists, including writers, journalists, cartoonists, and actors. For example, the journalist Sāmī Kamāl al-Dīn (2008) chooses this expression for the title of his collection of anecdotes about famous Egyptian humourists. To give another example, a newspaper article commemorating the actor Saʿīd Ṣāliḥ (1938–2014) (A. Sh. A. 2014) quotes the satirical writer Maḥmūd al-Saʿdanī, who used this idiomatic expression to describe Ṣāliḥ in his book *al-Muḍḥikūn* (1991, Humourists).

101 In *Thieves in Retirement*, there are more references to religion to sarcastically expose the false morality and corruption of society. In particular, the Copt ʿĀdil, nicknamed Koftes, remains an outsider both in his village and the urban fringes, questioning religious harmony and equality in Egyptian society, taken for granted in the official discourse.

Muslim Brotherhood leading the students' demonstrations (105/114), the narrator tells the story of a religious leader escaping the police in Fayyūm City in the 1980s:

> I heard the tales – or rather, the divine miracles – of Sheikh Omar Abd al-Rahman, who used to preach at the mosque under the noses of State Security agents and then walk the streets surrounded by a throng of supporters. State Security was unable to arrest him due to the press of people and the multitude of blind doubles dressed like the Sheikh. Each time they thought they'd finally arrested the sightless sage and each time their victim would tell them he was a look-alike and that the sly old fox [il-dāhiyya] had fled to Asyut or Minya or some other place. (126/134)

Despite its brevity, this anecdote exploits many humour-generating techniques: the ruse of the look-alikes evokes the artificial nature of doubles; the action is repetitive and thus mechanical; blindness, usually associated with wise preachers, might be a handicap but turns into an advantage; finally, the colloquial word *"il-dāhiyya"* (literally 'calamity, sly devil'), used to describe the *shaykh*, reflects the security forces' frustration. This episode's playful tone mocks the difficulties of the national authorities in facing resisting communities, who more or less consciously employ humour as a weapon or are portrayed with irony to challenge the narrative of peaceful coexistence.

6.4 Conclusion: new forms of nomadism

Since *A Dog with No Tail* does not follow a clear plot, the humorous anecdotes contribute to the development of the narrative, covering various aspects of the narrator's identity as a young man, worker, aspiring writer, and urbanized Bedouin. These accounts exploit humour on two levels: on the level of action, humour is performed by lively characters, almost outcasts, who are put in amusing situations; on the level of narration, a certain ironic distance unmasks the contradictions in life and social relations. The narrating voice oscillates between involvement and detached observation, moving from autobiography to the biography of multiple groups.

The first section reconstructs Ḥamdī's migration and his struggle to find his place in the urban underworld of construction work. While providing many realistic details about the precarious living and working conditions, he also depicts some eccentric characters in an attempt to break his dull routine and be recognized as a writer. The second section explores the other pole of his displacement: Ḥamdī reconstructs the story of his Bedouin family which abandoned nomadism to settle down. In this counter-narrative (from official historiography to family history), he rejects nostalgic clichés and reveals the funny side in his ancestors' legendary tales. They revive the proverbial figures of the sly Bedouin and the villager at loss in the city. While humour is found in some migration novels to comment on the subject's integration in a new culture or to balance the hardship of some sad experiences, in *A Dog with No Tail* it becomes a survival strategy employed by the narrator to find a new sense of belonging in these alternative communities. Elaborating on this collective dimension, the third section argues that comedy is the common ground for integration at college and in prison, where it works as an almost unconscious form of resistance.

The anecdotes about the co-workers and ancestors examined in this chapter share some humour-generating techniques. They revolve around characters that duplicate the narrator's displacement and his life on the margins. Thus, his experience is compared to other migration trajectories, never entirely successful, which provides a sort of consolation. Being an articificial projection of the self and suggesting a sense of repetition, these doubles remind of Bergson's concept of the mechanical encrusted on the living. Furthermore, the narrator remarks their odd behaviour and usually provides a brief physical description that gives them a certain fixity, as if they were captured by a camera. In the descriptions and the actions, the focus is on the lower parts of the body or some grotesque physical features, accompanied by some sexual references and vulgar expressions, although not as frequent as in *Thieves in Retirement*. These stories tell us something also about the narrator who adopts liminality as his existential condition and self-mockery as his main communicative strategy.

Language plays a significant role in creating the humorous tone of this novel. The Bedouin dialect and the workers' jargon are distinctive traits of the communities portrayed in *A Dog with No Tail*; similarly, *Thieves in Retirement* characterizes the inhabitants of the informal neighbourhood with a colloquial register, coarse words, and the jargon of hashish smokers. When these registers are juxtaposed with the formal ones, there is room for ironic asides. Besides this, the narrator dialogues with official historiography and historical novels – for instance, Maḥfūẓ's literary representation of the 1919 revolution (Heshmat 2020) – to elaborate his counter-narrative. He also reinterprets Bedouin folklore, strengthening the community ties on the one hand, and on the other questioning its reliability to project a skeptical attitude on storytelling and his own writing. Several of these elements have already appeared in *Thieves in Retirement* but *A Dog with No Tail* relies less on sarcasm and more on irony and playfulness.

7 A comparative look

> We only talk about things that will lighten the mood: films we've seen recently, some interesting new music, tales of the wonders and oddities recited by taxi drivers, the jesters of the city. [. . .]
>
> Ihab had with him the English translation of Khairy Shalaby's novel *The Lodging House*.
>
> A. Naji, *Using Life*, 2017: 122, 143

After having examined the four novels as separate case studies, this chapter will compare them to illustrate how the combination of textual elements generates the overall humorous effect. It will identify similarities and differences while focusing on the interplay of humour with narratological categories, intertextual references, and style. These considerations will help draw the final conclusions in the next chapter and reflect on the impact of this sub-genre on contemporary Egyptian fiction.

7.1 Narratological aspects

7.1.1 Narrators

All four novels employ first-person narrators who are established or aspiring writers. Their attitude toward the story ranges from direct involvement to detachment, which in turn triggers different mechanisms of humour: the narrators of *Time-Travels*, *The Hashish Waiter*, and *A Dog with No Tail* may be described as participant observers of the community they satirize, whereas the narrator of *The Secret History* is more detached. The latter embodies many incongruities that turn him into the victim of irony.

The participant observers seek to identify with the characters and setting in order to involve the readers in a verisimilar story close to their experience. However, the degree of their complexity differs: in *Time-Travels* the narrator is a fictional projection of the implied author, whereas in *A Dog with No Tail* the narrating voice is a fragmented self. To achieve this identification, they function as authoritative guides and choose evocative names or, by contrast, anonimity.

Time-Travels's narrator is called Ibn Shalabī to evoke *adab*, a pre-modern Arabic genre aimed at entertaining while instructing. This name is also reminiscent of modern prose narratives known for their satirical vein: in *Ḥadīth*, al-Muwayliḥī names his narrator ʿĪsā ibn Hishām to recall the classical *maqāma*, whereas al-Shidyāq crafts a semi-autobiographical name (Fāriyāq and his wife Fāriyāqa) for the protagonist of his travelogue *al-Sāq ʿalā al-sāq*, which parodies multiple

https://doi.org/10.1515/9783110725414-008

literary genres including the *maqāma*. Basing the narrator's name on the author's surname facilitates the identification with the implied author. Furthermore, this name is extended to all Egyptians (called *banū Shalabī*) to identify with the implied reader. Ibn Shalabī, in fact, is both an ordinary man like them and the best representative of his national community. Similarly, al-Tūnisī named the protagonists of his dialogic narratives is-Sayyid and Sayyida, two proper names that literally mean 'Mr.' and 'Mrs.' respectively, and therefore represent Everyman and Everywoman (Booth 1990: 315).[102]

While *Time-Travels*'s narrator presents himself as a gullible participant, he is also an acute social observer. Having gained some experience and critical distance from his own society thanks to time-travelling, he plays the role of the mentor. When he reports about his journeys, he acts as a guide examining various facets of Egyptian society to expose its shortcomings. This didactic dimension of satire is well integrated with the fictional events and the overall humorous effect is not reduced by any claim for social or moral reform. Since this role is more effective with dialogic interactions, Ibn Shalabī splits himself into two (a savvy commentator and a naïve victim) or encounters some characters of the past with whom he exchanges questions and answers, thus drawing a comparison between the two periods. His view of contemporary Egyptian society virtually coincides with that of the implied author and implied reader: his way of relating the events confirms their knowledge of social injustice, oppression, and hardship in everyday life. Sometimes a certain distance with the implied author emerges, revealing that the narrator acts like a know-it-all and someone who complains about the situation but does not fight to change it.

Unlike Ibn Shalabī, the narrator of *The Hashish Waiter* is anonymous. The narrator seeks identification with his coterie, a subaltern group representing changes in the Egyptian society. He guides the reader into the urban underworld of the hash den, which becomes a familiar environment thanks to his internal perspective. Throughout the novel, this narrating voice increases his knowledge about the events but, conversely, becomes more introspective.

Even more introspective is the narrator of *A Dog with No Tail*, who starts his account as an anonymous Bedouin and later says that his name is Ḥamdī. He introduces himself as a liminal observer oscillating between being involved in the events and judging them from the outside. Indeed, when he tells the stories of his Bedouin family and co-workers, he mixes admiration and contempt: he shares some features with them but feels somehow superior. In other words, he

102 These dialogic narratives do not include any diegetic dimension but are entirely based on the protagonists' exchange of ideas via direct speech.

distances himself from the narrated events, revealing their contradictions and the other characters' naïveté. The same ambivalence is found in Ḥamdī's attitude toward himself, ranging from admiration to self-mockery.

The narrating voice of *The Secret History* is very complex since it is the narrator-author of Nuʿmān's biography that oscillates between scholarly and fictional writing conventions. As a first-person narrator, he is a character witnessing the story from a certain distance: he is an anonymous scholar originally from Dayrūṭ who collects information about a boy of the same village. As a writer, he arranges oral and written sources, classifies them as reliable or non-reliable, and declares that his aim is to defend Nuʿmān from his detractors. Sometimes he hides and the events appear on the foreground, as though they were presented from an external perspective. Still, most of the time he is intrusive: he makes commentaries about the villagers' accounts because he knows more than the sources and characters; however, in some cases he admits to knowing less than the characters because he has had no access to the correct sources.

Thus, he embodies many contradictions: he wants to be authoritative but the story slips through his fingers; he relates the events in an apparently detached way but his opinion appears from the way he arranges the sources and footnotes; finally, his aim is informative but his style is redundant. Unlike Ibn Shalabī, the narrator-biographer is not a social observer who ridicules his own society. It is rather the novella's implied reader who notes the incongruity of his reports and the fictional world's absurdity. Instead of being the agent of humour, this narrator becomes the object of ridicule. He is laughable for his flowery prose and the big efforts he puts in documenting a trivial story. Still, the reader sympathizes with him because he tries to craft a positive image of Nuʿmān but hopelessly fails.

By arranging the events, describing the characters, and reporting their words, these narrators shape the characters' script and orient the reader's affiliations. These two aspects are relevant in humorous novels because they correspond to the cognitive processing and attitudinal positioning respectively, which are necessary for the creation and appreciation of verbal humour. Larkin-Galinañes (2002: 145) argues that the narrating voice of humorous novels is consistent in its attitude toward the characters. The narrator seeks the implied reader's positive identification with himself and those characters he favours, and negative identification with the opposing characters.

When dialogues prevail, the characters' script is shaped by the content and diction of their utterances. For example, the hashish waiter attracts a positive affiliation because he speaks in a direct way and supports freedom. Moreover, the narrator and the clique, whose internal perspective is adopted, admire him. The reader is thus oriented to side with him and forgive his excesses. On the contrary, in *The Secret History* dialogues are scarce and the village's voices are filtered by the narrator. This narrative technique breaks the illusion of realism by creating a certain distance between the events on the one hand and the narrator and implied reader on the other. While this narrator focuses on the external dimension of events and utterances, as if they did not affect him, they happen in the same society he belongs to. Like Nuʿmān, he is the product of the rural world he distances himself from thanks to his knowledge and command of language.

Finally, all four narrators are writers or aspiring writers who belong to the community of Egyptian intellectuals.[103] This status allows them to ridicule the literary establishment: Shalabī targets some renowned writers and journalists as well as the internal dynamics of the intellectual circles, whereas the narrators of Mustajāb's and Abū Julayyil's novels look at their own intellectual endeavours with self-mockery.

To sum up, two narrative strategies can be identified: the narrator either seeks identification with the portrayed community and implied reader or distances himself to judge the world from the outside. In both cases, some experimental writing techniques break the illusion of realism. As has been illustrated, these narrators are in-between members of marginal groups within the Egyptian national community. Therefore, they offer an eccentric perspective on society by revealing its incongruities. On a formal level, the narrators of *The Hashish Waiter* and *A Dog with No Tail* adopt their group's jargon and storytelling techniques. These communities may experience displacement, but they identify with a specific place, as illustrated in the next section.

7.1.2 Space and time

Homology between space and characters is a common feature in all four novels. In the first place, marginal spaces host unconventional subjects like vagrants, hash smokers, and daily workers, whose survival strategies are reminiscent of picaresque characters. This underworld bursts with vitality and follows its own internal logic: it appears as a topsy-turvy world in comparison to official spaces. Secondly, this homology highlights the indigenousness of both places and characters. Villages and popular districts are the homeland of authentic Egyptians,

103 The anonymous biographer of *The Secret History* mentions some historians and existentialist writers, but no information about his own recognition as a scholar is available; Ibn Shalabī is a journalist who knows many contemporary writers and intellectuals; the anonymous narrator of *The Hashish Waiter* is an aspiring novelist who works as a journalist and knows some intellectuals; the narrators of *A Dog with No Tail* and *Thieves in Retirement* are aspiring writers.

like the villager, Bedouin, and urban *ibn al-balad*, who become the stereotypical representatives of their communities. Therefore, they talk in a local form of colloquial Arabic and their sense of humour mirrors their folk and street culture.

This technique is exemplified by Ṣāliḥ, whose existence coincides with that of the den, and the labourers of *A Dog with No Tail* who work and live in dilapidated houses. A single building like the hash den in *The Hashish Waiter* or buildings with similar features in *A Dog with No Tail* are depicted as microcosms embodying urban and social changes. The den and the apartment building, in fact, mirror the characters' precarious living conditions, sense of crowded alienation, and semi-legal status. Combining nostalgia and criticism, this representation is extended to the depiction of the Bedouin village by Abū Julayyil.

This shift from the village to the city coincides with the main trends of spatial representation in modern and contemporary Egyptian fiction, starting with the village novel, then focusing on the margins, and finally returning to the city centre. The four novels respectively depict an Upper Egyptian village, Old Cairo, and the informal urban districts where countryside and city merge.

These settings revive the traditional narrative trope of the rural-urban rivalry in a humorous way. For example, *The Secret History* does not portray the village and the city in detail but links them with idyllic nature and awe-inspiring buildings respectively. When the two worlds encounter, they are contrasted: the village preserves the beauty of nature but is reluctant to implement social change, whereas the city is the site of refinement and education, as well as exploitation of the dispossessed. In *A Dog with No Tail*, the Bedouin village and the city become the sites of a double alienation. This alienation starts with the previous generations whose misadventures across the desert, village, and city shape a family story of migrations. While reinterpreting the rural-urban rivalry, these novels do not employ another canonical spatial opposition found in Egyptian satirical writings and fiction, *i.e.* the comparison between Egypt and the West.

With their focus on recent urban changes in liminal neighbourhoods, Shalabī and Abū Julayyil give a new meaning to the public space. For instance, the café is commonly depicted in Egyptian literature as a site of aggregation, cultural debate, and political activism. While preserving this function of social gathering, the hash den in *The Hashish Waiter* hosts an alternative sub-culture, whereas the café in *A Dog with No Tail* becomes a transit place where daily workers are hired. To give another example, Abū Julayyil's novel ridicules the empowering role of the university as a cultural institution and site for students' political engagement, thus challenging the literary conventions and the reader's encyclopaedic knowledge. In his novel, instead, the university is the site where the protagonist fails both in his studies and relation with the other sex. There he joins a group of friends who are unconcerned with politics but is arrested because of his accidental involvement in a students' demonstration.

Prison is another place that carries two opposite scripts in these writings: the negative script of torture and humiliation is subverted by the positive image of a supportive community that adopts the counterculture of laughter. In *A Dog with No Tail*, the sense of humour shared among the prisoners dispels their fear, whereas the Storehouse of Banners in *Time-Travels* is initially designed as a prison but later becomes a state within the state. There Ibn Shalabī joins an alternative community of people who enjoy buffoonery, practical jokes, sarcasm, breaking social conventions, and entertainment by means of intoxication (mainly drinking).

To use a metaphor taken from *A Dog with No Tail*, urban spaces undergo a process of demolition and construction. By mapping the city, all three writers preserve the urban heritage and record the changes made by the population and the authorities. This strategy is relevant in *Time-Travels*, in which Shalabī brings back to life the monuments of Old Cairo, a traditional district that was neglected by urban modernization and recently renovated as a touristic attraction. Shalabī digs beneath the touristic image of Khān al-Khalīlī bazar, al-Fīshāwī Café, Fatimid mosques, Ayyubid citadel, and Mamluk palaces to suggest that these monuments preserve the national history and identity. His archaeological recovery of the past coincides with his appraisal of Arab cultural heritage and folk culture, in an attempt to link Egyptianness to the genius of the place.

An image symbolizing urban change is the earthquake. *A Dog with No Tail* portrays how the 1992 earthquake caused displacement for the Cairene population without affecting the protagonist. *Time-Travels* mentions the earthquake that destroyed al-Ḥakīm mosque in 1303 and metaphorically refers to this natural phenomenon to describe the boisterous guffaw of some grotesque characters.

Like spatial displacement, anachronism can lead to some laughable misunderstandings. This is a key humorous strategy in *Time-Travels*, whose characters travel across time, bringing their values, way of speaking, and material culture with them. Furthermore, the protagonist's parents in *A Dog with No Tail* can be considered out of place in the city's hospital, as if they were relics of the past.

Even if the analysis has focused more on space than time, it is worth remarking that the novels of the corpus move from chronological to fragmented time. While *The Secret History* follows the chronological order of biographies, *Time-Travels*'s protagonist bounces back and forth the between Fatimid and Ayyubid periods (ch.1–7) and then follows the chronological order, when he enters the Mamluk era (ch.8–24). *The Hashish Waiter* portrays the routine at the hash den in a repetitive present and explores the past with some flashbacks. The time of the discourse accelerates in the last part of the novel, in which the narrator briefly summarizes and partially omits (ellipsis) what happens after Ṣāliḥ's arrest. Finally, time is fragmented and there is no chronological progression in *A Dog with No Tail.* It rather follows the narrator's mental associations giving the novel a circular structure.

In all four novels, it is possible to isolate small temporal units corresponding to the main character's adventures. As Propp (2009: 158–160) remarks, this anecdotic structure is typical of travelogues and biographical accounts, in which the main narrative thread can be divided into self-contained episodes whose brevity favours the explosion of humour. Moreover, the Italian literary critic Brioschi (2006: 115–128) considers the literary sketch or vignette (bozzetto) as the typical narrative unit in Italian humorous literature: while the short story follows the progression from an initial situation to one or more situations in an organic way, the sketch depicts the phases of a single situation, usually with an exemplary purpose and a playful morality. Brioschi finds this structure in some novels whose weak plot is balanced by the regularity of the characters.

Indeed, the novels of the corpus fit into the genres of the travelogue and the biography of an individual or a group. Since there is little plot progression, it is possible to trace humour-generating mechanisms in short self-contained narrative units. *The Secret History* and *Time-Travels* rely heavily on the juxtaposition of self-enclosed episodes that increase the humorous effect because of their structural features (brevity and repetition/variation), while reviving the Arab comic tradition of anecdotes and *maqāmāt*. The juxtaposition of narrative units is balanced by a recognizable character, whose clearly defined traits will be illustrated in the next section.

7.1.3 Characters

Beside their function in relation to the narrating voice, time, and spatial representation, characters may be examined as a specific narratological category. Each novel is constructed around the (mis)adventures of a male protagonist who maintains a clearly defined and consistent image throughout the episodes of his biographical account or travelogue.

This coincides with Larkin-Galinañes's considerations about the construction of humorous types. Starting from the opening chapters, such characters are presented through a broad range of illocutionary acts (their physical descriptions, actions and reactions, reported speech) pointing at a limited range of salient characteristics, which are repeatedly confirmed in the subsequent episodes (Larkin-Galinañes 2002: 144–145). In other words, these fictional personae are well-defined, uncomplicated, and consistent in their behaviour. Every time these characters appear in the narrative, they evoke a specific script in the reader's mind, *i.e.* a set of defined traits and expectations as to their behaviour. Throughout the novel, these expectations may be incongruous with the external level of discourse based on the reader's encyclopaedic knowledge of the world, but such incongruities are playfully solved. The high degree of internal coherence creates in the readers expectations of doom for the characters; however, their fate is not perceived as tragic because of the awareness of incongruity on the level of discourse and the textual markers indicating that we are in a comic genre.

For example, Nuʿmān is the perfect victim: he is an orphan of humble origins who does not receive any formal education and is at the mercy of other people. Since he is a naïve and simple character, he is the target of what Muecke calls *ingénu* irony, which is recurrent across literatures. Referring to Muecke (1969: 91), Paniconi (2006a: 144–145) describes Dhāt – the female protagonist of the homonymous novel by Ṣunʿallāh Ibrāhīm – as an *ingénue*, who appears eccentric to society but flashes an ironic glance on society itself. She appears naïve because she has a lower capacity of judgement than the narrator and implied reader. In Nuʿmān's case, this asymmetrical relation is brought to its extreme since one may wonder whether he has any capacity of judgement at all. To this effect, the narrator rarely mentions Nuʿmān's feelings and thoughts or, if he does, dismisses them as inappropriate. Furthermore, he reifies the boy as if he were a puppet, like when he is tossed in the air in the lady's house or is carried back and forth on the mule's back.

From the beginning, *The Secret History* creates expectations of doom for Nuʿmān so, in the subsequent episodes, the reader wants to know what else will happen to him. The reader's awareness of dealing with a humorous fictional text creates a certain distance that enables him/her to enjoy situations that are patently unenjoyable to the protagonist (Larkin-Galinañes 2002: 151). The opposite of the innocent victim is the trickster, like Ibn Shalabī: every time he appears, the reader knows that he will succeed and wants to know how. Both types of characters employ one of Triezenberg's humour enhancers, *i.e.* repetition and variation.

Another humour enhancer is the use of shared stereotypes, including stock characters. When we read a story about a popular agent or victim of humour, we feel a pleasant expectation of amusement. All four novels exploit some stock characters of the Arab cultural heritage and attach to them some stereotypes shared within Egyptian culture.

In *Time-Travels*, several stock characters are transferred into the modern context. Ibn Shalabī revives the model of the trickster, epitomized by Juḥā and traditionally found in the *maqāmāt*, shadow plays, folkloric and *adab*-anecdotes. Ibn Shalabī evokes this type of character because, in his time-travels, he plays different roles and is mistaken for somebody else, until he reveals his innate nature, thus turning the events to his advantage. His picaresque features are adapted to everyday life in contemporary Egypt, where he is preoccupied with poverty, traffic, overpopulation, political oppression, tourism, and mediatic communication. Thus, the social issues and setting are familiar to the reader, although the story takes place in the past. Furthermore, his adventures point at the continuity between the two historical periods, as though the stereotypical image of the Egyptians was rooted in the past.

The interplay with the past makes the satirical criticism of the present more effective, yet indirect. To express this satire, Ibn Shalabī embodies the idiosincrasies of contemporary ordinary Egyptians and turns into the stereotypical representative of his group: he does a humble job, but is educated since he is also a journalist; he experiences the socio-political changes of his time, like consumerism, corruption, Westernization, and the increasing gap between the rich and the poor; he is generous, patient, artful, and witty; his qualities balance his defects, such as opportunism and a certain passivity to politics, which are justified as survival strategies (Bushnaq 2002: 502–505). While this ordinary Egyptian is usually praised in the novel, a moderate degree of criticism toward him, emerging from the fictional events and the narrator's guiding attitude, can be tolerated. The main targets of such criticism are his opponents, *i.e.* the rulers who oppress the lower classes. Like Ibn Shalabī, the opponents are characterized by a set of well-defined and consistent features: they are despotic, corrupted, cruel, and unconcerned with the risk of falling into disgrace. The two social groups (the rulers and the oppressed, *al-awāʾil wa-l-awākhir*) are constructed as monolithic categories responding to the clear-cut us/them opposition.

One of the rulers in *Time-Travels* is Qarāqūsh, a stock character who epitomizes whimsical rule and unfair justice. When the protagonist meets Qarāqūsh, he ridicules him by evoking both popular anecdotes and the modern vaudeville theatre. Similarly, when Ibn Shalabī plays the proverbial role of the court jester, he mixes references to classical literature and contemporary popular humour. While his performance is anachronistic for the times of the Mamluk sultan and falls flat on the level of the story, on the level of discourse the implied readers are amused by his efforts and laugh with him. They appreciate Ibn Shalabī's humour thanks to their common knowledge, which is superior to that of the opposing characters.

The court jester is traditionally considered as a wise fool, who speaks truth to power without fear of reprisal thanks to his supposed lunacy and entertaining abilities (Otto 2001). Ibn Shalabī alternates wisdom and foolishness as survival strategies in his daily life, as Juḥā usually does: sometimes he resorts to his intelligence and eloquence, and sometimes he pretends to be a fool. Even when he acts like a fool, his naïveté can reveal the shortcomings of society.

Unlike Ibn Shalabī, the hashish waiter embodies the two qualities simultaneously: he is a sage in a fool's clothing whose unintelligible words contain a proverbial wisdom. He knows that playing the fool is an effective survival strategy but does not apply it in a conservative way. On the contrary, he pushes freedom of speech to its limits. He is forgiven by the well-off customers of the den that he ridicules but pays the consequences for defying the political authorities.

While Ibn Shalabī is an outsider in the halls of power, Ṣāliḥ, Nuʿmān, and Ḥamdī are somehow outsiders in the city. They are genuine Egyptians on the one hand, but on the other they belong to marginal social, regional, and ethnic groups who are exposed to ridicule. *The Secret History* and *A Dog with No Tail* revive the type of the village yokel and Bedouin respectively, two stock characters of *adab*-anecdotes and regional popular humour.

Nevertheless, the protagonist is not alone in being ridiculed or mocking his opponents, since his belonging to a small community is central in generating the humorous effects. The analysis includes some comic episodes depicting circles of friends having fun, such as the guests at the lady's house, the aspiring intellectuals at the den, and Ḥamdī's cliques at university and in prison. Furthermore, the protagonist's belonging to the community is reinforced by some characters that have been described as doubles: Nuʿmān's doubles are his father and the narrator; Ṣāliḥ is imitated by the members of the coterie, including a female character; and Ḥamdī's doubles are his co-workers and male relatives. Therefore, *The Hashish Waiter* is not only the story of the king of the rundown, but also the biography of the coterie; similarly, *A Dog with No Tail* places the protagonist's autobiography into a Bedouin and a national history of rural-urban migration.

7.2 Intertextuality

7.2.1 Literary heritage

Through their clearly defined script, stock characters revive the popular and literary humorous traditions. Mustajāb, Shalabī, and Abū Julayyil share with other contemporary novelists a broad interest for the Arab cultural heritage, comprising literary models, oral storytelling, and folk culture. The analysis has focused on two types of interaction with classical literary models to generate the humorous effect. The first one is recalling those established forms that are already inscribed into the comic tradition and using them as a broad hypotext. This concerns not only stock characters, but also the textual structure and thematic focus. The second type of interaction consists in re-elaborating a specific text or writing tradition with parodic effects.

The first trend is exemplified by *Time-Travels*, which revives the *maqāma* in its humorous aspects: the trickster, episodic structure, journeys into the urban world, eloquent display, and dramatic irony of playing a ruse at somebody's expense. Literary criticism suggests that the classical *maqāma* portrayed the Muslim society of its day and parodied some established discoursive genres through the eloquent display, two aims that are also found in Shalabī's comic narrative. Even though Shalabī does not reproduce the rhetorical patterns of the classical *maqāma*, he combines other textual and linguistic elements to achieve formal virtuosity.

Moreover, *Time-Travels* gives a new form to the modern travelogue, which is sometimes seen as a neo-*maqāma* for its episodic structure and unconventional ideas subverting the social norms. In the modern travelogue, the physical displacement and multiple encounters are the narrative devices that are employed for the satirical dissection of society and comparison of different lifestyles. Following this tradition and developing the sub-genre of time-travelling, *Time-Travels* juxtaposes several episodes integrating social observation with fictional events.

A Dog with No Tail can be placed within the same trend of intertextuality since it features the literary type of the Bedouin in self-contained anecdotes to develop the theme of nomadic identity in a contemporary city. The humorous anecdotes about the Bedouin in pre-modern literature and Egyptian folklore are the hypotext. Sadan (1989) argues that the literary figure of the Bedouin in *adab* compilations is admired and ridiculed at the same time. While the wise fool and the farmer are treated with a similar ambivalence in the anecdotes, the Bedouin attracts those motifs that other folkloric traditions attach to them. Sadan suggests that this ambivalence reflects later echoes of the process of acculturation, which he defines as "the adaptation of the Arab elements to the civilization of the sedentary countries which they conquered in the seventh century." (Sadan 1989: 473)

The anecdotes convey admiration for the Bedouin's hospitality, self-control, and *murūwa* (the ideal of manhood, including all-knightly virtues, such as manliness, generosity, and sense of honor). Furthermore, the Bedouin displays his eloquence in sharp retorts and his cleverness by tricking the gullible sedentary man. Sadan suggests that the Bedouin is comparable to the literary figure of the poet for his sharp retorts and improvisation in invective poetry. This positive image alternates with mockery for his ignorance in matters of religion, ugly appearance, and primitive manners (eliciting also scatological humour). Since the Bedouin is not familiar with the comforts of life, when he is invited to the table of a refined man, he does not follow the hygienic rules, behaves like a glutton, and is shocked by new types of food, wine, and music. Sometimes he turns these ridiculous situations in his favour and is therefore praised.

Going back to *A Dog with No Tail*, the anecdotes about the narrator's forefathers stress both the contrast of nomad *vs* sedentary and that of villager *vs* city dweller. The narrator admires his ancestors and proudly transmits their legendary stories. However, the positive image rooted in a legendary past is challenged by the negative reality that the narrator sees, which reveals opportunism, cowardice, internal rivalry, and ignorance of city life. Since the narrator retells the same story in different versions, interrupting them with his commentaries, he also mocks the conventions of storytelling and folk epics.

Similarly, *The Hashish Waiter* revives the anecdotic tradition about intoxication induced by wine or drugs, which may lead to elation and a euphoric mood. The connection between hashish and humour, well-established in classical and Mamluk literature, is still alive in Egyptian popular culture. Shalabī reinterprets this tradition by developing the main narrative thread as a series of gatherings at the hash den. He depicts these sessions, the smokers' idle talk, and their collective culture of humour.

7.2.2 Historiography

The second type of interaction with previous writing models concerns both classical and modern historiography. *Time-Travels* and *The Secret History* reproduce the formal conventions of classical historical and biographical writing by means of parody, *i.e.* the transformation of elements in the hypotext. The aim is not to ridicule the hypotext, but rather to create a synthesis of the two texts engaging the reader in the creation of a new meaning.[104]

Classical biography is not humorous in itself, although it may alternate serious information about its subject with some amusing anecdotes. *The Secret History* follows the biographical literary conventions in the presentation of the material, evaluation of the sources' reliability, reported speech, and use of passive voice. It also reproduces the annalistic style to summarize different events that happen in the village in a certain period. Taken out of their context, these conventions create a different effect in the novel. For example, reported speech reproduces the village's polyphony to substitute an authoritative narrating voice with a collective

104 Kassem-Draz (1981), Mehrez (1994), and Paniconi (2006a), who have studied parody and pastiche in al-Ghiṭānī's novels, refer to the concept of parody as discussed in Genette (1982) and Hutcheon (2000) [1985].

voice and internal perspective. The same technique creates the impression of objectivity, needed in classical biography, but also disrupts the mimetic conventions of realist fiction. The overall effect is comic because this biographical model is anachronistic, too refined for the trivial subject, and mixed with other narrative discourses (such as the folk epics and the village novel).

Time-Travels is the other novel of the corpus that re-elaborates the stylistic features of pre-modern historiography to create its fictional world. It employs the writings of two Mamluk historians as a hypotext (Ibn Taghrībirdī and al-Maqrīzī) to give some degree of continuity to the novel's historical setting despite the protagonist's time-travels. These historical sources provide some information about certain specific aspects: the *khiṭaṭ* maps the urban architecture and social history, whereas the court chronicle follows the political events of the Mamluk dynasty.

Shalabī quotes these sources *verbatim*, sometimes reproducing long passages. The serious purpose of using historical sources to understand the past becomes a parodic game revealing the fictional nature of the text: the historical accounts are 'out of place', since they are presented as direct or reported speech of fictional characters, such as the chroniclers themselves as fictional personae, the narrator, and even Emir Khazʿal. This creates confusion as to time (anachronism between the story and historical sources) and subjectivity (who is the author?), which blurs the boundaries between documentary and fictional writing, original and falsification. Furthermore, the quotations are digressions interrupting the main narrative but may also be interrupted in turn. For instance, some historiographical passages are followed by a commentary or witty repartee in Egyptian Colloquial Arabic. It is exactly this juxtaposition of multiple textual models and registers that generates the humorous effect.

The Hashish Waiter and *A Dog with No Tail* do not reproduce the conventions of historical writing but are concerned with problematizing official historiography through the stories of the coterie and family respectively. Told from the internal perspective of subaltern groups, these accounts reveal what official historiography has erased. *The Hashish Waiter* challenges the official discourse about the Arab-Israeli conflict and the impact of liberalization in the 1970s, whereas *A Dog with No Tail* questions the integration of the Bedouin community into the nation state.

The interest in crafting a historical counter-discourse leads to re-write some significant events. A common trend in the novels is the focus on episodes of political upheaval and mass protest. Both *The Secret History* and *A Dog with No Tail* reconsider the involvement of marginal communities in the 1919 revolution. *The Secret History* mentions the assault to the British train in Dayrūṭ only to deny that Nuʿmān's father was involved; it also confounds this political upheaval with other national and local "troubles". The narrator of *A Dog with No*

Tail, instead, claims that his family took part in the upheaval only to revenge a relative who had been exiled with the nationalist Saʿd Zaghlūl. Far from being politically conscious, the Bedouin contribution aimed at destroying the railway line and looting the police stations. It ended with some family members imprisoned and no recognition as revolutionaries. This alternative version also challenges the fictional and cinematic representations of the events, such as Maḥfūẓ's *Trilogy* and the films based on it, which are mentioned in the novel.

Finally, *Time-Travels* portrays mass protests by focusing on the throng with a mixture of criticism for its irrationality and admiration for its subversive culture of laughter. These episodes employ the carnivalesque and obscene side of humour since the temporary subversions of power relations is celebrated with excesses and insolent language.

7.2.3 Across genres

Intertextuality in these novels includes other forms of cultural production, such as poetry, drama, and cinema. These can be interpreted as references to the Egyptian cultural scene and political satire to reinforce the novels' sense of humour.

The first example is the metaphor of theatre in *The Hashish Waiter*. As the members of the clique imitate the hashish waiter, comedy actors draw inspiration from popular culture to revive the type of the wise fool and simpleton. Thus, theatre can be seen as a mirror reflecting society. The fictional events lead to some metanarrative commentary about the interplay of popular and literary humour and the mechanism of identification in satirical theatre. This metanarrative metaphor is well-integrated in the plot, since the clique loves theatre, cinema, and other forms of popular culture. Shalabī's appreciation of popular culture may also be seen in his parody of Western films, when the protagonist of *Time-Travels* enters the Storehouse riding a horse. This parody mocks the protagonist and the language of commercial cinema itself. Furthermore, Abū Julayyil chooses a famous Egyptian comedy for a bitterly humorous episode: his cousin watches *Khallī bālak min Zūzū* (1972) several times, till the cinema's ceiling collapses on his head leaving him injured. All these references, easily deciphered by the Egyptian audience, are linked to the realm of entertainment.

In a few cases, poetic invective is employed. In *The Secret History* only a few lines of the invective are presented against Nuʿmān's father. The poem is so dull that the reader's attention is diverted toward its authors, *i.e.* the religious authorities who condemn the father as an outcast but are fooled in the subsequent episodes. In *The Hashish Waiter*, the poem praising Ṣāliḥ and mocking the oppressors is the product of a collective oral creation. It is one of the references to colloquial poetry (*shiʿr al-ʿāmmiyya*) in this novel. Finally, *A Dog with No Tail* links invective to Bedouin identity. The narrator mentions the foul-mouthed slang he crafts with his university friends to mock those who do not understand their code language. He also refers to the local rivalry between his native village and the neighbouring hamlets, expressed in idioms, one anecdote, and one line of poetry. Moreover, the Bedouin poetic tradition is found in his forefather's habit to host poets and singers who composed "[p]raise poems and songs of scorn" (147/155).

These trans-generic references are not humorous in themselves, but facilitate the perception of comedy and satire of the themes they are associated with.

7.3 Themes and style

Despite their different styles, all four novels in the corpus share certain features that contribute to the production of humour. Shalabī's novels contain a constant flux of humour in the form of witty dialogues, the narrator's jabs, and characters performing as entertainers. In contrast, in Mustajāb's novel dialogues are almost absent and humour is found at the intersection of the formal, discoursive, and semantic levels. These levels create incongruity thanks to the complex narrative structure that includes footnotes and repetition, as in the case of the three interrupted rituals analysed as comic episodes. Abū Julayyil adopts an intermediate strategy, since humour emerges in some performances and anecdotes that the narrator observes with a certain degree of self-mockery.

Being interested in the lower classes and the texture of ordinary life, all three authors tackle similar social issues in their novels, such as injustice, inclusion/exclusion, and precarious living conditions. Within this context, approaches toward these topics have evolved over the three decades between the publication of *The Secret History* and that of *A Dog with No Tail*. For example, the underworld moves from central Cairo in *The Hashish Waiter* to other neighbourhoods in *A Dog with No Tail*. However, the thematic focus remains the interplay of the self and the community in times of socio-political change. In this context, humour serves to criticize the shortcomings of the Egyptian society, while reconsidering the representation of the self and revealing the absurdities of life. Collective humour in *The Hashish Waiter* and *A Dog with No Tail* has an affiliative and relief function, whereas the stereotypes employed in *Time-Travels* criticize several aspects of society with a comforting effect on the audience.

The novels of the corpus employ humour for social rather than overtly political satire. For instance, all four novels target the incongruity between appearance and lack of morality, especially in religious matters. This is achieved through different styles: *The Secret History* condemns superstition and ignorance through the contradictory anecdotes contained in the main text and footnotes, as well as one anecdote ridiculing a futile religious dispute; *Time-Travels* resorts to the carnivalesque in the fight between the Storehouse and the authorities; *The Hashish Waiter* contains one anecdote about an opportunistic *shaykh*; and *A Dog with No Tail* mocks the government's attempts to repress the religious opposition. In the latter novel and *Time-Travels*, political satire is indirect because it focuses on the effect of politics on ordinary people, whereas *The Hashish Waiter* attacks specific authorities and policies. All three novels contain some episodes that employ humour to temporarily subvert power relations on an individual or collective level.

To achieve these effects, the authors employ two recurrent stylistic features: repetitions and physical descriptions. Repetition is a humour enhancer on the macro-level of the structure, whereas it conveys the effect of mechanical actions on the micro-level of single episodes. As suggested by Bergson, human beings are comical when they give the same impression of an object or mechanism. This is exemplified in the comic scenes of *The Secret History* that contain formulaic names, repeated gestures with a magical effect, and irrelevant details interrupting the tension, whereas *A Dog with No Tail* employs repetition both within single anecdotes (especially the one about the landlord) and metanarrative commentaries.

A similar mechanical effect is conveyed by the focus on single parts of the body, as if they were reified. This is very frequent in *The Secret History*, where focusing on the lower parts of the body, especially in the rituals, mocks the superstitions and social control of sexuality. Moreover, in *A Dog with No Tail* the narrator briefly describes the characters with a detached style to set the stage for the humorous episodes. Some unusual or grotesque details of the descriptions trigger the comic effect, as though the body externalized their moral defects. The lower parts of the body elicit the obscene side of humour to ridicule the victim's social standing. Shalabī makes a different use of descriptions: picturesque details link the subjects to the setting and, especially in *Time-Travels*, the grotesque features of some characters place them within the world of horror and fantasy.

Shalabī is a master of the humorous techniques that are found, to a lesser extent, in the other authors. Among these techniques are anachronism, misunderstandings, metaphors with animals, nicknames, and descriptions of the characters' laughter. As regards language, his dialogues and narrative sequences are full of wordplay, double-entendre, neologism, parallelism, and assonance. Moreover, Shalabī resorts to Egyptian Colloquial Arabic as a literary language with its wide range of nuances and registers. The creative resistance of dialect is one of the themes of *The Hashish Waiter*, fictionalized by the protagonist's participation in the dictionary project, as well as a linguistic transgression in parallel with the humorous transgression of the stories. In *Time-Travels*, instead, this linguistic variety interrupts the official discourse of authorities and historians.

Similarly, in *A Dog with No Tail* the colloquial expresses some ironic commentaries on laughable situations and is juxtaposed to the high register. Like in *The Hashish Waiter*, this linguistic variety is one of the components of the jargon characterizing the group of friends. Initially the reader perceives the estranging effect of this jargon but is soon involved in the logic of that community. Mustajāb's novel, instead, is written in an elaborated literary Arabic. It is significant that the only dialogues in the text, interrupting the three rituals, are in Egyptian Colloquial Arabic.

To sum up, this chapter has illustrated the main humour-generating strategies in *The Secret History*, *Time-Travels*, *The Hashish Waiter*, and *A Dog with No Tail*. It has looked at the interplay of humour and narratological categories by focusing on the construction of characters in relation to the narrating voice, space, and time. Moreover, in terms of narrative structure, the episodic nature of these novels highlights the characters' (mis)adventures. Then, this chapter has examined the appropriation of the comic tradition, comprising both the literary heritage and popular culture, to portray social behaviours and power relations. While this tradition provides some motifs and characters, other writing conventions established for serious purposes are parodied. In particular, these four novels challenge official historiography. Finally, this chapter has looked at the novels' thematic and stylistic features. This aspect is related to the context since it identifies the targets of humour and illustrates how the representation of Egyptian society is combined with formal innovations. All these elements render sense of humour in an artistic way: beside characterizing the literary output of these authors, they could be schematized to define a humorous sub-genre in Egyptian fiction.

Conclusions

> Some two decades earlier, in the mid-eighties, the city of Alexandria saw the opposition strike a blow that was, back then, quite unprecedented anywhere in Egypt. It was in a number of summer theaters – where troupes would put on plays starring comedians of the first rank, like Sayyid Zayyan, Mohamed Nigm, Waheed Saif, and a very young Mohamed al-Heneidi – that the seeds of Alexandria's first political protest against its oppressors in the modern era took root. Audiences took to whistling at and applauding any scene that bore a trace, however faint, of political subversion. And if we bear in mind that these were family theaters first and foremost – since throughout the eighties and nineties Egyptian families would spend the summer months in Alexandria – then we can add to this the fact that they raised a generation of children who received their first political lessons there and later, as tumultuous youths, would put them into practice.
>
> N. Eltoukhy, *Women of Karantina*, 2014: 31–32

In all four novels, humour emerges from the depiction of eccentric characters in marginal environments: Nuʿmān is a simpleton turned into an antihero in an Upper Egyptian village; Ibn Shalabī is a trickster moving across time between the centres of power and the underworld; Ṣāliḥ is a wise fool and the leader of the community meeting at the hash den; and Ḥamdī is a Bedouin in the precarious underworld of daily labourers facing migration as a collective experience. This type of characterization and the culture of laughter it embodies is a central aspect in defining a humorous sub-genre in Egyptian fiction. Although this is not the only trend in Egyptian humorous and satirical writings, the four novels by Muḥammad Mustajāb, Khayrī Shalabī, and Ḥamdī Abū Julayyil are representative of a compositional method combining humour, satirical criticism, and aesthetic qualities. As illustrated in the analysis, humour structures these literary texts, allowing the progression of the story and featuring in some metanarrative commentaries.

This sub-genre interacts with the main literary innovations since the late 1970s, combining social realism with non-mimetic modes of representation. In this respect, Mustajāb challenges the conventions of scholarly writing and the village novel, whereas Shalabī experiments with the nuances of orality and folk culture, and Abū Julayyil resorts to fragmentation and the focus on the self. As Caiani notes for other Arab writers (§2.2), their interest in the cultural heritage does not only provide a vehicle for irony in view of political criticism, but it is part of a broad aesthetic and ideological project. Like some of their contemporaries, these three novelists appropriate the literary heritage and popular culture through direct or indirect manipulation. Therefore, analyzing humour in these novels reveals something about other compositional aspects of their works, in terms of language, spatial representation, and intertextuality.

https://doi.org/10.1515/9783110725414-009

While establishing a dialogue with the formal innovations of contemporary Egyptian fiction, these writings employ a set of humour-generating techniques that differentiate them from other novels with a more serious tone and plot progression. Firstly, all four novels construct their comic characters with clearly defined traits which are consistent throughout the story. To this aim, they resort to some stereotypes about the Egyptians and stock characters taken from traditional Arabic literature and folklore. These proverbial characters, including tricksters, wise fools, court jesters, sly Bedouin, village yokels, and whimsical rulers, heighten the humorous effect when they are adapted to the contemporary context. In this way, they redefine the boundaries of Egyptianness in a playful way and allow a certain degree of self-mockery, since the audience can identify with them. They emerge as comic types through their physical descriptions, dialogues, reported speech, collective comedy performances, and anecdotes. In fact, the narrator's discursive construction resorts to both identification and ironic distance: Shalabī privileges identification, Mustajāb adopts detaching techniques, whereas Abū Julayyil oscillates between the two.

Besides the episodic structure and stock characters belonging to the comic tradition, these novels subvert the conventions of historical writing, especially in the form of biography, court chronicle, and topography. The parodic interplay with the historical sources in Mustajāb and Shalabī disrupts the mimetic representation: parodying or de-contextualizing the high register of the sources challenges their official narrative. Even when no historical sources are mentioned, humorous anecdotes about a certain social group question official historiography, as happens with the Bedouin in *A Dog with No Tail* and the aspiring intellectuals at the hash den in *The Hashish Waiter*. Other strands of the cultural heritage employed to craft this counter-narrative are storytelling and popular culture. The family legends in Abū Julayyil's novel challenge the official narrative about the sedentarization of the Bedouin, whereas Shalabī and Mustajāb re-elaborate popular entertainment and village gossip respectively.

Among the recurrent stylistic features, repetition is found both in the episodic structure and within the single anecdotes. The characters can be considered as doubles, especially in *The Hashish Waiter* and *A Dog with No Tail* which portray the collective experience of humour. As frequently happens in verbal and visual humour, the body becomes a vehicle for the comic effect. In the novels of the corpus, physical features are exaggerated, reified, described from a detached perspective, or linked with the sexual sphere. Yet, obscene and scatological humour is limited to the public protests activating the carnivalesque culture of laughter in Shalabī and mild sexual allusions in Abū Julayyil.

The eccentricity of the characters and events is conveyed by means of a vivid language, the juxtaposition of registers, and the jargon of the margins, all of which defies the literary conventions. Shalabī crafts abundant wordplay with different nuances of Egyptian Colloquial Arabic permeating the dialogues and affecting the narrating voice. The jargon of hash smokers is comparable to Abū Julayyil's jargon of construction workers and Bedouin dialect. In contrast, Mustajāb achieves the humorous effect by juxtaposing the refined literary language of his composition with trivial deeds in *The Secret History*.

Similar themes are tackled in all four novels yet evolving with the socio-political context at the time of publication: rural-urban rivalry, migration, crisis of the national community and affiliation to alternative communities, corruption, and social injustice. Politics has a different weight in these narratives. *The Hashish Waiter* is the most direct in its satirical criticism of the Egyptian leaders, with the second part of this novel relying on dark humour and sarcasm, whereas *The Secret History* and *Time-Travels* adopt oblique strategies. The former confines the political scenario, characterized by wars and revolutionary change, to the background; while the latter criticizes the leaders as a monolithic group whose negative traits are not attached to a specific person, but are rather interchangeable. Finally, *A Dog with No Tail* exemplifies the critical attitude of all three authors: political negligence manifests itself in everyday life and the attitude of ordinary people, which is marked by wide-spread opportunism and incongruity between appearance and ethics. In other words, satirical criticism becomes a satire of mores, exposing the flaws of both rulers and ordinary people. In these novels, the subversion of power relations is not limited to the relation between citizens and rulers, but also involves the notions of central/marginal and licit/illicit.

This study of literary humour allows the claim that al-Ṭūkhī's *Women of Karantina*, discussed in the introduction of this book, does not appear in a vacuum. Rather, its innovative combination of sense of humour and aesthetic qualities is anticipated by other Egyptian authors whose literary output could be further investigated. This sub-genre negotiates its place within the canon with its interplay of high and low registers, references to popular and literary heritage, humorous style and satirical representation of society. These elements should be taken into account to define a canon of humour in Egyptian fiction, thus remarking ruptures and continuities over the decades and exploring the mutual influences across generations of writers.

Some of the humour-generating techniques that were found in the corpus are also employed in *Women of Karantina*. This novel depicts a topsy-turvy world where rogues and criminals become heroes. While resorting to an epic tone for trivial deeds, it plays both with the conventions of the folk epics and the generational novel, the latter being an established genre of Egyptian fiction that boasts Najīb Maḥfūẓ as its best representative. The narrator is a historian who struggles to grasp the flow of the story slipping through his hands, so he oscillates between being objective and siding with the characters. Even though no specific proverbial figures are revived, the fictional personae are mainly constructed as doubles and history repeats itself one generation after the other.

The characters' contradictions are embodied by their physical appearance: their grotesque portrait umasks their false morality, conveying a biting satire of religious extremism. The transgressive choice of placing women at the top of the criminal empire lampoons both religious extremism and patronising discourse about women's empowerment. Another form of grotesque distortion is the pervasive presence of crime in all its forms, which loses its terrifying effect by becoming absurd. Moreover, the novel's hybrid language highlights the characters' idiosyncrasies while parodying some literary and cultural clichés. *Women of Karantina* makes an extensive use of Egyptian Colloquial Arabic and explicit imagery.

In the novels of the corpus, liminal spaces provide a stage for eccentric characters and their culture of laughter. Completing the evolution from the countryside to the city and those who are in-between, *Women of Karantina* exposes the social contradictions enclosed in a marginal environment and mocks the possibility of writing the history of Alexandria once it has been turned into a literary and cinematic cliché. To deconstruct the cosmopolitan myth attached to this city, the novel inserts some incongruous family legends and references to popular culture. The latter technique is exemplified by a new version of the story of the criminal sisters Rayā and Sakīna, already popular in the press, theatre, and television (Chiti 2020). Moreover, comedy theatre and cartoons are mentioned in metanarrative comments about the functions of humour in the Egyptian society: by representing a form of evasion and indirect political criticism, comedy theatre worked as a safety valve in the 1980s and influenced subsequent generations until the 2011 revolution; cartoons and blogs are presented as new media circulating regional humour aimed at ridiculing the reputation of a city or social group.

Women of Karantina includes some episodes that are overtly funny, but it is the manipulation of language and narrative that crafts this dark comedy. Commenting on the style of his own novel, al-Ṭūkhī mentions the broad targets of humour:

> Many writers describe [Women of Karantina] as sarcastic, but I [don't] think [so]. Its sense of humour is not sarcastic because [. . .] sense of humour is more innocent. When I become sarcastic, I have a target and shoot to it. But [when I use] sense of humour, I have the whole world as a target.[105] (Eltoukhy 2014 video)

105 The interview is in English and the transcription is mine.

The study of humour in Arabic literature may proceed in many different directions. Literary criticism may ascribe other novels to the humorous sub-genre, thus exploring the stylistic and thematic peculiarities of each contribution. Conversely, the analytical framework of this study may be applied to other types of satirical writings that subvert the canons of fiction even more openly. In fact, the analysis does not focus only on the literary value, but also on textual strategies and humour enhancers. Among the selected authors, Shalabī is known for his witticism and extensive knowledge of popular culture; therefore, a comprehensive study of his literary output would help define his contribution to Egyptian fiction. In the continuum between seriousness and jest, his novels tend toward the pole of prototypical comic stories. Thus, some humorous passages taken from his novels would make a good case for the analysis of linguistic features to ground the stylistic interpretation in order to be compared with more recent satirical short stories and visual productions.

Future research may focus on specific genres within one literary tradition, for instance the travelogue genre and semi-autobiographical accounts. To give just two examples from Egyptian literature briefly mentioned in this book, the travelogue form allows a satirical dissection of society in *Fallāḥ miṣrī fī bilād al-faranja* (1978b, An Egyptian peasant in the land of the Franks) by Shalabī and *Riḥla ilā Isrā'īl* (A journey to Israel) by the playwright ʿAlī Sālim. As regards semi-autobiographical accounts, the satirical journalist Maḥmūd al-Saʿdanī wrote a series books featuring *al-walad al-shaqī* (naughty boy or *enfant terrible*) to portray his work experience and later his political exile. Admired by the new generation of satirists, al-Saʿdanī began his career as a short story writer and later became popular as a critical voice in Egyptian journalism.

Another possible path would be the comparison of humour-generating strategies across Arabic literatures from different countries. This comparative look may examine how stock characters are adapted across different literary traditions: the village yokel or simpleton is a suitable lens to examine the village novel,[106] whereas professional entertainers such as the court jester make use of the local tradition of popular humour to subvert different power relations according to the political context.[107] More attention should be devoted to the gender

---

106 Besides Mustajāb's The Secret History, other village novels whose main protagonist is an outcast who breaks the community's rules in social include: *ʿUrs al-Zayn* (1966; *The Wedding of Zein and Other Stories*, 1968) by the Sudanese al-Ṭayyib Ṣāliḥ (1929–2009) and *Laylat ʿurs* (2002; *Wedding Night*, 2006) by the Egyptian Yūsuf Abū Rayya (1955–2009).

107 In this respect, it is worth considering *Qiṭṭ abyaḍ jamīl yasīru maʿaī* (2011; *A Beautiful White Cat Walks with Me*, 2016) by the Moroccan Yūsuf Fāḍil (b. 1949). Longlisted for the *International Prize for Arabic Fiction* in 2014, this novel is based on the conflict between the father,

dimension of literary humour in a two-fold way: rediscovering the role played by women humourists in the early modern and contemporary period; and looking at gender issues in humorous productions as a critical response to social constraints or a didactic tool to perpetuate some ideological stances. Moreover, the analysis of political and literary humour in the contemporary Arab context provides new meanings to the notions of creative resistance in times of rebellion and resilience in times of distress. To avoid the normalization of these concepts, it is worth exploring the culture of laughter across different cultural productions, if possible, from an intercultural perspective.

The interplay of humour, literature, and satirical criticism engages the authors and the readers in a complex game. Besides being a weapon of oblique criticism, humour adds amusement to the reading experience, strengthens positive affiliation, and reveals something about the absurdity of life.

who used to be the court jester of King Ḥassan II (1961–1999) but is fired, and the son, a stand-up comedian disillusioned by Marxism.

Bibliography

Primary sources

ʿAbd al-ʿĀl, Ghāda. 2008. *ʿAyza itgawwiz*. Cairo: Dār al-shurūq. Translated in English by Nora Eltahawy as: Abdel Aal, Ghada. 2010. *I want to get married!* Austin: University of Texas Press.

ʻAbd al-Laṭīf, Ḥamza (ed.). 2015. *Fāshūsh fī ḥukm Qarāqūsh al-mansūb ilā Ibn Mammātī, wa-yalīhi al-Fāshūsh fī aḥkām wa-ḥikāyāt Qarāqūsh bi-riwāyat al-imām al-Suyūṭī* [Stupidity in the decisions of Qarāqūsh attributed to Ibn Mammātī and Stupidity in the decisions and stories of Qarāqūsh compiled by al-Suyūṭī]. Beirut: Manshūrāt al-Jamal.

ʿAbd al-Majīd, Ibrāhīm. 1993 [1986]. *Bayt al-yāsamīn*. Alexandria: Dār wa-maṭābiʿ al-mustaqbal bi-l-Iskandariyya. Translated in English by Noha Radwan as: Abdel Meguid, Ibrahim. 2012. *The House of Jasmine*. Northampton, MA: Interlink Books, Kindle edition.

Abou-Golayyel, Hamdi & Elisabetta Ciuccarelli. 2010. La nouvelle littérature égyptienne. Entretien avec Hamdi Abou Golayyel par Elisabetta Ciuccarelli. *Afkar/Idees IEMed* 24. 34–35. http://www.iemed.org/observatori/arees-danalisi/arxius-adjunts/afkar/afkar-ideas-24/afkar24_Hamdi_Elisabetta_entrevista_fr.pdf (accessed 19 October 2020).

Abū Julayyil, Ḥamdī. 1997. *Asrāb al-naml: qiṣaṣ* [Swarms of bees]. Cairo: al-Hayʾa al-ʿāmma li-quṣūr al-thaqāfa.

Abū Julayyil, Ḥamdī. 2000. *Ashyāʾ maṭwiyya bi-ʿināya fāʾiqa: qiṣaṣ* [Items folded with great care]. Cairo: al-Hayʾa al-misṛiyya al-ʿāmma li-l-kitāb.

Abū Julayyil, Ḥamdī. 2002. *Luṣūṣ mutaqāʿidūn*. Cairo: Dār Mīrīt. Translated in English by Marilyn Booth as: Abu Golayyel, Hamdi. 2006. *Thieves in Retirement*. Syracuse, N.Y.: Syracuse University Press. Translated in French by Stéphanie Dujols as: Hamdi Abou-Golayyel, 2005. *Petits voleurs à la retraite*. Paris: Editions de l'Aube. Translated in Spanish by Álvaro Abella Villar as: Hamdi Abu Golayyel. 2008. *Ladrones jubilados*. Barcelona: Ediciones de París.

Abū Julayyil, Ḥamdī. 2003. *al-Qāhira: shawāriʿ wa-ḥikāyāt* [Cairo: streets and stories]. Cairo: al-Hayʾa al-misṛiyya al-ʿāmma li-l-kitāb.

Abū Julayyil, Ḥamdī. 2010a. *Ṭayy al-khiyām: qiṣaṣ* [Folding the tents]. Cairo: Dār Mīrīt.

Abū Julayyil, Ḥamdī. 2010b. Khayrī Shalabī: harabtu min al-ḥadāthiyyīn alladhīna shawwahū al-thaqāfa al-gharbiyya ilā l-maqābir [Khayrī Shalabī: I moved away from the Modernists who distorted Western culture]. *al-Safīr*, 28 September. http://assafir.com/Article/212/214040/AuthorArticle (accessed 19 October 2020).

Abū Julayyil, Ḥamdī. 2011 [2008]. *al-Fāʿil*. Beirut and London: Dār al-Sāqī. Translated in English by Robin Moger as: Abu Golayyel, Hamdi. 2015 [2009]. *A Dog with No Tail*. Cairo and New York: AUC Press.

Abū Julayyil, Ḥamdī. 2012. *Fursān zamān* [Heroes of old days]. Cairo: Dār Ṭībār li-kutub al-aṭfāl.

Abū Julayyil, Ḥamdī. 2013. *al-Qāhira: jawāmiʿ wa-ḥikāyāt* [Cairo: mosques and stories]. Cairo: al-Hayʾa al-misṛiyya al-ʿāmma li-l-kitāb.

Abū Julayyil, Ḥamdī. 2017. *Naḥnu ḍaḥāyā ʿAkk. Riwāya ukhrā fī l-tārīkh al-islāmī* [We are all victims of the ʻAkk tribe. A different account of Islamic history]. Cairo: Manshūrāt Battāna, 2017.

https://doi.org/10.1515/9783110725414-010

Abū Julayyil, Ḥamdī. 2018. *Qiyām wa-inhiyār al-ṣād shīn* [Rise and fall of S.Sh.]. Cairo: Dār Mīrīt.

Abū Rayya, Yūsuf. 2008 [2002]. *Laylat ʿurs*. Cairo: al-Hayʾa al-misṛiyya al-ʿāmma li-l-kitāb. Translated in English by Neil R. Hewison as: Abu Rayya, Yusuf. 2006. *Wedding Night*. Cairo and New York: AUC Press.

al-ʿĀydī, Aḥmad. 2003. *An takūn[a] ʿAbbās al-ʿAbd*. Cairo: Dār Mīrīt. Translated in English by Humphrey Davies as: Alaidy, Ahmed. 2009. *Being Abbas el Abd*. Cairo and New York: AUC Press.

Flammarion, Camille. 1865. *Lumen*. Paris.

Gaspar, Enrique. 1887. *El Anacronópete. Viaje a China*. Barcelona.

Ghali, Waguih. 1964. *Beer in the Snooker Club*. New York: Knopf.

al-Ghīṭānī, Jamāl. 1981. *Khiṭaṭ al-Ghīṭānī* [al-Ghīṭānī's topography]. Beirut: Dār al-masīra.

al-Ghīṭānī, Jamāl. 1989 [1971]. *al-Zaynī Barakāt*. Cairo: Dār al-shurūq. Translated in English by Farouk Abdel Wahab as: al-Ghitani, Jamal. 2006. *Zayni Barakat*. Cairo and New York: AUC Press.

al-Ghīṭānī, Jamāl. 1985 [1976]. *Waqāʾiʿ ḥārat al-Zaʿfarānī*. Cairo: Maktabat Madbūlī. Translated in English by Farouk Abdel Wahab as: al-Ghitani, Jamal. 2009 *The Zafarani Files*. Cairo and New York: AUC Press.

Grīs, Samīr. 2011. Ḥiwār maʿa al-adīb Ibrāhīm Aṣlān: Khayrī Shalabī kāna mutakhawwaf[an] an tuṣbiḥa Miṣr dawla dīniyya [Interview with the writer Ibrāhīm Aṣlān: Khayrī Shalabī was worried that Egypt would become a religious state]. *Qantara.de*, 13 September. https://ar.qantara.de/node/12981 (accessed 19 October 2020).

Ḥabībī, Imīl. 1998 [1974]. *al-Waqāʾiʿ al-gharība fī ikhtifāʾ Saʿīd Abī l-Naḥs al-Mutashāʾil*. Cairo: Dār al-hilāl. Translated in English by Salma Khadra al-Jayyusi & Trevor Le Gassick as: Habiby, Emile. 2002. *The Secret Life of Saeed: The Pessoptimist*. New York: Interlink Books.

al-Ḥakīm, Tawfīq. 1958 [1937]. *Yawmiyyāt nāʾib fī l-aryāf*. Cairo: Dār Miṣr li-l-ṭibāʿa. Translated in English by Abba Eban as: al-Hakim, Tawfik. 1989 [1947]. *Maze of Justice. Diary of a Country Prosecutor*. Austin: University of Texas Press.

al-Ḥarīrī. 2020. *Impostures*. Translated by Michael Cooperson. Foreword by Abdelfattah Kilito. New York: NYU Press.

Ibn al-Jawzī. 1990. *Akhbār al-ḥamqā wa-l-mughaffalīn* [Fools and simpletons]. Edited by ʿAbd al-Amīr Muhannā. Beirut: Dār al-fikr al-lubnānī.

Ibn Khallikān. 1968–1972. *Wafayāt al-aʿyān wa-anbāʾ abnāʾ al-zamān* [Obituaries of celebrities and news about the author's contemporaries]. Edited by Iḥsān ʿAbbās. 8 vols. Beirut: Dār al-thaqāfa.

Ibn Taghrībirdī. 1929–1972. *al-Nujūm al-ẓāhira fī mulūk Miṣr wa-l-Qāhirah* [The flowing stars, on the kings of Egypt and Cairo]. 16 vols. Cairo: al-Muʾassasa al-miṣriyya al-ʿāmma li-l-taʾlīf wa-l-ṭibāʿa wa-l-nashr.

Ibrāhīm, Ṣunʿallāh. 1974. *Najmat Aghusṭus* [The star of August]. Damascus: Ittiḥād al-kuttāb al-ʿarab.

Ibrāhīm, Ṣunʿallāh. 1981. *al-Lajna*. Beirut: Dār al-kalima. Translated in English by Mary St. Germain & Charlene Constable as: Ibrahim, Sonallah. 2002. *The Committee*. Cairo and New York: AUC Press.

Ibrāhīm, Ṣunʿallāh. 1998 [1992]. *Dhāt*. Cairo: Dār al-mustaqbal al-ʿarabī. Translated in English by Anthony Calderbank as: Ibrahim, Sonallah. 2001. *Zaat*. Cairo and New York: AUC Press.

Idrīs, Yūsuf. 1971. A-kāna lā-budd[a] yā Līlī an tuḍī'ī al-nūr? In *Bayt min laḥm wa-qiṣaṣ ukhrā* [House of flesh and other stories]. Cairo: ʿĀlam al-kutub. Translated in English by Wadida Wassef as: Idris, Yusuf. 2009. Did You Have to Turn on the Light, Li-Li? In Denys Johnson-Davies (ed.), *The Essential Yusuf Idris. Masterpieces of the Egyptian Short Story*, 109–121. Cairo and New York: AUC Press.

Idrīs, Yūsuf. 1980. Ḥikāya miṣriyya jidd[an]. In *Anā sulṭān qānūn al-wujūd* [I am the sultan of the law of existence]. Cairo: Maktabat Gharīb. Translated in English by Lena Jayyusi & Christopher Tingley as: Idris, Yusuf. 2005. A Very Egyptian Story. In Salma Khadra Jayyusi (ed.), *Modern Arabic Fiction. An Anthology*, 403–405. New York: Columbia University Press.

al-Jāḥiẓ. 1971. *Kitāb al-bukhalāʾ*. Edited by Ṭāhā al-Ḥājirī. Cairo: Dār al-maʿārif. Translated in English by R. B. Sergeant as: al-Jāḥiẓ. 1997. *The Book of Misers. A Translation of al-Bukhalāʾ*. 2 vols. Reviewed by Ezzedin Ibrahim. Reading: Garnet Publishing.

al-Khamīsī, Khālid. 2006. *Taksī. Ḥawādīt al-mashāwīr*. Cairo: Dār al-shurūq. Translated in English by Jonathan Wright as: Al Khamissi, Khaled. 2011 [2008]. *Taxi*. Doha: Bloomsbury Qatar Foundation.

al-Khaṭīb al-Baghdādī. 1983. *Kitāb al-taṭfīl wa-ḥikāyāt al-ṭufayliyyīn wa-akhbāruhum wa-nawādir kalāmihim wa-ashʿārihim*. Cairo: Maktabat al-qudsī. Translated in English by Emily Selove as: al-Khatib al-Baghdadi. 2012. *Selections from the Art of Party-Crashing in Medieval Iraq*. Syracuse, N.Y.: Syracuse University Press.

al-Maqrīzī. 2002–2004. *al-Mawāʿiẓ wa-l-iʿtibār fī dhikr al-khiṭaṭ wa-l-āthār* [Admonitions and reflections on the quarters and monuments]. Edited by Ayman Fuʾād Sayyid. 4 vols. in 5. London: Al-Furqan Islamic Heritage Foundation.

al-Maqrīzī. 1934–1973. *al-Sulūk li-maʿrifat duwal al-mulūk* [The path to knowledge of dynasties and kings]. Edited by M. M. Ziyāda & S. ʿA. ʿĀshūr. 12 vols. Cairo.

al-Māzinī, Ibrāhīm ʿAbd al-Qādir. 2009 [1929]. *Ṣundūq al-dunyā* [Peep show]. Cairo: Dār al-shurūq.

al-Māzinī, Ibrāhīm ʿAbd al-Qādir 2009 [1931]. *Ibrāhīm al-kātib*. Cairo: Dār al-shurūq. Translated in English by Marsden Jones & Magdi Wahba as: al-Māzinī, Ibrāhīm. 1976. *Ibrahim the Writer*. Cairo: General Egyptian Book Organization.

al-Māzinī, Ibrāhīm ʿAbd al-Qādir. 2006 [1935]. *Khuyūṭ al-ʿankabūt* [Spider's webs]. Cairo: Dār al-hudā li-l-nash wa-l-tawzīʿ.

al-Māzinī, Ibrāhīm ʿAbd al-Qādir 2009 [1943]. *Ibrāhīm al-thānī* [Ibrahim II]. Cairo: Dār al-shurūq.

Mubārak, ʿAlī. 1882. *ʿAlam al-Dīn* [The sign of religion]. Alexandria: Maṭbaʿat Jarīdat al-Maḥrūsa.

Mubārak, ʿAlī. 1988. *al-Khiṭaṭ al-tawfīqiyya al-jadīda* [The new topography of the reign of Tawfiq]. Cairo: Bulāq.

Mustajāb, Muḥammad. 1982. *Min al-tārīkh al-sirrī li-Nuʿmān ʿAbd al-Ḥāfiẓ* [The secret history of Nuʿman Abd al-Hafiz]. Cairo: Maktabat al-Nīl li-l-ṭabʿ wa-l-nashr.

Mustajāb, Muḥammad. 1986 [1984]. *Dayrūṭ al-sharīf* [Dayrūṭ the noble]. Cairo: Maktabat Madbūlī.

Mustajāb, Muḥammad. 1986. *Dayrūṭ al-sharīf wa-Nuʿmān ʿAbd al-Ḥāfiẓ*. Cairo: Maktabat Madbūlī. Translated in English by Humphrey Davies as: Mustagab, Mohamed. 2008. *Tales from Dayrut: Short Stories*. Cairo and New York: AUC Press. Translated in Dutch by Djûke Poppinga as: Moestagaab, Mohammed. 1989. *Uit de geheime geschiedenis van Noeʿmaan Abd al-Hafiz. 3 Verhalen uit Egypte*. Baarn, Den Haag, and Brussel: Ambo/NOVIB/NCOS.

Translated in French by Stéphanie Dujols & Nashwa El-Azhari as: Mostagab, Mohamed. 1997. *Les tribulations d'un égyptien en Egypte*. Arles: Actes Sud. Translated in German by Hartmut Fähndrich & Edward Badeen as: Mustagab, Muhammad. 2009. *Irrnisse Und Wirrnisse des Knaben Numân*. Basel: Lenos Verlag.

Translation of excerpts: Mostagab, Mohamed. 1994. Les Gaber. Translated by Frédérique Gourdan & Raafat al-Malatawi. *Égypte/Monde arabe*, Première série, 17 – Soudan 2. 185–193. https://ema.revues.org/651 (accessed 19 October 2020). – Mustagab, Mohamed. 2001. Two Short Stories "The Exit" and "Hulagu" with Profile by Mona Zaki. Edited and translated by Mona Zaki. *Banipal* 12 (Autumn). 44–47 – Mustagab, Mohamed. 2012. Naked He Went Off. In Denys Johnson-Davies (ed.), *Homecoming: Sixty Years of Egyptian Short Stories*, 244–247. Cairo and New York: AUC Press.

Mustajāb, Muḥammad. 1998. *Qiyām wa-inhiyār āl Mustajāb* [Rise and fall of the Mustagabs]. Cairo: Maktabat al-usra.

Mustajāb, Muḥammad. 1999–. *Nabsh al-ghurāb* [The crow digs up]. 3 vols. Cairo: Kitāb al-ʿArabī.

Mustajāb, Muḥammad. 2003. *Innahu al-rābiʿ min āl Mustajāb* [Mustagab the Fourth]. Cairo: Maktabat al-usra.

Mustajāb, Muḥammad. 2004. *Kalb āl Mustajāb* [The Dog of the Mustagabs]. Cairo: al-Hayʾa al-ʿāmma li-quṣūr al-thaqāfa.

Mustajāb, Muḥammad. 2005. *al-Lahw al-khafī* [Hidden amusement]. Cairo: Dār Mīrīt.

Translation of Mustajāb's short stories: Mustagab, Muhammad. 2003. Der Bergzahn. Translated by Hartmut Fähndrich & Edward Badeen. *LiteraturNachrichten. Afrika-Asien-Lateinamerika* 79 (Oktober – Dezember). 12–13. (Reprinted in: Taufiq Suleman (ed.). 2004. *Arabische Erzählungen*, 65–69. München: Verlag.) – Mustagab, Mohamed. 2006. A Story "The Hired Killer" and a True Account "Ola the Hit Man" with Introduction by Mona Zaki. Edited and translated by Mona Zaki. *Banipal* 25 (Spring). 124–130. – Mustajab, Muhammed. 2012. The Battle of the Rabbits. Translated by Robin Moger. *Qisasukhra*, 28 August. https://qisasukhra.wordpress.com/2012/08/28/the-battle-of-the-rabbits/ – Id. 2015. Mustajab VII. Translated by Robin Moger. *Qisasukhra*, 4 April. https://qisasukhra.wordpress.com/2015/04/04/mustajab-vii/ (accessed 19 October 2020).

al-Muwayliḥī, Muḥammad. 1912 [1907]. *Ḥadīth ʿĪsā b. Hishām, aw Fatra min al-zaman*. Cairo. Edited and translated into English by Roger Allen as: al-Muwayliḥī, Muḥammad. 2015. *What ʿĪsā Ibn Hisham Told Us or, A Period of Time, Volume One*. New York: New York University Press.

Nājī, Aḥmad. 2014. *Istikhdām al-ḥayāh*. Illustrated by Ayman al-Zurqānī. Beirut: Dār al-tanwīr. Translated in English by Benjamin Koerber as: Naji, Ahmed. 2017. *Using Life*. Illustrated by Ayman Al Zorqany. Austin: Center for Middle Eastern Studies at The University of Texas.

Rakhā, Yūsuf. 2011. *Kitāb al-ṭughrā*. Cairo: Dār al-shurūq. Translated in English by Paul Starkey as: Rakha, Youssef. 2015. *The book of the Sultan's seal: strange incidents from history in the city of Mars*. New York: Interlink Books.

Robida, Albert. 1892. *Kerbiniou le très madré. Voyage au pays des saucisses. Jadis chez Aujourd'hui*. Paris.

Ṣāliḥ, al-Ṭayyib. 1966. *ʿUrs al-Zayn*. Bayrūt: Dār al-ʿawda. Translated in English by Danys Johnson-Davies as: Salih, Tayeb. 1968. *The Wedding of Zein and Other Stories*. London: Heinemann Educational.

Sālim, ʿAlī. 1994. *Riḥla ilā Isrāʾīl* [A journey to Israel]. Maktabat Madbūlī al-ṣaghīr.

Schalabi, Khairi & Abier Bushnaq. 2006. Reise im Zeitraum. Khairi Schalabi im Gespräch mit Abier Bushnaq. *Lisan. Zeitschrift für arabische Literatur* 2. 16–24.

al-Shāfiʿī, Majdī. *Mītrū*. Cairo: Dār malāmiḥ li-l-nashr, 2008. Translated in English by Chip Rossetti as: El Shafee, Magdy. 2012. *Metro: A Story of Cairo*. New York: Metropolitan.
Shalabī, Khayrī. 1972. *Muḥākamat Ṭāhā Ḥussayn: dirāsa* [Taha Hussein's trial]. Beirut: al-Muʾassasa al-ʿarabiyya li-l-dirāsāt wa-l-nashr.
Shalabī, Khayrī. 1973. *Fatḥ al-Andalus: dirāsa* [The conquest of Andalusia]. Cairo: al-Hayʾa al-miṣriyya al-ʿāmma li-l-kitāb.
Shalabī, Khayrī. 1978a. *al-Awbāsh* [The riff raff]. Cairo: Rūz al-Yūsuf.
Shalabī, Khayrī. 1978b. *Fallāḥ miṣrī fī bilād al-faranja: riḥlāt* [An Egyptian peasant in the land of the Franks]. Cairo: Dār al-maʿārif.
Shalabī, Khayrī. 1981. *Fī-l-masraḥ al-miṣrī al-muʿāṣir: dirāsa* [Egyptian contemporary theatre]. Cairo: Dār al-maʿārif.
Shalabī, Khayrī. 1982. *Masraḥiyyat ṣuyyād al-lūlī: masraḥiyyatān ghināʾiyyatān* [The pearl fisher: two musical plays]. Cairo: al-Hayʾa al-miṣriyya al-ʿāmma li-l-kitāb.
Shalabī, Khayrī. 1985. *ʿAmāliqa ẓurafāʾ: siyar wa-tarājim* [Refined people: biographies]. Cairo: Dār al-maʿārif.
Shalabī, Khayrī. 1986. *al-ʿArāwī* [Buttonholes]. Cairo: Dār al-mustaqbal al-ʿarabī.
Shalabī, Khayrī. 1989. *al-Shāʿir Najīb Surūr: masraḥ al-azma* [Najīb Surūr: The theatre of crisis]. Cairo: al-Hayʾa al-miṣriyya al-ʿāmma li-l-kitāb.
Shalabī, Khayrī. 1991a [1981/83]. *Riḥlāt al-ṭurshajī al-ḥalwajī*. Cairo: Maktabat Madbūlī. Translated in English by Michael Cooperson as: Shalaby, Khairy. 2010. *The Time-Travels of the Man Who Sold Pickles and Sweets*. Cairo and New York: AUC Press. Translation of excerpts: Schalabi, Khairi. 2006. Die Reisen des Gurkeneinlegers und Süßwarenhändlers at-Turschagi al-Halwagi. Translated by Abier Bushnaq. *Lisan – Zeitschrift für arabische Literatur* 2. 26–37.
Shalabī, Khayrī. 1991b. *Wikālat ʿAṭiyya*. Cairo: Dār sharqiyyāt. Translated in English by Farouk Abdel Wahab as: Shalaby, Khairy. 2006. *The Lodging House*. Cairo and New York: AUC Press.
Shalabī, Khayrī. 1996. *Baṭn al-baqara* [The cow's belly]. Cairo: Dār al-mustaqbal al-ʿarabī.
Shalabī, Khayrī. 2000. *Ṣāliḥ Hēṣa*. Cairo: Dār al-hilāl. Translated in English by Adam Talib as: Shalaby, Khairy. 2011. *The Hashish Waiter*. Cairo and New York: AUC Press. Translated in French by Frédéric Lagrange as: Shalaby, Khairy. 2006. *Le Temps du kif*. Arles: Actes Sud, 2006. Translation of excerpts: Id. 2004. Le Barouf. Translated by Frédéric Lagrange. *La pensée de midi* 12. 25–32.
Shalabī, Khayrī. 2010a. *Isṭāsiyya* [Ecstasy]. Cairo: Dār al-shurūq.
Shalabī, Khayrī. 2010b. *Thulāthiyyat al-amālī li-Abī ʿAlī Ḥasan walad khālī* [The trilogy of hopes]. 3 vols. Cairo: Dār al-shurūq.
Shalabī, Khayrī. 2011. *Uns al-ḥabāyb: al-shukhūṣ fatrat al-takwīn* [In company of the loved ones: people in my formative years]. Cairo: al-Hayʾa al-miṣriyya al-ʿāmma li-l-kitāb.
Shalabi, Khairi. 2012. Pissing over the Imam's Head. Translated by Robin Moger. *Qisasukhra*, 7 September. https://qisasukhra.wordpress.com/2012/09/07/pissing-over-the-imams-head/ (accessed 19 October 2020).
Shalaby, Khairy. 2000. The Clock. In Denys Johnson-Davies (ed.). *Under the Naked Sky: Short Stories from the Arab World*. Cairo and New York: AUC Press. (Reprinted in Denys Johnson-Davies (ed.). 2014. *Homecoming. Sixty Years of Egyptian Short Stories*, 292–293. Cairo and New York: AUC Press).

al-Sharqāwī, ʿAbd al-Raḥmān. 1954. *al-Arḍ*. Cairo: Rūz al-Yūsuf. Translated in English by Desmond Stewart as: al-Sharqawi, Abdel Rahman. 2005. *Egyptian Earth*. London: Saqi Books.

al-Shaykh, Ḥanān. 2011. *Innahā Lundun yā ʿazīzī*. Beirut: Dār al-ādāb. Translated in English by Catherine Cobham as: al-Shaykh, Hanan. 2001. *Only in London*. New York: Pantheon Books.

al-Shidyāq, Aḥmad Fāris. 1855. *al-Sāq ʿalā al-sāq fīmā huwa al-Fāryāq*. Paris. Edited and translated in English by Humphrey Davies as: al-Shidyāq, Aḥmad Fāris. 2013–2014. *Leg over Leg*. 4 vols. New York: New York University Press.

al-Taḥāwī, Mīrāl. 1997. *al-Khibāʾ*. Cairo: Dār sharqiyyāt. Translated in English by Anthony Calderbank as: al-Tahawy, Miral. 1998. *The Tent*. Cairo and New York: AUC Press.

al-Ṭahṭāwī, Rifāʿa Rāfiʿ. 1993 [1834]. *Takhlīṣ al-ibrīz fī talkhīṣ Bārīz*. Cairo: al-Hayʾa al-miṣriyya al-ʿāmma li-l-kitāb. Translated in English by Daniel L. Newman as: al-Tahtawi, Rifa'a Rafi'. 2002. *An Imam in Paris. Account of a Stay in France by an Egyptian Cleric (1826–1831)*. London: Saqi Books.

al-Ṭūkhī, Nāʾil. 2013. *Nisāʾ al-Karantīnā*. Cairo: Dār Mīrīt. Translated in English by Robin Moger as: Eltoukhy, Nael. 2014. *Women of Karantina*. Cairo and New York: AUC Press.

Twain, Mark. 1983 [1889]. *A Connecticut Yankee in King Arthur's Court*. Berkeley: University of California Press.

Volney, Constantin-François. 1791. *Les ruins ou Méditations sur les révolutions des empires*. Paris.

Wells, Herbert George. 1888. *The Chronic Argonauts*. London.

al-Yāzijī, Nāṣīf. 1885 [1856]. *Majmaʿ al-baḥrayn* [The meeting-point of the two seas]. Beirut: al-Maṭbaʿa al-amīrikāniyya.

Secondary sources

Abdel Nasser, Tahia. 2011. al-Arshīf al-ʿarabī fī l-wāqiʿiyya al-siḥriyya / The Arabic Archive of Magic Realism. *Alif: Journal of Comparative Poetics*, 31. 185–214. http://www.jstor.org/stable/23216067 (accessed 19 October 2020).

Abdel Nasser, Tahia. 2015. Revolution and *Cien Años de Soledad* in Naguib Mahfouz's *Layālī Alf Laylah*. *Comparative Literature Studies* 52 (3). 539–561. www.jstor.org/stable/10.5325/complitstudies.52.3.0539 (accessed 19 October 2020).

Abdou Mohamed, Hayam. 2015. Leer a Hamdi Abu Golayyel en español. El papel del traductor. In Noureddine Achiri, Álvaro Baraibar & Felix K. E. Schmelzer (eds.), *Actas del III Congreso Ibero-Africano de Hispanistas*, 53–65. Pamplona: Servicio de Publicaciones de la Universidad de Navarra. http://dadun.unav.edu/handle/10171/38307 (accessed 19 October 2020).

Aboubakr, Randa. 2013. The Role of New Media in the Egyptian Revolution of 2011. Visuality as an Agent of Change. In Walid El Hamamsy & Mounira Soliman (eds.), *Popular Culture in the Middle East and North Africa: A Postcolonial Outlook*, 231–245. New York: Routledge.

Aboubakr, Randa. 2015. Mock Translation in the Blogosphere: The Creation of an Alternative Discourse. Paper presented at the workshop Researching Translation in the Context of Popular Culture: Theoretical and Methodological Perspectives, Univeristy of Manchester,

13 February 2015. https://artisinitiative.org/events/events/manchester2015/presentations-and-videos/ (accessed 19 October 2020).
Abou El Naga, Shereen. 2009. Satirical Weapons, Egyptianized Kings. In Georges Tamer (ed.), *Humor in der arabischen Kultur / Humor in Arabic Culture*, 291–298. Berlin: de Gruyter.
Abou Saif, Laila. 1973. Najīb al-Rīḥānī: From Buffoonery to Social Comedy. *Journal of Arabic Literature* 4. 1–17. http://www.jstor.org/stable/4182904 (accessed 19 October 2020).
Abu-Lughod, Janet. 1961. Migrant Adjustment to City Life: The Egyptian Case. *American Journal of Sociology* 67 (1). 22–32. http://www.jstor.org/stable/2772954 (accessed 19 October 2020).
Alexander, Richard. 1997. *Aspects of Verbal Humour in English*. Tubingen: Gunter Narr Verlag.
Allen, Roger. 1992. *A Period of Time: A Study and Translation of Hadith 'Isa Ibn Hisham by Muhammad al-Muwaylihi*. London: Ithaca Press.
Allen, Roger (ed.). 1994. *Critical Perspectives on Yusuf Idris*. Colorado Springs, CO: Three Continents Press.
Allen, Roger. 2007. Rewriting Literary History: The Case of the Arabic Novel. *Journal of Arabic Literature* 38 (3). 247–260. http://www.jstor.org/stable/25597955 (accessed 19 October 2020).
Ammann, Ludwig. 1993. *Vorbild und Vernunft: Die Regelung von Lachen und Scherzen im mittelalterlichen Islam*. Hildesheim: Georg Olms Verlag.
Antoon, Sinan. 2014. *The Poetics of the Obscene in Premodern Arabic Poetry. Ibn al-Ḥajjāj and Sukhf*. New York: Palgrave Macmillan.
ʿAṣfūr, Jābir. 1999. *Zaman al-riwāya* [The time of the novel]. Damascus: Dār li-l-thaqāfa wa-l-nashr.
A. Sh. A. 2014. Saʿīd Ṣāliḥ. . . Wadāʿan "li-l-mubhij wa-l-mubtahij wa-l-muthaqqaf bi-lā iddiʿāʾāt" [Saʿīd Ṣāliḥ. Farewell to the charming intellectual without pretense]. *Al-Dustūr*, 6 August. http://www.dostor.org/654758 (accessed 19 October 2020).
Attardo, Salvatore. 1994. *Linguistic Theories of Humor*. Berlin Mouton de Gruyter.
Attardo, Salvatore. 2001. *Humorous Texts: A Semantic and Pragmatic Analysis*. Berlin and New York: Mouton de Gruyter.
Attardo, Salvatore. 2008. A Primer for the Linguistics of Humor. In Victor Raskin (ed.), *The Primer of Humor Research*, 101–155. Berlin and New York: Mouton de Gruyter.
Attardo, Salvatore. 2020. *The Linguistics of Humor: An Introduction*. Oxford: Oxford University Press.
Attardo, Salvatore, and Victor Raskin. 1991. Script Theory Revis(it)ed: Joke Similarity and Joke Representation Model. *Humor – International Journal of Humor Research* 4 (3–4). 293–348. doi:10.1515/humr.1991.4.3-4.293 (accessed 19 October 2020)
Avallone, Lucia. 2011. Autori egiziani degli anni Duemila. Blogosfera, graphic e postmoderno: nuovi linguaggi nel panorama letterario arabo. *Kervan – Rivista Internazionale di studii afroasiatici* 13/14. 25–46. https://www.ojs.unito.it/index.php/kervan/article/view/1396 (accessed 19 October 2020).
Ayalon, D. al-Djabartī. *EI2*.
Badarneh, Muhammad A. 2011. Carnivalesque Politics: A Bakhtinian Case Study of Contemporary Arab Political Humor. *Humor – International Journal of Humor Research* 24 (3). 305–327. doi:10.1515/humr.2011.019 (accessed 19 October 2020).
Badawi, El-Said & Martin Hinds. 1986. *A Dictionary of Egyptian Arabic*. Beirut: Librairie du Liban.

Badawi, M. M. 1973. Al-Māzinī the Novelist. *Journal of Arabic Literature* 4. 112–145. http://www.jstor.org/stable/4182911 (accessed 19 October 2020).

Badawi, M. M. [Badawī, Muḥammad Muṣṭafā]. 2008. Riwāyat "al-Fā'il" li-l-miṣrī Ḥamdī Abū Julayyil. Sard mutaqaṭṭi' yatabādalu al-maraḥ ma'a al-'ālam [*The Labourer* by the Egyptian Ḥamdī Abū Julayyil. Fragmented prose exchanging mirth with the world]. *al-Ḥayāh*, 26 April. http://www.sahafi.jo/arc/art1.php?id=0f42ad4fba da49405523ff8f82357bd194456a12 (accessed 19 October 2020).

Bahrawi, Sayed. 2005. Une nouvelle génération d'écrivains en Egypt. L'écriture pour la vie. In Elisabetta Bartuli (ed.), *Egitto oggi. I quaderni di Merifor*, 143–148. Bologna: Il Ponte.

Bakhtin, Mikhail. 1984. *Rebelais and His World*. Bloomington: University of Indiana Press. [Translation of *Tvorchestvo Fransua Rable i narodnaia kultura srednevekovia i Renessansa*, 1965]

Bakīr, Āmāl. 2001. Al-kūmīdiyā al-Nu'māniyya. Al-muwāṭin al-miṣrī al-basīṭ wa-mu'ānātuhu 'abra kull al-'uṣūr [Nu'mān's comedy. The simple Egyptian citizen and his preoccupations across time]. *al-Ahram*, 22 June. http://cedej.bibalex.org/DocumentFrm.aspx?documentID=78266&lang=en&Author=Eid+Abd+Al+Hamid&Publisher=Al-Ahram (accessed 19 October 2020).

Barbaro, Ada. 2013. *La fantascienza nella letteratura araba*. Roma: Carocci.

Bashandī, Hind. 2016. Nabīh Sarḥān. . . Min «jundī miṣrī» ilā «mudhī' isrā'īlī» [Nabīh Sarḥān, from Egyptian soldier to radio host in Israel]. *al-Ghad TV*, 11 July. https://www.alghad.tv/-نبية سرحان-من-جندي-مصري-إلى-مذيع-إس/ (accessed 19 October 2020).

Bassiouney, Reem. 2008. *Arabic Sociolinguistics*. Edinburgh: Edinburgh University Press.

Bauden, Frédéric. 2010. al-Maqrīzī. In Dunphy & Bratu (eds.), *Encyclopedia of the Medieval Chronicle*, 1074–1076. Leiden and Boston: Brill. http://dx.doi.org/10.1163/2213-2139_emc_SIM_01768 (accessed 19 October 2020).

Bauden, Frédéric. Ibn 'Abd al-Ẓāhir. *EI3*.

Bayyūmī, Musṭạfā. 1994. *al-Fukāha 'inda Najīb Maḥfūẓ* [Humour in Najīb Maḥfūẓ]. Cairo: al-Sharika al-misṛiyya al-'ālamiyya li-l-nashr.

Bencheneb, Saadeddine. 1944. Edmond About et Al-Muwailihi. *Revue africaine* 88. 270 ff.

Benigni, Elisabetta. 2009. *Il carcere come spazio letterario: ricognizioni sul genere dell'*adab al-suğūn *nell'Egitto tra Nasser e Sadat*. Roma: Nuova Cultura.

Benstock, Shari. 1983. At the Margin of Discourse: Footnotes in the Fictional Text. *PMLA* 98 (2). 204–225. https://www.jstor.org/stable/i219754 (accessed 19 October 2020).

Bergson, Henri. 1911. *Laughter: An Essay on the Meaning of the Comic*. New York: Macmillan. [Translation of *Le rire: essai sur la signification du comique*, 1901]

Binay, Sara. 2009. "Why Will Hassan Nasrallah Win the Nobel Prize for Education?" Zeitgenössische politische Witze im Libanon. In Georges Tamer (ed.), *Humor in der arabischen Kultur / Humor in Arabic Culture*, 299–311. Berlin: de Gruyter.

Binay, Sara. 2013. "Where Are They Going?": Jokes as Indicators of Social and Political Change. In von Hees, von Maltzahn & Weinrich (eds.), *Orient Institute Studies* 2 – *Inverted Worlds: Cultural Motion in the Arab Region*. http://www.perspectivia.net/publikationen/orient-institut-studies/2-2013/binay_jokes (accessed 19 October 2020).

Black, Ian. 2015. Arab Cartoonists Pen Their Response to Charlie Hebdo Affair. *The Guardian*, 15 January. https://www.theguardian.com/world/2015/jan/15/arab-cartoonists-response-charlie-hebdo-affair (accessed 19 October 2020).

Booth, Marilyn. 1990. *Bayram al-Tunisi's Egypt: Social Criticism and Narrative Strategies*. London: Ithaca Press.

Booth, Marilyn. 1992. Colloquial Arabic Poetry, Politics, and the Press in Modern Egypt. *International Journal of Middle East Studies* 24 (3). 419–440. doi:10.1017/S0020743800021966 (accessed 19 October 2020).
Booth, Marilyn. 1993. Poetry in the Vernacular. In M. M. Badawi (ed.), *Modern Arabic Literature. The Cambridge History of Arabic Literature*, 463–482. Cambridge: Cambridge University Press.
Booth, Marilyn. 2006. Introduction. On the Fringes of Cities (Cairo) and Languages (Arabic). In Abu Golayyel, *Thieves in Retirement*, xi–xviii. Syracuse, N.Y.: Syracuse University Press.
Booth, Marilyn. 2011. House as Novel, Novel as House: The Global, the Intimate, and the Terrifying in Contemporary Egyptian Literature. *Journal of Postcolonial Writing* 47 (4). 377–390. doi:10.1080/17449855.2011.590310 (accessed 19 October 2020).
Booth, Marilyn. 2013a. Insistent Localism in a Satiric World: Shaykh Naggār's 'Reed-Pipe' in the 1890s Cairene Press. In Hans Harder & Barbara Mittler (eds.), *Asian Punches. A Transculural Affair*, 187–218. Heidelberg: Springer.
Booth, Marilyn. 2013b. What's in a Name? Branding *Punch* in Cairo, 1908. In Hans Harder & Barbara Mittler (eds.), *Asian Punches. A Transculural Affair*, 271–303. Heidelberg: Springer.
Bora, Fozia. Ibn Ṭuwayr. *EI3*.
Bourdieu, Pierre. 1992. *Les regles de l'art: genese et structure du champ litteraire*. Paris: Seuil.
Branca, Paolo, Barbara De Poli & Patrizia Zanelli. 2011. *Il sorriso della mezzaluna. Umorismo, ironia e satira nella cultura araba*. Roma: Carocci.
Brioschi, Franco. 2006. Letteratura umoristica e umorismo letterario. In Id., *La mappa dell'impero. Problemi di teoria della letteratura*, 115–128. Milano: Il Saggiatore.
Broadbridge, Anne F. 2003. Royal Authority, Justice, and Order in Society: The Influence of Ibn Khaldūn on the Writings of al-Maqrīzī and Ibn Taghrībirdī. *Mamluk Studies Review* 7 (2). 231–247.
Brockelmann, Carl & Charles Pellat. Maḳāma. *EI2*.
Brookshaw, Dominic Parviz (ed.). 2012. *Ruse and Wit: The Humorous in Arabic, Persian, and Turkish Narrative*. Boston and Washington: Ilex Foundation and the Center for Hellenic Studies.
Brugman, Jan. 1984. *An Introduction to the History of Modern Arabic Literature in Egypt*. Leiden: Brill.
Bushnaq, Abier. 2002. *Der historische Roman Ägyptens: Eine literaturwissenschaftliche Untersuchung am Beispiel der Mamlukenromane*. Berlin: Klaus Schwarz Verlag.
Cachia, Pierre. 2011. *Exploring Arab Folk Literature*. Edinburgh: Edinburgh University Press.
Caiani, Fabio. 2007. *Contemporary Arab Fiction: Innovation from Rama to Yalu*. London and New York: Routledge.
Camera D'Afflitto, Isabella. 2007. *Cento anni di cultura palestinese*. Roma: Carocci.
Campanini, Massimo. 2005. *Storia dell'Egitto contemporaneo: dalla rinascita ottocentesca a Mubarak*. Roma: Lavoro.
Campbell, Ian. 2018. *Arabic Science Fiction*. New York: Palgrave Macmillan.
Carrell, Amy. 2008. Historical Views of Humour. In Victor Raskin (ed.), *The Primer of Humor Research*, 303–332. Berlin and New York: Mouton de Gruyter.
Casini, Lorenzo. 2003. Introduzione. In Id. (ed.), *Fuori Degli Argini. Racconti Del '68 Egiziano*, vii–xvi. Roma: Edizioni Lavoro.
Casini, Lorenzo, Maria Elena Paniconi & Lucia Sorbera. 2012. *Modernità arabe. Nazione, narrazione e nuovi soggetti nel romanzo egiziano*. Messina: Mesogea.

Chelala, Rania. 2010. *Border-Crossing Laughter: Humor in the Short Fiction of Mark Twain, Mikhail Naimy, Edgar Allan Poe, and Emile Habiby*. Chapel Hill: University of North Carolina Ph.D. dissertation.

Chenou, Marianne. 1995. Dramatische Strukturen in den Maqāmen al-Hamadānīs und al-Ḥarīrīs. In Johann Christoph Bürgel & Stephan Guth (eds.), *Gesellschaftlicher Umbruch und Historie im zeitgenössischen Drama der islamischen Welt*, 87–100. Beirut and Stuttgard: Beiruter Texte und Studien 60.

Chiti, Elena. 2016. 'A Dark Comedy': Perceptions of the Egyptian Present between Reality and Fiction. *Journal of Arabic and Islamic Studies* 16. 273–289. https://journals.uio.no/JAIS/article/view/4752 (accessed 19 October 2020).

Chiti, Elena. 2020. Building a National Case in Interwar Egypt: Raya and Sakina's Crimes through the Pages of *al-Ahrām* (Fall 1920). *History Compass* 18 (2). 1–13. https://onlinelibrary.wiley.com/doi/full/10.1111/hic3.12607 (accessed 19 October 2020).

Chłopicki, Władysław. 2017. Humor and Narrative. In Salvatore Attardo (ed.), *The Routledge Handbook of Language and Humor*, 143–157. New York: Routledge.

Cobham, Catherine. 2006. Enchanted to a Stone: Heroes and Leaders in *The Harafish* by Najīb Maḥfūẓ. *Middle Eastern Literatures* 9 (2), 123–135. https://doi.org/10.1080/14752620600814160 (accessed 19 October 2020).

Cooperson, Michael. 1998. Remembering the Future: Arabic Time-Travel Literature. *Edebiyat* 8 (2), 171–189.

Cooperson, Michael. 2008. Safar. The Early History of Time Travel Literature: Al-Muwayliḥī's *Ḥadīth ʿĪsā b. Hishām* and Its Antecedents. In Beatrice Gruendler & Michael Cooperson (eds.), *Classical Arabic Humanities in Their Own Terms*, 419–446. Leiden and Boston: Brill.

Corrao, Francesca Maria. 1991. *Giufà: il furbo, lo sciocco, il saggio*. Milano: Mondadori.

Corrao, Francesca Maria. 1996. *Il riso, il comico e la festa al Cairo nel XIII secolo: il teatro delle ombre di Ibn Dāniyāl*. Roma: Istituto per l'Oriente C. A. Nallino.

Craig, Bruce, Marlis J. Saleh & Warren C. Schultz (eds.). 2003. Al-Maqrizi [Special Issue]. *Mamluk Studies Review* 7 (2). http://mamluk.uchicago.edu/MamlukStudiesReview_VII-2_2003.pdf (accessed 19 October 2020).

Daly, Martin W. 1998. The British Occupation, 1882–1922. In Id. (ed.), *The Cambridge History of Egypt, Volume 2: Modern Egypt, from 1517 to the End of the Twentieth Century*, 239–251. Cambridge: Cambridge University Press.

Damir-Geilsdorf, Sabine. 2020. "Candies from Eastern Ghouta". Dark Humor in Visualizing the Syrian Conflict. In Ead. & Stephan Milich (eds.). *Creative Resistance. Political Humor in the Arab Uprisings*, 191–221. Bielefeld: transcript Verlag.

Damir-Geilsdorf, Sabine & Stephan Milich (eds.). 2020. *Creative Resistance. Political Humor in the Arab Uprisings*. Bielefeld: transcript Verlag.

Darwīsh, ʿAbīr. 2001. al-Adab al-sākhir. Li-mādhā ikhtafā min ḥayātinā al-thaqāfiyya? [Satirical literature. Why did it disappear from our cultural life?]. *al-Sharq al-awsaṭ*, 29 August. http://archive.aawsat.com/details.asp?article=54777&issueno=8310#.V266YjVZ3IU (accessed 19 October 2020).

Ḍayf, Shawqī. 1999. Kitāb al-Fāshūsh [The book of stupidity]. In *Fī l-shiʿr wa-l-fukāha fī Miṣr* [Poetry and humour in Egypt], 92–99. Cairo: Dār al-maʿārif, 1999.

De Angelis, Francesco. 2007. *La letteratura egiziana in dialetto nel primo '900*. Roma: Jouvence.

De Angelis, Francesco. 2015. Graphic Novels and Comic Books in Post-Revolutionary Egypt: Some Remarks. *La Rivista di Arablit* V (9–10), 23–37.

De Poli, Barbara. 2011. Umorismo e censura nel mondo arabo: il caso "Demain". In Paolo Branca, Barbara de Poli & Patrizia Zanelli, *Il sorriso della mezzaluna. Umorismo, ironia e satira nella cultura araba*, 143–176. Roma: Carocci.

Devi, Gayatri & Najat Rahman (eds.). 2014. *Humor in Middle Eastern Cinema*. Detroit: Wayne State University Press.

Dorigo Ceccato, Rosella. 1987–1988. Un diverso approccio al *Ḫayāl al-ẓill* nella letteratura araba tra Ottocento e Novecento. *Quaderni di Studi Arabi* 5/6. 208–225. https://www.jstor.org/stable/25802604 (accessed 19 October 2020).

Dové, Peter. 2009. Satire und schwarzer Humor im Werk von Zakariyyā Tāmir. In Georges Tamer (ed.), *Humor in der arabischen Kultur / Humor in Arabic Culture*, 279–290. Berlin: de Gruyter.

Dozio, Cristina. 2018. Il Cairo: luoghi semi-ufficiali e personaggi eccentrici nei romanzi di Shalabī e Abū Julayyil. *Annali di Ca' Foscari Serie Orientale* 54. 77–106. https://edizionicafoscari.unive.it/it/edizioni/riviste/annali-di-ca-foscari-serie-orientale/2018/1/il-cairo-luoghi-semi-ufficiali-e-personaggi-eccent/ (accessed 19 October 2020).

Dozio, Cristina. 2019. Old Characters in New Clothes: Bilāl Faḍl's Satirical Writings. In Stephan Guth & Teresa Pepe (eds.). *Arabic Literature in a Post-Human World. Proceedings of the 12th Conference of the European Association for Modern Arabic Literature (EURAMAL), May 2016, Oslo*, 289–308. Wiesbaden: Harrassowitz Verlag.

Dūss, Madīḥa & Humphrey Davies (eds.). 2013. *al-ʿĀmmiyya al-miṣriyya al-maktūba: mukhtārāt min 1401 ilā 2009* [Written Egyptian Arabic: an anthology from 1401 to 2009]. Cairo: al-Hayʾa al-miṣriyya al-ʿāmma li-l-kitāb.

EAL = *Encyclopedia of Arabic Literature* → Meisami, Julie Scott & Paul Starkey (eds.)

EI2 = *Encyclopaedia of Islam*, Second Edition, ed. P. Bearman, Th. Bianquis, C. E. Bosworth, E. van Donzel, W. P. Heinrichs. Leiden: Brill online 2012. Online edition of print version published 1955–2005.

EI3 = *Encyclopaedia of Islam, THREE*, ed. Kate Fleet, Gudrun Krämer, Denis Matringe, John Nawas and Everett Rowson. Leiden: Brill online 2015–.

Elad, Ami. 1994. *The Village Novel in Modern Egyptian Literature*. Berlin: Klaus Schwarz Verlag.

El-Ariss, Tarek. 2013. *Trials of Arab Modernity. Literary Affects and the New Political*. New York: Fordham University Press.

El-Ariss, Tarek. 2017. Teaching Humor in Arabic Literature and Film. In Muhsin J. al-Musawi (ed.), *Arabic Literature for the Classroom*, 130–144. London and New York: Routledge.

El-Assyouti, Mohamed. 2000. Khairi Shalabi: The Narrative Eye. *Al-Ahram Weekly*, Issue No. 463, 6–12 January. https://www.arabworldbooks.com/authors/khairy-shalaby (accessed 19 October 2020).

El Hakim, Zaki. 1961. Goha chez les écrivains égyptiens d'expression française. *La Revue égyptienne de littérature et de critique* 1. 79–94.

El Sadda, Hoda. 2012. *Gender, Nation, and the Arabic Novel: Egypt, 1892–2008*. Syracuse, N.Y.: Syracuse University Press.

El-Shamy, Hasan M. 1995. *Folk Traditions of the Arab World: A Guide to Motif Classification*. Indianapolis: Indiana University Press.

El-Shamy, Hasan M. 2006. *A Motif Index of The Thousand and One Nights*. Indianapolis: Indiana University Press.

El-Wardani, Mahmoud. 2013. Book Review: The Secret World of Alexandria. *Ahram Online*, 26 May. http://english.ahram.org.eg/NewsContent/18/62/72333/Books/Review/Book-review-The-secret-world-of-Alexandria.aspx (accessed 19 October 2020).

Ermida, Isabel. 2008. *The Language of Comic Narratives: Humor Construction in Short Stories*. Berlin: Mouton de Gruyter.

Ettmüller, Eliane Ursula. 2012a. Caricature and Egypt's Revolution of 25 January 2011. *Zeithistorische Forschungen/Studies in Contemporary History* 9 (1). 138–148. https://zeithistorische-forschungen.de/1-2012/4469 (accessed 19 October 2020).

Ettmüller, Eliane Ursula. 2012b. *The Construct of Egypt's National-Self in James Sanua's Early Satire and Caricature*. Berlin: Klaus Schwarz Verlag.

Ettmüller, Eliane Ursula. 2013. Abū Nazzāra's Journey from Victorious Egypt to Splendorous Paris: The Making of an Arabic *Punch*. In Hans Harder & Barbara Mittler (eds.), *Asian Punches. A Transculural Affair*, 219–303. Heidelberg: Springer.

Fahmy, Ziad. 2011. *Ordinary Egyptians: Creating the Modern Nation through Popular Culture*. Stanford: Stanford University Press.

Fähndrich, Hartmut (ed.). 2012. Humor [Special Issue]. *SGMOIK SSMOCI Bulletin* 34.

Faraj, Muḥammad. 2013. Malḥama "Nisāʾ al-Karantīnā" al-sākhira [The sarcastic epic of Nisāʾ al-Karantīnā]. *Al-Mudun*, 5 May. https://www.almodon.com/culture/2013/5/5/ملحمة-نساء-الكرنتينا-الساخرة (accessed 19 October 2020).

al-Fāris, Muḥammad. 1990. al-Ightirāb fī adab Khayrī Shalabī [Estrangement in Khayrī Shalabī's writings]. *Al-Qāhira*, 109, 15 October. https://archive.alsharekh.org/Articles/26/2614/303442/4 (accessed 19 October 2020).

Fatḥī, Ibrāhīm. 1986. *Muʿjam al-muṣṭalaḥāt al-adabiyya* [Arabic-English dictionary of literary terms]. s.l.: al-Muʾassasa al-ʿarabiyya li-l-nāshirīn al-muttaḥidīn.

Fayed, Shaimaa. 2010. Oppression, Wealth Gaps Spurs Satire in Egypt. *Reuters Africa*, 13 October. https://www.reuters.com/article/us-egypt-satire/oppression-wealth-gaps-spurs-satire-in-egypt-idUSTRE69C3ON20101013 (accessed 19 October 2020).

Fenoglio, Irène. 1991. Caricature et représentation du mythe: Goha. In Jean-Claude Vatin (ed.), *Images d'Égypte. De la fresque à la bande dessinée*, 133–143. Cairo: CEDEJ.

Fenoglio, Irène, & François Georgeon (eds.). 1995. L'humour en Orient [Special Issue]. *Revue du monde musulman et de la Méditerranée* 77–78. www.persee.fr/issue/remmm_0997-1327_1995_num_77_1 (accessed 19 October 2020).

Ferroni, Giulio. 1974. *Il comico nelle teorie contemporanee*. Roma: Bulzoni.

Franke-Ziedan, Claudia. 2013. *Satire und Kontext: Gesellschaftskritik in den Dramen des ägyptischen Autors Ali Salem*. Wiesbaden: Reichert Verlag.

Freud, Sigmund. 1960. *Jokes and Their Relation to the Unconscious*. New York: Norton & Company. [Translation of *Der Witz und seine Bezieung zum Unbewussten*, 1905]

Freud, Sigmund. 1995 [1910]. *Eine Kindheitserinnerung des Leonardo da Vinci*. Edited by Janine Chasseguet-Smirgel. Frankfurt am Main: Fischer. Translated in Arabic by Aḥmad ʿUkāsha as: Freud, Sigmund. 1970. *Leonardo Da Vinci: dirāsa taḥlīliyya li-Sigmund Freud*. Cairo: Anglo-Egyptian Bookshop.

Genette, Gérard. 1982. *Palimpsestes*. Paris: Editions du Seuil.

Genette, Gérard. 1987. *Seuils*. Paris: Editions du Seuil.

Georgeon, François. 1995. Rire dans l'Empire ottoman? In Irène Fenoglio & François Georgeon (eds.), L'humour en Orient [Special Issue]. *Revue du monde musulman et de la Méditerranée* 77–78. 89–109.

Gheissari, Ali. 2012. Despots of the World Unite! Satire in the Iranian Constitutional Press: The *Majalla-Yi Istibād*, 1907–1908. In Dominic Parviz Brookshaw (ed.), *Ruse and Wit: The Humorous in Arabic, Persian, and Turkish Narrative*, 98–118. Boston and Washington: Ilex Foundation and the Center for Hellenic Studies.

Ghersetti, Antonella. 1993. I paradigmi della stupidità: *ḥumq* e *ḥamqā* nella letteratura d'*adab*. *Annali di Ca' Foscari* XXXII (3), 83–95. http://lear.unive.it/jspui/handle/11707/1708 (accessed 19 October 2020).

Guo, Li. 2012. *The Performing Arts in Medieval Islam: Shadow Play and Popular Poetry in Ibn Daniyal's Mamluk Cairo*. Leiden: Brill.

Guo, Li. Ḥarāfīsh. *EI3*.

Guth, Stephan & Teresa Pepe (eds.). 2019. *Arabic Literature in a Post-Human World. Proceedings of the 12th Conference of the European Association for Modern Arabic Literature (EURAMAL), May 2016, Oslo*. Wiesbaden: Harrassowitz Verlag.

Gutiérrez de Terán, Ignacio. 2009. Taxistas y proletarios de Egipto: ¡leed a Dostoievski! *Revista de Libros* 155: 44–45. https://www.revistadelibros.com/articulo_imprimible.php?art=4493&t=articulos (accessed 19 October 2020).

Guyer, Jonathan. 2015. Translating Egypt's Political Cartoons. In Mona Baker (ed.), *Translating Dissent: Voices From and With the Egyptian Revolution*, 208–220. New York: Routledge.

Haeri, Niloofar. 2002. *Sacred Language, Ordinary People: Dilemmas of Culture and Politics in Egypt*. Basingstoke: Palgrave Macmillan.

Hafez, Sabry. 2000. The Novel, Politics and Islam. Haydar Haydar's *Banquet for Seaweed*. *New Left Review* II (5). 117–141. https://newleftreview.org/issues/II5/articles/sabry-hafez-the-novel-politics-and-islam (accessed 19 October 2020).

Hafez, Sabry. 2001. Jamāliyyāt al-riwāya al-jadīda: al-qaṭī'a al-ma'rifiyya wa-l-naz'a al-muḍādda li-l-ghinā'iyya / Aesthetica of the New Novel: Epistemological Rupture and Anti-Lyrical Poetics. *Alif: Journal of Comparative Poetics* 21. 184–246. www.jstor.org/stable/1350042 (accessed 19 October 2020).

Hafez, Sabry. 2010. The New Egyptian Novel. Urban Transformation and Narrative Form. *New Left Review* II (64). 47–62. https://newleftreview.org/II/64/sabry-hafez-the-new-egyptian-novel (accessed 19 October 2020).

Håland, Eva Marie. 2017. *Adab sākhir* (Satrical Literature) and the Use of Egyptian Vernacular. In Jacob Høigilt & Gunvor Mejdell (eds.), *The Politics of Written Language in the Arab World. Writing Change*, 142–165. Leiden – Boston: Brill. https://www.duo.uio.no/handle/10852/65062 (accessed 19 October 2020).

Hamarneh, Walid. 2010. Aḥmad Fāris al-Shidyāq. In Roger Allen (ed.), *Essays in Arabic Literary Biography: 1850–1950*, 317–328. Wiesbaden: Harrassowitz Verlag.

Hamdan, Mas'ud. 2004. The Carnivalesque Satires of Muhammad al-Maghut and Durayd Lahham: A Modern Layer of Comic Folk Drama in Arab Tradition. *Journal of Dramatic Theory and Criticism* XVIII (2). 137–148.

Hämeen-Anttila, Jakko. 2002. *Maqama: A History of a Genre*. Wiesbaden: Harrassowitz Verlag.

Hammoud, Dalia E. 2014. Egyptianising Politics/Politicising Egyptians: An Analysis of Political Jokes. *IOSR-JHSS Journal of Humanities and Social Science* 19 (6). 20–31. https://www.iosrjournals.org/iosr-jhss/papers/Vol19-issue6/Version-7/D019672031.pdf (accessed 19 October 2020).

Ḥamūda, 'Ādil. 1990. *al-Nukta al-siyyāsiyya. Kayfa yaskharu al-miṣriyyūn min ḥukkāmihim* [Political Jokes. How Egyptians mock their rulers]. Cairo: Dār Sfinks.

Hart, Stephen M. & Wen-chin Ouyang (eds.). 2005. *A Companion to Magical Realism*. Colección Támesis. Rochester, N.Y: Tamesis.

Heerbaart, Fabian. 2020. "We Started to Celebrate Being Egyptian". Humor in the Work of Younger Egyptian Artists. In Sabine Damir-Geilsdorf & Stephan Milich (eds.), *Creative Resistance. Political Humor in the Arab Uprisings*, 103–129. Bielefeld: transcript Verlag.

Helmy, Heba. 2011. Streets of Cairo: Emad Eddin, Once a Hub of Entertainment in Downtown. *Egypt Independent*, 21 May. http://www.egyptindependent.com/news/streets-cairo-emad-eddin-once-hub-entertainment-downtown (accessed 19 October 2020).

Helmy Ibrahim, Amr. 1995. La *nokta* égyptienne ou l'absolu de la souveraineté. In Irène Fenoglio & François Georgeon (eds.), L'humour en Orient [Special Issue]. *Revue du monde musulman et de la Méditerranée* 77–78. 199–212.

Heshmat, Dina. 2004. *L'évolution des représentations de la ville du Caire dans la littérature égyptienne moderne et contemporaine*. Paris: Université Sorbonne Nouvelle – Paris 3 Ph. D. dissertation.

Heshmat, Dina. 2006. *al-Qāhira fī l-adab al-miṣrī al-ḥadīth wa-l-muʿāṣir: min ḥulm al-madīna al-kabīra ilā ʿuzlat al-ḍawāḥī* [Cairo in modern and contemporary Egyptian literature: from the dream of the megalopolis to isolated suburbs]. Cairo: al-Majlis al-aʿlā li-l-thaqāfa.

Heshmat, Dina. 2012. Istasiya de Khayri Shalabi. Le retour du héros engagé pour le changement. Paper presented at the 10th Conference of the European Association for Modern Arabic Literature (EURAMAL), Inalco Paris, 9–12 May.

Heshmat, Dina. 2020. *Egypt 1919. The Revolution in Literature and Film*. Edinburgh: Edinburgh University Press.

Høigilt, Jacob. 2019. *Comics in Contemporary Arab Culture. Politics, Language, and Resistance*. London: I. B. Tauris.

Holcomb, Christopher. 1992. Nodal humor in comic narrative: a semantic analysis of two stories by Twain and Wodehouse. *Humor – International Journal of Humor Research* 5 (3). 233–250. https://doi.org/10.1515/humr.1992.5.3.233 (accessed 19 October 2020).

Hussein, Nashaat Hassan. 1990. *The Sub-Culture of Hashish Users in Egypt: A Descriptive Analytic Study*. Cairo Papers in Social Science 13. Cairo: The American University in Cairo.

Hutcheon, Linda. 2000 [1985]. *A Theory of Parody: The Teachings of Twentieth-Century Art Forms*. Urbana and Chicago: University of Illinois Press.

Hutchins, William. 2010. Ibrāhīm ʿAbd al-Qādir al-Māzinī. In Roger Allen (ed.), *Essays in Arabic Literary Biography: 1850–1950*, 219–225. Wiesbaden: Harrassowitz Verlag.

Irwin, Robert. 2006. Mamluk History and Historians. In Roger Allen & D. S. Richards (eds.), *Arabic Literature in the Post-Classical Period. The Cambridge History of Arabic Literature*, 159–170. Cambridge: Cambridge University Press.

Jacquemond, Richard. 2008. *Conscience of the Nation. Writers, State, and Society in Modern Egypt*. Cairo and New York: AUC Press.

Jacquemond, Richard. 2013. *The Yacoubian Building* and Its Sisters: Reflections on Readership and Written Culture in Modern Egypt. In Walid El Hamamsy & Mounira Soliman (eds.), *Popular Culture in the Middle East and North Africa: A Postcolonial Outlook*, 144–161. New York: Routledge.

Jacquemond, Richard. 2016. Satiric Literature and Other 'Popular' Literary Genres in Egypt Today. *Journal of Arabic and Islamic Studies (JAIS)* 16. 349–367. https://journals.uio.no/JAIS/article/view/4756 (accessed 19 October 2020).

Junge, Christian. 2019. *Die Entblößung der Wörter. aš-Šidyāqs literarische Listen als Kultur- und Gesellschaftskritik im 19. Jahrhundert. Mit historischen Paratexten im Anhang*. Wiesbaden: Reichert Verlag.
Kamāl al-Dīn, Sāmī. 2008. *Alladhīna aḍḥakū ṭūb al-arḍ* [Those who made us laugh] Cairo: Dār al-kitāb al-ʿarabī li-l-nashr wa-l-tawzīʿ.
Kassem-Draz, Céza [Qāsim Draz, Sīzā]. 1981. In Quest of New Narrative Forms: Irony in the Works of Four Egyptian Writers: Jamāl Al-Ghīṭānī, Yaḥyā Al-Ṭāhir ʿAbdallah, Majīd Ṭūbyā, Ṣunʿallah Ibrāhīm (1967–1979). *Journal of Arabic Literature* 12. 137–159. https://www.jstor.org/stable/4183051 (accessed 19 October 2020).
Kassem-Draz, Céza [Qāsim Draz, Sīzā]. 1982. al-Mufāraqa fī l-qaṣṣ al-ʿarabī al-muʿāṣir [Irony in contemporary Arabic prose]. *Fuṣūl* 2. 143–151.
Kazarian, Shahe S. 2011. Humor in the Collectivist Arab Middle East: The Case of Lebanon. *Humor – International Journal of Humor Research* 24 (3). 329–348. https://doi.org/10.1515/humr.2011.020 (accessed 19 October 2020).
Kazazian, Anna. 1995. Saroukhan ou la satire amère de l'histoire. Les débuts d'un caricaturiste arménien en Égypt. In Irène Fenoglio & François Georgeon (eds.), L'humour en Orient [Special Issue]. *Revue du monde musulman et de la Méditerranée* 77–78. 175–189.
Kebede, Tewodros Aragie, Kristian Takvam Kindt & Jacob Høigilt. 2013. *Language Change in Egypt: Social and Cultural Indicators* Survey. *A Tabulation Report*. Fafo-report 39. https://www.fafo.no/index.php/zoo-publikasjoner/fafo-rapporter/item/language-change-in-egypt-social-and-cultural-indicators-survey (accessed 19 October 2020).
Keith-Spiegel, Patricia. 1972. Early Conceptions of Humor: Variety and Issues. In Jeffrey H. Goldstein & Paul E. McGhee (eds.), *Psychology of Humor. Theoretical Perspectives and Empirical Issues*, 4–34. New York and London: Academic Press.
Kennedy, Philip F. 2006. The *Maqāmāt* as a Nexus of Interests. Reflections on Abdelfattah Kilito's *Les Séances*. In Julia Bray (ed.), *Writing and Representation in Medieval Islam: Muslim Horizons*, 153–214. London and New York: Routledge.
Khayr, Muḥammad. 2013. Nisāʾ al-Karantīnā. al-sukhriyya min al-mustaqbal [Nisāʾ al-Karantīnā – satire from the future]. *Al-Taḥrīr*, 8 June. http://www.masress.com/tahrirnews/339223 (accessed 19 October 2020).
Kilito, Abdelfattah. 1983. *Les Séances: récits et codes culturels chez Hamadhânî et Harîrî*. Paris: Sindbad.
Kilpatrick, Hilary. 1993. The Egyptian Novel from Zaynab to 1980. In M. M. Badawi (ed.), *Modern Arabic Literature. The Cambridge History of Arabic Literature*, 223–269. Cambridge: Cambridge University Press.
Kilpatrick, Hilary. 1998. The "genuine" Ashʿab. The relativity of fact and fiction in early adab texts. In Stefan Leder (ed.), *Story-Telling in the Framework of Non-Fictional Arabic Literature*, 94–117. Wiesbaden: Harrassowitz Verlag.
Kishtainy, Khalid. 1985. *Arab Political Humour*. London: Quartet Books.
Kishtainy, Khalid. 2009. Humor and Resistance in the Arab World and Greater Middle East. In Maria J. Stephan (ed.), *Civilian Jihad: Nonviolent Struggle, Democratization, and Governance in the Middle East*, 53–64. New York: Palgrave Macmillan.
Koestler, Arthur. 1975 [1964]. *The Act of Creation*. New York: Macmillan.
Kolk, Mieke & Freddy Decreus (eds.). 2005. *The Performance of the Comic in Arabic Theatre: Cultural Heritage, Western Models and Postcolonial Hybridity*. Gent: Documentatiecentrum voor Dramatische Kunst, Universiteit Gent.

Lagrange, Frédéric. 2015. Le marginal comme modèle national. Fumeurs de haschich et gueux sublimes dans le *Ṣāliḥ Hēṣa* de Ḫayrī Šalabī. In Ève Feuillebois-Pierunek & Zaïneb Ben Lagha (eds.), *Étrangeté de l'autre, singularité du moi. Les figures du marginal dans les littératures*, 567–588. Paris: Classiques Garnier.
Lane-Poole, Stanley. 1898. *Saladin and the Fall of the Kingdom of Jerusalem*. New York and London: G.P. Putnam's Sons.
Lane-Poole, Stanley. 1901. *A History of Egypt in the Middle Ages*. London: Methuen.
Lane-Poole, Stanley. 1906. *The Story of Cairo*. London: J. M. Dent & co.
Larkin-Galiñanes, Cristina. 2000. Relevance Theory, Humour, and the Narrative Structure of Humorous Novels. *Revista Alicantina de Estudios Ingleses* 13. 95–106. http://hdl.handle.net/10045/5334 (accessed 19 October 2020).
Larkin-Galiñanes, Cristina. 2002. Narrative Structure in Humorous Novels: The Case of *Lucky Jim*. *Babel afial: Aspectos de filología inglesa y alemana* 1 Extra. 141–170.
Larkin-Galiñanes, Cristina. 2017. An Overview of Humor Theory. In Salvatore Attardo (ed.), *The Routledge Handbook of Language and Humor*, 4–16. New York: Routledge.
Larsen, Egon. 1980. *Wit as a Weapon: The Political Joke in History*. London: F. Muller.
Larzul, Sylvette. 1995. Un récit comique des *Mille et une nuits*: l'«histoire d'Abû l-Ḥasan, ou le dormeur éveillé». In Irène Fenoglio & François Georgeon (eds.), L'humour en Orient [Special Issue]. *Revue du monde musulman et de la Méditerranée* 77–78. 29–39.
Lindsey, Ursula. 2010a. Book Review: "Why Did You Leave the Village?" *The National*, 7 January. http://www.thenational.ae/arts-culture/book-review-why-did-you-leave-the-village (accessed 19 October 2020).
Lindsey, Ursula. 2010b. Abu Golayyel: Wrestling with Identity. *Egypt Independent*, 23 February. http://www.egyptindependent.com/news/abu-golayyel-wrestling-identity (accessed 19 October 2020).
Lindsey, Ursula. 2010c. And Then Cairo Turned Itself Inside Out. *The National*, 4 March. http://www.thenational.ae/world/middle-east/and-then-cairo-turned-itself-inside-out (accessed 19 October 2020).
López-Bernal, Desirée. 2015. El humor en la literatura árabe medieval (de Oriente a al-Andalus). *Sociedad Española de Estudios Árabes. Actas de Simposios* 1. 171–182. http://hdl.handle.net/10481/42356 (accessed 19 October 2020).
Lynx Qualey, Marcia. 2010a. One-Minute Review: A Dog with No Tail. *ArabLit*, 7 March. http://arablit.org/2010/03/07/one-minute-review-a-dog-with-no-tail/ (accessed 19 October 2020).
Lynx Qualey, Marcia. 2010b. The Rise of Egyptian Satiric Literature: Good, Bad, Indifferent? *ArabLit*, 14 October. http://arablit.org/2010/10/14/the-rise-of-egyptian-satiric-literature-good-bad-indifferent/ (accessed 19 October 2020).
Lynx Qualey, Marcia. 2011a. Q&A with Adam Talib, Translator of Khairy Shalaby's "The Hashish Waiter". *ArabLit*, 8 July. https://arablit.org/2011/07/08/qa-with-adam-talib-translator-of-khairy-shalabys-the-hashish-waiter/ (accessed 19 October 2020).
Lynx Qualey, Marcia. 2011b. Q&A with Michael Cooperson, Translator of Shalaby's "Time Travels". *ArabLit*, 9 July. https://arablit.org/2011/07/09/qa-with-michael-cooperson-translator-of-shalabys-time-travels/ (accessed 19 October 2020).
Lynx Qualey, Marcia. 2011c. "The Hashish Waiter": Freedom and Escape in the Era of Camp David. *Egypt Independent*, 28 August. http://www.egyptindependent.com/news/hashish-waiter-freedom-and-escape-era-camp-david (accessed 19 October 2020).

Lynx Qualey, Marcia. 2014. Discussing "Women of Karantina": A Savage Comic Epic, Relentlessly Ironic, Uncompromisingly Rude, Profoundly Moral, Totally True. *ArabLit*, 13 October. https://arablit.org/2014/10/13/discussing-women-of-karantina-a-savage-comic-epic-relentlessly-ironic-uncompromisingly-rude-profoundly-moral-totally-true/ (accessed 19 October 2020).

Malti-Douglas, Fedwa. 1980. Humor and Structure in Two "Buḫalāʾ" Anecdotes: Al-Ǧāhiẓ and Al-Ḫaṭīb Al-Baghdādī. *Arabica* 27 (3). 300–323. http://www.jstor.org/stable/4056575 (accessed 19 October 2020).

Malti-Douglas, Fedwa. 1983. Min al-tārīkh al-sirrī li-Nuʿmān ʿAbd al-Ḥāfiẓ wa-tadmīr ṭuqūs al-ḥayāh wa-l-lugha [The Secret History and the rupture of the rituals of life and language]. *Ibdāʿ* 6–7. 86–92.

Malti-Douglas, Fedwa. 1993. Mahfouz's Dreams. In Michael Beard & Adnan Haydar (eds.), *Naguib Mahfouz: From Regional Fame to Global Recognition*, 126–143. Syracuse, N.Y: Syracuse University Press.

Mannone, Nathanael. 2020. Beyond *Tanfis*: Performativity and Quotidian Humor in Revolutionary Tunisia. In Sabine Damir-Geilsdorf & Stephan Milich (eds.), *Creative Resistance. Political Humor in the Arab Uprisings*, 53–77. Bielefeld: transcript Verlag.

Marino, Danilo. 2016. Raconter l'ivresse à l'époque mamelouke. Les mangeurs de haschich comme motif littéraire. *Annales islamologiques* 49: 55–80. http://journals.openedition.org/anisl/1595 (accessed 19 October 2020).

Marszalek, Agnes. 2020. *Style and Emotion in Comic Novels and Short Stories*. London: Bloomsbury Academic.

Martin, Rod A. 2007. *The Psychology of Humor: An Integrative Approach*. Burlington, MA: Elsevier Academic Press.

Marzolph, Ulrich. 1983. *Der Weise Narr Buhlūl*. Wiesbaden: Steiner.

Marzolph, Ulrich. 1992. *Arabia Ridens: die humoristische Kurzprosa der frühen adab-Literatur im internationalen Traditionsgeflecht*. 2 vols. Frankfurt am Main: Vittorio Klostermann.

Marzolph, Ulrich. 1996. *Nasreddin Hodscha. 666 Wahre Geschichten*. München: Beck.

Marzolph, Ulrich. 1998. "Focusees" of Jocular Fiction in Classical Arabic Literature. In Stefan Leder (ed.), *Story-Telling in the Framework of Non-Fictional Arabic Literature*, 118–129. Wiesbaden: Harrassowitz Verlag.

Marzolph, Ulrich. 2002. Sanitizing Humor: Islamic Mediterranean Jocular Tradition in a Comparative Perspective. In Michele Bernardini et al. (eds.), *Europa e Islam tra i secoli XIV e XVI / Europe and Islam between [the] 14th and 16th Centuries*, vol. 2: 757–782. Napoli: Istituto Universitario Orientale.

Marzolph, Ulrich. 2005. Juḥā in the *Arabian Nights*. *Journal of Arabic Literature* 36 (3). 311–322. https://www.jstor.org/stable/4183553 (accessed 19 October 2020).

Marzolph, Ulrich. 2009. Provokative Grenzbereiche im klassischen arabischen Witz. In Georges Tamer (ed.), *Humor in der arabischen Kultur / Humor in Arabic Culture*, 153–166. Berlin: de Gruyter.

Marzolph, Ulrich. 2010a. Buhlūl. *EAL*, 160–161.

Marzolph, Ulrich. 2010b. hazl. *EAL*, 281.

Marzolph, Ulrich. 2010c. humour. *EAL*, 294–295.

Marzolph, Ulrich. 2015. The Story of Abū al-Ḥasan the Wag in the Tübingen Manuscript of the Romance of ʿUmar Ibn al-Nuʿmān and Related Texts. *Journal of Arabic Literature* 46 (1). 34–67. https://www.jstor.org/stable/44072434 (accessed 19 October 2020).

Marzolph, Ulrich. Naṣr al-Dīn Khodja. *EI2*.

Marzolph, Ulrich, Richard van Leeuwen & Hassan Wassouf (eds.). 2004. *The Arabian Nights Encyclopedia*. 2 vols. Santa Barbara, California: ABC-CLIO.

Mauritz, Hans. 2009. Autorenforum: Muhammad Mustagab – Der böse Spötter aus Oberägypten. *Leben in Luxor*. http://www.leben-in-luxor.de/luxor_essays_mauritz_mustagab.html (accessed 19 October 2020).

Mehrez, Samia. 1993. Kitābat al-qariyya fī l-adab al-muʿāṣir [Writing the village in contemporary literature]. *Mawāqif* 70–71. 162–175.

Mehrez, Samia. 1994. *Egyptian Writers between History and Fiction. Essays on Naguib Mahfouz, Sonallah Ibrahim and Gamal al-Ghitani*. Cairo: AUC Press.

Mehrez, Samia. 2010a. *Egypt's Culture Wars. Politics and Practice*. Cairo and New York: AUC Press.

Mehrez, Samia. 2010b. *The Literary Atlas of Cairo. One Hundred Years on the Streets of the City*. Cairo and New York: AUC Press.

Meisami, Julie Scott & Paul Starkey (eds.). 2010 [1998]. *Encyclopedia of Arabic Literature*. London and New York: Routledge.

Mersal, Iman. 2011. Revolutionary Humor. *Globalizations* 8 (5). 669–674.

el-Messiri, Sawsan. 1978. *Ibn al-Balad: A Concept of Egyptian Idenity*. Brill: Leiden.

Metwally, Mohammed. 2014. *Margins in the Center. Reading Thresholds of the Egyptian Novel. A Study of Structure and Significance*. Berlin: Freien Universität Ph.D. dissertation.

Milich, Stephan & Leslie Tramontini. 2018. Writing against Injustice and Oppression: On the Literary Commitment of Muẓaffar al-Nawwāb and Muḥammad al-Māghūṭ. *al-Abhath* 62–63. 103–133.

Mizzau, Marina. 1984. *L'ironia. La contraddizione consentita*. Milano: Feltrinelli.

Monaco, Arturo. 2019. Comic Folk Literature in the Time of Facebook: Luqmān Dayrakī and His Posts on Facebook. In Stephan Guth & Teresa Pepe (eds.). *Arabic Literature in a Post-Human World. Proceedings of the 12th Conference of the European Association for Modern Arabic Literature (EURAMAL), May 2016, Oslo*, 331–353. Wiesbaden: Harrassowitz Verlag.

Monroe, James T. 1983. *The Art of Badīʿ az-Zamān al-Hamadhānī as Picaresque Narrative*. Beirut: AUB Press.

Montgomery, James E. 2009. *Al-Jāḥiẓ* on Jest and Earnest. In Georges Tamer (ed.), *Humor in der arabischen Kultur / Humor in Arabic Culture*, 209–239. Berlin: de Gruyter.

Montgomery, James E. 2013. *Al-Jāḥiẓ: In Praise of Books*. Edinburgh: Edinburgh University Press.

Moreh, Shmuel. 1992. *Live Theatre and Dramatic Literature in the Medieval Arabic World*. Edinburgh: Edinburgh University Press.

Moreh, Shmuel. 2010. shadow-play. *EAL*, 701–702.

Muecke, D. C. 1969. *The Compass of Irony*. London: Methuen.

Muftī, Bashīr. 2011. "Al-Fāʿil" li-Ḥamdī Abū Julayyil: riwāyat al-maqāṭiʿ al-dhātiyya [*Al-Fāʿil* by Ḥamdī Abū Julayyil: a novel of autobiographical fragments]. *Al-Ḥayāh*, 10 December. (link no longer available)

Müller, Kathrin. 1993. *Und der Kalif lachte bis er auf den Rücken fiel: ein Beitrag zur Phraseologie und Stilkunde des klassischen Arabisch*. Munich: Bayerischen Akademie der Wissenschaften.

al-Musawy, Muhsin. 2006. Pre-Modern Belletristic Prose. In Roger Allen & D. S. Richards (eds.), *Arabic Literature in the Post-Classical Period. The Cambridge History of Arabic Literature*, 101–133. Cambridge: Cambridge University Press.

Musca, Giosuè. 1996. *Carlo Magno e Hārūn al-Rashīd*. Bari: Dedalo.

Mustajāb, Muḥammad Muḥammad. 2016. ʿAn tafāṣīl al-ḥayāh al-yawmiyya. Muḥammad Mustajāb al-ibn yastaʿīdu dhikrayyāt Mustajāb al-ab fī l-sadd al-ʿālī [The details of everyday life. Mustajāb's son revives his father's memories of the High Dam]. *Al-Ahram*, 16 January. https://www.masress.com/ahram/1468895 (accessed 19 October 2020).
Naaman, Mara. 2011 *Urban Space in Contemporary Egyptian Literature. Portraits of Cairo.* New York: Palgrave Macmillan.
Nadā, Aḥmad. 2013. Nisāʾ al-Karantīnā. al-wuṣūl ilā l-malḥama [Nisāʾ al-Karantīnā all the way to epics]. *Akhbār al-adab*, 5 October. https://www.masress.com/adab/7193 (accessed 19 October 2020).
Neuwirth, Angelika. 2009. Ayyu ḥarajin ʻalā man ansha'a mulaḥan? Al-Ḥarīrī's plea for the legitimacy of playful transgression of social norms. In Georges Tamer (ed.), *Humor in der arabischen Kultur / Humor in Arabic Culture*, 241–254. Berlin: de Gruyter.
Nicolas, Michèle. 1995. La comédie humaine dans le Karagöz. In Irène Fenoglio & François Georgeon (eds.), L'humour en Orient [Special Issue]. *Revue du monde musulman et de la Méditerranée 77–78*. 75–87.
Nilsen, Alleen & Don Nilsen. 2008. Literature and Humor. In Victor Raskin (ed.), *The Primer of Humor Research*, 243–280. Berlin and New York: Mouton de Gruyter.
Olson, Elder. 1968. *The Theory of Comedy*. Bloomington, IN: Indiana University Press.
Osti, Letizia. 2006. Scholarly Competition in Third/Ninth Century Baghdad: The Case of Thaʿlab and al-Mubarrad. *Quaderni di Studi Arabi* 1. 87–112. https://www.jstor.org/stable/25802989 (accessed 19 October 2020).
Osti, Letizia. 2013. A Grammarian's Life in his own Voice. Autobiographical Fragments in Arabic Biographical Literature. In Monique Bernards (ed.), *ʿAbbasid Studies IV. Occasional Papers of the School of ʿAbbāsid Studies – Leuven, July 5–July 9, 2010*, 142–179. Warminster: Gibb Memorial Trust.
Ott, Claudia. 2009. Worüber lacht *Tausendundeine Nacht*?. In Georges Tamer (ed.), *Humor in der arabischen Kultur / Humor in Arabic Culture*, 255–262. Berlin: de Gruyter.
Otto, Beatrice K. 2001. *Fools Are Everywhere. The Court Jester around the World*. Chicago and London: University of Chicago Press.
Ouyang, Wen-chin. 2013. *Poetics of Love in the Arabic Novel: Nation-State, Modernity and Tradition*. Edinburgh: Edinburgh University Press.
Paniconi, Maria Elena. 2006a. *Narrare il disincanto. L'ironia nel romanzo egiziano deli anni Ottanta e Novanta*. Venezia: Università Ca' Foscari Ph.D. dissertation.
Paniconi, Maria Elena. 2006b. Il romanzo sperimentale egiziano degli anni Novanta: gli esempi di Muṣṭafā Ḏikrī, Muntaṣir Al-Qaffāš, May al-Tilmisānī. *Annali di Ca' Foscari* XLV (3). 65–91.
Pepe, Teresa. 2012. Autofiction on Screen: Self-representation of an Egyptian 'Spinster' in a Literary Blog, *Journal of New Media Studies in MENA* 1. 1–10.
Pérès, Henri. 1944. Les origines d'un roman célèbre de la littérature arabe moderne: «Ḥadīṯ ʿĪsā ibn Hišām» de Muḥammad al-Muwailiḥī. *Bulletin d'études orientales* 10. 101–118.
Perho, Irmeli. 2001. Al-Maqrīzī and Ibn Taghrī Birdī as Historians of Contemporary Events. In Hugh Kennedy (ed.), *The Historiography of Islamic Egypt (c. 950– 1800)*, 107–120. Leiden: Brill.
Pomerantz, Maurice A. & Bilal W. Orfali. 2013. A Lost Maqāma of Badīʿ al-Zamān al-Hamaḏānī? *Arabica* 60 (3–4). 245–271.
Popper, William. Abū 'l-Maḥāsin, Ibn Taghrībirdī. *EI2*.

Poulet, Solange. 1995. Cinéma et politique en Égypte: une stratégie du rire. In Irène Fenoglio & François Georgeon (eds.), L'humour en Orient [Special Issue]. *Revue du monde musulman et de la Méditerranée* 77–78. 213–224.

Propp, Vladimir. 2009. *On the Comic and Laughter*. Toronto, Buffalo, and London: University of Toronto Press. [Translation of *Problemy komizma i smekha*, 1976]

Rabbat, Nasser. Khiṭaṭ. *EI3*.

Radwan, Noha. 2012. *Egyptian Colloquial Poetry in the Modern Arabic Canon. New Readings of* Shiʿr al-ʿĀmmiyya. New York: Palgrave Macmillan.

Rakha, Youssef. 1999. Ibrahim Mansour: The Duke in His Domain. *Al-Ahram Weekly*, Issue No. 452, 21–27 October. (link no longer available)

Rakha, Youssef. 2000. End of an Era. *Al-Ahram Weekly*, Issue No. 499, 14–20 September. https://www.arabworldbooks.com/e-zine/end-of-an-era (accessed 19 October 2020).

Ramadan, Yasmine. 2019. *Space in Modern Egyptian Fiction*. Edinburgh: Edinburgh University Press.

Raskin, Victor. 1985. *Semantic Mechanisms of Humor*. Dordrecht: D. Reidel.

Reynolds, Dwight F. 2006. Sīrat Banī Hilāl. In Roger Allen & D. S. Richards (eds.), *Arabic Literature in the Post-Classical Period. The Cambridge History of Arabic Literature*, 307–318. Cambridge: Cambridge University Press.

Rosenbaum, Gabriel M. 2011. The Rise and Expansion of Colloquial Egyptian Arabic as a Literary Language. In Rakefet Sela-Sheffy & Gideon Toury (eds.), *Culture Contacts and the Making of Cultures: Papers in Homage to Itamar Even-Zohar*, 323–343. Tel-Aviv: Unit of Culture Research, Tel Aviv University.

Rosenthal, Franz. 1971. *The Herb: Hashish Versus Medieval Muslim Society*. Leiden: Brill.

Rosenthal, Franz. 2011 [1956]. *Humor in Early Islam*. With an introduction by Geert J. van Gelder. Leiden: Brill.

Rosenthal, Franz. al-Maḳrīzī. *EI2*.

Rowson, E. K. 2010a. mujūn. *EAL*, 546–548.

Rowson, E. K. 2010b. sukhf. *EAL*, 743.

Rundgren, Frithiof. 1970–1971. Arabische Literatur Und Orientalische Antike. *Orientalia Suecana* 19–20. 81–124.

Ruocco, Monica. 1987. Il Teatro e la Storia nel Masrah al-Tasyis di Sa'd Allah Wannus. *Oriente Moderno* VI (LXVII). 7–12.

Ruocco, Monica. 2010. *Storia del teatro arabo. Dalla* nahḍah *a oggi*. Roma: Carocci.

Sadan, Joseph. 1984. *Al-adab al-ʿarabī al-hāzil wa-nawādir al-thuqalāʾ* [Humorous Arabic literature and anecdotes about simpletons]. Acre: Maktabat wa-maṭbaʿat al-Sarūjī.

Sadan, Joseph. 1989. An Admirable and Ridiculous Hero: Some Notes on the Bedouin in Medieval Arabic Belles Lettres, on a Chapter of Adab by al-Râghib al-Iṣfahânî, and on a Literary Model in Which Admiration and Mockery Coexist. *Poetics Today* 10 (3). 471–492. https://www.jstor.org/stable/1772901 (accessed 19 October 2020).

al-Saʿdanī, Maḥmūd. 1991. *al-Muḍḥikūn* [Humourists]. Cairo: Dār al-hilāl, 1991.

Salem, Heba & Kantaro Taira. 2012. *al-Thawra al-daHika*: The Challenges of Translating Revolutionary Humor. In Samia Mehrez (ed.), *Translating Egypt's Revolution: The Language of Tahrir*, 183–211. Cairo and New York: AUC Press.

Schapiro, Meyer. 1956. Leonardo and Freud: An Art-Historical Study. *Journal of the History of Ideas* 17 (2). 147–178.

Schmidt, Jean-Jacques. 2013a. *Historiettes, anecdotes et bons mots*. Arles: Sindbad/Actes Sud.

Schmidt, Jean-Jacques. 2013b. *Le Livre de l'humour arabe*. Arles: Babel/Actes Sud.
Selaiha, Nehad. 2001. From Page to Stage. Nehad Selaiha is Bewitched and Repelled by a Stage Version of a Popular Satirical Novel. *Al-Ahram Weekly*, 5–11 July 2001. (link no longer available)
Selim, Samah. 2003. The Narrative Craft: Realism and Fiction in the Arabic Canon. *Edebiyat: Journal of Middle Eastern Literatures* 14 (1–2). 109–128. doi:10.1080/03646550332000173361 (accessed 19 October 2020).
Selim, Samah. 2004. *The Novel and the Rural Imaginary in Egypt, 1880–1985*. London and New York: Routledge.
Shehata, Samer S. 1992. The Politics of Laughter: Nasser, Sadat, and Mubarek in Egyptian Political Jokes. *Folklore* 103 (1). 75–91.
Simpson, Paul. 2003. *On the Discourse of Satire*. Amsterdam: John Benjamins.
Simpson, Paul & Derek Bousfield. 2017. Humor and stylistics. In Salvatore Attardo (ed.), *The Routledge Handbook of Language and Humor*, 158–173. New York: Routledge.
Somekh, Sasson. 1993. Colloquialized *fuṣḥā* in modern Arabic prose fiction. *Jerusalem Studies in Arabic and Islam* 16. 176–194.
Starkey, Paul. 2001. Egyptian History in the Modern Egyptian Novel. In Hugh Kennedy (ed.), *The Historiography of Islamic Egypt (c. 950–1800)*, 251–262. Leiden: Brill.
Starkey, Paul. 2006a. Book Reviews – Women of Karantina. *Banipal* 53. http://www.banipal.co.uk/book_reviews/125/women-of-karantina/ (accessed 19 October 2020).
Starkey, Paul. 2006b. "Heroes" and Characters in the Novels of Ṣunʿallāh Ibrāhīm. *Middle Eastern Literatures* 9 (2). 147–157. doi:10.1080/14752620600814228 (accessed 19 October 2020).
Starkey, Paul. 2016. *Sonallah Ibrahim. Rebel with a Pen*. Edinburgh: Edinburgh University Press.
Stavrakopoulou, Anna. 2012. Ottoman Karagöz and Greek Shadow Theatre: Communicational Shifts and Variants in a Multi-Ethnic and Ethnic Context. In Dominic Parviz Brookshaw (ed.), *Ruse and Wit: The Humorous in Arabic, Persian, and Turkish Narrative*, 146–157. Boston and Washington: Ilex Foundation and the Center for Hellenic Studies.
Stewart, Devin. 2006. The Maqāma. In Roger Allen & D. S. Richards (eds.), *Arabic Literature in the Post-Classical Period. The Cambridge History of Arabic Literature*, 145–158. Cambridge: Cambridge University Press.
Stewart, Devin. 2015. Humor. In Dwight F. Reynolds (ed.), *The Cambridge Companion to Modern Arab Culture*, 224–248. Cambridge: Cambridge University Press.
Talib, Adam. 2018. *How Do You Say "Epigram" in Arabic? Literary History at the Limits of Comparison*. Leiden: Brill.
Talib, Adam, Marlé Hammond & Arie Schippers (eds.). 2014. *The Rude, the Bad and the Bawdy. Essays in Honour of Professor Geert Jan van Gelder*. Cambridge: Gibb Memorial Trust.
Tamer, Georges (ed.). 2009. *Humor in der arabischen Kultur / Humor in Arabic Culture*. Berlin: de Gruyter, 2009. In this volume: Tamer, Georges. Introduction, ix–xx; The Qurʾān and Humor, 3–28.
Tamer, Georges. 2014. Arabic culture, humor in. In Salvatore Attardo (ed.), *Encyclopedia of Humor Studies*, vol.1, 55–59. Los Angeles: SAGE.
Tarbush, Susannah. 2007. Book Reviews – The Lodging House by Khairy Shalaby. *Banipal* 30. http://www.banipal.co.uk/book_reviews/32/the-lodging-house-by-khairy-shalaby/ (accessed 19 October 2020).

Tarbush, Susannah. 2009. "Tales from Dayrut": Feudalism, Folklore and Fantasy. *Saudi Gazette*, 9 March. http://thetanjara.blogspot.com/2009/03/auc-press-publishes-tales-from-dayrut.html (accessed 19 October 2020).

Tarbush, Susannah. 2012. Book Reviews – The Hashish Waiter by Khairy Shalaby. *Banipal* 44. http://www.banipal.co.uk/back_issues/82/issue-44/ (accessed 19 October 2020).

Temlali, Yassin. 2008. «Al Faîl» de Hamdi Abou Golayyel, ou le Caire souterrain des déracinés. *BabelMed*, 20 December. http://www.babelmed.net/letteratura/236-algeria/3846-al-fa-l-de-hamdi-abou-golayyel-ou-le-caire-souterrain-des-d-racin-s.html (accessed 19 October 2020).

Thompson, Stith. 1989. *Motif-Index of Folk-Literature: A Classification of Narrative Elements in Folktales, Ballads, Myths, Fables, Mediaeval Romances, Exempla, Fabliaux, Jest-Books, and Local Legends*. 6 vols. Bloomington, IN: Indiana University Press.

Triezenberg, Katrina. 2004. Humor Enhancers in the Study of Humorous Literature. *Humor – International Journal of Humor Research* 17 (4). 411–418. doi:10.1515/humr.2004.17.4.411 (accessed 19 October 2020).

Triezenberg, Katrina. 2008. Humor in Literature. In Victor Raskin (ed.), *The Primer of Humor Research*, 523–542. Berlin and New York: Mouton de Gruyter.

Truitt, E. R. 2015. *Medieval Robots. Mechanism, Magic, Nature, and Art*. Philadelphia: University of Pennsylvania Press.

van Gelder, Geert J. 1988. *The Bad and the Ugly. Attitudes Toward Invective Poetry* (Hijā') *in Classical Arabic Literature*. Leiden: Brill.

van Gelder, Geert J. 1992a. Mixtures of Jest and Earnest in Classical Arabic Literature. Part I. *Journal of Arabic Literature* 23 (2). 83–108. https://www.jstor.org/stable/4183266 (accessed 19 October 2020).

van Gelder, Geert J. 1992b. Mixtures of Jest and Earnest in Classical Arabic Literature. Part II. *Journal of Arabic Literature* 23 (3). 169–190. https://www.jstor.org/stable/4183275 (accessed 19 October 2020).

van Gelder, Geert J. 2010a. hijāʾ. *EAL*, 284–285.

van Gelder, Geert J. 2010b. satire, medieval. *EAL*, 693–695.

van Leeuwen, Richard. 2005. Lies, Illusions and Authority. The Thousand and One Nights and Arabic Comic Theatre. In Mieke Kolk & Freddy Decreus (eds.), *The Performance of the Comic in Arabic Theatre: Cultural Heritage, Western Models and Postcolonial Hybridity*, 210–224. Gent: Documentatiecentrum voor Dramatische Kunst, Universiteit Gent.

Wedel, Gerhard. Ibn Khallikān. *EI3*.

Winter, Michael. 2006. Historiography in Arabic During the Ottoman Period. In Roger Allen & D. S. Richards (eds)., *Arabic Literature in the Post-Classical Period. The Cambridge History of Arabic Literature*, 171–188. Cambridge: Cambridge University Press.

Zaki, Mona. 2007. Mona Zaki reviews "Thieves in Retirement" by Hamdi Abu Golayyel. *Banipal* 29. http://www.banipal.co.uk/book_reviews/16/thieves-in-retirement-by-hamdi-abu-golayyel/ (accessed 19 October 2020).

Zanelli, Patrizia. 2011. Egitto, mitica terra della risata. In Paolo Branca, Barbara de Poli & Patrizia Zanelli, *Il sorriso della mezzaluna. Umorismo, ironia e satira nella cultura araba*, 103–141. Roma: Carocci.

Zargar, Cyrus Ali. 2006. The Satiric Method of Ibn Dāniyāl: Morality and Anti-Morality in "Ṭayf al-Khayāl". *Journal of Arabic Literature* 37 (1), 68–108. www.jstor.org/stable/4183560 (accessed 19 October 2020).

Websites and videos

Abou Naddara Collection. http://kjc-sv016.kjc.uni-heidelberg.de:8080/exist/apps/naddara/project.html (accessed 19 October 2020).

Centre de recherche sur les médiation (crem). Colloque International Humour et politique dans l'espace arabe de la Nahda à aujourd'hui. Nancy: Université de Lorraine, 5–6 December 2019. https://crem.univ-lorraine.fr/humour-et-politique-dans-lespace-arabe-de-la-nahda-aujourdhui (accessed 19 October 2020).

Eltoukhy, Nael interviewed by AUC Press. 2014. *The man behind 'Women of Karantina'*. 3 December. Video available at: https://www.youtube.com/watch?v=3_KCjH6Bi5w (accessed 19 October 2020).

Eltoukhy, Nael interviewed by Nataša Ďurovičová. 2016. *On the Map 2015: Nael Eltoukhy*. Interviews with Writers in Residence (The University of Iowa). 16 February. Video available at: https://www.youtube.com/watch?v=3_KCjH6Bi5w (accessed 19 October 2020).

Guyer, Jonathan. *Oum Cartoon*. http://oumcartoon.tumblr.com/?og=1 (accessed 19 October 2020).

Mamluk Studies Resources. http://mamluk.uchicago.edu/ (accessed 19 October 2020).

Mamluk Bibliography Online. http://mamluk.lib.uchicago.edu/index.html (accessed 19 October 2020).

https://doi.org/10.1515/9783110725414-011

Index

ʿAbd al-ʿĀl, Ghāda 47
Abū Julayyil, Ḥamdī 56–67
– *al-Fāʿil (A Dog with No Tail)* 157–180
– *Luṣūṣ mutaqāʿidūn* (*Thieves in Retirement*) 62, 64–66, 158–160, 180
Abū Nuwās 25, 34, 94
Abū Ṭāḥūn (Bedouin village) 170–173
adab hazlī (jocular literature) 10, 12
adab sākhir (satirical literature) 2, 3, 10, 39, 48, 57
affiliative function (also group affiliation) 53, 54, 121, 122, 128, 143, 176, 195
Alexandria 3, 56, 105, 198, 201
alienation 49, 50, 158, 162, 170, 185
– crowded alienation 163, 185
antihero 29, 49, 50, 53, 54, 63, 82–92, 96, 98
Arabian Nights (*Alf layla wa-layla*) 33–35, 113
ʿashwāʾiyya (pl. *ʿashwāʾiyyāt*, shantytown) 50, 131, 163, 164
Aṣlān, Ibrāhīm 50, 58, 59, 61
Attardo, Salvatore & Raskin, Victor see General Theory of Verbal Humour (GTVH)
Attardo, Salvatore see narrative humour and register humour
al-ʿĀydī, Aḥmad 47, 113, 117

Bakhtin, Mikhail
– carnivalesque 1, 41, 51, 87, 104, 125–127
– comic scarecrow 125
– grotesque realism 104, 126
Bergson, Henri 15, 16, 196
biographical genre 68, 76, 83, 187, 192, 193
Bourdieu, Pierre see literary field

Chłopicki, Władysław see narrative humour
court chronicle 108, 109, 193, 199
creative resistance 1, 14, 41, 196, 203
cultural heritage (*turāth*) 8, 24, 46, 54, 94, 131, 186, 188, 190, 198, 199

Dayrūṭ (also Deirut, Upper Egypt) 55, 68, 73, 193
dictionary 137, 149, 196
diglossia 43
donkey 32, 33, 42, 79, 83, 90, 91
double 32, 102, 103, 109–114, 122, 123, 137, 139, 153, 155, 165, 166, 179, 180, 190, 199

earthquake 118, 161, 162, 186
Egyptian Colloquial Arabic (ECA) xiii, 2, 89, 97, 120, 124, 126, 128, 130, 148–150, 159, 193, 196, 197, 200, 201
– literature in the colloquial 37, 46–48, 106
– colloquial poetry see *shiʿr al-ʿāmmiyya*
Egyptianness (also authenticity) 126, 133, 153, 156, 186, 199
epic (*sīra*) 54, 56, 58, 60, 68, 76, 82, 83, 134, 192, 193, 200
– *al-sīra al-hilāliyya* (epic of the Banū Hilāl) 94, 134, 175
Ermida, Isabel see narrative humour

fantasy 13, 50, 61, 63, 71, 75, 87, 97, 103, 125, 196
Fayyūm (northern Upper Egypt) 56, 171, 173, 179
flyting (*naqīḍa*, pl. *naqāʾiḍ*) 14, 176
frame narrative 28, 100, 109, 127
Freud, Sigmund 9, 15, 16, 41, 86
fukāha see humour

General Theory of Verbal Humour (GTVH) 6, 18–20
– Knowledge Resources (KR) 18
Generation of the Nineties 4, 45, 50, 62, 66
Generation of the Sixties 4, 45, 49–52, 60
Genette, Gérard 50, 77, 192
al-Ghīṭānī, Jamāl 5, 49–51, 54, 61, 65, 108, 109

https://doi.org/10.1515/9783110725414-012

Ḥabībī, Imīl 3, 11, 44, 54, 82, 105
al-Ḥakīm, Tawfīq 47, 48, 57, 63, 68, 75
al-Hamadhānī 27–29, 28, 105
al-Ḥarīrī 27
hashish 34, 128–130, 135, 142, 143, 148, 155, 156, 192
– hash den (*ghurza*) 131–133, 182, 185
Ḥaqqī, Yaḥyā 60, 118
hēṣa (rowdiness) 130, 148, 150–153
hijā' (also *hawj*, invective) 13, 14, 25
horror 75, 76, 89, 91, 96, 97, 196
house narrative 162, 163
humour 8–23
– dark humour 14
– humour enhancer 6, 8, 19, 20, 44, 54, 168, 188, 196, 202
– humorous novel 4, 10, 17, 21, 51, 183
– narrative humour 10, 11, 18–23
– political humour (also political jokelore) 1, 38–43
– register humour 23, 44
Ḥussayn, Tāhā 58, 63, 77

Ibn ʿAbd al-Ẓāhir 106, 107, 115
ibn al-balad (authentic Egyptian) 64, 110, 185
Ibn Iyās 49, 116
Ibn al-Jawzī 26, 27, 29
Ibn Khallikān 106, 107, 116, 123
Ibn Taghrībirdī 107, 108, 116, 124, 125, 193
Ibn al-Ṭuwayr 99, 107, 111, 115
Ibrāhīm, Ṣunʿallāh 3, 5, 39, 40, 49–51, 53, 188
Idrīs, Yūsuf 45, 48, 60, 127
interrupted ritual 70, 86–92, 195
irony 12, 23, 28, 44, 49–51, 54, 61, 69, 72, 75, 81, 91, 97, 154, 169, 178–181, 188, 191, 198

al-Jabartī 107
al-Jāḥiẓ 15, 25, 26, 29, 30, 32, 44
jargon 20, 54, 57, 135, 148, 150, 156, 161, 180, 184, 197, 199, 200
al-jidd wa-l-hazl (jest and earnest) 13, 25–27
jocular anecdote 12–15, 24–27, 29, 30, 34

karagöz see *khayāl al-ẓill* (shadow theatre)
khabar (pl. *akhbār*, narrative unit) 17, 125
al-Khamīsī, Khālid 47, 106
al-Khaṭīb al-Baghdādī 15, 29
khayāl al-ẓill (shadow theatre) 14, 24, 35, 36
– Ibn Dāniyāl 35
khiṭaṭ (topography) 54, 65, 107–109, 193, 199
– *Khiṭaṭ al-Ghīṭānī* (al-Ghīṭānī's topography) 108, 109
– *al-Khiṭaṭ al-tawfīqiyya al-jadīda* (The new topography of the reign of Tawfiq) 108
– *al-Mawāʿiẓ wa-l-iʿtibār fī dhikr al-khiṭaṭ wa-l-āthār* (Admonitions and reflections on the quarters and monuments) 108
– *al-Rawḍa al-bahiyya al-ẓāhira fī khiṭaṭ al-muʿizziyya al-Qāhira* (The magnificent garden in the topography of al-Muʿizz's Cairo) 107
Koestler, Arthur 15, 16

labour (also construction work) 160–162, 169
Lane-Poole, Stanley 107
Larkin-Galiñanes, Cristina see humorous novel and narrative humour
literary field 45–47

Madrasat al-mushāghibīn (The school for troublemakers) 154
Maḥfūẓ, Najīb 48, 60, 104, 116, 118, 180, 194, 200
Manshiyyat Nāṣir (Cairo) 56, 64, 66, 158, 163
Manṣūr, Ibrāhīm 61, 116, 136
maqāma (pl. *maqāmāt*) 7, 27–29, 46, 100, 110, 117, 127, 181, 191
– neo-*maqāma* (pl. neo-*maqāmāt*) 46, 48, 101, 106, 110, 191
al-Maqrīzī 65, 106–108, 113, 115, 116, 193
Maʿrūf quarter (Cairo) 129, 131–134, 138, 164
al-Māzinī, Ibrāhīm ʿAbd al-Qādir 46, 48, 57
Mubārak, ʿAlī 65, 101, 108
mufāraqa (ironic distance, paradox) 49, 141, 160
Mustajāb, Muḥammad 46, 55–61, 78

– *Min al-tārīkh al-sirrī li-Nu'mān 'Abd al-Ḥāfiẓ* (*The Secret History*)
– *Dayrūṭ al-sharīf* (Dayrūṭ the noble) 63, 75, 76
al-Muwayliḥī, Muḥammad 46, 100–106, 109, 181

al-Nadīm, 'Abd Allāh 37, 46, 47, 101
nādira (pl. *nawādir*) see jocular anecdote
nahḍa (Arab Renaissance) 46, 48, 100, 101, 105
Nājī, Aḥmad 62, 181
nonsense 13, 27, 81, 97, 144

Old Cairo 118, 185, 186

parody 12, 23, 49, 50, 54, 91, 125, 159, 192, 194, 199
picaresque 29, 54, 65, 100, 103, 105, 106, 109, 112, 119, 127, 166, 184, 189
Propp, Vladimir 15, 16, 187
prison 122, 123, 158, 177, 178, 180, 186, 190
puppet 93–96, 188

Qarāqūsh 8, 30, 98, 123, 124, 189

Raskin, Victor see Semantic Script Theory of Humour (SSTH)
Rayā and Sakīna 201
relief (*tanfīs*) 6, 9, 15, 16, 41, 141, 143, 155, 176, 195
repetition 19, 20, 23, 43, 44, 62, 66, 74, 82, 87, 91, 95, 97, 109, 127, 157, 163, 168, 180, 187, 188, 195, 196, 199
revolution
– 1888-82 'Urābī revolt 37, 84, 101
– 1919 revolution 37, 77, 84, 174, 180, 193
– 1952 revolution 69, 71
– 2011 revolution (also January/Tahrir revolution) 1, 2, 39, 41, 201
al-Rīḥānī, Najīb 94, 124
ruler 43, 94, 103, 114, 117, 119, 122, 123, 128, 146, 189, 199, 200
rural vs urban 73, 132, 185

al-Sa'danī, Maḥmūd 51, 57, 178, 202
Sālim, 'Alī 38, 51, 57, 154, 202
Ṣanū', Ya'qūb (also Sanua, James) 4, 37, 46, 47, 101
satire 12–14, 23, 38, 46, 50, 53, 92–96, 150–153, 195, 196
– satirical press 36–38
self-mockery 37, 53, 66, 111, 122, 142, 143, 145, 151, 169, 180, 183, 184, 195, 199
Semantic Script Theory of Humour (SSTH) 8, 17, 18
Shalabī, Khayrī 51, 52, 54–65
– *Riḥlāt al-ṭurshajī al-ḥalwajī* (*Time-Travels*) 98–129
– *Ṣāliḥ Hēṣa* (*The Hashish Waiter*) 129–156
al-Sharqāwī, 'Abd al-Raḥmān 60, 63, 77, 116
al-Shidyāq, Aḥmad Fāris 46, 101, 181
shi'r al-'āmmiyya (colloquial poetry) 146, 147, 195
slang 2, 48, 62, 148, 160, 195
stereotype 10, 12, 20, 22, 34, 36, 44, 53, 100, 122, 127, 128, 151, 156, 188, 195, 199
stock character (also proverbial character) 29–33, 44, 54, 128, 188–190, 199
– Bedouin 30, 34, 180, 190–192
– court jester 11, 31, 99, 112, 113, 189, 202
– focusee 30
– Juḥā 30–33, 35, 44, 188, 189
– miser 15, 26, 29
– simpleton (also village yokel) 26, 29, 54, 84, 154, 170, 190, 194, 198, 199, 202
– trickster 29–31, 35, 36, 44, 109–112, 166, 188, 191, 199
– wise fool 30, 31, 44, 82, 112, 130, 138–142, 189–191
Storehouse of Banners (*khizānat al-bunūd*) 99, 118, 125, 126, 186, 196
storytelling 7, 36, 50, 55–58, 63, 65, 66, 72–75, 79, 94, 97, 110, 119, 135, 176, 180, 184, 190, 192
sukhriyya see satire and *adab sākhir* (satirical literature)
suspense of form 69, 96

Tāmir, Zakariyyā 38, 44
"the caliph/sultan laughed. . ." 11, 113

travelogue genre (*riḥla*) 38, 46, 59, 100–104, 109, 114, 127, 181, 187, 191, 202
– time-travelling 100, 103, 113–115, 127, 191
Triezenberg, Katrina see humour enhancer
al-Ṭūkhī, Nāʾil
– *Nisāʾ al-Karantīnā* (*Women of Karantina*) 3, 4, 62, 198, 200, 201
al-Tūnisī, Bayram 3, 37, 46, 53, 106, 182

university (also college) 158, 160, 176, 177, 180, 185, 190

village novel 55, 62–64, 68, 70–77, 97, 185, 193, 198, 202

zajal (strophic colloquial poetry) 37, 46

www.ingramcontent.com/pod-product-compliance
Lightning Source LLC
Chambersburg PA
CBHW031425150426
43191CB00006B/402
* 9 7 8 3 1 1 1 2 6 7 2 6 5 *